THE SETTLEMENT COOK BOOK

Compiled by
MRS. SIMON KANDER

THIS IS THE 1910
FOURTH EDITION

→»» · «←

This is a Mary Perks Book

THE AMERICAN CRAYON COMPANY

SANDUSKY, OHIO • 9 ROCKEFELLER PLAZA, NEW YORK, N. Y.

PRINTED AND BOUND IN THE UNITED STATES OF AMERICA

CONTENTS

	PAGE
Appetizers	58
Beverages, Hot and Cold	20
Biscuits and Breakfast Cakes	39
Bread, Rolls and Toast	28
Cake	336
Cake Frostings and Fillings	325
Candies	386
Canning Fruits and Vegetables	422
Cereals	17
Chafing Dish Recipes	229
Cookies and Kisses	368
Dumplings and Garnishes for Soups	81
Eggs, Omelets and Pancakes	47
Entrees	213
Fish and Oysters	96
Fruits, Fresh and Stewed	397
Fruit Syrups, Juices and Wines	402
Household Rules	3
Ice Creams and Frozen Puddings	282
Invalid Cookery	444
Jelly	408
Kuchen	311
Meat	113
Mehlspeise	179
Pastry and Pies	299
Pickles and Catsups	432
Potatoes	172
Poultry and Game	137
Preserving and Pickling	412
Puddings, Hot	246
Puddings, Cold	264
Salads	194
Salad Dressings	188
Sandwiches	235
Sauces for Fish, Meat and Vegetables	87
Sauces for Puddings	241
Soups	66
Stuffing for Meat and Poultry	134
Tartlets and Fried Cakes	320
Vegetables	149

INDEX

APPETIZERS

Appetizer of Artichoke, 63.
Anchovy, Butter on Toast, 60.
Caviere with Eggs, 64.
Crab or Lobster Canapes, 60.
Crawfish, Butter on Toast, 60.
Egg Appetizer, 65.
Egg and Tomato Appetizer, 64.
Egg Timbales, 64.
Filled Tomatoes, 63–64.
Fruit Salad, 59.
Grape Fruit Salad, 59.
Herring Appetizer, 61.

Herring Salad, 62.
Kippered Herring, 61.
Lobster Cocktail, 58.
Marrow Bones, 65.
Oyster Cocktails, 58.
Pear Salad, 59.
Pears, Stuffed, 60.
Pickled Herring, 62.
Sardine Appetizer, 63.
Sardellen Appetizer, 61.
Strawberry Cocktail, 59.
Sweetbread Cocktail, 58.

BEVERAGES, HOT

Cocoa, 22.
Coffee, 21.
Chocolate, 22.
General Rules, 20.

Glueh Wine, 22.
Milk, 20
Punch Imperial, 23.
Tea, 21–22.

BEVERAGES, COLD

Champagne Punch, 26.
Claret Cup, 25.
Egg Milk Punch, 27.
Fruit Punch, 24.
Ginger Punch, 25.
Gin Fizz, 27.
Grape Punch, 24.
Iced Tea, 23.
Jackson Cocktail, 27.
Lemonade, 23.

Manhattan Cocktail, 27.
Mint Julep, 26.
Moselle Punch, 26.
Orangeade, 24.
Orange Julep, 27.
Pineapple Punch, 24.
Pousse Cafe, 27.
Strawberry Punch, 25.
Washington Punch, 26.

BISCUITS, MUFFINS, SHORT CAKES, ETC.

Baking Powder Biscuits, 39.
Baking Powder Doughs, 39.
Cinnamon Rolls, 42.
Cornmeal Muffins, 41.
Dutch Apple Cake, 43.
English Muffins (Yeast), 41.
Fried Rye Muffins, 41.
Graham Gems, 40.

Lemon Puffs, 42.
Popovers, 42.
Rhubarb Pudding, 43.
Strawberry Short Cake, 42–43.
Twin Mountain Muffins, 40.
Wheat Muffins, 40.
Whole Wheat Muffins, 40.

BISCUITS AND ROLLS (YEAST)

Bread Sticks, 34.
Parker House Rolls, 34.
Potato Biscuits, 36.
Salad Rolls, 36.

Rolls, 34.
Tea Rolls, 35.
Yellow Biscuits, 35.
Zwieback, 36.

INDEX

BREAD

General Rules, 28.
Boston Brown Bread, 32.
Braided Bread, 28.
Bread, 28.
Corn Bread, 31–32.
Currant Bread, 31.

Entire Wheat Bread, 30–31.
Ginger Bread, 33.
Glazed Bread and Rolls, 29.
Gluten Bread, 30.
Rye Bread, 30.

BREAD—STALE AND TOAST

Bread Patties or Canapes, 37.
Crisped Crusts, 37.
Croutons, 37.
Crumbs, 37.
Dry Toast, 37.

French Toast, 38.
Matzos Dipped in Eggs, 38.
Milk Toast, 38.
Soup Sticks, 37.
Water Toast, 37.

CAKE FROSTINGS

Boiled Chocolate Frosting, 328–329.
Boiled Icing, 327–328.
Boiled Maple Sugar Frosting, 328.
Butter Icing, 327–328.
Caramel Frosting, 329.
Chocolate Frosting, 326.
Egg Frosting, 326.
Fruit Frosting, 326.

Lemon Frosting, 325.
Marshmallow Frosting, 329.
Nut Frosting, 329.
Orange Icing, 325–326.
Plain Icing, 325.
Royal Icing, 326.
Water Icing, 325.

CAKE FILLINGS

Banana Filling, 333.
Brod Torte Filling, 332.
Butter Filling, 334.
Caramel Filling, 330.
Chocolate Filling, 331.
Chocolate Nut Filling, 332.
Cocoanut Lemon Filling, 338.
Custard Fillings, 330.
Fig Filling, 334.

Marshmallow Filling, 334.
Nut Filling, 332.
Nut or Fruit Filling, 329.
Orange Filling, 333.
Orange or Lemon Filling, 333.
Sour Cream Filling, 330.
Sponge Cake Filling, 331.
Whipped Cream Filling, 335.

CAKES WITH BUTTER

General Rules, 336.
Blackberry Cake, 343.
Blitz Kuchen, 340–341.
Butter Cakes, 337.
Caramel Layer Cake, 347.
Cheap Cup Cakes, 338.
Chocolate Nut Cake, 343.
Chocolate Layer Cake, 346.
Coffee Cakes, 342–343.
Devil's Food Cakes, 345–346.
Fruit or Wedding Cake, 344.

Gold Cakes, 340.
Hickory Nut Cake, 343.
Layer Cake, 345.
Marble Cake, 341.
Molasses Layer Cake, 345.
Oven, Testing for Cake, 337.
Plain Cake, 339.
Quick Cake, 339.
Sand Torte, 341.
Streusel for Blitz Kuchen, 341.
White Cakes, 339–340.

CAKES—SPONGE

Angel Food, 349.
Cake without Butter, 347.
Chocolate Sponge Cake, 349.
Cream Filling, 352.
Delicate Zwieback, 350.
Jelly Roll (Sponge), 357.
Matzos Sponge Cake, 350–357.
Mocha Layer Cake, 353.
Orange Layer Cake, 353.

Potato Flour Cake, 350.
Seven Layer Cake, 355.
Sour Cream Cake, 357.
Sour Cream Chocolate Cake, 350.
Sponge Cake (Boiled), 348.
Sponge Layer Cake, 352.
Sponge Cake (with Water), 347.
Sunshine Cake, 349.

CAKES—TORTES

Almond Tortes, 354.
Almond Torte with Lady Fingers, 355.
Angel Torte, 355.
Brod Torten, 355.
Cheese Tortes, 356.
Chestnut Torte, 356.
Chocolate Torte, 357.
Chocolate Zwieback Torte, 357.
Coffee Cream Torte, 357.
Daisy Torte, 358.
Date Torte, 358.
Date and Walnut Torte, 358.
Farina Torte, 359.
Filbert Torte, 359.
Filled Torte, Cherries, 359.
Filled Torte, Macaroon, 359.
Himmel Torte, 360.

Karmeliter Torte, 360
Kiss Torte, 360.
Lady Finger Torte, 361.
Laver Torte, 361.
Macaroon Torte, 361.
Martzepan Torte, 361.
Matzos Torte, 362.
Matzos Chocolate Torte, 362.
Moss Torte, 362.
Mushkazunge, 363.
Orange Torte, 363.
Potato Chocolate Torte, 363.
Poppyseed Tortes, 364.
Rum Torte, 364.
Rye Bread Tortes, 365.
Walnut Tortes, 366.
Zwieback Torte, 367.

CAKES—SMALL

Brownies, 370.
Bundte Schuessel, 370.
Cake Baskets, 370.
Chocolate Eclair's, 369.
Chocolate Drop Cakes, 371.
Cocoanut Drop Cakes, 371.
Cream Puffs or Eclairs, 369.

Ginger Drops, 371.
Lady Fingers, 368.
Othellos, 368.
Peanut Drops Cake, 372.
Small Strawberry Cream Cakes, 370.
Sponge Drops, 368.

CAKES—FRIED

Apple Fritters en Surprise, 323.
Butter for Frying, 322.
Doughnuts, 322.

Hesterliste, 324.
Rose Tarts, 323.
Snow Balls, 323.

CANDIES

General Rules, 386.
Almond or Peanuts, Salted, 396.
Butter Scotch, 390.
Chocolate Caramels, 389.
Chocolate Cream Drops, 392.
Chocolate Dipped Cherries, 392.
Chocolate Dipped Grapes, 393.
Chocolate Sausage, 394.
Cinnamon Balls, 391.
Cocoanut Candy, 388.
Daisy Cream Candy, 390.
Date or Fig Chocolates, 394.
Date Sausage, 394.
Dates, Stuffed, 393.
Figs, Stuffed, 394.
Fondant, 391–392.
Fudges, 388.
Glaced Nuts or Fruits, 395.

Gumdrops, 396.
Marshmallow Fudge, 388.
Marshmallows Toasted, 396.
Marron Glace, 395.
Molasses Candy, 390–391.
New Orleans Pralines, 390.
Opera Caramels, 389.
Orange Sticks, 395.
Peanut Brittle, 387.
Penoche, 387.
Pepperm't or Wintergr'n Wafers, 391.
Popcorn Balls, 396.
Prunes, Stuffed, 394.
Seafoam, 389.
Spanish Sweets, 394.
Strawberries (Fresh) Dipped, 393.
Sugar, Effects of Too Much, 386–387.
Turkish Candy, 389.

CANNING FRUITS

General Rules, 422.
Apples Canned, 425.
Blackberries, 427.
Canned Fruit (Baked), 424.
Canned Fruit (Steamed), 425.
Canned Fruit (Stewed), 424.
Canned Peaches (Steamed), 426.
Canned Peaches (Stewed), 425.
Cherries Canned, 425.
Directions for Canning, 423.

Pears, Canned, 426.
Pineapples, Canned, 427.
Raw Rhubarb, Canned, 427.
Raspberry or Blueberry, Canned, 428.
Strawberries and Raspberries, Canned, 427.
Strawberries, Canned without Fire, 428.
Table for Canning Fruit, 422.
To Prepare Syrup, 423.
To Sterilize Jars, 423.

CANNING VEGETABLES

Asparagus, to Can, 428.
Beans, (String), to Can, 429.
Beets, to Can, 429.
Cauliflower, to Can, 429.
Corn, to Can, 430.
Corn on Cob, to Can, 430.

Peas, to Can, 430.
Tomatoes, (Stewed), to Can, 431.
Tomatoes, (Whole), to Can, 431.
Soup, (Tomato), to Can, 431.
Vegetables, to Can, 428.

CATSUPS AND RELISHES

Beet and Horse-radish Relish, 443.
Chili Sauce, 440.
Corn Relish, 442.
Cucumber Relish, 442.
English Chutney Sauce, 441.
Green Pepper Relish, 442.

Green Tomato Relish, 441.
Horse-radish for the Table, 443.
Mustard for the Table, 443.
Tomato Catsups, 439–440.
Tomato Relish, 441.

CEREALS

General Rules, 17.
Barley, Tapioca, Sago, 18.
Cereal with Sliced Bananas, 18.
Cornmeal, 18.

Cream of Wheat, 17.
Rice, 19.
Rolled Oats or Wheat, 17.
Turkish Pilaf, 19.

COOKIES

Almond Cookies, 385.
Anise Cookies, 377.
Butter Cookies, 373–374.
Cardamom Cookies, 377.
Card Gingerbread, 381.
Chocolate Cookies, 374.
Chocolate Sticks, 375.
Clove Cookies, 377.
Crisp Cookies, 375.
Fig Cookies, 378.
Fruit Cookies, 379.
Ginger Snaps, 376.
Honey Cakes, 381.
Jelly Cookies, 380.

Koumiss Bread, 381.
Lebkuchen, 381–382.
Matzos Anise Cookies, 378.
Nut Patties, 379.
Oat Meal Cookies, 375.
Orange Cookies, 378.
Pfeffernuesse, 378.
Rolled Date Cookies, 380.
Rolled Wafers, 380.
Rocks, 379.
Soft Molasses Cookies, 376.
Spice Cookies, 376.
Sugar Cookies, 373.

COOKIES—KISSES

Almond Pretzels, 382.
Chocolate Kisses, 384.
Cocoanut Kisses, 383.
Cocoa Kisses, 384.
Cinnamon Stars, 384.
Date Macaroons, 384.

Hickory-nut Kisses, 383.
Kisses, 382.
Kisses with Whipped Cream, 382.
Marguerites, 385.
Nut and Fruit Kisses, 383.

CHAFING DISH RECIPES

Cake Canapes, 234.
Chafing Dishes, 229.
Cheese on Toast, 229.
Chicken a la Newburg, 232.
Chicken a la King, 233.
Crab-meat and Green Peppers, 231.
Creamed Crab Meat, 230.
Deviled Almonds or Chestnuts, 234.
English Monkey, 232.
Frog Legs a la Newburg, 233.
Grilled Sardines, 234.
Hot Ham Sandwiches, 234.

Lobster a la Newburg, 233.
Lobster a la Thackery, 231.
Macaroni with Tomato Sauce, 230.
Minced Meat and Jelly Sauce, 234.
Mock Crab on Toast, 231.
Oyster a la Poulette, 231.
Oyster Rarebit, 231.
Rictum-Dity, 232.
Sardines on Toast, 234.
Scotch Woodcock, 232.
Welsh Rarebit, 230.

INDEX

CHEESE

General Rules, 220.
Boiled Cheese (Koch Kase), 221.
Cheese Balls, 221–222.
Cheese Fondue, 222.
Cheese Ramikins, 223.

Cheese Souffle, 223.
Cottage Cheese, 221.
Prepared Cheese, 221.
Toasted Crackers and Cheese, 223

DUMPLINGS AND GARNISHES FOR SOUP

Baking Powder Dumplings, 82.
Creplech, 86.
Cracker Balls, 82.
Cracker Dumplings, 82.
Crisped Crackers, 81.
Croutons, 81.
Drop Dumplings, 82.
Egg Balls, 84.
Egg Barley, Pfarvel, 86.
Egg Custard, 84.
Ein Lauf, 81.
Farina Balls, 84.

Fingerhuetchen, 86.
Fritter Beans, 85.
Mandel Kloesse, 83.
Matzos for Soup, 81.
Matzos Kloesse, 83.
Matzos Marrow Balls, 84.
Meat Dumplings, 82.
Noodles, 85.
Plaetzchen, 85.
Spatzen, 81.
Sponge Dumplings, 85.

EGGS

General Rules, 47.
Buttered Eggs, 48.
Cooked Eggs, Soft, 47.
Cooked Eggs, Hard, 47.
Composition of Eggs, 47.
Curried Eggs, 52.
Deviled Eggs, 52.
Eggs in Baked Potatoes, 50.
Eggs a la Buckingham, 51.
Eggs a la Columbus, 50.
Eggs au Gratin, 49–50.
Eggs a la Martin, 50.

Eggs in a Nest, 49.
Eggs a la Tarcat, 52.
Eggs in Tomato Sauce, 50.
Fried Eggs, 48.
Golden Rod Toast, 51.
Poached or Dropped Eggs, 48.
Poached Eggs and Cheese, 49.
Scrambled Eggs, 48.
Scrambled Eggs with Tomato Sauce, 51.
Scotch Eggs, 52.
Shirred Eggs, 48.
Steamed Eggs, 48.

ENTREES

Apple Fritters, 214.
Batter for Fritters, 213.
Brunswick Stew, 227.
Canned Corn Timbales, 218.
Chestnut Croquettes, 217.
Chicken Croquettes, 215.
Chicken Liver Timbales, 220.
Chicken Timbales, 220.
Chicken or Sweetbreads with Mushrooms, 224.
Chili Con Carne, 228.
Chop Suey, 227.
Cooking in Deep Fat, 213.
Crab Meat Chops, 216.
Egg Cutlets, 217.
Egg Timbales, 218.
Fillet of Beef with Artichoke, 227.
Halibut Timbales, 219.
Hot Tamales, 228.
Lobster Chops, 216.
Lobster in Shells, 225.

Fish and Cheese in Timbales, 218.
Fruit Fritters, 214.
Goose Liver Patties, 226.
Macaroni in Tomato Cases, 226.
Oyster and Macaroni, 223.
Patties, 226.
Pine-apple Fritters, 214.
Queen Fritters, 214.
Rice Croquettes, 215.
Salmon Croquettes, 216.
Salmon Timbales, 219.
Scalloped Fish in Ramikins, 224.
Shrimp a la Creole, 225.
Shrimp in Tomato Cases, 225.
Shrimp Spanish, 224.
Shrimp Wiggle Patties, 227.
Spanish Rice, 228.
Swedish Timbale Cases, 217.
Sweetbread Timbales, 219.
To Egg and Crumb Croquettes, 215.
Tomato Souffle, 225.

INDEX

FISH

General Rules, 96.
Baked Black Bass, 98.
Baked Fish with Sardelles, 99.
Baked Trout, 99.
Boiled Fish, 100.
Boiled Fish with Lemon Sauce, 103.
Boiled Salt Mackerel, 107.
Bone a Fish, 97.
Broiled Fish, 97.
Broiled Salt Mackerel, 108.
Broiled Sardines, 98.
Broiled Smelts, 98.
Codfish Balls, 108.
Composition of Fish, 96.
Creamed Codfish, 108.
Creamed Salmon, 101.
Filled Fish, 102.
Fillet De Sole, 100.
Fish Balls, 102.
Fish Cakes, 102.
Fish Glace, 107.
Fish with Horse-radish Sauce, 104.

Fish a la Macedoine, 105.
Fish Pudding, 104.
Fish Salad, 106.
Fish Salad in Jelly, 106.
Fish a la Tartare, 105.
Fried Fish, 97.
Halibut Steak, 98.
Halibut with Lobster a la Newburg, 104.
Halibut with Shrimp a la Newburg, 103.
Halibut with Tomato Sauce, 103.
Moulded Fish Salad, 106.
Planked Fish, 99.
Salmon Mould, 101.
Salmon Pudding, 101
Salmon Trout, Boiled, 100.
Salt Herring, 108.
Sauted Fish, 97.
Sharfe Fish, 100.
Stuffing for Fish, 99.
Sweet and Sour Fish, 104.
Trout with Mayonnaise, 105.

FISH—SHELLFISH

Broiled Live Lobster, 112.
Broiled Oysters, 109.
Clams a la St. Louis, 111.
Escalloped Oysters, 110.
Fried Oysters, 110.
Fricasseed Oysters, 109.
Frog Legs, Fried, 111.
Lobster a la Bordelaise, 112.

Lobster Rissoles, 112.
Lobster, Stewed, 112.
Oysters, 109.
Oysters in Blankets, 111.
Oysters au Gratin, 110.
Oysters, Manhattan Style, 111.
Oysters and Mushrooms, 111.
Oysters on Toast, 110.

FISH, MEAT AND VEGETABLE SAUCES

Bearnaise Sauce, 92.
Brown Sauce, 89.
Caper Sauce, 89.
Catsup Sauce, 89.
Creole Sauce, 90.
Cream Sauce, 88.
Cucumber Sauce, 94.
Curry Sauce, 93.
Drawn Butter Sauce, 91.
Egg Sauce for Boiled Fish, 94.
Hollandaise Sauce, 91.
Horseradish Sauce, 95.
Jelly Sauce for Game, 91.
Lemon Sauce, for Fish or Meat, 95.
Maitre D'Hotel Sauce, 91.
Mint Sauce, 93.

Mustard Sauce, 94.
Mushroom Sauce, 89.
Newburg Sauce for Fish or Lobster, 95.
Parsley Butter, 91.
Port Wine Sauce, 90.
Piquante Sauce, 90.
Sardellen Sauce, 90.
Sauce for Boiled Tongue or Fish, 95.
Sweet and Sour Sauce, 88, 89.
Tartar Sauce, 92.
Tomato Sauce, 93.
What Sauces Contain, 87.
White Sauce, 87.
White Sauce, Thick, 88.
White Sauce, Thin, 87.
Whipped Cream Sauce, 94.

FRUIT—FRESH AND STEWED

Apples, Baked, 398.
Apples, Steamed, 399.
Apple Sauce, 399.
Bananas, Baked, 401.
Canned Fruit Compote, 401.
Cranberry Sauce, 400.
Cranberry Compote, 400.
Cranberry Jelly, 400.
Ginger Figs, 401.
Grape Fruit, 398.

Musk Melons, 398.
Orange, to Serve, 397.
Peach or Pear Compote, 400.
Pineapple, Fresh, 398.
Prunes, Stewed, 399.
Rhubarb Sauce, 399.
Steamed Dates, 401.
Strawberries, Natural, 397.
Watermelon, to Serve, 398.

FRUITS—SPICED

Apples, Pickled, 418.
Cherries, Brandied, 421.
Cherries, Pickled, 420.
Cherries, Spiced, 420.
Gooseberries, Spiced, 420.
Peaches, Brandied, 421.

Peaches, Pickled, 419.
Pears, Brandied, 421.
Pears, Pickled, 419.
Plums, Pickled, 419.
Watermelon, Sweet Pickled, 420.

FRUIT SYRUPS, JUICES AND WINES

Blackberry Cordial, 405.
Cherry Bounce, 405.
Chocolate Syrup, 403.
Currant and Raspberry Juice, 404.
Dandelion Wine, 406.
Dripping Bag, to Make, 402.
Fruit Syrups and Juices, 402.
Grape Wine, 406.

Lemon Syrup, 402.
Orange Syrup, 403.
Raspberry Shrub, 405.
Raisin Wine, 406.
Rosel, Beet Vinegar, 407.
Sugar Syrup, 402.
Tarragon Vinegar, 407.
Unfermented Grape Juice, 403.

GRIDDLE CAKES AND WAFFLES

Baking Powder Batters, 44.
Bread Griddle Cakes, 45.
Buckwheat Cakes, 46.
Cornmeal Griddle Cakes, 45, 46.
Plain Griddle Cakes, 44.

Rice Griddle Cakes, 45-46.
Sour Milk Griddle Cakes, 45.
Sugar Syrup, 46.
Waffles, 46.

HOUSEHOLD RULES

Building a Fire, 11.
Cooking, 4.
Dishes, Washing, 8.
Food Classification, 4-5.
Food, Relative Value, 6.
Fireless Cooker, to Make, 11.
Fireless Cooker, to Use, 12.
Fireless Cooker, Recipes, 13, 14, 15.
Fireless Cooker, Time Table, 16.
Gas Range, to Use, 11.

How to Measure, 3.
Removing Stains, 10.
Room, Airing, 10.
Room, Dusting, 9.
Room, Sweeping, 9.
Sink, Care of, 9.
Table, to Clear, 8.
Table, to Lay, 6.
Table, Waiting on, 7.
Weights and Measures, 3.

ICE CREAM

General Rules, 282.
Apricot or Peach Ice Cream, 283.
Banana Ice Cream, 283.
Brown Bread Ice Cream, 284.
Caramel Ice Cream, 284.
Coffee Ice Cream, 284.
Chestnut Ice Cream, 285.
Chocolate Ice Cream, 285.
Fancy Ice Cream, 285.
Frozen Egg Nog, 286.
Grape Ice Cream, 286.
Macaroon Ice Cream, 286.

Maple Ice Cream, 286.
Orange Ice Cream, 286.
Peach Ice Cream, 286-287.
Peaches Melba Ice Cream, 287.
Pistachio Ice Cream, 287.
Raspberry or Strawberry Ice Cream, 288.
Strawberry Ice Cream, 288.
Sauce, Chocolate for Ice Cream, 289.
Sauce, Claret for Ice Cream, 289.
Sauce, Maple for Ice Cream, 289.
Sauce, Strawberry for Ice Cream, 290.
Vanilla Bean for Ice Cream, 288.

ICES AND SHERBETS

Cafe Parfait, 290.
Champagne Sherbet, 290.
Cranberry Frappe, 290.
Creme De Menthe Ice, 290.
Fruit Ice, 291.
Grape Frappe, 291.
Lemon Ice, 291.

Lemon Milk Sherbet, 292.
Mint Sherbet, 292.
Orange Frappe, 292.
Pineapple Sherbet, 292.
Raspberry or Currant Ice, 292.
Strawberry Ice, 293.
Vanilla Sauce for Ice Cream, 291.

ICE CREAMS, FROZEN PUDDINGS

Angel Mousse, 294.
Baked Alaska, 294.
Chestnut Pudding, Frozen, 295.
Chocolate Pudding, Frozen, 295.
Coffee Pudding, Frozen, 295.
Cranberry Parasade, 294.
Frozen Dessert, 296.
Frozen Diplomat, 296.
Frozen Pudding, 293.

Frozen Kiss Pudding, 296.
Frozen Nesselrode, 296.
Frozen Strawberry Pudding, 297.
Ice Puddings, 293.
Lalla Rookh Pudding, 297.
Maple Mousse, 297.
Raspberry Bombe Glace, 297.
Strawberry Parfait, 298.
To Mold Frozen Mixture, 293.

INVALID COOKERY

Apple Water, 447.
Barley Water, 448.
Beef Tea, 449.
Brown Flour Soup, 450.
Egg Nog, 446.
Flaxseed Tea, 449.
Flour Ball, Prepared, 451.
Fruit Tablets, 452.
Grape or Currant Juice, 447.
Gruel, Cracker, 452.
Gruel, Farina, 451.
Gruel, Oatmeal, 451.
Ice Cream for One, 446.
Invalid Cookery, 444.
Irish Moss Lemonade, 449.
Junket Custard, 447.
Koumiss, 445.
Lemonade or Orangeade, 447.
Lemon Whey, 448.

Lime Water, 445.
Milk, 444.
Milk Albumenized, 445.
Milk, Certified, 445.
Milk, Modified, 445.
Milk Punch, 446.
Milk for the Sick, 445.
Mustard Plaster, 452.
Mutton Broth, 450.
Rhubarb Water, 448.
Rice Water, 448.
Saccharin Solution, 452.
Scraped Beef, 451.
Serving Food, 444.
Toast Water, 448.
Wine Soup, 450.
Wine Soup, Cream, 450.
Wine, Red, Soup, 450.
Wine Whey, 448.

JELLY

General Rules, 408.
Bar-Le-Duc, 411.
Cherries in Currant Jelly, 411.
Crabapple Jelly, 409.
Crabapple and Cranberry Jelly, 410.
Crabapple and Plum Jelly, 409.

Currant Jelly, (without Cooking) 410.
Currant and Raspberry Jelly, 410.
Filling the Glasses, 409.
Grape Jelly, 410.
Mint Jelly, 411.
Plum Jelly, 411.

KUCHEN

Berliner Pfann Kuchen, 317.
Bohemian Kolatchen, 315.
Bundt Kuchen, 314-315.
Cinnamon Rolls, 313.
Coffee Kuchen, 312.
Filled Walnut Kipfel, 314.
Ice Kolatchen, 316.
Kuchen Dough, 311-312.
Kuchen Roll, 314.
Kuchen Tarts, 313.
Poppy Seed Roll, 314.

Raised Doughnuts, 316.
Russian Tea Cakes, 315.
Savarin, 315.
Sour Cream Kipfel, 314.
Sour Cream Kolatchen, 315.
Spice Roll, 314.
Stolla, 313.
Turnovers, Kipfel, etc., 313.
Vienna Kipfel, 314.
Yeast Kipfel, 314.

MEAT—BEEF

General Rules, 114.
Beef en Casserole, 119.
Beef Loaf, 116.
Beefsteak and Onions, 115.
Beef Stew, 117.
Beef a la Mode, 120.
Beef's Tongue, 121.
Boiled Smoked Tongue, 122.
Braised Beef, 117.
Braised Calves' Liver, 123.
Brisket of Beef, 118.
Broiled Steak, 114.
Broiled Tenderloin, 115.
Calf's Heart, 123.
Division of Side of Beef, 113.
Fillet of Beef, 117.

Fried Liver, 122.
Hamburg Steak, 116.
Lyonnaise Tripe, 123.
Mock Birds or Beef Rolls, 119.
Mock Roast Duck, 120.
Pan Broiled Steak, 115.
Pickled Beef, 221.
Pot Roast, 120.
Roast Beef, 116.
Roast Meats, with Gas, 116.
Round Steak, 115.
Steak in Casserole, 115.
Steak for Oven, 115.
Stewed Tripe, 123.
Sweet and Sour Beef, 121.

MEAT—LAMB AND MUTTON

Broiled Lamb Chops, 124.
Crown of Lamb, 124.
Cutlets, Lamb, 124.

Mutton, Stewed, 124.
Pan Broiled Chops, 124.
Roast Lamb, 125.

MEAT—PORK

Bacon, 125.
Boiled and Baked Ham, 126.
Boiled Sausage, 126.
Fried Ham and Eggs, 126.

Fried Sausage, 126.
Liver and Bacon, 125.
Pork Chops, 125.

MEAT—VEAL

Cutlets, Veal, 128.
Fricassee of Veal, 127.
Hungarian Goulash, 128.
Roast Veal, 127.

Roast Veal Breast, 127.
Veal Loaf, 129.
Veal Pot Pie, 128.
Veal Rolls, 128.

MEAT—SWEETBREADS

Baked Sweetbreads, 129.
Boiled Sweetbreads, 129.
Broiled Sweetbreads, 130.

Calf's Brains, 129.
Fried Sweetbreads, 130.
Sweetbreads with Mushrooms, 130.

MEATS, WARMED OVER

Casserole of Rice and Meat, 132.
Chicken a la Waldorf, 133.
Croquettes, 132.
Dried Beef with Eggs, 133.
Dried Beef in Sauce, 130.
Hash, 131.
Meat Pie with Potato Crust, 131.

Minced Meat on Toast, 131.
Potato and Meat Pie, 131.
Roast Beef with Gravy, 130.
Rissoules, 132.
Sausage and Eggs, 133.
Scalloped Meat, 132.

OMELETS AND PANCAKES

Asparagus Omelet, 54.
Bohemian Pancakes, 56–57.
Bread Omelet, 54.
Bread Pancake, 57.
Creamy Omelet, 53.
French Omelet, 53.
French Pancake, 55.

German Pancake, 55–56.
Matzos Pancakes, 57.
Omelet with Flour, 53.
Omelet with White Sauce, 53.
Orange Omelet, 54.
Potato Pancakes, 57.
Spanish Omelet, 54.

PASTRY FOR PIES

General Rules, 299.
Cookie Dough for Pies, 301.
Matzos Pie Crust, 302.
Murbeteig, 301–302.

Plain Pastry, 300.
Puff Paste, 301.
Short or Flaky Pastry, 300.

PIES AND KUCHEN FILLINGS

Apple Pie, 302–303.
Apple, Peach or Plum Pie or Kuchen, 303.
Blueberry Pie or Kuchen, 303–304.
Cheese Pie or Kuchen, 304–305.
Cherry Pie or Kuchen, 305.
Chocolate Pie, 306.
Custard Pie, 306.
Custard for Kuchen, 310.
Currant Pie, 306.

Gingerbread Filling for Kuchen, 309.
Lemon Pie, 307.
Mince Meat for Pies, 307.
Mock Cherry Pie, 308.
Poppy Seed Filling for Kuchen, 309.
Prune Filling for Pie or Kuchen, 309.
Pumpkin Pie, 308.
Streusel for Kuchen, 310.

PIES, TARTLETS

Cheese Fingers, 321.
Cheese Straws, 321.
Lady Locks, 320.
Lemon or Orange Tarts, 320.

Macaroon Tarts, 321.
Strawberry Tarts, 320.
Tarts, 320.

INDEX

PICKLES

Beans, Pickled, 437.
Beans, Dill, 434.
Beets, Pickled, 437.
Cabbage, Pickled, 437.
Cauliflower, Pickled, 436.
Chow-Chow, 435.
Cucumber Pickles, Sliced, 432.
Dill Green Tomatoes, 435.
Dill Pickles, 434.
Dill Pickles Small, 433.

Estregan Pickles, 433.
Mixed Pickles, 435.
Mock Olives, 439.
Mustard Pickles, 433.
Onions, Pickled, 438.
Peppers, Pickled, 438.
Ripe Cucumber Pickles, 432.
Sweet Pickles, 432.
Sauerkraut, 439.
Tomato (Delmonico), Pickles, 436.

POULTRY

Birds en Casserole, 142.
Braised Breast and Legs of Goose, 145.
Clean and Dress Poultry, 137.
Chicken Cut into Pieces, 137.
Chicken en Casserole, 141.
Chicken Cream, 142.
Chicken Fricassee, 140.
Chicken with Madeira Sauce, 140.
Chicken a la Maryland, 141.
Chicken and Rice, 140.
Goose Fricassee, 145.
Goose Greben, 144.
Gravy for Roast Chicken, 138.

Kischtke, 145.
Liver Goulash, 147.
Pressed or Jellied Chicken, 141.
Preserved Goose Meat, 144.
Rendered Fat, 144.
Roast Chicken, 138.
Roast Goose or Duck, 143.
Roast Turkey, 142.
Spring Chicken, Broiled, 139.
Spring Chicken, Fried, 139.
Squabs, Broiled, 143.
Stuffed Goose Necks, 145.

POULTRY, GAME

Belgian Hare, 148.
Hazen Pfeffer, 148.
Rabbit, 148.

Venison, 148.
Wild Duck, 147.
Quail, 147.

POULTRY—STUFFING FOR MEAT AND POULTRY

Apple Stuffing for Goose or Duck, 136.
Bread Stuffing, 134.
Bread Stuffing for Goose or Duck, 135.
Chestnut Stuffing, 135.
Game, Stuffing for, 136.

Oyster Stuffing, 135.
Potato Stuffing, 135.
Prune or Apple Stuffing, 136.
Squabs, Stuffing for, 135.

PRESERVES

Cherry or Raspberry Preserves, 413.
Cherry Conserve, 416.
Crabapple Preserves, Baked, 413.
Cranberries or Cherries, Baked, 413.
Ginger Apples, 414.
Ginger Pears, 414.
Gooseberry Preserve, 414.
Gooseberry Conserve, 417.
Grape Marmalade, 414.
Orange Marmalade, 414.
Pear Conserve, 417.

Pear and Apple Conserve, 418.
Preserving Small Fruits, Raw, 412.
Plum Conserve, 417.
Quince Preserve, 415.
Radish or Beet Preserve, 415.
Rhubarb Conserve, 417.
Strawberry Preserve, 415.
Sunshine Strawberries, 416.
Sunshine Currants or Cherries, 416.
Tomato Preserves, 416.
Tomato Preserves, Green, 416.

PUDDING SAUCES

Brandy Sauce, 241.
Caramel Sauce, 241.
Chocolate Sauce, 241.
Coffee Sauce, 241.
Cream Sauce, 242.
Creamy Sauce, 242.
Custard Sauce, 242.
Hard Sauce, 243.
Jelly Sauce, 243.

Kirsch Sauce, 243.
Lemon Sauce, 243.
Sauce for Matzos Pudding, 243.
Sauce, for Steamed Pudding, 244.
Strawberry Sauce, 244.
Strawberry Hard Sauce, 244.
Vanilla Sauce, 244.
Wine Sauce, 244–245.

PUDDINGS—HOT

Apple Pudding, 248.
Baked Indian Pudding, 249.
Bread and Fruit Pudding, 246.
Bread Pudding, 246–247.
Chocolate Bread Pudding, 247.
Grant Thomas, Pudding, 249.
Ice Cream Pudding, 249.

Potato Pudding, for Easter, 250.
Rice Pudding, 248.
Roly Poly, 249.
Scalloped Apples, 247.
Scalloped Rhubarb, 248.
Stale Bread Dessert, 246.

PUDDINGS—GRANDMOTHER'S

Apple Charlotte, 225.
Auf Lauf, 253.
Dampf Noodles, 253.
Dimpes Dampes, 254.
Kugel, 254.
Matzos Crimsels, 256.
Matzos Crimsels, Filled, 257.
Matzos Pudding, 255.
Matzos Schalet, 255.
Matzos Schalet, with Apples, 255.

Noodle Kugel, 254.
Noodle Pudding, 251–252.
Rice Kugel, 254.
Snitz, Kloes or Hutzle, 253.
Spritz Krapfen, 257.
Steamed Noodles, 253.
Strudel, Apple, 250–251.
Strudel, Cabbage, 251.
Strudel, Rahm, 251.

PUDDINGS—STEAMED

General Rules, 257.
Bread Pudding, 259.
Chocolate Pudding, 261.
Date Pudding, 260.
English Plum Pudding, 261.
Fig Pudding, 259.
Fruit Dumplings, 259.
Plum Pudding, 260.
Rice Snow Balls, 259.
Sponge Pudding, 262.

Steamed Fruit Pudding, 260.
Steamed Caramel Pudding, 261.
Souffle, Coffee, 262.
Souffle, Chestnut, 262.
Souffle, Chocolate, 263.
Souffle, Macaroon, 262.
Souffle, Lemon, 263.
Souffle, Walnut, 263.
Suet Puddings, 258.
Whole Wheat Pudding, 258.

PUDDINGS—CUSTARDS

General Rules, 264.
Apple Tapioca, 268.
Baked Tapioca Pudding, 268.
Blanc Mange, 267.
Caramel Custard, 266.
Cocoanut Custard, 264.
Coffee Custard, 266.
Cornstarch Pudding, 268.
Chocolate Blanc Mange, 267.
Chocolate Custard, 264.

Cup Custard, Baked, 265.
Custard with Caramel Sauce, 266.
Floating Island, 265.
Orange Custard, 265.
Pineapple Cornstarch, Pudding, 269.
Reunet Custard or Junket, 268.
Rothe Gritze, 269.
Soft Custard, 264.
Tapioca Cream, 267.

PUDDINGS—GELATINE

Angel Charlotte Russe, 273.
Banana Cream, 274.
Banana Sponge, 274.
Chocolate Cream, 274.
Chocolate Charlotte, 275.
Coffee Jelly, 275.
Cream Pudding, 275.
Danish Rice Pudding, 276.
Delmonico Dessert, 276.
Easter Egg Dessert, 277.
Gelatine Pudding, 277.

Lemon Jelly, 278.
Macaroon and Chocolate Pudding, 278.
Macaroon Dessert, 278.
Nesselrode Pudding, 279.
Orange Jelly, 279.
Orange or Strawberry Charlotte, 279.
Pineapple Jelly, 280.
Prune Pudding, 280.
Rice a la Dresden, 280.
Snow Pudding, 280.
Wine Jelly, 281.

PUDDINGS—WHIPS

Apple Dessert, 270.
Apple Snow, 269.
Banana Whip, 271.
Banana Pudding, 273.
Bohemian Cream, 273.
Chestnut Flake, 271.
Fig and Pineapple Dessert, 270.
Fruit Dessert, 269.

Heavenly Hash, 272.
Marshmallow Dessert, 272.
Prune or Date Whip, 271.
Queen of Trifles, 272.
Rice with Apples or Pineapple, 270.
Swiss Rice, 271.
Wine Syllabub, 273.

SALADS

General Rules, 194.
Artichokes Salad, 201.
Asparagus Salad, 201-202.
Aspic Jelly, 208-209.
Banana Croquette Salad, 204.
Bird's Nest Salad, 202.
Cabbage Salad, 197.
Cabbage Rose Salad, 197.
Cauliflower and Beet Salad, 201.
Celery and Cabbage Salad, 199.
Celery and Nut Salad, 203.
Chestnut Salad, 201.
Cherry Salad, 203.
Chicken Salad, 206.
Chicken Salad in Tomatoes, 207.
Chicken, Sweetbreads and Mushroom Salad, 207.
Conquard Salad, 204.
Cucumber Salad, 195.
Cucumber and Tomato Salad, 196.
Egg Salad, 200.
Endive Salad, 195.
German Celery Salad, 199.
Ham or Tongue Salad, 206.
Homemade Ring Mould, 209.
Jellied, Cucumber Salad, 212.
Lamb and Mint Salad, 205.
Lettuce Salad, 195.
Lemon Jelly, 210.
Liver and Egg Salad, 206.

Moulded Salad Jelly, Mixed, 211.
Moulded Jelly Salad, 211.
Moulded Sweetbread and Cucumber Salad, 211.
Mushroom Salad, 207.
Orange or Grape Fruit Salad, 204.
Oyster Salad, 204.
Pineapple Salad, 203.
Potato Salad, 197-198.
Potato Salad with Bacon, 198.
Red and White Cabbage Salad, 197.
Russian Vegetable Salad, 200.
Salmon Salad, 205.
Shad Roe Salad, 205.
Sherry's Salad, 202.
Shrimp and Cucumber Salad, 204.
Stuffed Tomato Salad, 196.
Stuffed Beet Salad, 200.
Sweetbread, Cucumber and Tomato Salad, 208.
Sweetbread and Mushroom Salad, 207.
Sweetbread and Pea Salad, 208.
Tomato Salad, 195-196.
Tomato Aspic Salad, 212.
Tomato Aspic with Salad, 210.
Tomato Baskets, 196.
Tongue Salad, 206.
Waldorf Salad, 203.
Water Lily Salad, 200.
Wax Bean Salad, 199.
Wine Jelly, 210.

SALAD DRESSINGS

Boiled Mayonnaise Dressing, 190-191.
Boiled Oil Mayonnaise, 191.
Cream Mayonnaise Dressing, 189.
Delmonico Salad Dressing, 192.
French Salad Dressing, 188.
Gargoyle Sauce, 192.
German Salad Dressing, 189.

Mayonnaise for Cold Meats, 189-190.
Mixed Seasonings, 188.
Oil Mayonnaise Dressing, 192.
Sweet and Sour Cream Dressing, 189.
Vinaigrette Dressing, 188.
White, Green, Red Mayonnaise, 193.

SANDWICHES

Bread and Butter, 235.
Cheese Sandwiches, 235.
Cheese Sandwiches Hot, 235.
Cheese and Anchovy, 236.
Cheese Mixture for Sandwiches, 236.
Checker Board Sandwiches, 237.
Chicken Sandwiches, 236.
Chicken and Nut Filling, 236.
Cottage Cheese Sandwiches, 236.
Date, Fig or Plum Sandwiches, 237.
Egg Sandwiches, 237.
Egg and Sardine Sandwiches, 237.
Ham Sandwiches, 238.

Jelly Sandwiches, 238.
Lettuce Sandwiches, 238.
Lobster Sandwiches, 238.
Nut Butter, for Sandwiches, 239-240.
Pate de Foie Gras Sandwiches, 238.
Ribbon Sandwiches, 238.
Rolled Bread Sandwiches, 235.
Sandwiches, 235.
Stuffed Olive Sandwiches, 239.
Sweet Bread Sandwiches, 239.
Swiss Cheese Sandwiches, 236.
Veal Mixture for Sandwiches, 239.

SOUPS WITH MEAT STOCK

Barley, Soup, 70.
Bouillon, 67.
Chicken Soup, 68.
Consomme, 67.
Dried Pea Soup, 71.
Green Kern Soup, 71.
Lentil Soup, 71.

Mulligatawny Soup, 70.
Mutton Soup, 68.
Ox Tail Soup, 69.
Soup Stock, 66-67.
Turkey or Goose Soup, 68.
Vegetable Soup No. 1, 69.

SOUPS WITHOUT MEAT STOCK

Almond Soup, 74.
Baked Bean Soup, 75.
Black Bean Soup, 75.
Beet Soup, 79.
Corn Soup, 74–75.
Cherry Soup, 80.
Clam Chowder, 77.
Cream of Asparagus Soup, 73.
Cream of Barley or Rice Soup, 75.
Cream of Celery Soup, 74.
Cream of Herring Soup, 79.
Cream of Mushroom Soup, 74.
Crabfish Cream Soup, 76.

Fish Chowder, 77.
Lobster Bisque, 77.
Milk Soup, 72.
Mock Bisque, 78.
Mock Clam Chowder, 77.
Mock Turtle, 78.
Oyster Stew, 76.
Potato Soup, 72.
Salmon Soup, 78.
Tomato Soup, 72.
Vegetable Soup No. 2, 69.
Wine Soup, 79.

VEGETABLES

General Rules, 147.
Artichokes, 151–152.
Asparagus, 150.
Bananas, Fried, 152.
Beans, Baked, 152.
Beans and Barley, 153.
Beans, Lima, 153.
Beans, String, 154.
Beans, String, and Tomatoes, 155.
Beans, String, Sweet and Sour, 154.
Beets, Boiled, 155.
Beets, Pickled, 155.
Brussel's Sprouts, 155.
Cabbage, 155–157.
Carrots, 158–159.
Cauliflower, 155–156.
Celery, 160.
Chestnuts, 160.
Corn, 161.
Corn Fritters, 162.
Cucumbers, 160.
Dandelions, 163.

Dill Pickle Vegetable, 161.
Egg Plant, Baked, 163.
Endive, 163.
German Celery, 160.
Kohlrabi, 163.
Macedoine, 165.
Mushrooms, 164.
Onions, 165.
Oyster Plant, 166.
Parsnips, 166.
Peas, 166–167.
Pea Puree, 153.
Peppers, Stuffed, 167–168.
Radishes, 168.
Sauerkraut with Brisket of Beef, 158.
Spinach, 169.
Squash, 169–170.
Succotash, 162.
Time Table for Vegetables, 147.
Tomatoes, 170–171.
Turnips, 171.

VEGETABLES—POTATOES

Baked Potatoes, 173.
Baked Mashed Potatoes, 175.
Boiled Potatoes, 172.
Boston Browned Potatoes, 174.
Composition of Potatoes, 172.
Creamed Potatoes, 176.
Duchesse Potatoes, 176.
Franconia Potatoes, 174.
French Fried Potatoes, 174.
Fried Potatoes, 175.
Hashed Browned Potatoes, 175.

Lyonnaise Potatoes, 175.
Mashed Potatoes, 173.
Potato Balls, 173.
Potato Cakes, 175.
Potato Croquettes, 174.
Potatoes au Gratin, 177.
Potato Puffs, 174.
Saratoga Potatoes, 174.
Scalloped Potatoes, 176.
Surprise Balls, 175.

VEGETABLES—SWEET POTATOES

Baked Sweet Potatoes, 177.
Boiled Sweet Potatoes, 177.
Croquettes of Sweet Potatoes, 178.

Glazed Sweet Potatoes, 177.
Mashed Sweet Potatoes, 177.
Southern Style, Sweet Potatoes, 178.

VEGETABLES—MEHLSPEISE

Baking Powder Dumplings, 180.
Baked Noodles with Cheese, 184.
Beef and Liver Dumplings, 182.
Boiled Broad Noodles, 183.
Dumplings, 179–180.
Egg Barley, 184.
Filled Dumplings, 184–185.
Garnishes for Dumplings, 179.
Liver Dumplings, 182.
Matzos Kloese, 183.

Mock Asparagus, 181.
Macaroni, Boiled, 185.
Macaroni and Cheese, 185.
Macaroni with Eggs, 187.
Macaroni and Tomatoes, 185.
Macaroni with Tomatoes and Mushrooms, 186.
Mushroom Sauce, 186.
Potato Dumplings, 181.
Spaghetti Italienne, 187.
Yeast Dumplings, 180.

"THE SETTLEMENT" COOK BOOK

"THE SETTLEMENT" COOK BOOK

CHAPTER I

HOUSEHOLD RULES

HOW TO MEASURE

All measurements should be made LEVEL.

Accurate measurement is essential to insure good cooking.

A half-pint cup is the standard. They can be had with fourths and thirds indicated.

A cupful is a cup filled LEVEL with the top. To measure a cupful, fill lightly with a spoon, taking care not to shake the cup; then level with the knife.

A spoonful is a spoon filled LEVEL with the top. First sift the material into the bowl, dip in the spoon, lift it slightly heaping, and level it by sliding the side of a knife across the top of the spoon. Do not level by pressing it.

Half a spoonful is obtained by dividing through the middle lengthwise.

A speck of anything is what will lie within a space ¼ inch square.

TABLE OF WEIGHTS AND MEASURES

2 cups	1 pint
2 pints	1 quart
4 quarts	1 gallon
8 quarts	1 peck
4 cups flour	1 pound
2 cups solid butter	1 pound
2 cups granulated sugar	1 pound
3 cups corn meal	1 pound
2⅔ cups powdered sugar	1 pound
2⅔ cups brown sugar	1 pound
2 cups solid meat	1 pound
16 ounces	1 pound
2 tablespoons butter, sugar, salt	1 ounce
4 tablespoons flour	1 ounce
16 tablespoons	1 cup
60 drops	1 teaspoon
8 salt spoons	1 teaspoon
3 teaspoons	1 tablespoon
4 tablespoons	¼ cup
4 tablespoons	1 wine glass

COOKING

Cooking is the art of preparing food by the aid of heat, for the nourishment of the human body. The principal ways of cooking are boiling, broiling, stewing, roasting, baking, frying, sauteing, braising, fricasseeing and steaming.

Boiling: Cooking in boiling water. Boiling point, 212° F.

Broiling: Cooking over a glowing fire.

Steaming: Cooking over boiling water.

Stewing: Cooking for a long time in water below the boiling point. Simmering point, 185° F.

Roasting: Cooking before a glowing fire.

Baking: Cooking in an oven.

Frying: Cooking in hot deep fat, deep enough to cover article to be cooked.

Sauteing: Cooking in a small quantity of fat.

Braising: A combination of stewing and baking.

Fricasseeing: A combination of frying and stewing.

FOOD

Food is anything that nourishes the body. Food is necessary for growth, repair and energy. The substances comprising the body are obtained from food.

All food is changed into liquid before it can be carried about by the blood, to build up the worn-out tissues.

Digestion of Food—First step: In the mouth the food is crushed and some of the starch is changed to sugar by the saliva.

Second step: In the stomach the gastric juice dissolves the proteids.

Third step: In the intestines the bile, pancreatic and intestinal juices act upon the food.

    (a) The rest of the starch is changed to sugar.
    (b) The rest of the proteids are dissolved.
    (c) The fat is divided into small drops and mixed all through the food, just as cream is mixed through milk before it rises to the top.

FOOD CLASSIFICATION

ORGANIC

- **I PROTEIDS**
  1. Albumen — Eggs, Meat, Fish
  2. Casein
     - Animal — Milk, Cheese
     - Vegetable — Peas, Beans, Lentils, Peanuts
  3. Gluten — Cereals
  4. Gelatine — Bones and Fish
  5. Fibrine — Muscle of Meat

  Use — To build up tissue and repair worn out tissue.

- **II CARBOHYDRATES**
  1. Starch — Cereals, Vegetables, Fruits
  2. Sugar — Vegetables, Sugar

- **III FATS AND OILS**
  1. Butter
  2. Cream
  3. Fat of meat
  4. Fish
  5. Cereals
  6. Nuts
  7. Olive Oil

  Use — To furnish energy and maintain heat.

INORGANIC

- **I MINERAL MATTER**
  1. Sodium
  2. Iron
  3. Lime
  4. Potash
  5. Sulphur

  Use — To build up bone and other tissue, to aid digestion, to purify the blood.

- **II WATER** — Use
  1. Regulates temperature
  2. Aids in carrying off waste
  3. Acts as a carrier
  4. Aids in digestion
  5. Acts as a solvent

RELATIVE VALUE OF FOOD

This table shows the quantities of various foods that are required to equal a quart of milk in total nutrients.

A quart of standard milk weighing 34.4 ounces contains 3.3 per cent Proteid, 4 per cent Fat, 5 per cent Starch and Sugar, and .7 per cent Mineral matter, or 13 per cent Total Nutrients equal to 4.47 ounces.

Kind of Food.	Total nutrients. Per cent.	Amount required. Ounces.	Net cost. $
Beef, Round, medium fat	32.1	13.9	$0.104
Oysters	11.7	38.2	.382
Codfish, boneless, dried	42.7	10.4	.065
Eggs at 20¢ per doz	23.3	19.1	.172
Cheese, Cheddar	72.6	6.1	.061
Wheat, Flour	87.2	5.1	.008
Macaroni	89.7	4.9	.046
Cornmeal, granular	87.5	5.1	.017
Potatoes at 60¢ per bu	17.4	25.7	.016
Beans, navy, dried	87.4	5.1	.017
Cabbage	7.3	61.2	.076
Cauliflower	7.7	58.0	.276
Apples at $1.15 per bu	11.4	39.2	.049
Bananas at 15¢ per doz	16.1	27.7	.111
Prunes	66.0	6.8	.051

LAYING THE TABLE

General Directions—Cover the table with a silence cloth of felting or Canton flannel. Over this spread a spotless table cloth evenly, the middle crease dividing the table exactly in half.

Position of Host and Hostess—Position of the host, at the head of the table near entrance door. Hostess at the foot of the table opposite.

Placing Knives, Forks and Spoons—Place the knife or knives at the right of each place, the sharp edge toward the plate; the fork or forks, next, tines up, one inch from the edge, being careful to have the spacing the same at every place. Soup spoons over the plate, handles to the right. Teaspoons to left of forks, bowls up.

Place silver in the order in which it is to be used, counting from the outside toward the plate.

Placing of Glasses—Place the water glass at right of plate, at end of knife blade.

Placing Napkins, Pepper, Salt—Place napkins at left of plate. Pepper and salt near corners, or one of each between the places for two people.

Sideboard and Side-table—Object: To hold all extras that may be needed during a meal.

WAITING ON TABLE

The table should look as neat and attractive as possible. Place everything straight upon the table. Turn no dishes upside down.

Always heat the dishes in which warm food is served.

Never fill the glasses and cups more than three-quarters full.

When passing a plate, hold it so that the thumb will not rest on the upper surface. When refilling the glasses, take hold of them near the bottom and draw them to the edge of the table, then remove them from the table.

A waiter passes food to the left side of each person, except beverages, which should be placed at the right.

In placing a dish in front of a person, the waiter should stand at the right. Food and dishes are removed from the right.

In passing dishes from which a person is to help himself to a portion, pass it always from the left side, so that it may be taken with the right hand.

In passing individual dishes from which the person does not help himself—such as coffee, etc.—set it down slowly and easily from the right hand side.

When the dishes are being served by a person at the table, stand at the left hand of that person, hold your tray low and near the table, and take on the tray one plate at a time and place it before the person for whom it is intended, setting it down from the right side.

Serve first the most honored guest.

When one course is finished, take the tray in the left hand, and stand on the left side of the person you are waiting upon, and remove with your right hand the spoons, knives and forks. Then remove the plate and small dishes, never piling them on top of each other, but removing them one at a time. Fill the glasses before every course. Before the dessert is served, remove the crumbs from the cloth, either with a brush or crumb knife. Do not let the table become disordered during the meal. The hostess should serve the soup, salad, dessert and coffee, and, at a family dinner, the vegetables and entrees. The host serves the fish and meat.

To clear the table remove all dishes from each place, then the meat and vegetables. Remove crumbs from the cloth before bringing in dessert.

TO CLEAR THE TABLE AFTER A MEAL

Brush the crumbs from the floor. Arrange the chairs in their places. Collect and remove the knives, forks and spoons. Empty the cups and remove them. Scrape off the dishes—never set any food away on the dishes used for serving—pile them up neatly and remove to the place where they are to be washed. Brush the crumbs from the cloth and fold it carefully in the old crease, as it lays on the table. If the napkins are used again, place them neatly folded in their individual rings.

WASHING DISHES

Have the dishes scraped.

Pile all articles of each kind together; plates by themselves, the largest at the bottom; cups by themselves; silver articles together, and steel knives and forks by themselves.

Soaking dishes:

Cold water should be used for soaking dishes which have been used for milk, eggs and starchy foods. Hot water for dishes used for sugar substances and for sticky, gummy substances like gelatine. Greasy dishes of all kinds, including knives, are more easily cleaned if first wiped with soft paper, which should be burned.

Order: 1. Glassware; 2. Silver; 3. Cups and saucers; 4. Plates; 5. Platters, vegetable dishes, etc.; 6. Cooking utensils (if not washed first).

To wash dishes:

Have a pan half filled with hot soapy water. Slip glasses and fine China in sideways, that the hot water will touch outside and inside at once, and thus avoid danger of breaking. If dishes are very dirty or greasy, add a little washing soda, ammonia or soap.

Rinse all dishes in clean hot water (except cut glass), drain and wipe with clean dry towels.

A Dover egg-beater should not be left to soak in water, or it will be hard to run. Keep the handles clean, wipe the wire with a damp cloth immediately after using.

Kitchen knives and forks should never be placed in dish water. Scour them with brick dust, wash with dish cloth, and wipe them dry.

Tinware, granite ironware should be washed in hot soda water, and if browned, rub with sapolio, salt or baking soda. Use wire dish cloth if food sticks to dishes.

Keep strainer in sink, and pour all dish water, etc., in it, and remove contents of strainer in garbage pail.

Wash towels with plenty of soap, and rinse thoroughly every time they are used.

Hang towels up evenly to dry. Wash dish cloths.

When scrubbing, wet brush and apply soap with upward strokes, working with the grain of the wood; rinse and dry.

Wash dish pans, wipe and dry.

Wash your hands with white (castile or ivory) soap, if you wish to keep smooth hands, and wipe them dry.

Wash teakettle; polish faucets; scrub sink with clean hot suds.

CARE OF THE SINK

When dish-washing is finished, wash every part of the sink with hot, soapy water. Wash above and around the sink. Use a skewer to clean behind the sink pipes.

Flush the sink with boiling water every day and about once a week with a strong solution of washing soda.

SWEEPING A ROOM

How to Sweep: Before beginning to sweep, see that no food is left uncovered in the room and that all movable articles and furniture are taken out of the room. Sweep from the edges of the room toward the center. Sweep with short strokes, keeping the broom close to the floor. Turn it edgewise to clean cracks. Always sweep a floor before washing or scrubbing it.

DUSTING A ROOM

Begin at one corner and take each article in turn as you come to it. Dust it from the highest things to the lowest, taking up the dust in the cloth.

Dust the woodwork, furniture and movable articles with a soft cotton cloth. Shake it frequently out of the windows.

AIRING A ROOM

Lower the upper sash of a window, to let out the foul air, which always rises to the top.

Raise the lower sash of an opposite window, of same or an adjoining room, to admit fresh air.

This will create a draft, that will thoroughly air the room.

Bed room windows should always be open at night from the top.

REMOVING STAINS

When possible remove all stains while they are fresh, as they are less obstinate before dried into the cloth.

If a stain has been overlooked and washed in, it is difficult to remove and should be bleached on the grass.

Blood Stains—Wash in cold water until the stain turns brown, then rub with Fels Naphtha soap and soak in warm water.

If the goods are thick make a paste of cold raw starch and apply several times until the stain is removed.

Brass Stains—Rub either lard or olive oil on the stain, then wash with warm water and soap.

Fruit and Coffee Stains—Stretch the stained part over a bowl, and pour boiling water through it from a height until the stain disappears.

Tea and Chocolate Stains—Are hard to remove, therefore soak them in cold water and borax and then apply the boiling water as for coffee stains.

Milk Stains—Wash them out while fresh in cold water.

Glue Stains—Apply vinegar with a cloth.

Grease Stains—Place a blotter over the stain and iron with a very hot iron.

Grass Stains—Wash with Fels Naphtha soap and water, or if the colors are not delicate, apply ammonia and water at once. If cotton, wash in alcohol.

Ink Stains—Soak in sweet or sour milk, or wet stains in oxalic acid and rinse.

Mildew Stains—If the stain is not too old it may be removed by applying soft soap and powdered chalk, keeping it moist and laying it in the sun.

Rust—Soak spot with lemon juice, then cover with salt. Let stand in the sun for several hours, or, soak spots in oxalic acid until stain disappears. Rinse thoroughly. Oxalic acid should be used on white material only. Oxalic acid is a poison, should be marked poison and kept out of reach of children.

BUILDING A FIRE

It is necessary to have:
1st, Fuel.—Something to burn.
2nd, Heat.—To make fuel hot enough to burn.
3rd, Air.—To keep the fire burning.

DIRECTIONS FOR THE USE OF A GAS RANGE

Don't use blacking. When dry and still warm, rub thoroughly inside and out with an oily cloth, using a tiny bit of lard, suet or olive oil. Never clean when the stove is cold. Plunge a wire into the burner holes occasionally to see that they are free from dirt.

Wash the wire rack and drip-pan every time you roast or broil.

Make test of time required to cook certain things; study the degree of heat required. Such tests will, in a short time, give you definite knowledge of your range, which can be acquired in no other way.

Don't light the gas until you are ready to use it. Put it out when you take the things from the stove. When boiling or bubbling begins, the contents of the vessel have reached the boiling point. You can turn down the burner and still maintain boiling.

How to Bake in a Gas Range. The degree of heat required for various foods depends so much upon the shape and size of the loaf of bread, or the pie, or whatever it may be, that specific directions cannot be given, which will exactly fit every case. However, every housewife, if she uses a modern, efficient gas range, should get a hot oven in five minutes after lighting both burners and closing the oven door.

TO MAKE A FIRELESS COOKER

Material:
A large, closely fitted covered box or pail,
Wire netting,
Granite iron cooking kettles, with straight sides and closely fitted covers,
10 to 50 lbs. mineral wool, for padding.
Cotton cloth or galvanized iron fitted lining.

Place hinges on cover of box, and see that box or pail to be used as the cooker is large enough to hold one, two or three closely covered granite kettles or pails, allowing at least 2 inches of space all around and at the top and bottom of kettles.

If your kettles are not of the same height, place enough packing, not necessarily mineral wool, underneath the shorter ones to bring the tops of the kettles on a level.

Cut a framework of wire netting for each kettle, 3 inches longer than the height of the kettle, fit it loosely around the sides, that it may be lifted out easily. Sew down the sides with twine.

Fold over 1 inch of wire, all around the top, to make a smooth finish. At the bottom of the wire, 2 inches apart, make 2 inch cuts, upward, all around the bottom. Bend the pieces thus formed, outward, as a foundation on which the framework stands.

Place this wire framework in the cooker box on a layer of mineral wool 2 or 3 inches deep, allowing 2 inch space between kettles and the side of box or pail. Slip kettles in the wire frames and pack mineral wool solidly in all empty spaces, until tops of kettles are reached.

Lift out kettles. Make bags of Canton flannel to fit loosely over each cooking kettle.

Take piece of goods, size of box or pail, cut out spaces where kettles belong and sew in the fitted bags.

Slip this covering over the mineral wool and tack it neatly to the sides of the box or pail. Cover the 3 inch deep cushions that fit over tops of kettles with the flannel.

A galvanized iron lining, made by a tinsmith, would be easier kept clean, than the home made cloth affair.

Mineral wool sells at about 2 cts. per pound and can be bought at any hardware store. It retains heat a long time. Sawdust, scraps of newspapers, hay or baled shavings may be used in place of the mineral wool.

INSTRUCTIONS FOR USING FIRELESS COOKER

The food is placed in the granite kettles, covered closely and cooked over fire, on a gas, wood, oil, or coal stove, until piping hot (see table, page 16), and immediately slipped into spaces in which they fit. If you use only one of the cooking kettles or pails for food, have the others filled with hot water. Cover pails quickly to retain all the heat and steam possible and place mineral wool cushion over all. Close box quickly and the food will cook evenly and tender.

The principle is first to bring the food to the BOILING point on the STOVE, then put it in the Cooker. To secure the best results, the covered kettle should always be filled nearly to the TOP, excess of water to be poured off later. The most important point to be observed, is to have the contents of the covered kettle thoroughly HOT before placing it in the "COOKER."

The length of all STOVE cooking should be guided by the SIZE of the article to be cooked.

In preparing small quantities, it is best to use a SMALL vessel, and when properly heated place it in the Cooker vessel, already filled with BOILING water.

It is IMPORTANT to keep the cover on the Cooker kettle until contents are cooked, and not open during time of COOKING.

Everything that is usually cooked on TOP of a stove and some that are cooked in the OVEN, can be prepared to better advantage in the Fireless Cooker, as the slow boiling makes everything more tender and delicate, retains all the flavors and has the added advantage that no odors escape into the house.

As it is impossible to scorch or overcook any article, it is not necessary to remove the kettle at any fixed time.

For infants and the sick who require hot nourishment at all hours of the night, the cooker is invaluable.

A dinner can be prepared at noon, then you can go out for the afternoon, and on your return at any time, you can immediately serve your dinner, steaming hot.

RECIPES FOR FIRELESS COOKER

SOUPS

Soups are prepared as usual, only no allowance should be made for evaporation. Boil twenty minutes on the stove, put in the Cooker five or six hours or all night, the next morning add vegetables to flavor, cook five minutes more, return to Cooker and let remain until noon. In soups the economy of the Cooker is especially noticeable, as the only expensive item, the long cooking over a fire, is avoided.

BOILED MEATS

Season meat with salt, pepper, roll in flour and place in hot, greased frying pan; brown on both sides. Cover with boiling water, boil steadily and slowly for ½ hour or until meat is hot in center. Boil hard with cover for a few seconds then slip in Fireless Cooker and allow it to remain 6 or more hours or over night, according to the weight.

POT ROAST

For four or five pound rump roast of beef. Place in an iron kettle two tablespoons of suet. When melted, brown the roast in the fat. Remove the meat to the cooker kettle and cover with boiling water. Boil slowly thirty minutes, with a little salt. Without removing the cover, place in the cooker for four hours. Add a little of the liquor to the fat, and place the meat in and brown for a few minutes on the stove. Thicken the gravy with flour. The liquor can be used for soup.

POTATOES BOILED

Pare and cut potatoes in quarters if large. Cover with boiling water. Boil five minutes and remove to the Cooker for one and one-half hours. Potatoes can be left in the Cooker five or six hours without becoming soggy.

SAUER KRAUT

Take one quart of sauer kraut and two pounds of brisket of beef or fresh pork. Cut the meat in slices and mix with the kraut in the kettle. Cover with boiling water and boil ten minutes without lifting the cover. Remove to the Cooker for eight or ten hours. A little salt should be added before cooked, if needed. Drain, and serve on hot platter.

TO FRY OLD CHICKEN

Singe and cut up in small pieces. Place in Cooker kettle. Cover with boiling water, add a little salt and boil 25 minutes. Remove to the Cooker for six or eight hours, or over night. Leave in liquor until ready to serve, then brown in hot fat, season with salt and pepper. Serve with mushroom sauce.

ROAST BEEF OR ROAST CHICKEN

Have the bones removed from a rib roast and rolled. Chicken is prepared as for roasting. Place either roast or chicken in hot oven for twenty or thirty minutes until well browned, then place in 4 quart kettle and place that in 8 quart kettle partly filled with boiling water. Have lids on both kettles, and when all is well heated, put into Fireless Cooker for three or four hours. The time in the oven and in the Cooker is dependent on whether the roast is liked well done or rare, and on the size and age of the chicken.

BAKED BEANS

Wash and pick over one quart of white beans. Soak over night. In the morning let them come to a boil, add a pinch of soda and drain. Put them into the kettle with one-half pound of salt pork, slash the rind and cover with boiling water. Boil five minutes and remove to the Cooker for five or six hours. Remove the beans to a baking dish. Cut the pork in slices and lay over the top. Season with salt, pepper and four tablespoons of molasses or brown sugar. Bake until a nice brown.

BOSTON BROWN BREAD

Follow recipes on Page 32.

Pour into well buttered moulds; have mould three-fourths full, with the top buttered. Place on wire rack in Cooker kettle, fill nearly to top of mould with boiling water, boil thirty minutes, remove to Cooker for five or more hours. Place in a hot oven five or ten minutes to form dry crust. By adding half a cup of raisins you have fruit bread.

STEWED PRUNES

Wash the prunes and cover with cold water, and soak over night. The next morning put them with the water in which they were soaked on the stove and boil five minutes. Sweeten to taste. Remove to the Cooker without removing the cover, for five or six hours. When done, remove prunes to dish and boil syrup ten minutes, and pour over the prunes.

TIME TABLE FOR USING FIRELESS COOKER

SOUPS

Variety	Time Boiling on Fire	Time in Cooker
Celery Soup,	5 Minutes,	2 Hours or More.
Vegetable Soup,	15 Minutes,	4 Hours or More.
Chicken Soup,	15 Minutes,	4 Hours or More.
4 lbs. Veal Soup,	15 Minutes,	4 or 5 hrs. or over night.
4 lbs. Beef Soup,	25 Minutes,	4 or 5 hrs. or over night.

MEATS

Boiled Ham,	30 Minutes,	6 Hours or More.
Corned Beef,	30 Minutes,	6 Hours or More.
Boiled Beef or Mutton,	25 Minutes,	4 Hours or More.
Boiled Young Chicken,	15 Minutes,	3 Hours or More.
Boiled Old Chicken,	30 Minutes,	5 Hours or More.
Boiled Fish,	10 Minutes,	2 Hours or More.

VEGETABLES

Peas (green),	2 Minutes,	2 Hours or More.
Cauliflower,	5 Minutes,	1 Hour or More.
String Beans,	5 Minutes,	2 Hours or More.
Potatoes,	6 Minutes,	1½ Hours or More.
Turnips,	10 Minutes,	2 Hours or More.
Beets,	15 Minutes,	3 Hours or More.
Cabbage, (winter),	10 Minutes,	3 Hours or More.

FRUITS

Fresh Fruits,	5 Minutes,	1½ Hours or More.
Dried fruit, (after soaking),	10 Minutes,	2 Hours or More.

CEREALS

Rice, 1 part to 3 of water,	5 Minutes,	1½ Hours or More.
Wheatena,	5 Minutes,	2 Hours or More.
Quaker Oats,	5 Minutes,	2 Hours or More.

1 Part of these last two cereals to 2½ parts water.

CHAPTER II

Cereals

Cereals or grains are seeds of certain members of the grass family; they form a very important part of the food of man. Cereals are wheat, Indian corn or maize, oats, rice, rye and barley. From these are prepared various breakfast foods, oatmeal, wheatena, etc. They all contain more or less starch.

For family use, cereals should be bought in small quantities and kept in tightly covered jars.

GENERAL RULES

Boiling water and salt should always be added to cereals—one teaspoon salt to one cup of cereal.

They should be cooked directly over heat the first five minutes and then over boiling water in a double boiler.

Long cooking improves the flavor and makes them more easily digested.

ROLLED OATS OR WHEAT

1 cup rolled oats or wheat, 2 cups boiling water,
1 teaspoon salt.

Boil ten minutes, stirring constantly; then over boiling water one hour longer. A better flavor is developed by longer cooking. One-fourth pound of dates, stoned and cut in pieces and stirred in the mush, may be added, and served as a dessert for dinner or luncheon.

CREAM OF WHEAT

½ cup cream of wheat, 1 teaspoon salt,
4 cups boiling water.

See that the water is actually boiling in a saucepan. Add salt, then cream of wheat gradually. Stir constantly until thick. Cook ½ to ¾ hour over hot water.

CORN MEAL MUSH

4 cups boiling water, 2½ teaspoons salt,
1 cup cornmeal.

Add the salt to the boiling water. Add the meal gradually, so that the water will not stop boiling, and stir continually, keeping it directly over the heat 10 minutes. Cook over boiling water ½ to 3 hours longer. Long cooking improves the flavor.

SAUTED CORNMEAL MUSH

Put left over mush into a dish and smooth it over the top. When cold cut into slices ½ inch thick. Dip each slice into flour. Melt ½ teaspoon dripping in a frying pan, and be careful to let it get smoking hot. Brown the floured slices on each side. Drain if necessary and serve on a hot plate with syrup.

BAKED CORN CAKE

1 pint cornmeal, 2 teaspoons salt,
2 quarts boiling water, 1 oz. butter.

Scald cornmeal with water and add salt. Spread about one-fourth inch thick on greased baking pan; finish in hot oven till quite dry.

CEREAL WITH SLICED BANANAS

1 pint cooked oatmeal, 4 bananas sliced.
1 pint whipped cream,

Pour left-over breakfast cereal into after-dinner coffee cups rinsed in cold water and set aside. When cold and ready to use, turn from the cups on to a buttered pan, and heat in the oven. To serve surround with sliced bananas; whipped cream, clotted cream or plain cream with sugar.

BARLEY, TAPIOCA, SAGO, ETC.

½ cup barley or other hard grain, 1 qt. boiling water,
1 teaspoon salt.

Add salt to the boiling water and pour gradually on the barley, or other hard grain and boil until tender from 1 to 2 or more hours, according to the grain, and have each kernel stand out distinct when done.

Add more boiling water as it evaporates. Use as a vegetable, or in soups. Pearl barley, tapioca and sago cook quicker than the ordinary large grains.

BOILED RICE

1 cup rice,   2 qts. boiling water,
1 teaspoon salt.

Pick over rice and wash thoroughly.

Add slowly to boiling, salted water so as not to check boiling of water. Boil rapidly for 30 minutes or until kernels are soft. Drain in coarse strainer.

STEAMED RICE

1 cup rice,   4 cups boiling water,
2 teaspoons salt.

Pick over and wash the rice in three or four waters. Put it with the boiling water and salt into the double boiler. Steam 40 minutes or until tender. Serve with milk or cream.

CURRIED RICE

1 cup rice,   3 cups hot chicken or veal
1 onion,   broth,
2 teaspoons curry powder,   butter.

Cover rice with cold water, bring quickly to boiling point, drain and rinse in cold water. Then cook in the chicken or veal broth and when half done add the onion finely chopped and sauted in butter and the curry powder creamed with a little butter. Mix thoroughly, add more stock if needed, and finish cooking in a slow oven. Serve with hot chicken or veal.

TURKISH PILAF

½ cup washed rice,   ¾ cup tomatoes, stewed and
1 cup brown soup stock   strained,
   highly seasoned,   3 tablespoons butter.

Add tomato to stock, and heat to boiling point; add rice and steam until rice is soft; stir in butter with a fork and keep uncovered that steam may escape. Serve in place of vegetables or as a border for curried or fricasseed meat.

CHAPTER III

BEVERAGES

HOT DRINKS
GENERAL RULES

A beverage is any drink. Water is a beverage, and is an essential to life. All beverages contain a large percentage of water, and aid to quench thirst, to introduce water into the system and regulate the temperature; to assist in carrying off waste; to nourish; to stimulate the nervous system and various organs. Freshly boiled water should be used for making hot beverages; freshly drawn water for making cold beverages.

MILK

Vessels used for milk must be thoroughly cleansed; they should be first washed in clear, cold water. Fill them with water in which a teaspoon of borax or bicarbonate of soda has been dissolved, and let stand one hour. Then scald, wipe thoroughly, and stand in the sun or near the stove to dry.

Cover milk with muslin and keep in a cold place. Milk may be sterilized or pasteurized to destroy disease germs.

In summer, milk should be sterilized twice a day, for babies or young children.

PASTEURIZED MILK

Sterilize milk bottles or jars by boiling them twenty minutes in water.

Fill sterile bottles or jars nearly full of milk, cork them with baked cotton, place on rings in a deep pan and fill with cold water so that the water may be as high outside the jars as the milk is inside, place the pan over the fire and heat until small bubbles appear around the top of the milk (about 155° F); remove to the back of the fire and allow the bottle to stand there 15 minutes, then reduce the temperature as quickly as possible, and when milk is cold remove the bottles from the water and keep in a cold place. In summer milk should be pasteurized twice a day for babies.

COFFEE AND TEA

Coffee, the seeds of the berry of the coffee tree, are roasted in order to develop the aroma. Coffee contains a stimulating substance, called caffeine, and tannin. The tannin is an injurious substance found in tea and coffee. Long steeping develops the tannin.

Tea is made from the leaves of the tea plant. Tea leaves have to be wilted, rolled and dried by artificial heat in order to develop their flavor. Green tea is made from freshly picked young leaves, which are prepared quickly. Ex.: Gunpowder, Hyson and Japan. Black tea is made from leaves left in a heap on the ground, in order to darken and develop the flavor. Ex.: Oolong, English Breakfast, Orange Pekoe.

Tea and coffee should never be taken on an empty stomach unless for medicinal purposes.

Coffee should be bought in small quantities and kept in airtight cans.

FILTERED COFFEE

1 cup coffee, finely ground.   6 cups freshly boiling water.

Place coffee in strainer, strainer in coffee pot and pot over slow fire. Add gradually the boiling water and allow it to filter or drip. Cover between additions of water. If desired stronger, refilter. Serve at once, with cut sugar, cream or scalded milk. Put sugar and cream in cup, then add the hot coffee.

BOILED COFFEE

1 heaping teaspoon ground coffee to
1 cup of freshly boiling water.

1 cup ground coffee to
1 quart freshly boiling water.

Mix the coffee with a clean eggshell and a little cold water, and place in a well aired coffee pot. Add the freshly boiling water, and boil five minutes. Let stand on back of stove ten minutes. Add one-half cup cold water.

NOTE—Coffee should be freshly ground and kept in air-tight cans. A favorite coffee is ⅔ Java and ⅓ Mocha.

CHOCOLATE

1½ ounces bitter chocolate,   1 cup boiling water,
4 tablespoons sugar,   3 cups milk.
Few grains salt,

Scald milk; melt chocolate in small saucepan over hot water; add sugar, salt and gradually boiling water; when smooth, place on range and boil 1 minute; add scalded milk. Beat and serve.

If the sweet chocolate is used, omit the sugar.

COCOA

1 cup milk,   2 teaspoons cocoa,
1 cup boiling water,   2 scant teaspoons sugar.

Scald the milk. In a saucepan put the cocoa, sugar and boiling water. Boil one minute, then add it to the scalded milk. Taste, and add more sugar, if needed.

COCOA SHELLS

1 cup cocoa shells   6 cups boiling water.

Boil shells and water three hours; as water boils away, add more water. Strain and serve with milk and sugar. By adding ⅓ cup of cocoa nibs a much more satisfactory drink is obtained.

TEA

3 teaspoons tea,   2 cups boiling water.

Scald an earthen or china teapot. Put in tea and pour on boiling water. Let stand on back of range or in a warm place 5 minutes. Strain and serve immediately with or without sugar and milk.

RUSSIAN TEA

Russian tea is made and served in dining or drawing room; the water is kept hot in a Samovar and the tea steeped in a teapot. The tea may be served hot or cold, but always without milk. A thin slice of lemon or a few drops of lemon juice is allowed for each cup. Preserved strawberries, cherries or raspberries are considered an improvement.

GLUEH WINE

1 quart claret,   ½ teaspoons whole cloves,
1 pint water,   1 teaspoon whole cinnamon,
2 cups sugar,   lemon rind cut thin and in
                                 small pieces.

Mix all, boil steadily for 15 minutes and serve hot.

PUNCH IMPERIAL

1 sliced pineapple,	grated rind of 1 lemon,
1 bottle of champagne, (or seltzer and claret),	4 oranges cut into pieces, grated rind of 1 orange,
1 bottle of red wine,	1 stick of cinnamon, (broken into pieces),
½ bottle or arrak or rum,	
juice of 4 lemons,	1 stick of vanilla bean, (about 4 inches long),
½ quart of boiling water,	
1 pound of sugar,	½ cup maraschino cherries if desired.

Boil spices thoroughly with the water. Remove them and pour water into large earthen dish. Add lemon and orange juice and rind, also pineapple and sugar, (sugar and fruit to be prepared in a separate dish) then add wine and arrak, cover and heat on back of stove, add champagne before serving.

COLD DRINKS

ICED TEA

Strain freshly made tea into glasses one-third full of cracked ice. Sweeten to taste. A slice of lemon may be added, seeds removed. The flavor is much finer by chilling the infusion quickly.

LEMONADE

1 lemon,	2 cups water.
4 tablespoons sugar,	

Extract the juice of one lemon with a lemon squeezer. Add the sugar and water and stir till dissolved. Add chipped ice if desired. The water may be poured over the sugar boiling hot, in which case, cover and allow to stand until cool, and then add the lemon juice.

LEMONADE FOR 150 PEOPLE

5 doz. lemons, squeezed,	6 pounds sugar,
1 doz. oranges, sliced,	6 gallons water,
1 can or a fresh pineapple,	ice.

The rule is one pound of sugar to every dozen of fruit. If pineapple is fresh, add one more pound of sugar. Mix sugar with fruit and juice, and let stand. When ready to serve add water and ice, to keep cool. The sugar and some water may be boiled to a syrup, allowed to cool, and the fruit and juices added afterward.

ORANGEADE

Follow same rule as for lemonade, adding a little lemon juice.

PINEAPPLE PUNCH

1 quart cold water,
2 cups sugar,
1 cup orange juice,
½ cup lemon juice,
2 cups chopped pineapple.

Boil water and sugar and pineapple 20 minutes; add fruit juice; cool, strain and dilute with ice water.

FRUIT PUNCH FOR 50 PEOPLE

1 cup water,
2 cups sugar,
1 cup tea infusion,
1 quart apollinaris,
2 cups strawberry syrup,
juice of 5 lemons,
juice of 5 oranges,
1 can grated pineapple,
1 cup maraschino cherries.

Boil water and sugar to a syrup, 10 minutes, add tea, strawberry syrup, lemon juice, orange juice and pineapple; let stand ½ hour. Strain and add ice water to make 1½ gallons of liquid. Add cherries and Apollinaris, serve in punch-bowl with large piece of ice.

GRAPE PUNCH

No. 1

¼ cup grape juice,
1 teaspoon lemon juice,
¾ cup cold water,
sugar to taste.

Mix sugar with strained grape juice, add lemon juice and water. A slice of orange or pineapple may also be added.

No. 2

1 pound sugar,
1 cup water,
6 lemons, juice,
1 quart unsweetened grape juice.

Boil sugar and water until it spins a thread when dropped from a spoon. Take from fire and when cool add the juice of the lemons and the grape juice. Let stand over night. When ready to serve add Apollinaris or soda water.

STRAWBERRY PUNCH

2 quarts strawberries,
2 pounds sugar,
juice 2 oranges,
juice 1 lemon,
ice water,
1 cup champagne,
2 whites of eggs,
ice.

Crush the berries with the sugar. Let stand 2 hours; strain through a bag. Add orange and lemon juice and let stand on ice until wanted, then add an equal measure of ice water—the champagne and whites of egg beaten stiff. Place in punchbowl with large piece of ice and serve in tall glasses.

GINGER PUNCH

1 quart cold water,
1 cup sugar,
½ cup lemon juice,
½ pound Canton ginger,
½ cup orange juice,
chopped ice.

Chop ginger, add to water and sugar and boil 15 minutes. Add orange and lemon juice, cool, strain and add chopped ice to dilute.

CLARET CUP

No. 1

3 pints claret wine,
½ cup curacoa,
3 lemons (juice),
½ cup sugar,
1 bunch fresh mint,
1 orange finely sliced,
12 strawberries,
4 slices pineapple,
1 pint Apollinaris,
1 slice cucumber rind.

Mix ingredients except Apollinaris; stand on ice to chill and just before serving add the chilled Apollinaris.

No. 2

1 pint claret,
1 cup sugar,
1 pint sparkling Moselle,
1 orange (juice),
1 slice cucumber rind,
1 pint Apollinaris.

Mix ingredients except Apollinaris; stand on ice to chill and just before serving add the chilled Apollinaris.

WASHINGTON PUNCH FOR 12 PEOPLE

1 pint pineapple, sliced,
1 cup sugar,
½ bottle Moselle wine,
2 bottles Rhine wine,
1 bottle claret wine,
1 pint pineapple, sliced fine,
1 quart champagne,
large piece of ice.

Sprinkle the sugar over the pineapple, add the half bottle Moselle and let stand 24 hours. Strain, add the rest of the Rhine and the claret wine and the other ½ sliced pineapple. Place on ice, just before serving add the champagne and serve from punch-bowl with large piece of ice.

CHAMPAGNE PUNCH FOR 12 PEOPLE

3 pints champagne,
¼ pint maraschino,
½ pint imported brandy,
¼ pound loaf sugar,
½ cup maraschino cherries,
2 lemons,
2 oranges,
pineapple slices,
Ice.

Dissolve the sugar in a little water. Slice oranges and lemons and mix all except champagne and cherries. Place in punch-bowl with large piece of ice and add the cherries and the champagne, chilled. Serve in glasses.

MOSELLE PUNCH

4 bottles Moselle wine,
2 quarts pineapple, chopped,
1 pound sugar,
1 quart champagne,
1 quart seltzer,
ice.

Sugar the chopped pineapple, pour the wine over and let stand several hours on ice to ripen. Place in punch-bowl, add a large piece of ice and the chilled champagne and seltzer. Will serve 25 people.

MINT JULEP

1 teaspoon sugar,
1 teaspoon water,
4 sprigs mint,
1 cup shaved ice,
¼ cup brandy or whiskey,
1 teaspoon maraschino.

Dissolve sugar, water and liquors. Press the mint in to extract the flavor. Stir well, then withdraw the mint and add the fine ice; replace the mint, stems down, leaves above. Trim with fruits in season and serve, in a large thin glass with a straw.

ORANGE JULEP

Rind ½ orange shaved fine,
1 tablespoon powder sugar,
1 cup chopped ice,
2 sprigs fresh mint,
1 teaspoon creme de menthe,
¼ cup whiskey.

Mix orange rind, sugar and a little of the ice for two minutes to extract the oil. Add rest of ice, the fresh mint, stems down, leaves above and the rest of the ingredients. Serve in a large glass with a straw.

GIN FIZZ

½ tablespoon sugar,
½ lemon (juice),
¼ cup gin,
½ cup fine ice,
½ cup Vichy or seltzer water.

Mix sugar, gin and lemon juice, add the ice, stir well. Strain in a tall seltzer glass and fill with Vichy or seltzer water. Serve at once.

EGG MILK PUNCH

1 egg,
3 teaspoons sugar,
½ cup shaved ice,
2 tablespoons St. Croix Rum,
⅓ cup milk,
a grating of nutmeg,
¼ cup brandy.

Mix in the order given, cover tightly, shake well and strain into large tall glass, with the nutmeg on top.

MANHATTAN COCKTAIL

⅓ whiskey (Sheridan rye),
fine ice,
⅓ Vermuth bitters,
⅓ water.

A dash of Angostura, apricotine and orange bitters, and a slice of lemon peel. Stir well and serve in cocktail glasses. Sweeten to taste.

JACKSON COCKTAIL

⅔ glass grape fruit juice,
⅓ glass sherry,
1 tablespoonful maraschino,
1 cherry.

Have all at the very point of freezing.

POUSSE CAFE

⅔ creme de cafe,
⅙ creme de menthe,
⅙ apricotine or vanilla.

Pour the cafe first and slowly add apricotine or vanilla and then the mint, being careful to keep the colors distinct; do not mix.

CHAPTER IV

BREAD, ROLLS AND TOAST

GENERAL RULES

Flour should be kept in a dry atmosphere. It makes better bread if heated just before using. The yeast must be fresh. Scald the milk or water, then cool until lukewarm. The heat of the oven should be increased slightly the first twenty minutes, then kept even for twenty minutes, and the last twenty minutes it should decrease. Bread should be kept in a clean tin box, and not exposed to moisture.

Yeast is a plant, the small, invisible germs of which are floating in the air. They settle in various places, and when they find a warm, moist, sweet, strength-giving or nitrogenous mixture, they begin to grow. Hot water kills the yeast plant; cold water chills it. Lukewarm liquids should be used.

When the yeast plant grows it causes fermentation, which changes some of the starch into sugar, and then some of the sugar into alcohol and carbon-dioxide or carbonic acid gas. This carbon-dioxide gas raises the dough. If it rises too long, it will make the bread sour.

Dough is made light in four ways:
1. By the use of yeast.
2. By the use of baking powder.
3. (a) By the use of soda and molasses.
   (b) By the use of soda and sour milk.
4. By beating air into a mixture:

BREAD

2 cups scalded milk, or boiling water,
1 tablespoon salt,
1 tablespoon sugar,
1 tablespoon butter or other fat,
½ oz. compressed yeast dissolved in ½ cup lukewarm water,
6 to 6½ cups flour.

Put salt, sugar and butter in large mixing bowl; pour on the hot milk or water; when lukewarm add dissolved yeast and five cups flour, mix and stir well with knife or mixing spoon. Add remaining flour, mix and turn the dough out on a floured board and knead until soft and elastic. Put it back into the bowl, moisten, cover, and let it rise in a warm place until double its bulk, cut down, toss on floured board, then divide into loaves, and place into greased or floured pans. Cover the bread and again allow it to double in bulk, then bake one hour in a hot oven, twelve seconds by the hand. Biscuits require more heat and less time to bake. Remove from pans and place in draft if you wish a hard crust. If a soft crust is desired, roll bread in a clean cloth. If set in day time, use 1 cake yeast. This recipe makes 2 loaves. If set at night, use ½ cake yeast. For 4 large loaves take 3 pints milk or water, 3 tablespoons each of salt, sugar, fat or butter, 5 quarts flour, 1 oz. yeast dissolved in ½ cup lukewarm water.

BRAIDED BREAD (BARCHES)

Take bread dough when ready to shape into loaves. Divide into halves, thirds, fourths, etc., according to the number of strands desired for each loaf. Knead slightly and roll the strands evenly, prick with a fork, then twist into braid. Place each braided loaf—into a pan (floured) to rise until very light. Brush top of bread over with yolk of well beaten egg to which a tablespoon of cold water has been added and sprinkle with poppy seeds. Bake in hot oven forty-five to sixty minutes, and cool in a draft to form a hard crust.

TO GLAZE BREAD AND ROLLS

Brush top of bread or rolls over with yolk of egg, to which a pinch of sugar and a tablespoon of cold water has been added. Bake in hot oven and cool in a draft, if you wish a hard crust; if a soft crust is desired, brush over with a little melted butter or sweet cream as soon as it comes out of the oven, or put 2 teaspoons of cornstarch into a saucepan, add 2 tablespoons cold water, mix and add half cup of boiling water. Stir over the fire till it cooks for 5 minutes. Shortly before the bread and rolls are ready, brush the top over with cornstarch mixture, then return to the oven to dry. Repeat this process in 5 minutes and a soft, rich crust will result. For sweetened rolls and buns dredge the top plentifully with granulated sugar, then baste with the cornstarch preparation, then return to the oven to dry, repeat these processes several times and an exceedingly beautiful tasty crust is produced.

RYE BREAD

Rye bread is made same as wheat bread, using rye in place of the wheat flour. If desired, one-fourth to one-half the quantity of wheat flour may be mixed with the rye. Caraway seeds sprinkled in the dough makes a desirable flavor. Bake longer than the wheat bread. Oven must be hot, and the crust should be hard. Brush loaves with water to make them shine.

SOFT GRAHAM BREAD

3 cups graham flour,
1 cup white flour,
1 teaspoon salt,
½ cup molasses, or
¼ cup sugar,
2 tablespoons butter,
¾ yeast cake,
1½ cups warm water.

Dissolve the yeast with a little of the lukewarm water, mix the other ingredients in the order given, and add sufficient lukewarm water to make a soft dough. Cover bowl and set in warm place. When the dough is light beat it and pour into the bread pans, filling them half full. When light, bake in a moderate oven.

GLUTEN BREAD

3 cups milk or water,
½ oz. yeast (1 cake),
About 3 pints gluten flour,
1 egg,
2 tablespoons melted butter,
½ teaspoon salt,
2 tablespoons sugar, if agreeable.

Make a sponge, with the milk or water lukewarm, the yeast crumbled and softened, and a pint of flour. When light, add salt, butter, sugar, if used, the beaten egg and gluten flour to knead. Knead until smooth and elastic. Shape into loaves. Bake about 1 hour.

ENTIRE WHEAT BREAD

2 cups scalded milk,
¼ cup sugar, or
⅓ cup molasses,
1 teaspoon salt,
1 yeast cake, dissolved in ¼ cup lukewarm water,
4⅔ cups of coarse entire wheat flour.

Add sweetening and salt to the milk; cool, and when lukewarm, add the dissolved yeast cake and flour; beat well, cover, and let rise to double its bulk. Beat again and turn into greased bread pans, having pans one-half full. Let rise and bake. Entire wheat bread should not quite double its bulk during last rising. This mixture may be baked in gem pans.

GRAHAM BREAD OR WHOLE WHEAT BREAD

1 cup boiling water,
1 cup fresh milk,
½ oz. yeast (1 cake),
2 tablespoons warm water,
2 teaspoons salt,
2 tablespoons sugar,
Whole wheat flour.

Select whole wheat flour, free from outside bran, pour ½ the boiling water into the fresh milk. When lukewarm add yeast, dissolved in 2 tablespoons of warm water, salt and sugar. Mix and stir in sufficient whole wheat flour to make a batter that will drop from a spoon, beat well, cover securely to exclude air and let stand in a warm place (about 75°) for 3 hours, or until quite light, then stir in sufficient flour to make a soft dough, knead lightly for about 10 minutes, making a softer loaf than for white bread. Mould 2 loaves, place in greased pans, cover and let stand in a warm place until the loaves are double their bulk, about 1 hour. Bake in a slow oven for about 1½ hours.

Add 1 cup nuts when moulding into loaves, if desired.

CURRANT BREAD

2 pints of flour,
3 teaspoons baking powder,
¼ teaspoon salt,
2 cups milk,
1 cup currants,
1 egg,
1 tablespoon sugar.

Mix dry ingredients; wash and dry currants, dredge with flour. Add egg to milk and combine the mixtures. Bake in a deep pan in a hot oven ½ hour.

CORN BREAD

No. 1

2 cups yellow corn meal,
½ teaspoon salt,
3 teaspoons baking powder,
2 cups milk,
2 tablespoons butter,
2 eggs.

Sift together the corn meal, salt and baking powder. Scald the milk, and add the butter to it. When the butter is melted add the milk to the meal together with the yolks of the eggs. Beat the whites of the eggs to a stiff froth, and fold lightly in, just before putting into the oven. Bake in a deep pan, in a hot oven about half an hour.

CORN BREAD

No. 2

1 cup flour,	4 teaspoons baking powder,
1 cup cornmeal,	1 cup sweet milk,
4 tablespoons sugar,	2 tablespoons butter melted,
1 egg,	1 teaspoon salt.

Mix the dry ingredients by sifting them together. Add the milk, the well beaten eggs and the butter. Beat well and bake in a shallow pan in a hot oven, twenty minutes.

No. 3

2 cups corn meal,	1/4 cup sugar,
1 cup flour,	1 egg,
1 1/4 teaspoon soda,	1/2 cup sour cream,
1/2 teaspoon salt,	2 cups sour milk.

Mix the dry ingredients, add the egg beaten lightly and the sour cream and milk. Beat well and bake in shallow pans, in a hot oven about half an hour.

STEAMING BROWN BREAD

Brown bread may be steamed by letting stand in a steamer over boiling water, or on a trivet, in a kettle of boiling water. The water should rise to about half the height of the mould. In either case, the mixture is to be placed in a greased, tightly closed mould. The best results are secured when the water is gradually raised to the boiling-point. After this point is once reached, it needs to be maintained until the cooking is finished, about three hours. Even longer cooking is of no disadvantage.

BOSTON BROWN BREAD

No. 1

1 cup rye meal,	1 teaspoon salt,
1 cup corn meal,	3/4 cup molasses,
1 cup graham flour,	1 3/4 cups sweet milk, or warm
3/4 teaspoon soda,	water.

Mix and sift dry ingredients; add milk and molasses, and place in a covered, greased mould and steam two and one-half hours, or steam in small cups one hour. Fill cups two-thirds full.

No. 2

1 egg,	1 cup sour milk,
1/2 cup sugar,	2 teaspoons soda,
1/2 cup molasses,	1 teaspoon salt,

2 3/4 cups graham flour.

Beat egg slightly, add sugar and molasses and the rest of the ingredients. Mix well and place in 3 one pound greased baking

GINGERBREAD

powder cans (tight covers), and steam one hour. Then bake in moderate oven 25 minutes.

No. 1

½ cup sugar,
3 tablespoons butter,
1 egg,
1½ cups flour,
⅛ teaspoon salt,
1 teaspoon ginger,
1 teaspoon cinnamon,
1 teaspoon soda,
½ cup milk or hot water,
½ cup molasses.

Mix butter and sugar to a soft, creamy paste; add beaten egg. Mix spices, salt and soda with flour, and add a small portion. Add molasses and milk mixed together, and flour alternately. Pour into buttered shallow pans. Bake thirty to forty-five minutes.

No. 2

1 egg,
1 cup sugar,
1 cup molasses,
1 cup sour milk, butter, or
1 cup butter and lard, mixed,
1 teaspoon spices, (cinnamon and cloves),
½ teaspoon ginger,
1 teaspoon of soda, a little salt,
3 cups flour,
½ cup currants, or in season 1 quart blueberries.

Mix soda and sour milk and add to molasses. Cream butter add sugar, then the egg; sift remaining dry ingredients. Combine mixtures. Pour into buttered shallow pans and bake in a moderately hot oven.

GINGERBREAD FOR KUCHEN FILLINGS

5½ cups flour,
1 pt. New Orleans Molasses,
2 tablespoons butter or goose oil.
1 cup warm water,
1 teaspoon soda,

Place flour in bowl; make cavity in center. Add molasses, butter or goose oil, soda dissolved in the warm water.

Mix well and beat thoroughly, about 20 minutes. Pour into buttered bread pans and bake in a moderately hot oven about one hour.

Will keep for months in a dry place.

When stale, grate and use as a garnish for Mehlspeisa, page 179, a filling for Spice Kuchens and as a flavor for Sweet and Sour Sauce, No. 3, page 89.

ROLLS

Take Bread dough, page 28, when ready to shape into loaves, and make a long, even roll. Cut into small even pieces, and shape with thumb and fingers into round balls. Set close together in a shallow pan, let raise until double the bulk, and bake in hot oven from ten to twenty minutes. If crusty rolls are desired, set far apart in a shallow pan, bake well, and cool in draft.

CRESCENT ROLLS

Take Bread dough, page 28, or Kuchen dough, page 311, and when well risen, toss on floured baking board, roll into a square sheet ¼ inch thick. Spread with melted butter, and cut into 6 inch squares, then cut each square into two equal parts through opposite corners, thus forming two triangles. Roll over and over from the longest side to the opposite corner and then shape the rolls into half moons or crescents. Place in floured or greased pans, rather far apart; brush with beaten yolk to which a little cold water has been added and sprinkle tops of crescents or horns with poppy seed. Set in warm place to rise and when double its bulk, bake in hot oven until brown and crusty.

BREAD STICKS

1 cup scalded milk,
¼ cup butter,
1½ tablespoon sugar,
1 yeast cake,
1 egg (white),
3¾ cups flour,
½ teaspoon salt.

Add butter, sugar and salt to milk; when lukewarm add yeast cake, white of egg well beaten, and flour.

Knead, let rise, roll, shape and size of a lead pencil. Place in floured pan, far apart, brush tops with beaten yolk of egg and sprinkle with poppy seed (if desired). Let raise and bake in hot oven until brown and crisp.

PARKER HOUSE ROLLS

2 cups scalded milk,
3 tablespoons butter,
2 tablespoons sugar,
1 teaspoon salt,
1 ounce compressed yeast,
¼ cup lukewarm water,
5½ cups flours.

Add butter, sugar and salt to milk; when lukewarm, add yeast dissolved in the lukewarm water, and 3 cups of flour. Beat thoroughly, cover and let rise until light; cut down and add the rest of the flour or enough to knead. Let rise again in a warm place, toss on slightly floured board, knead, pat and roll out to ⅓ inch thickness. Shape into rounds, with biscuit cutter; dip the handle of a knife in flour and with it make a crease through the middle of each piece; brush over one-half of each piece with melted butter, fold and press edges together. Place in greased pan one inch apart, cover, let rise and bake in a hot oven 12 to 15 minutes.

SALAD ROLLS

Use same ingredients as for Parker House Rolls. Shape in small biscuits, place in rows on a floured board, cover with cloth and let rise until light and well puffed. Flour handle of wooden spoon and make a deep crease in middle of each biscuit, take up, and press edges together. Place close together in buttered pan, cover, let rise and bake 15 to 20 minutes in a hot oven. From this same mixture crescents, small braids, bow knots and other fancy shapes may be made.

TEA ROLLS

1 cup milk,
1½ cups flour,
1½ teaspoons salt,
⅓ cup butter,

1 oz. compressed yeast,
¼ cup sugar,
2 eggs,
flour.

Scald milk, when lukewarm dissolve yeast cake and add 1½ cups flour. Beat thoroughly, cover and allow to stand until light. Add sugar, salt, eggs, butter and enough flour to knead. Allow to rise again, until light. Shape into rounds or small oblong finger rolls, and place in buttered pans close together, when light, bake in hot oven.

YELLOW BISCUITS

1 cup lukewarm milk,
2 tablespoons butter,
1 tablespoon sugar,
1 tablespoon salt,

½ ounce compressed yeast,
3½ cups flour,
1 cup strained Hubbard Squash.

Crumble yeast with sugar in a little of the lukewarm milk, add the rest of the milk, the salt, butter and squash or sweet potato. Then add the flour, knead until smooth, add more flour if necessary. Let rise in a warm place. Roll and shape into biscuits and let rise again and bake in a moderate oven about ½ hour, or until thoroughly done.

FRIED POTATO BISCUITS

1 cup flour,
1 cup cold mashed potatoes,
¼ teaspoon salt,
1 oz. compressed yeast,
Milk.

Take flour, add the salt and mashed potato. Let yeast dissolve in a little lukewarm milk, mix all together and add rich milk enough to make like biscuit dough; roll out about one-half inch thick; cut into two-inch squares, let rise, and fry a golden brown in deep, hot fat.

POTATO BISCUITS

½ oz. compressed yeast,
1 cup warm milk,
1 tablespoonful sugar,
1 teaspoon salt,
1 quart sifted flour (scant).
2 large potatoes, (baked and grated),
2 eggs,
½ cup butter.

Dissolve yeast in the warm milk. Mix in the order given and knead while the potato is hot and set to rise. Add more flour if necessary. Roll thin and cut with small biscuit cutter. Lay two biscuits, one on top of the other in a pan and stand in a warm place. Bake about twenty minutes in a moderate oven. Brush over with sugar and water before placing in the oven.

ZWIEBACK

½ cup milk,
½ teaspoon salt,
1 oz. compressed yeast,
¼ cup sugar,
¼ cup melted butter,
3 eggs,
flour.

Scald the milk and when lukewarm add to the crumbled yeast. Add the sugar, butter, salt, and the eggs unbeaten, and enough flour to handle. Let rise until light. Make into oblong rolls the length of middle finger, and place close together in a buttered pan in parallel rows, two inches apart. Let rise again and bake 20 minutes. When cold, cut in half inch slices and brown evenly in the oven.

USES FOR STALE BREAD

Crusts and small pieces of bread should be dried in a cool oven until a light brown. Roll them on a pastry board, or put through a meat grinder. Crumbs must be sifted. Use them only to cover articles of food cooked in deep fat. Crumbs should be kept in jars with a piece of muslin tied over them.

CROUTONS

Cut pieces of stale bread into cubes, and brown in the oven.

CRISPED CRUSTS

Cut the crusts of bread into strips one inch wide, five inches long and one-half inch thick, and toast in oven to a golden brown.

SOUP STICKS

Cut stale bread in ⅓ inch slices, remove crusts, brown in the oven, and cut in ⅓ inch strips.

BREAD PATTIES OR CANAPES

Cut bread into pieces 2 inches thick; cut either round or 4½ inches long by 3 inches wide. Remove part of bread from center, butter and brown in the oven.

DRY TOAST

Cut stale bread one-fourth inch thick; dry in the oven. Then put on a toaster or fork, move it gently over heat until dry, then allow it to become a light brown by placing it nearer the heat and turning constantly; or, light gas oven, heat five to eight minutes. Place bread in toaster or pan, one inch from gas, in lower or broiling oven. When brown on one side turn and brown on the other. Serve with or without butter. Bread cut into triangles and toasted are called toast points, and are used for garnishing.

WATER TOAST

Dip slices of dry toast into boiling, salted water. Quickly remove and butter.

CREAM OR MILK TOAST

2 cups milk or cream, 2 tablespoon butter,
1 tablespoon flour, 1 teaspoon salt,

Cook the flour in the melted butter. Add salt and gradually stir in the hot milk. After it thickens, pour this sauce over slices of dry or water toast; or butter the dry hot toast, add ½ tablespoon salt to one cup of hot milk, and pour it over the toast. Serve hot.

FRENCH TOAST

2 eggs, ⅔ cup milk,
½ teaspoon salt, 6 slices of stale bread.

Beat the eggs slightly, add salt and milk, dip the bread in the mixture. Have a griddle hot and well buttered; brown the bread on each side. Serve hot with cinnamon and sugar or a sauce.

MATZOS DIPPED IN EGGS

4 matzos (unleavened bread), 2 tablespoons goose fat, or olive oil,
6 eggs, Sugar and cinnamon,
½ tablespoon salt,
Lemon, grated rind.

Beat eggs very light, add salt. Heat the fat in a spider. Break matzos into large, equal pieces. Dip each piece in the egg mixture and fry a light brown on both sides. Serve hot, sprinkled with sugar, cinnamon and a little grated lemon rind.

CHAPTER V

BISCUITS AND BREAKFAST CAKES

BAKING POWDER DOUGHS

All measurements are level.

Pastry flour should be used, if possible. Flour must be sifted before it is measured; then mix and sift dry ingredients.

Six teaspoons of baking powder will raise 1 qt. of flour.

The eggs are beaten whole and the milk added to them, then added to the dry ingredients. When fat is used, it is usually melted and added last, but may be worked into the flour with the tips of the fingers, or cut in with a knife.

The pans or muffin rings should be greased before the mixture is prepared. Iron gem-pans must be heated.

The oven must be ready for baking before mixtures are prepared; they must be put into the oven as soon as prepared and baked from 12 to 30 m. Bake on the floor of the oven; they may be raised to the shelf to brown.

BAKING POWDER BISCUITS

2 cups flour,
4 teaspoons baking powder,
½ teaspoon salt,
¾ to 1 cup mlik, or water,
2 tablespoons shortening.

Sift the dry ingredients together. Rub the butter into the flour with the tips of the fingers. Mix the milk into the flour with a knife adding the milk gradually until as soft as can be handled easily. Put it on a floured board and roll until ½ inch thick. Cut in small rounds and bake in hot oven 10 to 15 minutes.

Use as little flour as possible on the board when shaping the dough.

WHEAT MUFFINS

2 cups flour,
½ teaspoon salt,
3 teaspoons baking powder,
2 tablespoons sugar,
1 tablespoon butter,
1 teaspoon molasses,
1 egg,
1 cup milk.

Mix dry ingredients and sieve twice, rub in the butter. Separate the egg. Beat the yolk and add it to the milk and molasses. Mix with the dry ingredients and stir until smooth. Fold in the beaten white of egg and pour into hot, well greased muffin tins. Bake fifteen to twenty minutes in hot oven.

NOTE—Graham, rye, cornmeal, or whole wheat muffins are made the same way, by mixing with the wheat flour one-fourth to one-half the quantity of graham, rye, cornmeal or whole wheat flour.

WHOLE WHEAT MUFFINS

1½ cups whole wheat flour,
½ cup flour,
3 teaspoons baking powder,
½ teaspoon salt,
¼ cup sugar,
1 egg,
1 cup milk,
2 tablespoons butter, melted.

Mix dry ingredients; add egg, well beaten and the butter. Beat well and bake in buttered muffin tins 25 to 30 minutes in hot oven.

GRAHAM GEMS

½ cup flour,
1 cup graham flour,
¼ teaspoon salt,
3½ teaspoons baking powder,
1 egg,
¾ cup milk (about).

Sift the flour and do not use the bran left in the sifter. Sift again with the salt and baking powder; add the egg well beaten and enough milk to make a stiff batter. Bake in buttered gem pans, in hot oven 15 minutes.

TWIN MOUNTAIN MUFFINS

⅓ cup butter,
¼ cup sugar,
¼ teaspoon salt,
1 egg,
¾ cup milk,
2 cups flour,
4 teaspoons baking powder.
1 cup blackberries, in season.

Cream the butter; add the sugar gradually; then alternately the egg beaten and mixed with the milk and the flour sifted with the baking powder. Bake in buttered tin gem pans about 25 minutes. ¼ lb. dates, chopped fine, may be added to creamed butter and sugar for Date Muffins.

BISCUITS AND BREAKFAST CAKES

FRIED RYE MUFFINS

¾ cup rye meal,
¾ cup white flour,
2 teaspoons baking powder,
1 tablespoon sugar,
¼ teaspoon salt,
1 egg,
½ cup milk.

Mix in the order given, and drop from a small tablespoon into hot deep fat. Cook until the muffin will not stick when tried with a toothpick.

CORNMEAL MUFFINS

¼ cup butter,
½ cup sugar,
2 eggs,
1 cup milk,
2 cups flour,
1 cup cornmeal,
4 teaspoons baking powder,
½ tablespoon salt.

Cream the butter. Add sugar, then eggs, beaten, without separating, until light-colored and thick. Into this stir, alternately the milk, flour, and corn meal, sifted with the baking powder and salt. Beat thoroughly, and bake about twenty minutes in hot, well-buttered gem-pans.

ENGLISH MUFFINS WITH YEAST

1 cup scalded milk,
1 cup boiling water,
2 tablespoons butter,
¼ cup sugar,
¾ teaspoon salt,
½ yeast cake (¼ oz.),
1 egg,
4 cups flour.

Add butter, sugar and salt to milk and water; when lukewarm, add yeast cake, crumbled, and when dissolved, egg, well beaten and flour; beat thoroughly, cover and let rise over night. In morning fill buttered muffin ring ⅔ full, let rise until rings are full and bake ½ hour in a hot oven; or, if preferred, put the raised muffin mixture in buttered muffin rings on a hot greased griddle. Cook slowly until well risen and browned underneath; turn muffins and rings and brown on the other side.

Or, take plain Bread dough, page 28, and when light, divide into pieces and shape into small rounded biscuits. Place them on a layer of flour 2 inches thick on wooden trays and let them rise again; then place them carefully on a hot plate or stove and bake them until they are slightly browned, turn and brown them on other side. It takes from 20 minutes to ½ hour to bake them.

CINNAMON ROLLS

2 cups flour,
3 teaspoons baking powder,
⅓ teaspoon salt,
2 tablespoons butter,
⅔ cup milk,

2 tablespoons sugar,
½ cup stoned raisins chopped fine, or currants,
2 tablespoons citron, chopped fine,
⅓ teaspoon cinnamon.

Mix five first ingredients same as baking powder biscuits. Roll to one-fourth inch thickness, brush over with melted butter and sprinkle with the raisins, citron, sugar and cinnamon. Roll like a jelly roll. Cut in pieces three-fourths inch thick. Place in buttered tins endwise and bake ten minutes in a hot oven. Dried currants may be used in place of raisins.

DUTCH APPLE CAKE

2 cups flour,
3 teaspoons baking powder,
½ teaspoon salt,
3 tablespoons butter,

1 egg,
About ⅔ cup milk,
4 sour apples,
2 tablespoons sugar,
Little cinnamon.

Mix and sift the dry ingredients, work in shortening with tips of fingers, or cut in with knives; add milk with the well beaten egg, gradually mixing with a knife. Dough must be soft enough to spread in a shallow baking pan. Have ready, pared, cored and cut in quarters, the apples and when dough has been spread in pan, press apples into dough in parallel rows. Sprinkle the apples with the sugar and cinnamon. Bake in hot oven about ½ hour. Serve hot with a Lemon Sauce, page 95.

RHUBARB PUDDING

2 cups rhubarb, cut in ½ inch pieces,
1 egg,

⅔ cup sugar,
Baking powder biscuit crust.

Beat egg lightly, add sugar and rhubarb; pour this mixture into buttered baking dish, cover with Baking Powder Biscuit dough, page 39, and bake in hot oven until brown. Serve with Hard Sauce, page 243.

BISCUITS AND BREAKFAST CAKES

STRAWBERRY SHORTCAKE, No. 1

2 cups flour,
4 teaspoons baking powder,
½ teaspoon salt,
1 tablespoon sugar,
¾ cup milk,
¼ cup butter,
1 to 1½ qts. strawberries,
Cream.

Mix dry ingredients, work in butter with tips of fingers, and add milk gradually. Toss on floured board, divide in 2 parts. Pat, roll out and bake 12 minutes in hot oven in layer cake tins. Split and spread with butter. Sweeten strawberries to taste. Crush slightly and put between and on top of short cake. Allow from 1 to 1½ boxes berries to each short cake. Serve with cream, plain or whipped.

STRAWBERRY SHORTCAKE, No. 2

3 eggs, yolks,
1½ cups sugar,
1 teaspoon lemon juice,
½ cup water,
2 cups pastry flour,
2 teaspoons baking powder,
Whites 3 eggs,
1 qt. strawberries.

Beat yolks; add the sugar, lemon juice and water; then the flour, mixed with the baking powder, and lastly the whites of the eggs. Bake in shallow pans. When cool, split and fill with 1 pint of strawberries, which have been slightly crushed. Make a meringue, by beating the whites of 2 eggs stiff, and add gradually 4 tablespoons powdered sugar. Place on top of cake and garnish with the remainder of the strawberries.

POPOVERS

¼ teaspoon salt,
1 cup flour,
1 cup milk,
1 egg.

Sift flour and salt into a bowl. Beat the egg and add the milk to it, and stir gradually into the flour to make a smooth batter. Beat with egg-beater until full of air bubbles. Fill hot greased gem pans two-thirds full of the mixture. Bake in quick oven 30 to 40 minutes, until brown and popped over.

LEMON PUFFS

3 eggs,
½ cup powdered sugar,
¼ teaspoon salt,
½ lemon, grated rind,
2 cups flour.

Separate eggs; beat yolks well with sugar, add salt and lemon rind, then the whites beaten stiff and stir in the flour. Bake in muffin tins as soon as mixed, in a moderate oven.

BAKING POWDER BATTERS

Baking Powder is composed of baking soda and cream of tartar with a little flour or cornstarch.

Soda is an alkali.

Cream of Tartar is an acid.

Baking Powder $\begin{cases} \frac{1}{2} \text{ cream of tartar,} \\ \frac{1}{4} \text{ soda,} \\ \frac{1}{4} \text{ starch.} \end{cases}$

Batter is a mixture of flour with sufficient liquid to make it thin enough to be beaten.

Pour-Batter, 1 measure of liquid to 1 measure of flour.

Drop-Batter, 1 measure of liquid to 2 measures of flour.

General Directions for Batters and Doughs:

Sift flour before measuring. Put flour by spoonfuls into the cup; do not press or shake down. Mix and sift dry ingredients. Measure dry, then liquid ingredients, shortening may be rubbed or chopped in while cold, or creamed; or it may be melted and then added to dry ingredients, or added after the liquid. Use 2 teaspoons baking powder to 1 cup flour. If eggs are used, less baking powder will be required.

Baking powder mixture should be handled as little as possible.

Baking powder mixture requires a hot oven.

PLAIN GRIDDLE CAKES

2 teaspoons baking powder,
1 cup flour,
¼ teaspoon salt,
1 cup milk (scant),
1 egg,
1 teaspoon melted butter.

Sift the dry ingredients. Beat the egg. Add the milk, and stir it in gradually to make a smooth batter. If not thin enough, use more milk.

Heat an iron griddle and grease it with a piece of fat. Pour the cakes on the griddle from the end of a large spoon. When the cakes are full of bubbles, turn with a broad knife, and brown the other side. Wipe griddle with a dry cloth and grease again after each baking. The egg may be omitted.

Larger quantity: 3 cups flour, 1½ tablespoons baking powder, 1 teaspoon salt, ¼ cup sugar, 2 cups milk, 1 egg, 2 tablespoons melted butter.

SOUR MILK GRIDDLE CAKES

No. 1

1 egg,
1 cup sour milk,
1 cup flour (scant),
½ teaspoon soda, dissolved in a little water,
½ teaspoon salt.

Beat egg in pitcher or sauce pan; add milk, if not thick enough, add a little melted butter; add flour, salt and soda. Mix well and bake on a hot griddle as Plain Griddle Cakes, page 44.

No. 2

2½ cups flour,
½ teaspoon salt,
1 egg.
2 cups sour milk,
1¼ teaspoons soda,

Mix dry ingredients. Add milk and the egg well beaten. Drop by spoonfuls on a greased hot griddle. Brown well on both sides. Serve with butter and Maple Syrup or Sugar Syrup, page 46.

BREAD GRIDDLE CAKES

1½ cups fine bread crumbs,
1½ cups hot milk,
2 tablespoons butter,
2 eggs,
½ cup flour,
½ teaspoon salt,
3½ teaspoons baking powder.

Mix in the order given. One cup any cooked cereal may be used instead of bread crumbs. Cook as other Griddle Cakes.

RICE GRIDDLE CAKES

2 cups hot boiled rice,
2 cups flour,
3 teaspoons baking powder,
1 teaspoon salt,
1 pint of milk,
2 eggs.

Mix the dry ingredients. The beaten yolks are added to the milk. Combine the two mixtures and lastly fold in the beaten whites. Cook as Griddle Cakes.

CORNMEAL GRIDDLE CAKES

1 cup flour,
1 cup cornmeal,
1 tablespoon baking powder,
1½ teaspoons salt,
2 cups milk,
1 or 2 eggs,

Mix the dry ingredients. Beat egg well, add salt and the milk, and combine the two mixtures. A tablespoon of molasses may be added to the batter. Cook as other Griddle Cakes. One teaspoon soda and two cups sour milk may be used in place of the baking powder and sweet milk.

CORNMEAL AND RICE GRIDDLE CAKES

½ cup cornmeal,
½ cup flour,
1 cup boiled rice,
2 teaspoons baking powder,
½ teaspoon salt,
2 eggs,
1 cup milk.

Mix dry ingredients. The beaten yolks with the milk. Combine the two mixtures, and fold in the whites beaten stiff. Cook same as other Griddle Cakes.

BUCKWHEAT CAKES

1 qt. lukewarm water,
1 teaspoon salt,
3¼ cups buckwheat flour,
½ cup flour,
½ ounce compressed yeast,
2 tablespoons molasses.

Dissolve the yeast in a little warm water with 1 teaspoon sugar; add to the rest of the water and mix with the flour, salt and buckwheat to make a thin batter. Let raise over night, next morning, add molasses and bake on a hot greased griddle, in small cakes, browning on both sides. Serve with sugar or syrup.

Save a cupful of this batter each time and it will be equally as nice as fresh yeast. After using two mornings add ½ teaspoon saleratus or soda to two tablespoonfuls of boiling water, beat thoroughly in the dough. This can be continued each day for at least 3 weeks, before making fresh sponge.

WAFFLES

1 pint flour,
3 teaspoons baking powder,
½ teaspoon salt,
1 tablespoon melted butter,
2 eggs, yolks and whites beat separately,
1 cup milk.

Mix in the order given, and bake at once on hot, well greased waffle iron. If the batter is too stiff, more milk may be used. Serve with syrup.

SUGAR SYRUP

2 cups sugar,
⅔ cup boiling water.

Use brown, white or scraped maple sugar. Pour on the boiling water and stir until the sugar is dissolved, but not afterwards. Boil until clear, and then cool.

CHAPTER VI

EGGS, OMELETS AND PANCAKES

COMPOSITION OF EGGS

Proteids, 14.9 per cent. Mineral matter, 1 per cent.
Fat, 10.6 per cent. Water, 73.5 per cent.

GENERAL RULES

A stale egg rises in water; fresh eggs are heavy, and sink to the bottom. Wash eggs as soon as they come from the store. Eggs should never be boiled, as that renders them tough and difficult of digestion. They should be cooked just under the boiling point.

SOFT COOKED EGGS

Have the water boiling, drop in the eggs gently, and place on stove where they will simmer but not boil, for from five to eight minutes.

HARD COOKED EGGS

Place the eggs in boiling water, move to a warm place, where they will simmer, not boil, and let cook thirty minutes. Remove shells, cut in quarters lengthwise, and pour browned butter over them and serve hot.

POACHED OR DROPPED EGGS

Fill a pan with boiling, salted water. Break each egg into a wet saucer and slip it into the water; set the pan back where water will not boil. Dip the water over the eggs with a spoon. When the white is firm and a film has formed over the yolk, they are cooked. Take them up with a skimmer, drain and serve hot, on toast. Season with salt.

STEAMED EGGS

Break an egg into a buttered cup or in patent egg steamer. Sprinkle it with salt and pepper. Put cup or cups into a steamer and cook until the white is set (three to five minutes). Remove carefully from cup with teaspoon. Serve on toast garnished with toast points.

SCRAMBLED EGGS

3 eggs,
½ teaspoon salt,
⅓ cup milk or water,
spk. pepper,
1 teaspoon butter.

Beat the eggs slightly, add the milk and seasoning. Cook in a hot, buttered frying pan, stirring constantly until thick. Serve hot.

BUTTERED EGGS

Melt one tablespoon of butter, slip in an egg and cook until the white is firm. Turn over once while cooking, and use just enough butter to keep it from sticking.

FRIED EGGS

Fried eggs are cooked as buttered eggs without being turned. They are usually fried with bacon fat, which is taken by spoonfuls and poured over the eggs. Do not have the fat too hot as that will give the egg a hard, indigestible crust.

SHIRRED EGG

Butter an egg shirrer or small vegetable dish, cover bottom and side with fine bread crumbs. Add an egg very carefully, cover with seasoned bread crumbs, and bake in a slow oven until white is firm and crumbs are brown.

EGGS IN A NEST

Separate whites from yolks; beat whites until dry. Butter a small fancy dish in which eggs are to be served; sprinkle fine bread crumbs in bottom. Place beaten whites in dish, make hollow and slip in the yolks, set bowl in sauce pan containing boiling water, cover and cook until white is firm. If brown tint is desired, set in hot oven for 1 minute or hold dish under flame in broiling oven.

POACHED EGGS AND CHEESE

6 eggs, poached,
6 tablespoons grated cheese,
1 cup white sauce,
6 pieces toast.

Cut toast round and put a poached egg upon it. Cook the White Sauce, page 87, add the cheese and pour over the egg. Garnish with parsley. Serve hot.

EGGS AU GRATIN, No. 1

6 hard cooked eggs,
1 pint White Sauce,
¾ cup grated American cheese,
¼ cup stale bread crumbs.

Remove shells of eggs, cut off a thin slice at each end, then cut in half crosswise. Remove yolks and stand the white cups or baskets on a shallow buttered dish or in ramikins. Rub the yolks to a smooth paste; add ¼ cup of grated cheese or, if preferred, an equal amount of minced ham, tongue or chicken, a speck of cayenne pepper, and moisten to shape with vinegar and olive oil or melted butter. Make into balls the size of the original yolks and fill the cups. Sprinkle eggs with grated cheese; pour over White Sauce, page 87, Cream Sauce, page 88, or Tomato Sauce, page 93, cover with bread crumbs, and sprinkle with grated cheese. Brown in the oven. Garnish with parsley. Serve hot.

Or, use whole eggs, eggs cut in halves, quarters, or slices, and cover with cream or tomato sauce, and then with buttered cracker crumbs. Set into the oven to reheat the mixture and brown the crumbs.

EGGS AU GRATIN (IN RAMIKINS)

3 hard cooked eggs,
3 tablespoons butter,
1 teaspoon onion, chopped fine,
1 teaspoon parsley, chopped fine,
¼ cup grated American cheese,
1 cup White Sauce,
Salt and cayenne to taste.

Cut hard cooked eggs in halves crosswise. Remove yolks and stand a white cup thus formed in each ramikin. Strain yolks through sieve or ricer; cream ½ of the sifted yolks with butter, add onion, parsley and salt and cayenne to taste, shape into balls the size of the original yolks and fill in the cups. Add the remaining yolk to the White Sauce, page 87, pour over eggs, sprinkle with the cheese and place in the oven to brown.

EGGS A LA MARTIN

1 cup white sauce,
6 eggs,
¼ pound grated American cheese.

Break the eggs carefully into a well buttered pudding dish, cover with the White Sauce, page 87, and sprinkle cheese over all. Bake 15 minutes in a moderate oven.

EGGS IN BAKED POTATOES

6 potatoes,
6 eggs,
6 tablespoons grated cheese,
6 teaspoons butter.

Bake the potatoes, cut off the top and remove half of the inside of potato, in its place drop an egg raw, salt, cayenne pepper, 1 tablespoon cheese in each and 1 teaspoon butter. Put back into a hot oven for 4 minutes.

EGGS IN TOMATO SAUCE

1 cup tomato sauce,
6 eggs,

Make Tomato Sauce, No. 1, page 93. Put in the bottom of a pudding dish—or take 2 tablespoons of the sauce and place in individual cups or ramikins, drop in the eggs or egg and cover with the Tomato Sauce. Bake in a moderate oven 8 to 10 minutes. Serve in the dishes in which they are cooked.

EGGS A LA COLUMBUS

Select green peppers or small tomatoes of uniform size. Plunge into boiling water, and remove the outer skin. Cut around the stem, and remove the seeds and veins. Set the peppers or tomatoes in small cake-pans, break a fresh egg into each, add salt and pepper and poach in a moderate oven about twelve minutes, or until the egg is set. Have ready a square of hot buttered toast for each egg. Serve with Tomato Sauce, page 93, poured round or in a dish apart.

EGGS A LA BUCKINGHAM

Make 5 slices milk toast and arrange on a platter. Use recipe for scrambled eggs—having eggs slightly underdone. Pour eggs over toast and sprinkle with 4 tablespoons grated mild cheese. Place in oven to melt cheese and finish cooking eggs.

SCRAMBLED EGGS WITH TOMATO SAUCE

5 eggs,
½ teaspoon salt,
2 tablespoons butter,
½ cup milk or water,
⅛ teaspoon pepper.

Beat eggs slightly with silver fork; add salt, pepper and milk. Heat omelet pan, put in butter, and when melted, turn in mixture. Cook until of creamy consistency, stirring and scraping carefully from bottom of pan. Have the following Tomato Sauce ready, stir it into the scrambled eggs, and serve hot on toast or crackers.

TOMATO SAUCE

2 tablespoons butter,
1 tablespoon chopped onion,
1¾ cups tomatoes,
1 tablespoon sliced mushrooms,
1 tablespoon capers,
¼ teaspoon salt,
Pepper.

Cook onions in butter until yellow, add tomatoes and cook until moisture has nearly evaporated. Add mushrooms, capers, salt, pepper. This is improved by a small piece of red or green pepper, finely chopped and cooked with onion and butter.

GOLDEN ROD TOAST

4 hard cooked eggs,
6 to 8 slices toast,
2 cups white sauce.

Separate the yolk and white of egg and chop the white. Put the yolk in a warm place. Make a White Sauce, page 87. Add the whites to the sauce. Heat thoroughly, and pour the mixture upon the toast. Press the yolk over the whole, through a fine strainer, and garnish with toast points and parsley.

CURRIED EGGS

6 hard cooked eggs,
2 tablespoons butter,
2 tablespoons flour,
¼ teaspoon salt,
½ teaspoon curry powder,
⅛ teaspoon pepper,
1 cup hot milk.

Melt butter, add flour and seasonings and gradually the hot milk. Slice the eggs, crosswise or in eighths lengthwise and reheat in the sauce. Garnish with bread Croutons, page 37. If you desire one teaspoon chopped onion may be browned in the butter.

DEVILED EGGS

4 hard cooked eggs,
¼ teaspoon salt,
½ teaspoon mustard,
¼ teaspoon Cayenne pepper,
1 teaspoon vinegar,
1 teaspoon olive oil or melted butter.

Take eggs when cold, remove shell and cut each in two lengthwise. Remove yolks and set whites aside. Rub yolks smooth and mix thoroughly with the rest of the ingredients and roll into balls size of original yolk. Place a ball in each half white of egg, and send to the table on a bed of crisp lettuce leaves.

EGGS A LA TARCAT

6 hard cooked eggs,
¼ pound chopped ham,
¼ onion chopped,
¼ teaspoon prepared mustard,
1 teaspoon salt,
a little red pepper.

Cut the eggs in half, lengthwise. Remove the yolk. Rub the yolks smooth with the rest of the ingredients, and refill the whites of eggs with this ham mixture. Serve cold on lettuce leaves with a little Mayonnaise, page 190, on each egg.

SCOTCH EGGS

1 cup lean ham, chopped very fine,
6 hard cooked eggs,
⅔ cup stale bread crumbs,
⅓ cup of milk,
½ teaspoon mustard,
1 raw egg,
Pepper to taste.

Cook bread crumbs in the milk and rub to a smooth paste. Mix it with the ham, add mustard, cayenne and the raw egg. Mix well. Remove the shells from the eggs and cover with the mixture; fry in hot fat 2 minutes, drain and serve hot or cold for lunch or picnics. Cut them in halves lengthwise and arrange each half on a bed of fine parsley. The contrast between the green, red, white and yellow gives a very pretty effect.

CREAMY OMELET

4 eggs,	½ teaspoon salt,
4 tablespoons milk, or water,	⅛ teaspoon pepper,
	1 teaspoon butter.

Beat eggs slightly, enough to blend the yolks and whites. Add milk and seasoning. Put butter in hot spider; when melted, turn in the mixture. As it cooks, draw the edges toward the center with a knife until the whole is set. If desired brown underneath, place on hotter part of the stove. Fold and turn on hot platter.

FRENCH OMELET

3 eggs,	spk. pepper,
½ teaspoon salt,	3 tablespoons hot water,
1 teaspoon butter.	

Beat the yolks of the eggs until thick; add salt, pepper and water. Fold in the whites of the eggs beaten stiff. Cook in a hot buttered omelet pan until it sets and is brown underneath. Finish cooking on the top grate of the oven. Chopped parsley, cheese, fruit jelly or meat may be placed in the center. Fold and turn upon a heated platter.

OMELET WITH WHITE SAUCE

½ tablespoon butter,	¼ cup milk,
½ tablespoon flour,	1 egg,
⅛ tablespoon salt,	½ teaspoon butter (for pan).
Pepper.	

Make a White Sauce, page 87, of the first five ingredients. Separate yolk and white of egg and beat them until light. When the sauce is cool, add the yolk and cut in the white. Turn on heated buttered pan and cook until set.

OMELET WITH FLOUR

3 eggs, beaten, separately,	2 tablespoons flour,
1 cup milk,	½ teaspoon salt.

Stir one-quarter of the milk with the flour and salt mixed, until smooth, add the rest of the milk and pour and stir over the beaten yolks, then fold in whites, beaten dry. Pour in a hot buttered spider and cook slowly on top of stove five minutes, set in a moderately slow oven and bake twenty minutes more or until set and a golden brown. Fold and serve on hot platter.

BREAD OMELET

2 tablespoons bread crumbs, 2 tablespoons of milk,
1 speck of salt, 1 egg,
1 speck of pepper, ½ teaspoon butter.

Soak the bread crumbs in the milk for fifteen minutes, then add the salt and pepper. Separate the yolk and the white of the egg and beat until light. Add the yolk to the bread and milk and cut in the white. Turn in the heated buttered pan and cook until set. Fold and turn on heated dish.

ASPARAGUS OMELET

Omlet, 1 can asparagus.
1 cup White Sauce,

Follow any of the above omelet recipes. Make White Sauce, page 87. Add asparagus, drained and rinsed, to the White Sauce, spread some of the mixture over half of the baked omelet, fold over the other half, turn on platter and pour over the rest of the sauce. Use the cut asparagus. Cooked peas, cauliflower, or remnants of finely chopped cooked chicken, veal or ham may be used in place of the asparagus.

ORANGE OMELET

Rind of ⅓ orange, 2 tablespoons powdered
1 egg, sugar.
1 tablespoon orange juice,

Beat the yolk of the egg and add the orange rind and juice. Add the sugar. Fold in the beaten white and turn on heated buttered pan and cook until set. Serve with powdered sugar.

SPANISH OMELET

French omelet, 1¾ cups tomatoes,
2 tablespoons butter, 1 tablespoon sliced mush-
1 tablespoon onion, finely rooms,
  chopped, 1 tablespoon capers,
6 olives chopped, ¼ teaspoon salt,
½ green pepper chopped fine, Few grains cayenne.

Make a French Omelet, page 53, with 4 eggs. First have ready the following sauce. Heat the butter in a spider, add the onions, olives and green pepper and cook a few minutes, then add the tomatoes and cook until moisture has nearly evaporated. Add the rest of the ingredients. Before folding the omelet, place spoonful on center, then fold and pour the rest of the sauce over and around.

FRENCH PANCAKE

3 eggs, separated,
¼ cup flour,
½ teaspoon salt,
1 cup cold water.

Stir yolks with the salt and flour, until smooth, add milk gradually, then fold in the beaten whites. Heat pan, add 2 tablespoons butter and when hot, pour in pancake; let cook slowly and evenly on one side, finish baking in oven.

GERMAN PANCAKE, No. 1

2 eggs,
1 cup milk,
½ teaspoon salt,
2½ tablespoons flour,
2 tablespoons butter.

Beat eggs very thoroughly without separating the yolks and whites; add salt, sift in the flour, add the milk gradually at first and beat the whole very well. Melt 1 tablespoon butter in a large frying pan, turn mixture in and cook slowly until brown underneath. Grease the bottom of a large pie plate, slip the pancake on the plate; add the other tablespoon of butter to the frying pan, when hot, turn uncooked side of pancake down and brown. Serve at once with sugar and lemon slices or with any desired preserve or syrup.

Or, when the pancake is nicely browned on the one side, the remaining tablespoon of butter may be heated in another spider and the uncooked side of the pancake turned down to brown slowly on this frying pan. Slip carefully on large heated platter and serve at once.

GERMAN PANCAKES No. 2

½ teaspoon salt,
½ cup flour,
2 eggs,
1 cup milk.

Beat eggs until very light, add the flour and salt and beat again, then add the milk slowly, and beat thoroughly.

Heat a generous quantity of butter in a frying pan, and pour all the batter into this at one time, place on a hot stove for one minute; then remove to a brisk oven, the edges will turn up on sides of pan in a few minutes; then reduce heat and cook more slowly until light, crisp and brown, about seven minutes. Take it out, slide it carefully on a hot plate, sprinkle plentifully with powdered sugar and send to the table with six lemon slices.

GERMAN PANCAKE, No. 3

3 eggs,
1 teaspoon salt,
2 cups flour,
1 cup milk,
Butter or lard for frying.

Take granite sauce pan with lip and handle; break in the eggs and beat until very light; add the salt, then the flour and milk alternately and beat very thoroughly. Have a large deep spider half full of lard almost to the boiling point. Pour all the batter gradually but quickly into the hot fat, starting from the center and pouring the batter around and around the circle, in one large cake, the size of the pan. It should fry crisp and brown. Then cook more slowly and allow it to raise; lift out the pancake with a pancake turner; return to the hot fat with the uncooked side of pancake down, fry until crisp and brown on this side, then reduce the heat somewhat and cook until thoroughly done on the inside. It takes considerable skill to have it come out in one smooth cake.

Lift out the pancake carefully, place on hot platter and serve hot, sprinkled plentifully with powdered sugar and lemon juice.

BOHEMIAN PANCAKES, No. 1

2 eggs, well beaten
1 tablespoon sugar,
1 cup lukewarm milk,
1¼ cups flour,
½ teaspoon salt,
½ oz. compressed yeast (1 cake) dissolved in a little lukewarm milk,
Grated rind of ½ lemon.

Put flour, sugar, salt and lemon rind in bowl, add well beaten eggs, the milk and mix well, then add the dissolved yeast. Beat thoroughly and set away in a warm place to raise, 1 or 2 hours or until very light. Lift the dough by spoonfuls, carefully from the top of the mixture, so as not to disturb the remainder.

Spread on griddle with back of spoon. Let bake slowly, that they may raise again, turn and bake on the other side.

Place baked pancakes singly on large platter or on individual plates.

Spread top of pancakes with a thick layer of Prune Filling, page 309, cover generously with grated Ginger Bread for Fillings, page 33, or gingersnaps, and over all spread whipped cream sweetened and flavored to taste, page 335. Makes 10 pancakes.

BOHEMIAN PANCAKES, No. 2

1¼ cups flour,
1 cup lukewarm water,
1 cake yeast (½ oz.)
¼ teaspoon salt.

Dissolve the yeast in a little lukewarm water and mix with the milk and the rest of the ingredients to a smooth batter.

Let raise in a warm place until very light and bake and serve as Bohemian Pancakes, No. 1. An egg may be added.

MATZOS PANCAKES

2 matzos,
2 tablespoons fat,
1 egg yolk, beaten,
1 tablespoon sugar,
1 cup milk,
1 beaten white of egg,
½ cup matzos meal for thin batter.

Mix the pancake batter of the last five ingredients, in the order given. Let water just run over the matzos, then place in oven for a minute. Heat the fat in the spider, spread one side of matzos with batter and fry, batter side down until nicely browned. Spread other side on brown. Serve hot, sprinkled with powdered sugar.

POTATO PANCAKES

6 raw grated potatoes,
3 whole eggs,
A pinch of baking powder,
1 teaspoon salt,
1 tablespoon flour,
A little milk.

Peel large potatoes and soak several hours in cold water; grate, drain, and for every pint, allow 2 eggs, about 1 tablespoon flour, ½ teaspoon salt, a little pepper. Beat eggs well and mix with the rest of the ingredients. Drop by spoonfuls on a hot buttered spider, in small cakes. Turn and brown on both sides. Serve with apple sauce.

BREAD PANCAKES

1 cup stale white bread,
1 egg,
¼ teaspoon salt,
pepper,
1 tablespoon flour.

Soak the bread in milk or water until thoroughly moistened. Mix with the rest of the ingredients, form in small cakes, and fry in a spider in a little hot butter on both sides until golden brown.

CHAPTER VII

APPETIZERS

OYSTER COCKTAIL, No. 1

1 pint small oysters,
12 tablespoons catsup,
3 tablespoons tarragon vinegar,
3 tablespoons Rhine wine,
Cayenne pepper and salt to taste,
Juice of 1 lemon.

Serve very cold with one-fourth teaspoonful grated horseradish on top of each portion.

OYSTER COCKTAIL, No. 2

18 oysters,
3 tablespoons tomato catsup,
6 drops tabasco sauce,
½ teaspoon lemon juice,
½ teaspoon sherry wine,
Salt to taste.

Mix and serve in sherbet glasses. Wipe the oysters dry. This quantity serves 3 people.

OYSTER COCKTAIL, No. 3

6 oysters,
1 tablespoon Snyder's cocktail catsup,
½ teaspoon grated horseradish root,
½ teaspoon lemon juice.

Place 5 or 6 small oysters in each glass, cover with catsup and lemon juice and place the fresh grated horseradish root on top. Serve very cold.

LOBSTER COCKTAIL

Two lobsters boiled, cut into pieces ½ inch square. Follow recipe for oyster cocktail No. 1, substituting the lobster in place of the oysters.

Serve very cold in cocktail glasses. This serves 6 people.

SWEETBREAD COCKTAIL

Soak a pair of sweetbreads in cold water one hour, drain and put into salted boiling water and cook slowly twenty to thirty minutes until tender; drain, plunge into cold water and when cold cut or break into pieces the size of small oysters. Put four or five pieces in each glass and cover with a highly seasoned lemon dressing and tomato catsup, one teaspoonful of each to a glass. Serve ice cold with a wafer.

Lemon Dressing. Juice of a lemon, equal quantity of water, salt and pepper to taste.

STRAWBERRY COCKTAIL

1 quart strawberries,
2 lemons, juice,
1 quart cold water,
2 cups sugar,
Ice.

Mash the berries well, add the water and lemon juice and let stand three hours. Strain, add sugar and stir until dissolved. Let stand on ice one hour. Serve at the beginning of a luncheon in tall narrow glasses reserving 3 or 4 whole berries, cut in two for each glass, or serve in thin glasses with shaved or crushed ice.

GRAPE FRUIT SALAD

Remove from the skin the cells and juice; add a little sugar, and if desired chopped pineapple and a few Maraschino cherries. Serve very cold in thin glasses, surrounded with crushed ice, or in fruit shells.

FRUIT SALAD

3 oranges,
3 bananas,
½ lb. Malaga grapes,
½ cup pineapple chopped,
Sugar to taste,
Juice of 1 lemon,
12 English walnut meats.

Cut the oranges in two crosswise, reserving the peels as salad cups. Remove pulp separately from each section. Remove skins and seeds from grapes. Mix orange pulp and grapes and pineapple, sprinkle with sugar, add lemon juice, and let stand in a cool place for several hours. Before serving, add the bananas sliced, and the walnut meats. Fill the orange shells with this mixture. One-fourth cup of wine may be added, if desired, or a wine dressing: One-half cup of sugar, one-third cup of sherry wine, and two tablespoons Madeira wine.

PEAR SALAD

Peel and core as many firm, sweet-flavored pears as there are persons to serve. Fill each pear with a Cream Mayonnaise

Dressing, page 189, into which has been mixed several chopped walnuts, chopped celery and a bit of chopped apple. Serve ice cold and garnish with Maraschino Cherries or cut pears in half lengthwise, core and put dressing in center.

CANNED PEARS, STUFFED

Fill the open spaces in canned pears, (halved) with preserved ginger, cut fine. Place pear on crisp lettuce leaves. Surround with whipped cream garnished with thin slices of preserved ginger, Canton ginger is the best.

CRABMEAT OR LOBSTER CANAPES

Spread rounds of toasted bread with finely chopped crab or lobster meat, seasoned with salt, cayenne and a few drops of lemon juice, moistened with Thick White Sauce, page 88. Cover with 2 tablespoons creamed butter to which 1 teaspoon white of egg has been added. Sprinkle with cheese and brown in the oven.

ANCHOVY BUTTER ON TOAST

4 boned anchovies,
2 hard boiled yolks of eggs,
¼ cup butter,
paprika.

Pound the above ingredients together in a mortar until smooth then pass through a puree sieve. If the anchovies were preserved in salt rather than oil, let stand some hours in milk or water to freshen.

Small, thin round pieces of toast, buttered; then spread very lightly with anchovy butter, and on this place a carefully fried or steamed egg. Garnish with lemon and parsley.

CRAWFISH BUTTER ON TOAST

Pick meat from the tails of twelve crawfish and set aside. Dry the shells and pound them all together in a mortar, adding 2 tablespoons good butter. Place in a sauce pan on moderate fire, stirring until it clarifies (about five minutes). Strain through a napkin, letting drop into cold water. When it congeals, take it out, place in warm basin, stir until it assumes the desired color. Mix with the picked meat, season highly with salt and cayenne, and serve on toast.

SARDELLEN APPETIZER, No. 1

6 pieces toast of rye bread, cut round,	3 hard boiled eggs,
	12 sardellen,
6 slices tomato,	Mayonnaise.

Cut bread round and toast and place on it a slice of tomato, on this put 4 half sardellen which have been soaked in water, then a half egg and over this a Mayonnaise dressing, page 190. It can also be served without the toast. Serve very cold.

SARDELLEN APPETIZER, No. 2

¼ lb. Sardellen,	12 small slices fresh rye bread or toast,
¼ lb. fresh butter, (scant),	
¼ teaspoon parsley, chopped fine,	2 hard cooked eggs.

Soak sardellen in cold water 4 hours, remove bones. Take equal parts of sardellen and fresh butter, creamed. Chop sardellen fine, mix with the butter, add the parsley and spread on fresh rye bread or toast. Separate egg, chop white fine and rice the yolk and decorate sandwiches with alternate rows; or

Soak one-half pound sardellen, bone and mash them and add two tablespoons Neufchatel cheese, two tablespoons sweet butter, a little grated onion, a pinch cayenne pepper. Spread on thin slices of toast.

HERRING APPETIZERS

Buy the prepared Bismark Herring, cut two half herrings into one inch pieces and surround by strips of Pimento (canned red peppers).

KIPPERED HERRING

1 can Bismark or pickled herring,	Lemon juice,
	Lemon slices,
A little pepper,	Parsley.
Melted butter,	

Remove herring from can, and arrange on a platter; sprinkle with pepper, brush over with lemon juice, and melted butter, and pour over the liquor left in the pan. Place in a moderate oven, heat thoroughly and garnish with parsley and lemon slices.

PICKLED HERRING

1 doz. milch herring,
4 large onions, sliced,
2 lemons, sliced,
2 tablespoons black peppercorns,
2 tablespoons mustard seed,
12 bay leaves,
1 tablespoon sugar,
3 cups vinegar,
1 cup water.

Soak herring in cold water over night, drain and remove entrails, reserving the roe and milt. If you desire, skin and bone them; cut off heads, run knife down center of back and skin towards the tail; scrape the meat off the bones, without cutting the bones, thus separating the herring in two parts.

Place herring in crock in layers, with sliced onion, lemon, a few pieces of bay leaf, a sprinkling of mustard seed and peppercorns.

Mix and mash the milt with the sugar, add a little vinegar to thin, strain through sieve, add the rest of the vinegar, or better still, in place of the vinegar 3 cups sour cream or milk, and pour over herring to cover.

Two medium sized sour apples, chopped fine, and 1 oz. of chopped almonds may be added; cover jar and keep in a cool, dry place. Will keep a long while. Serve with boiled potatoes in their jackets.

HERRING SALAD, No. 1

3 herring, cleaned and pickled to pieces,
3 apples,
3 boiled potatoes,
½ cup mixed nuts,
¼ cup chopped cooked veal
1 pickle,
A small onion,
Pepper,
¼ cup sugar,
A few capers,
4 hard boiled eggs.

Chop all fine, mix the yolks of the eggs with a little vinegar, and mix all together.

HERRING SALAD, No. 2

½ doz. milch herring,
½ lb. cold veal roast,
2 heaping cupfuls apples,
1½ heaping cupfuls beets, pickled,
¼ cup onions,
½ cup pickles,
¼ cup brandy,
2 stalks English celery,
½ cup cold boiled potatoes,
1 cup almonds,
4 hard boiled eggs,
2 tablespoons grated horse radish,
2 tablespoons chopped parsley,
1 cup granulated sugar,
1 cup vinegar.

Soak herring over night, skin and take out all the bones. Rub the milt through a colander, with some of the vinegar. Now chop all other ingredients but eggs to size of a large pea, add milt and mix thoroughly. Will keep a month in cold place. Decorate with sardellen, pickles, hard boiled eggs and beets, olives and parsley.

Or if you desire, mix all together and heap on platter. Separate the eggs. Rub yolks through a fine sieve and chop whites and decorate the mound of salad with alternate strips of white and yellow, keeping line distinct.

SARDINE APPETIZER

2 oil sardines,
1 tablespoon catsup,
1 tablespoon lemon juice,
A dash of Tabasco sauce,
1 round slice toast or buttered bread,
Lettuce leaf.

Drain, clean, skin and bone the sardines, place crisp lettuce leaf on bread and butter plate, place bread on top, lay the sardines across and spread over the whole the catsup, lemon juice and the Tabasco Sauce.

APPETIZER OF ARTICHOKE

6 slices of artichoke heart,
1 can caviere,
3 hard boiled eggs,
12 pimolas,
1 teaspoon chopped onion.

The artichokes can be bought in cans or bottles.

Cover each piece of artichoke with Caviere, chopped onion and pimolas (stuffed olives), also chopped white of egg and the yolk put through a ricer, and cover with a thin Mayonnaise, page 191.

FILLED TOMATOES, No. 1

6 tomatoes,
6 sardellen,
1 small box caviere,
2 hard boiled eggs,
½ green pepper,
½ dill pickle.

Scoop tomatoes and put on ice; when ready to serve fill with all above ingredients chopped fine, add some of the tomato that you scooped out—cover with Mayonnaise, page 190, and serve cold.

FILLED TOMATOES, No. 2

6 tomatoes,	1 tablespoon capers,
1 doz. anchovies, in oil,	1 tablespoon pearl onions,
2 slices of boiled ham,	½ green pepper,
2 hard boiled eggs.	

Scoop six tomatoes and put on ice while preparing the filling.
Take the inside of tomatoes, add anchovies, ham, peppers and chop together—then add onions, capers, teaspoon salt and fill the tomatoes, cover with the chopped eggs and pour over this a French dressing, page 188. Serve on lettuce leaf.

This can also be served in green peppers.

CAVIERE WITH EGGS AND CUCUMBERS

Butter rounds of Boston Brown Bread, page 32, press upon these rings of cold boiled egg, white, fill the rings with Caviere and place slices of fresh peeled cucumber, dressed with French Salad Dressing, page 188, above.

EGG TIMBALES

12 hard cooked eggs,	¼ teaspoon onion juice,
1 teaspoon salt,	Lettuce,
¼ teaspoon paprika,	Gargoyle Sauce.

Cook 3 fresh eggs 30 minutes just below the boiling point, remove shell and while warm pass through ricer or food grinder; add the seasoning to taste and pack while still warm into buttered timbale forms and place in ice chest 3 or more hours. Serve cold on a bed of crisp lettuce leaves and cover with Gargoyle Sauce, page 192. This serves 6 persons.

EGG AND TOMATO APPETIZER

2 or 3 hard cooked eggs,	3 large, ripe, firm tomatoes,
¼ teaspoon salt,	Gargoyle Sauce,
⅛ teaspoon paprika,	Lettuce.

Cook fresh eggs 30 minutes, just below the boiling point, remove shell and while warm, pass through ricer or food grinder. Add salt and paprika to taste and a few drops of onion juice if desired. Pack tightly into tall narrow glasses or in small baking powder tins, and set aside in cold place 4 or 5 hours. Remove from glass or case, cut into ½ inch slices. Cut tomatoes into thick slices crosswise; place lettuce leaf on serving plate; then the tomato slice, then the slice of egg on top of that and cover the whole with Gargoyle Sauce, page 192. This serves 6 persons.

EGG APPETIZER

6 steamed eggs,
6 round slices of buttered toast,
6 tablespoons Chili sauce,
Lettuce.

Spread round of freshly toasted bread with butter, place hot Steamed or Dropped egg, page 48, in center of each piece, cover each egg with a tablespoon of Chili sauce and serve hot on lettuce leaf.

MARROW BONES

6 marrow bones,
1 teaspoon salt,
parsley.

Have your butcher cut the marrow bones 3 inches thick and scrape the sides perfectly clean. Place in a hot oven for 6 minutes. Salt and send to table at once. Dress in a parsley bed and serve with toast points.

CHAPTER VIII

Soups

Long soaking in cold water, draws out the juices of meat and dissolves the gelatine. Soup stocks are prepared in this manner and then cooked at a low temperature. Celery leaves can be tied in a bunch and hung in a sunny place to dry, then placed in a paper bag, ready for use. The stalks and roots can be dried in a slow oven, powdered and bottled. Celery seed can be used for soups when the celery root or stalks are not at hand.

SOUP STOCK, No. 1

2½ lbs. beef plate or brisket
3 quarts cold water,
1 tablespoon salt,
¼ teaspoon pepper,
¼ cup each onion, carrot and celery, diced,
½ cup tomato, raw or stewed
1 teaspoon chopped parsley, grating of nutmeg.

Wipe and salt the meat; place in soup kettle and let stand 1 hour. Add the cold water and let stand ½ hour longer. Place on stove and let come to the boiling point. If you prefer clear soup, skim now. This scum contains the chief nutritive value to the soup. If allowed to remain a large part of it will pass through the strainer.

Let soup simmer 3 hours or longer, then add the vegetables, cook one hour longer, adding more hot water, if too much has evaporated. Strain, cool, skim off the fat, add seasonings, reheat and just before serving, add the parsley. If the meat is to be served at table remove from soup as soon as tender and serve with any well seasoned sauce. See Horseradish or Mustard Sauce, pages 94 and 95.

SOUP STOCK, No. 2

2 lbs. shin of beef, ½ meat, ½ fat and bone,
2 qts. cold water,
2 teaspoons salt,
1 small onion,
½ small carrot,
½ small turnip,
1 sprig parsley,
1 piece celery root.

Wipe the meat, cut it into small pieces. Put it, with the salt, into the cold water and let it stand ½ hour. Simmer 5 hours, then add the vegetables cut fine and the seasoning. Cook 1 hour longer, strain and cool. When ready to use, remove the cake of fat, bring the stock to a boil; adding more salt if necessary.

BOUILLON

2 lbs. lean beef, middle of round,
2 lbs. veal bone,
2 lbs. marrow bones,
3 lbs. chicken or fowl,
6 qts. cold water,
⅓ cup each of carrot, onion, celery,
1 tablespoon salt,
¼ teaspoon pepper,
¼ teaspoon nutmeg, grated,
A few grains of sugar.

Clean chicken, separate it at the joints, and place in soup kettle, with the veal bones. Cut beef into small pieces and brown in hot spider with the marrow from the marrow bones, and remove to soup kettle. Add the cold water. Heat quickly to the boiling point, skim if you want a clear soup. Let simmer slowly for 5 hours. Add the vegetables and let boil one hour longer. Strain and then season to taste. When cool remove the fat. Serve hot in bouillon cups with Fritter Beans, page 85.

The chicken should be removed as soon as tender. It can be served with any well flavored sauce or used for salads or croquettes.

CONSOMME

5 lbs. shin bone,
4 lbs. lean beef,
1 carrot, cut,
1 potato, cut,
$\frac{1}{16}$ teaspoon red pepper,
¼ cup celery, cut,
1 small onion, sliced,
1 bay leaf,
Chicken bones or cold left over chicken,
4 qts. water.

Place meat and bone in soup kettle, add the cold water, let stand 1 hour. Let slowly come to the boiling point and simmer slowly 4 or more hours. Add vegetables, boil 1 hour longer. Strain all through a sieve and season when cold; skim off fat. Serve hot.

CHICKEN SOUP

3 to 4 lbs. chicken,	2 stalks celery or,
3 to 4 qts. water,	¼ cup celery root, diced,
1 tablespoon salt,	¼ teaspoon pepper,
1 onion,	⅛ teaspoon nutmeg.

Select an old hen. Singe, clean and joint; then salt and let stand several hours or over night. Put on to boil in cold water and let it come to a boil quickly. Skim thoroughly, if you want a clear soup. Let simmer slowly 3 or more hours, add the vegetables, boil 1 hour longer, strain, remove fat and add seasoning to taste. Take out the chicken before it falls to pieces and use for salads, croquettes or with Brown Sauce, page 89. Serve soup hot with noodles, dumplings, or almost any of the Soup Garnishings, pages 81 to 86.

TURKEY OR GOOSE SOUP

Poultry bones and scraps of the meat,	1 teaspoon salt,
	⅛ teaspoon pepper,
Cold water to cover,	1 onion, sliced,
Stuffing,	¼ cup celery, diced,
	¼ cup carrot, sliced.

Take any left over poultry, break the carcass in pieces, removing all stuffing. Put into kettle with remnants of the meat; cover with cold water, bring slowly to the boiling point, and let simmer 4 or more hours; add onions and celery and let boil ½ hour longer. Strain, remove fat, add ½ cup stuffing to every quart of soup. Serve hot with dumplings, "Pfarfel," barley or green kern, pages 82 and 86, and barley and green kern with cereals, Chapter II.

MUTTON SOUP

½ lb. mutton (neck),	2 potatoes,
2 onions,	1 qt. cold water,
2 tablespoons rice,	Salt and pepper to taste.

Cut the mutton into small pieces and put into a stew pot with the cold water. Cook slowly 4 or 5 hours.

One hour before serving add the sliced potatoes, onions, rice and seasoning. Thicken, if desired, with a little flour wet in cold water.

VEGETABLE SOUP, No. 1

2 lbs. shin of beef, ½ meat, ½ fat and bone.

2 qts. cold water,	1 small onion,
2 teaspoons salt,	½ small carrot,
¼ teaspoon pepper,	½ small turnip,
1 teaspoon sugar,	1 sprig parsley,
1 cup tomato,	1 piece of celery root,
½ cup cabbage,	30 pods of shelled peas.

Wipe the meat, cut it into small pieces. Put it with the salt into the cold water and let it stand ½ hour. Simmer 4 hours; then add the vegetables cut fine and the seasoning. Cook 1 hour longer, strain and cool. When ready to use, remove cake of fat, bring the stock to a boil, adding more salt if necessary.

VEGETABLE SOUP, No. 2

1½ qts. boiling water,	4 tablespoons butter or other fat,
⅓ cup carrots, diced,	1 teaspoon sugar,
⅓ cup cabbage, cut,	4 cloves,
1½ cups potato, diced,	2 teaspoons salt,
¼ cup onion, sliced,	
1 cup strained tomatoes,	

1½ teaspoons chopped parsley.

Use all or any, and as many varieties of vegetables as you wish, using half as much vegetable as liquor.

Wash, pare, scrape and cut the vegetables fine. Then measure. Mix vegetables, all but the potatoes and tomatoes. Heat the fat in a spider, add the vegetables, cook 10 minutes, stirring constantly; add potatoes and cook 2 minutes longer, then add the boiling water and tomatoes and boil one hour or longer or until all the vegetables are tender, add the parsley, season to taste and serve hot. Any cold boiled vegetable (left overs) may be added to this soup.

OX TAIL SOUP

3 lbs. lean beef,	¼ cup celery root, diced,
2 ox tails,	1 tablespoon parsley root, diced,
6 qts. water,	
1 tablespoon salt,	2 tablespoons fat,
1 large onion, diced,	1 tablespoon flour,
	3 carrots.

Have the oxtails split and cut into small pieces and fry them lightly in the fat.

Put meat and oxtails in soup kettle, pour over the water and salt and let come slowly to a boil, then let cook slowly but steadily 4 hours or longer. Add the vegetables, boil 1 hour longer and reduce stock nearly ½. Strain, heat 1 tablespoon fat in a spider, add a tablespoon flour, brown, and gradually pour on a cup of the soup stock; stir this into the remaining stock and return the carrots cut in small dice. Serve hot with Croutons, page 81.

MULLIGATAWNY SOUP

3 lbs. raw chicken,
4 qts. cold water,
2 sour apples, sliced,
¼ cup onion, sliced,
¼ cup celery, cut in cubes,
¼ cup carrot, cut in cubes,
1 teaspoon curry powder,
1 tablespoon flour,
1 teaspoon salt,

2 cloves,
1 cup tomato, strained,
½ green pepper, chopped fine
⅛ teaspoon mace,
1 teaspoon chopped parsley,
1 teaspoon sugar,
A little pepper,
¼ cup butter or drippings.

Cook vegetables and chicken in the fat until browned; add flour, curry powder, cloves and all the rest of the ingredients and cook slowly until the chicken is tender. Remove chicken and cut the meat in small pieces. Strain the soup and rub the vegetables through a sieve. Add the chicken to the strained soup. Season and serve hot, with boiled rice.

BARLEY SOUP

2 qts. soup stock,
½ cup pearl barley,
1 quart boiling water;

1 teaspoon salt,
⅛ teaspoon pepper,
1 cup croutons.

Wash barley in cold water and then cook in 1 quart of boiling salted water until tender, 2 hours or more. When water has evaporated add Soup Stock, page 66. If you are making fresh soup, keep adding the "top soup," strained, to the barley and let boil until tender; ½ cup celery root or stalks, and ½ cup carrot, diced, boiled with the barley improves the flavor. Serve hot with Croutons, page 81.

DRIED PEA SOUP

2 cups dried split peas,
3 quarts cold water,
3 lbs. smoked brisket of beef, or
Scraps of dried beef, sausage,
   or a ham bone,
¼ cup celery, diced,
1 small onion, cut fine,
2 tablespoons butter,
1 teaspoon sugar,
2 teaspoons salt,
¼ teaspoon white pepper,
2 tablespoons flour.

Pick over and wash the peas. Soak them in cold water over night, drain, place in soup kettle with the smoked beef, ham bone or tongue, add the cold water and let boil slowly but steadily 4 hours or more; add the celery and cook until the peas and meat are tender. Remove meat when tender. Skim fat off the top of soup. Heat 2 tablespoons of the fat in a spider, add the onions and brown, add flour and gradually a cup of the soup. Add to the rest of the soup. Season to taste and serve with the smoked meat, adding Croutons, page 81. Or the peas may be cooked until tender and smoked sausage or dried beef may be boiled with them a few minutes and served hot with the soup. The soup should be quite thick; water, soup stock, milk or cream may be added to thin if desired.

GREEN KERN SOUP

2 qts. soup stock or poultry soup,
2 cups green kern,
2 cups boiling water,
⅛ teaspoon pepper,
¼ teaspoon celery, diced,
1 cup Croutons,
1 teaspoon salt,

Wash green kern in cold water, then cook in boiling salted water 2 hours or until tender, add the celery. As water evaporates add soup stock, page 66. If you are making fresh soup take the "top soup" and keep adding it strained to the green kern, until the desired consistency. Season to taste. Serve hot with Croutons, page 81. If you prefer, dry the green kern on back of stove, grind fine and cook until tender in the soup. Just before serving pour on one or two egg yolks well beaten and serve hot with Croutons.

LENTILS OR LINSEN SOUP

2 cups lentils,
3 qts. cold water,
3 lbs. brisket of beef, or
1 lb. smoked sausage, or
A ham bone,
¼ cup celery, diced,
1 small onion,
salt and pepper,
2 tablespoons flour,
Croutons.

The lentils are washed in cold water, then soaked in cold water over night. Made same as Dried Pea Soup, page 71. One cup of strained tomato improves the flavor.

POTATO SOUP

3 potatoes (cut small),
2 teaspoons chopped onions,
½ teaspoon salt,
1 quart boiling water,
⅛ teaspoon white pepper,
2 teaspoons chopped celery,
2 teaspoons parsley (chopped fine),
2 tablespoons butter,
1 tablespoon flour.

Heat one tablespoon butter, add the onions and celery, and let simmer ten minutes. Add potato, cover, and cook two minutes. Add the water and boil one hour. Add more boiling water as it evaporates. Bind the remaining flour and butter, add some potato liquid and cook. Combine the mixture and serve hot with the Croutons, page 81. Any cold cooked vegetable, left over, may be added.

MILK SOUP

2 tablespoons butter,
4 tablespoons flour,
1 quart hot milk, or
milk and water mixed,
1 teaspoon salt.

Brown the butter, add the flour and salt and pour some of the hot milk over the thickening, stirring all the time. Add the rest of the milk. Season to taste. Served with noodles, dumplings and other soup garnishes, see next chapter. Rye flour may be used in place of the wheat flour and one or 2 yolks of eggs may be added very gradually, just before serving.

CREAM OF POTATO SOUP

3 potatoes,
1 quart milk,
2 slices onion,
3 tablespoons butter,
2 tablespoons flour,
1½ tablespoons salt,
¼ tablespoon celery salt,
⅛ teaspoon pepper,
Few grains cayenne,
1 tablespoon chopped parsley.

Cook the potatoes till very soft. Scald the milk and onion in a double boiler. Drain the potatoes; add the milk, having removed the onion. Rub through a strainer and put back into double boiler over the fire. Melt the butter or dripping, add the flour, stirring all the time. Pour some of the hot milk mixture over the thickening, then return to the boiler and cook 5 minutes. Add 1 teaspoon finely chopped parsley and serve very hot. If the soup be too thick, add hot water or milk.

One-half cup cream, whipped stiff may be added to soup before serving.

TOMATO SOUP

1 can or quart of tomatoes,
1 pint of water,
4 cloves,
1 slice of onion,
2 teaspoons sugar,
1 teaspoon salt,
⅛ teaspoon soda,
2 tablespoons butter,
2 tablespoons flour.

Cook the first six ingredients twenty minutes; strain, reheat, add the soda, melt the butter, add the flour, and gradually the hot strained tomatoes.

CREAM OF TOMATO SOUP

½ can or pint tomatoes,
¼ teaspoon soda,
1 slice onion,
1 teaspoon salt,
2 teaspoons sugar,
¼ teaspoon white pepper,
2 tablespoons flour,
2 tablespoons butter,
1 quart milk or milk and water mixed.

Cook the onion with the milk. Heat butter, add flour and seasoning, ⅔ cup hot milk, then the rest gradually. Heat the strained tomatoes, add the soda, and when the bubbling stops, add the tomato to the white sauce.

CREAM OF ASPARAGUS

3 tablespoons butter,
3 tablespoons flour,
3 pints soup stock,
1 teaspoon salt,
1 teaspoon chopped parsley,
2 bunches green asparagus,
½ cup of cream,
1 slice onion.

Wash and drain asparagus, reserve tips and add stalks to 1 pt. cold water. Boil five minutes, drain, add Soup Stock, page 66, and one slice onion. Boil thirty minutes, rub through a sieve. Heat butter, add flour and seasoning and cook with the hot stock and milk; add the tips. If soup stock is not salted add more salt and a little pepper. Serve with the tips and Croutons, page 81.

One-half cup whipped cream may be added to the soup just before serving.

CREAM OF MUSHROOM SOUP

½ lb. mushrooms,
1 qt. chicken or veal broth,
1 slice onion,
2 tablespoons butter,
2 tablespoons flour,
1 cup cream,
Salt and pepper.

Chop mushrooms, add to chicken soup with onion, cook 20 minutes, and rub through a sieve. Reheat. Put butter in sauce pan, add flour when it bubbles add ⅔ cup mushroom and soup liquid, stir in the rest and then add the cream and seasonings.

ALMOND SOUP

½ lb. almonds,
3 pints chicken soup,
1½ tablespoons butter,
3 pints chicken or veal soup,
salt,
paprika,
1 cup cream.

Pour boiling water over almonds, slip off the skins. When cold put through meat chopper and grind until like coarse meal. Melt butter, add corn starch, add 1 cup chicken broth, and make a very smooth sauce. Then add the almonds to the remaining soup, cook for a few minutes, add seasoning of salt and paprika, and 1 cup cream. Serve in bouillon cups with spoonful whipped cream on top of each cup.

CREAM OF CELERY SOUP

3 stalks celery,
3 cups milk,
1 slice onion,
1 teaspoon salt,
2 tablespoons butter,
2 tablespoons flour,
¼ teaspoon pepper,
1 cup cream.

Break celery in one inch pieces, and pound in a mortar. Cook in double boiler with onion and milk 20 minutes. Remove onion, heat the butter, add flour and seasonings, first ⅔ cup and gradually the rest of the celery broth, and the cream, cook until smooth and slightly thickened and serve at once.

GREEN CORN SOUP

6 ears sweet corn or
1 pt. raw pulp,
1 pt. milk or cream,
1 teaspoon salt,
⅛ teaspoon white pepper,
1 teaspoon sugar,
1 teaspoon flour,
1 tablespoon butter.

Grate the corn. Cover the cobs with cold water, and boil 30 minutes, then strain. To 1 pint of this corn liquor add the raw corn pulp, cook 15 minutes, add the seasoning and milk, hot. Heat the butter, add the flour and gradually the corn mixture; cook 5 minutes longer and serve hot with crackers.

CREAM OF CORN SOUP

1 can corn,	2 tablespoons butter,
1 pt. water,	1 slice onion,
1 qt. hot milk,	2 tablespoons flour,
1 teaspoon salt,	1/8 teaspoon white pepper.

Heat the milk and onion, then remove onion. Chop the corn and cook it with the water 20 minutes. Melt the butter, add the flour, and when bubbling, add first 2/3 cup, then the rest of the milk gradually; cook till slightly thickened. Add this mixture to the corn and season with salt and pepper. If you wish rub the corn through a sieve. Serve hot, with crackers.

CREAM OF BARLEY OR RICE

1/2 cup pearl barley,	1/8 teaspoon pepper,
1 qt. soup stock,	1 cup hot cream,
1 slice onion,	2 yolks of egg,
1 teaspoon salt.	

Cook barley and onion in 1 quart of boiling water 45 minutes, add the soup stock and cook until tender. Strain, season and serve with thickening made of one cup hot cream stirred gradually into the two beaten yolks; add a handful of Croutons, page 81, and serve at once or it will curdle.

BAKED BEAN SOUP

1 qt. baked beans, or	2 qts. water,
1 can baked beans,	3 tablespoons butter,
1 medium onion,	3 tablespoons flour,
Salt and pepper to taste.	

Cook beans, water and onions until beans are soft. Put through a strainer. Melt butter, add flour, and when bubbling add 2/3 cup and then the rest of the soup. Season with salt and pepper, and reheat to boiling point and serve.

One cup strained tomatoes may be added.

BLACK BEAN SOUP

1 pint black beans,	1/8 teaspoon pepper,
2 qts. cold water,	1/4 teaspoon mustard,
2 tablespoons chopped onion,	A few grains cayenne,
	3 tablespoons butter,
2 stalks celery or piece celery root,	2 tablespoons flour,
	2 hard boiled eggs,
2 teaspoons salt,	1 lemon.

Soak beans over night; drain and add cold water and rinse thoroughly. Fry the onion in 2 tablespoons butter, put it with the beans, add the celery and the 2 quarts water. Cook slowly until the beans are soft, 3 or 4 hours, add more water as it boils away; rub through a strainer, add the seasonings and heat; heat the remaining butter in a saucepan, add the flour, then ⅔ cup and then the rest of the hot soup gradually; cut lemon (removing seeds) and eggs in thin slices and serve in the soup.

OYSTER STEW

2 cups scalded milk,
1 pt. oysters,
A little pepper,
½ teaspoon salt,
1 tablespoon butter.

When the milk is hot put the oysters and butter in a sauce pan and heat until the edges curl. Add the milk and seasoning. Cook one minute and serve at once.

CREAM OF OYSTER SOUP

1 pint of oysters,
½ cup cold water,
1 cup white sauce,
Salt and pepper to taste.

Wash oysters with ½ cup cold water, through colander, remove any bits of shell; reserve the liquid; heat gradually to the boiling point. Let oysters simmer until they look plump and the edges curl; drain and skim the liquid. Make a White Sauce, page 87, add the hot strained oyster liquid, salt and pepper to taste and cook until smooth. Add the oysters and serve hot with oyster crackers toasted in the oven just a few minutes.

CRABFISH CREAM SOUP

12 crab tails,
2 tablespoons butter,
1 qt. hot milk,
3 tablespoons flour,
1 cup cream,
Salt and pepper.

Take the crab meat out of 12 crabfish tails. Dry the shells and pound them together in a mortar; add the butter, place on fire until it clarifies, about 5 minutes, strain; add crab meat in pieces, salt and pepper to taste and add to the hot milk. Mix the flour with part of the cream to a smooth paste, add the rest of the cream, mix with the soup and boil and stir until all is smooth. Serve hot with oyster crackers toasted a few moments in the oven.

LOBSTER BISQUE

2 lbs. lobster,
2 cups cold water,
4 cups milk,
¼ cup flour,
1½ teaspoons salt.
A few grains cayenne.

Remove the meat from lobster shell. Add cold water to body bones and tough end of claws, cut in pieces; bring slowly to boiling point and cook twenty minutes. Drain, reserve liquor, and thicken with butter and flour cooked together. Scald milk with tail meat of lobster, finely chopped; strain and add to liquor. Season with salt and cayenne; then add tender claw meat, cut in dice, and body meat. When coral is found in lobster, wash, wipe, force through fine strainer, put in a mortar with butter, work until well blended, then add flour, and stir into soup. If a richer soup is desired, white stock may be used in place of water.

CLAM CHOWDER

1 qt. clams,
4 cups potatoes cut in dice ¾ inch square,
2 in. sq. fat salt pork,
1 sliced onion,
1 teaspoon salt,
⅛ teaspoon pepper,
4 teaspoons butter,
4 cups milk,
8 crackers.

Pick over and drain the clams to remove the pieces of shells. Cut the pork into fine pieces and try out; add the onions, fry 5 minutes, add the cubed potatoes, clam liquor and water enough to cover. Cook until nearly tender, pour into a sauce pan, and add the milk, butter, pepper and salt. When the potatoes are done and the milk is boiling hot, add the clams and lastly the crackers. The clams can be put in whole or cut up. They should not be cooked longer than three minutes, as long cooking makes them tough.

MOCK CLAM CHOWDER

Make the chowder like the above; only add a little more salt and leave out the clams. It should be cooked a little longer.

FISH CHOWDER

4 lbs. cod or haddock,
6 cups potato, cut in ¼ inch slices, or
4 cups potato, cut in ¾ inch cubes,
1 sliced onion,
1½ inch cubes fat salt pork,
1½ tablespoons salt,
¼ teaspoon pepper,
3 tablespoons butter,
4 cups scalded milk,
8 common crackers.

Order the fish skinned, but head and tail left on. Cut off head and tail and remove fish from backbone. Cut fish in two inch pieces and set aside. Put head, tail and back bone, broken in pieces, in stew pan; add two cups cold water and bring slowly to boiling point, cook twenty minutes. Cut salt pork in small pieces and try out, add onion, and fry five minutes; strain fat into stew pan. Parboil potatoes five minutes in boiling water to cover; drain and add potatoes to fat, then add two cups boiling water and cook five minutes. Add liquor, drained from bones, then add the fish, cover and simmer ten minutes. Add milk, salt, pepper, butter and crackers, split and soaked in enough cold milk to moisten, otherwise they will be soft on the outside but dry on the inside.

MOCK BISQUE

1 qt. tomatoes,
2 tablespoons cracker crumbs,
½ teaspoon salt,
3 pts. milk,
1 tablespoon butter,
speck pepper,
¼ teaspoon soda.

Heat the tomatoes and milk in separate dishes. Add to the tomatoes the salt, pepper, butter and bread crumbs. When the tomatoes are thoroughly cooked add the soda and milk at once and remove from the stove.

MOCK TURTLE

1 can tomatoes,
1 can Franco-American mock turtle,
1 qt. soup stock,
½ teaspoon paprika,
6 tablespoons Madeira wine,
6 thin slices lemon,
4 hard boiled eggs,
1 teaspoon salt,
4 cloves.

Heat tomatoes, mock turtle and soup, each separately, then mix together, add seasoning and boil all together. In the soup tureen, put the lemon slices, the white of the eggs chopped and the yellow ball of the eggs whole and pour the soup over it. This serves 12 people.

SALMON SOUP

⅓ can salmon,
1 qt. milk,
1 teaspoon salt,
2 tablespoons butter,
2 tablespoons flour,
⅛ teaspoon pepper.

Drain oil from the salmon, remove skin and bones and rub through a sieve. Heat the butter, add flour and seasoning, add ⅔ cup and then gradually the rest of the milk, scalded and the strained salmon. Cook until smooth and slightly thickened and serve hot with crackers.

BEET SOUP, Russian Style (Fleischik)

1 large beet,
½ lb. onions,
1 lb. fat meat; brisket of beef,
¾ cup sugar,
citric acid.

Cut the beet and onions in thick pieces and put in kettle with meat; cover with cold water and let cook slowly two hours; add sugar and citric acid to make it sweet and sour and let cook another hour; season and serve hot.

BEET SOUP, Russian Style (Milchik)

Cut two small beets in strips; cover with water and let cook until tender; add citric acid and a little sugar to make sweet and sour. Also a little salt; add ¾ cup sour cream. Serve cold.

Or—Sweet milk may be used and while hot gradually poured over 2 or more well beaten yolks of eggs, stirred constantly and kept over the fire until thick and smooth. Remove from stove and serve cold.

CREAM OF HERRING SOUP, Russian Style

2 cups milk,
2 cups water,
1 small onion,
Salt and pepper to taste,
2 herring (previously soaked).

Place milk, water, onion and seasoning in a saucepan. Boil for 10 minutes, add herring which has been previously soaked and cut in small pieces; cook until herring is tender.

WINE SOUP

4 cups claret wine,
2 cups water,
1 lemon, sliced fine,
1 tablespoon broken cinnamon,
1 tablespoon sugar,
2 tablespoons sago,
2 yolks of eggs.

Cook sago in one cup of boiling water until tender, as water evaporates add more.

Put the first five ingredients up to boil and let boil 18 minutes, or until well blended, add the cooked sago, let boil up and pour boiling hot gradually over the well beaten eggs. Serve cold.

CHERRY SOUP

1 qt. cherries,	1 tablespoon broken cinnamon,
1 qt. water,	½ lemon sliced fine,
¼ cup sugar,	2 tablespoons sago,
1 cup claret wine,	2 yolks of eggs.

Cook sago in one cup of boiling water until tender, add more, as water evaporates. Put the first six ingredients up to boil and let boil 15 minutes; add the cooked sago, let boil up and pour very gradually over the two well beaten yolks. Serve cold.

Strawberry, raspberry, currant, gooseberry, apple, plum or rhubarb soups are prepared the same way, each cooked until tender and sweetened to taste. The wine may be omitted and the juice of lemon may be added instead.

CHAPTER IX

DUMPLINGS AND GARNISHES FOR SOUPS

CROUTONS

In the oven—Cut stale bread into cubes, place in pan and brown in the oven; or butter the bread, cut into cubes and then brown the same way.

To Fry—Cook small cubes of stale bread in deep hot fat until brown or cook them in a little butter or fat in a hot spider until brown.

CRISPED CRACKERS

Split common crackers, place in pan in hot oven a few moments to heat through and freshen or crisp; or spread with creamed butter and place in pan, in a hot oven, a few moments with butter side up, until delicately browned.

MATZOS FOR SOUP

Break one or more matzos crackers into small pieces and drop into boiling soup one minute before serving.

EIN LAUF

1 egg,
¼ cup water,
⅛ teaspoon salt,
3 tablespoons flour.

Beat egg, add the salt and flour and stir until smooth. Pour slowly from end of spoon into boiling soup. Cook 2 or 3 minutes and serve hot; add 1 teaspoon chopped parsley to the soup.

SPATZEN

1 egg,
⅓ cup water,
½ teaspoon salt,
¾ cup flour.

Beat egg well, add salt, flour and water, stirring to a stiff, smooth batter. Drop by teaspoons into boiling soup 10 minutes before serving.

BAKING POWDER DUMPLINGS

1 cup flour,
2 teaspoons baking powder,
¼ teaspoon salt,
½ cup milk or water, scant.

Sift dry ingredients, stir in the milk or water and mix to smooth batter. Drop a teaspoonful at a time in the boiling soup; cover kettle, let boil 5 minutes and serve at once.

DROP DUMPLINGS

3 eggs,
½ cup milk,
2 tablespoons butter,
1 cup flour,
½ teaspoon salt,
$\frac{1}{16}$ teaspoon pepper,
A nutmeg grating.

Break the whites of the eggs into a cup and add enough milk to fill cup; mix with the butter and flour in a spider and stir as it boils until it leaves the spider clean. When cool stir in the yolks well and season to taste. Drop from teaspoon into boiling soup 5 minutes before serving.

CRACKER BALLS

6 tablespoons cracker crumbs,
1 egg,
2 tablespoons butter or fat,
1 teaspoon chopped parsley,
1 tablespoon milk or soup,
⅛ salt,
Nutmeg, ginger and pepper to taste.

Stir butter with the egg, add the seasoning, liquid and enough meal to shape into small balls. Drop into boiling soup 10 minutes before serving.

CRACKER DUMPLINGS

½ cup cracker crumbs,
1 egg,
½ cup hot water, milk or soup stock,
½ teaspoon salt,
$\frac{1}{16}$ teaspoon pepper,
1 teaspoon chopped parsley.

Scald the cracker crumbs with the hot soup or water, add the egg and seasonings. Drop with teaspoon into boiling soup 10 minutes before serving.

BREAD AND MEAT DUMPLINGS

¼ cup raw chopped calf's liver, beef, veal or poultry meat,
½ cup bread, cut in small squares,
1 teaspoon salt,
pepper and ginger to taste,
1 teaspoon chopped parsley,
1 teaspoon chopped onion,
1 tablespoon soup fat,
1 egg.

DUMPLINGS AND GARNISHES FOR SOUPS

Soak the bread in water 10 minutes; take it out and press dry. Add the egg, well beaten and the rest of the ingredients and with bread or cracker crumbs shape into balls size of a walnut. Drop into boiling soup, let cook 10 minutes and serve. Makes 20 dumplings.

MANDEL KLOESE

2 eggs,
½ teaspoon salt,
1/16 teaspoon pepper,
½ teaspoon chopped parsley.
6 almonds, grated,
½ teaspoon baking powder,
flour,

Beat yolks very light; add salt and seasoning, the blanched and grated almonds and enough flour and the baking powder to make a stiff batter. Add the beaten whites.

Drop from teaspoon into boiling soup 10 minutes before serving.

Test one in boiling water and if it boils apart, add more flour.

MATZOS KLOESE, No. 1

2 matzos or
1 cup soaked wheat bread,
2 tablespoons fat (goose),
2 eggs,
¼ onion, cut fine,
1 teaspoon chopped parsley,
½ cup matzos meal or
¾ cup cracker meal,
1 teaspoon salt,
⅛ teaspoon pepper,
¼ teaspoon ginger,
⅛ teaspoon nutmeg.

Soak the matzos a few minutes in cold water and then drain and squeeze dry. Heat the fat in a spider, add the onions, fry to a golden brown, then add the soaked matzos, stir until it leaves the spider clean, then add seasoning, the egg, slightly beaten and then the matzos or cracker meal, just enough to shape into balls the size of a walnut. Drop into boiling soup 15 minutes before serving.

Test one in boiling water and if it boils apart add more meal.

MATZOS KLOESE, No. 2

1 tablespoon poultry fat or butter,
3 eggs,
½ cup grated almonds,
½ teaspoon sugar,
⅛ teaspoon nutmeg,
⅛ teaspoon salt,
Matzos or cracker meal.

Beat the yolks very light, add seasoning, and the almonds and enough matzos or cracker meal to make a stiff batter, then add the beaten whites. Drop by teaspoon in deep hot fat, fry light brown; try one, and if they do not hold together, add more meal; place in oven to keep warm and put in soup just when sending to the table.

MATZOS—MARROW BALLS

2 tablespoons marrow fat, (beef),
2 eggs,
¼ cup matzos meal,
½ teaspoon salt,
A grating of nutmeg.

Split the bones and remove the marrow. Cream the marrow, add the eggs well beaten, season, and add only enough matzos meal to shape easily into balls, size of a walnut. Try one in boiling water, if it does not hold together, add more meal. Drop into boiling soup 15 minutes before serving. Cracker crumbs or bread crumbs may be used in place of the meal.

FARINA BALLS

1 cup hot milk,
½ cup farina,
1 tablespoon salt,
$\frac{1}{16}$ teaspoon pepper,
2 eggs.

Put butter and milk in double boiler, when hot add farina and stir until thick and smooth; take from stove and when cool add the yolks of the eggs and the whites beaten stiff. Season to taste and add ½ cup grated almonds, if desired. Roll into marbles. Drop them in boiling soup 10 minutes before serving and let them boil up once or twice.

EGG BALLS

2 yolks, cooked,
1 raw egg yolk,
⅛ teaspoon salt,
$\frac{1}{16}$ teaspoon pepper,
½ teaspoon melted butter.

Rub yolks through sieve, add seasoning and put together with raw yolk, just enough to shape into small balls. Roll in flour and fry in a little butter; and pour the hot broth over them, or drop them without frying, into boiling soup 5 minutes before serving.

EGG CUSTARD

2 eggs (yolks),
2 tablespoons milk,
Few grains salt.

Beat eggs slightly, add milk and salt, pour into a small buttered cup and place in pan of hot water and let cook until firm. Cool, remove from cup and cut into fancy shapes or squares. Pour the hot broth over them and serve.

SPONGE DUMPLINGS

¼ teaspoon salt, ½ teaspoon chopped parsley,
3 eggs, 1 cup soup stock.

Separate the egg; beat the yolk and add the soup stock; then add the beaten white. Pour into a buttered cup and place in pan of hot water and steam until firm; cool, remove from cup and cut into small dumplings with a teaspoon, pour the boiling soup over and just before serving add the parsley.

FRITTER BEANS

1 egg, ¾ teaspoon salt,
2 tablespoons milk or water, ½ cup flour.

Beat egg until light, add salt, flour and milk. Put through colander into hot deep fat and fry until brown. Drain and pour the hot broth over them and serve.

NOODLES

1 egg, ⅔ cup flour (about),
¼ teaspoon salt.

Beat egg slightly, add salt and enough flour to make a stiff dough. Roll out very thin, and set aside to dry for an hour or more. It must not be the least bit sticky and not so dry that it will break or be brittle.

Fold into a tight roll, or cut into 3 inch strips, placing the strips all together one on top of another. Now cut these long strips crosswise into very fine strips or threads. Toss them up lightly with fingers to separate well, and spread them out on the board to dry. When thoroughly dry, put in covered jars for future use. Drop by handfuls into boiling soup 5 minutes before serving.

"PLAETZCHEN"

1 egg, ⅔ cup flour (about),
¼ teaspoon salt.

Beat egg slightly, add salt and enough flour to make a stiff dough. Roll out very thin and let remain on board one hour or until it is quite dry, but not brittle. Cut into 3 inch strips and place strips on top of one another. Then cut these into ½ inch strips, crosswise, cut again to form ½ inch squares. When dough is all cut into these little squares, toss them up lightly and spread to dry on the board. Drop them by handfuls into boiling soup, let boil 5 minutes before serving.

FINGERHUETCHEN

1 egg,   2/3 cup flour (about),
1/4 teaspoon salt.

Beat egg slightly, add salt, and flour enough to make a stiff dough. Roll out thin, like noodle dough, and leave on board to dry.

Fold dough in three equal parts and cut into small circles with a floured thimble. Toss lightly with fingers to separate circles and fry in deep hot fat until brown, or place in a pan, plentifully greased, and bake in a very hot oven and cool and serve with soup.

Place in soup tureen or a few in each bouillon cup and pour the hot broth over them.

EGG BARLEY OR PFARVEL

1 egg,   7/8 cup flour,
1/4 teaspoon salt.

Beat egg slightly, add salt and enough flour to make a hard ball of dough or rub well with hollow of hand until small grains are formed.

Grate, chop or rub the dough through a colander. Dry a few moments in pan in the oven or on board. Drop a desired quantity gradually into boiling soup, let boil 5 to 10 minutes, then serve.

"Pfarvel" may also be used as a vegetable. This recipe makes one cup full of raw "pfarvel" or Eier graupen.

CREPLECH

Noodle Dough,   1 egg,
1 lb. lean raw beef, chopped   1 teaspoon salt,
     fine,   1/8 teaspoon pepper,
1/2 teaspoon onion juice.

Roll Noodle Dough, page 85, into pieces 1 1/2 inches square. Mix the meat with the egg and seasoning and place a teaspoon of this mixture on each square. Fold into three cornered pockets, pressing edges well together. Drop in boiling soup or salted water and boil 15 minutes.

Creplech may also be filled with prepared cottage cheese or prunes and used as a vegetable. See Mehlspeise, page 179.

CHAPTER X

SAUCES FOR FISH, MEAT AND VEGETABLES

WHAT SAUCES CONTAIN

Fat	Starch	Liquids	Seasoning
Butter,	Flour,	Milk,	Salt,
Beef dripping,	Corn Starch.	Water,	Pepper,
Oil.		Milk and Water,	Spices,
		Vegetable stock, with or without milk,	Sugar, Flavoring extracts,
		Fish stock,	Wines,
		Meat stock,	Acids.
		Fruit juices.	

THIN WHITE SAUCE

2 tablespoons butter,   ¼ teaspoon salt,
1½ tablespoons flour,   ⅛ teaspoon pepper,
   1 cup hot milk.

Scald the milk. Melt the butter in a saucepan. Remove from fire and mix with flour. Cook until it bubbles, then add ⅔ of the hot milk at once and the rest gradually and boil, stirring constantly, until the mixture thickens. Season and serve hot.

WHITE SAUCE

2 tablespoons butter,   ⅛ teaspoon pepper,
2 tablespoons flour,   ½ teaspoon salt,
   1 cup hot milk.

Melt the butter in a saucepan. Remove from fire and mix with flour. Cook until it bubbles, then add ⅔ of the hot milk at once and the rest gradually and boil, stirring constantly until the mixture thickens. Season and serve hot.

THICK WHITE SAUCE

(for Cutlets and Croquettes)

2½ tablespoons butter, ¼ teaspoon salt,
⅓ cup flour, ⅛ teaspoon pepper,
    1 cup hot milk or white soup stock.

Melt butter in hot frying pan, add flour and stir well and when it bubbles add ⅔ of the hot liquid at once and the rest gradually, stirring constantly until smooth. Season.

CREAM SAUCE

1 cup hot White Sauce, 2 yolks of eggs.

Pour the White Sauce, page 87, gradually over the beaten yolks and cook slowly until thick, stirring constantly, or add a little cold water to the beaten yolks and stir slowly into the gravy. Two tablespoons of wine may be added to flavor it. Serve at once, hot, over cooked green peas, asparagus, fish, meat or poultry.

SWEET AND SOUR SAUCE, No. 1

2 tablespoons butter, ¼ teaspoon pepper,
2 tablespoons flour, 2 tablespoons vinegar,
½ teaspoon salt, 1 cup of hot vegetable liquor
2 tablespoons sugar,   or soup stock.

Brown butter well, add flour and brown, then the seasoning, add ⅔ cup of the hot liquid, then the rest and vinegar and sugar to taste. Cook until smooth and serve hot as desired with cooked string beans, carrots, soup meat, etc.

SWEET AND SOUR SAUCE, No. 2

½ cup sugar, ¼ cup vinegar,
1 tablespoon flour, ½ teaspoon salt,
1 cup hot water, ⅛ teaspoon pepper.
Vegetable or soup stock,

Melt sugar in a hot spider, add the flour and stir, and very gradually add the boiling liquid, then the vinegar and the seasoning. Serve hot with boiled carrots, string beans, etc.

SWEET AND SOUR SAUCE, No. 3

4 ginger snaps,
½ cup brown sugar,
¼ cup vinegar,
½ teaspoon onion juice,
1 cup hot water, fish or soup stock,
1 lemon, sliced,
¼ cup raisins.

Mix all together and cook until smooth. It must taste strong of vinegar and sugar and more of either may be added to suit taste. Grated Gingerbread for Filling, page 33, may be used in place of the gingersnaps.

Served hot or cold with fish, meat, tongue and left over meats.

CATSUP SAUCE

1 cup white sauce,
3 tablespoons Catsup.

Make White Sauce, page 87. Mix with the catsup and serve hot or cold over fish or meat.

BROWN SAUCE

2 tablespoons butter or other fat,
2 tablespoons flour,
½ teaspoon salt,
⅛ teaspoon pepper,
1 cup hot water, meat, fish, or vegetable stock.

Brown the butter or fat and if desired add a small onion, chopped, and when brown add the flour, let brown, and add ⅔ cup of the hot liquid and gradually the rest of the seasoning. Let cook five minutes and serve with hot meat, vegetables, dumplings, etc. This makes one cup of sauce; if more is required, add the quantities in proportion.

MUSHROOM SAUCE

¼ can mushrooms,
1 cup brown sauce,
1 teaspoon chopped parsley.

Make Brown Sauce after above recipe and add to it the mushrooms, drained, rinsed and cut in quarters or slices, or make 1 cup of Brown Sauce using 1 cup of mushroom liquid in place of the other liquid and add 1 teaspoon chopped parsley. Serve hot over meat.

CAPER SAUCE

1 cup Brown Sauce,
¼ cup capers.

Drain the capers from their liquor and add to the Brown Sauce —recipe above. Serve hot with boiled mutton or fish.

CREOLE SAUCE

1½ cups Brown Sauce,
2 tablespoons butter,
2 tablespoons onion, chopped,
2 tablespoons chopped green peppers,
¼ cup mushrooms,
2 whole tomatoes, peeled and sliced, or
3 tablespoons canned tomato,
½ teaspoon salt,
½ teaspoon paprika,
1 teaspoon ketchup,
Bouquet.

Follow directions for Brown Sauce, page 89, increasing the proportions one-half. Heat butter, add the onion, let fry lightly, then the peppers, tomato and mushrooms; add this to the prepared Brown Sauce, season with the rest of the ingredients, cook altogether 20 minutes and serve hot over thick broiled steak.

Note—Kitchen Bouquet is a highly seasoned liquid, prepared for gravies and sold by grocers.

SARDELLEN SAUCE

4 to 6 Sardellen,
2 tablespoons butter,
2 tablespoons flour,
1 cup of fish or meat stock,
½ cup white wine,
juice of ½ lemon,
salt,
pepper,
yolks of 2 eggs.

Soak the Sardellen in cold water ½ hour, chop fine and rub through a sieve. Melt butter, add flour, ⅔ of the fish or meat stock, hot, stir until smooth, add the rest, and the wine, lemon and the strained Sardellen, cook slowly for 10 minutes, season with salt and pepper to taste and then stir in the yolks beaten with a little cold water, very gradually and remove from the stove. Serve with fish or meat.

PIQUANTE SAUCE

1 cup Brown sauce,
½ small onion, chopped fine,
2 tablespoons Sherry or Claret wine or vinegar,
1 tablespoon each of capers and pickles, chopped.

Make Brown Sauce, page 89, and while hot add the rest of the ingredients. Serve hot with beef.

PORT WINE SAUCE

1 cup Brown Sauce,
2 tablespoons Port wine.
⅛ cup currant jelly,

Make Brown Sauce, page 89, omitting onion, and when hot add jelly and wine. Cook until dissolved and serve hot with venison chops.

JELLY SAUCE FOR GAME

½ lemon cut in dice,
1 tablespoon chopped citron,
1 teaspoon butter,
½ wine glass sherry,
½ glass currant jelly,
⅛ teaspoon salt,
1/16 teaspoon red pepper.

Boil all together and serve hot with game.

DRAWN BUTTER SAUCE

2 cups boiling water, milk or fish stock,
8 tablespoons butter,
⅛ teaspoon pepper,
4 tablespoons flour,
½ teaspoon salt.

Melt 4 tablespoons butter into a saucepan. Remove from the fire and mix with flour. Add ⅔ cup of the boiling liquid, then the rest; the remainder of the butter in small pieces, and the salt and pepper. Boil 5 minutes and serve hot.

PARSLEY BUTTER

1 tablespoon butter,
1 teaspoon minced parsley,
1 teaspoon lemon juice,
¼ teaspoon salt,
A few grains pepper.

Rub butter to a cream, add salt, pepper, parsley and lemon juice. Spread over hot broiled fish or steak.

MAITRE D'HOTEL SAUCE

¼ cup butter,
½ teaspoon salt,
⅛ teaspoon pepper,
½ teaspoon finely chopped parsley,
¾ tablespoon lemon juice.

Put butter in a bowl, and with small wooden spoon or spatula work until creamy. Add salt, pepper and parsley, then lemon juice, very slowly. Spread over hot broiled fish or steak.

HOLLANDAISE SAUCE

½ cup butter,
2 eggs (yolks),
1 tablespoon lemon juice,
A few grains cayenne pepper,
¼ teaspoon salt,
½ cup boiling water.

With a wooden or silver spoon rub the butter to a cream, add the yolks one at a time. Beat well, add the lemon juice, salt and pepper. About 5 minutes before serving add the boiling water, and stir rapidly until it thickens. Cook the sauce in a double boiler, or set the bowl in a pan of boiling water until it thickens.

OR—Put butter in a bowl, cover with cold water and wash, using a spoon. Divide into three pieces; put one piece in a saucepan with the yolks of eggs and lemon juice, place saucepan in a larger one containing boiling water and stir constantly with a wire whisk until butter is melted; then add second piece of butter and as it thickens, third piece. Add water, cook 1 minute, remove from fire and then add salt and cayenne. Serve hot with fish or vegetables.

BEARNAISE SAUCE

To Hollandaise Sauce as above stir in 1 teaspoon each of fresh tarragon (Estregan) and parsley, chopped fine. Serve hot with chops, broiled squabs, salmon and the like.

TARTAR SAUCE

No. 1

1 tablespoon vinegar,
1 tablespoon lemon juice,
¼ teaspoon salt,
1 tablespoon Worcestershire sauce,
⅓ cup butter.

Mix vinegar, lemon juice, salt and Worcestershire in small bowl and heat over hot water. Brown the butter and strain into it. Serve cold over fish.

No. 2

1 teaspoon mustard,
⅛ teaspoon pepper,
Few drops onion juice,
Yolks 2 raw eggs,
½ cup olive oil,
3 tablespoons vinegar,
1 tablespoon chopped olives,
1 tablespoon chopped capers,
1 teaspoon powdered sugar,
¼ teaspoon salt,
1 tablespoon chopped cucumber pickles,
1 tablespoon parsley.

Mix seasonings in the order given; add the yolks, and stir well; setting the bowl in a pan of ice water, add oil slowly, then the vinegar and chopped ingredients. This will keep for several weeks if kept in a cool place. Serve cold over fish or meats.

No. 3

1 cup Mayonnaise dressing,
1 tablespoon chopped capers,
1 tablespoon tarragon vinegar,
1 tablespoon chopped olives,
1 tablespoon cucumber pickles.

Make any desired Mayonnaise, page 191, and add to it the rest of the ingredients. Serve cold with fish or cold meat dishes.

TOMATO SAUCE

No. 1

2 tablespoons butter,	½ cup water,
¼ teaspoon onion juice,	1 cup strained tomato,
2 tablespoons flour,	1 teaspoon salt,

spk. pepper.

Heat the butter, remove from the fire, stir in the flour. Add the water, stir well, add the tomato, the onion juice, salt and pepper, boil 5 minutes. Served hot with boiled macaroni, or with boiled or baked meat, or with baked eggs or fish.

No. 2

½ can tomatoes or	3 cloves,
1¾ cups fresh stewed tomatoes,	2 tablespoons butter or other fat,
2 slices onion,	2 tablespoons flour,
8 peppercorns,	1 tablespoon sugar,
1 bay leaf,	¼ teaspoon salt.

Cook tomatoes 15 minutes with the onion, peppercorns, bay leaf and cloves. Strain.

Heat the butter in a frying pan, add ⅔ cup flour and then the rest of the hot strained tomatoes. Season to taste.

Served over hot chops, fish, macaroni, etc.

MINT SAUCE

¼ cup chopped mint leaves,   1 tablespoon powdered sugar,
½ cup vinegar.

Add sugar to vinegar; when dissolved pour over mint and let stand thirty minutes over slow fire to infuse. If vinegar is strong dilute with water. Serve hot over hot lamb.

Or boil sugar and vinegar, throw in the mint leaves and let boil up once. Set aside and serve cold with lamb.

CURRY SAUCE

2 tablespoons butter,	½ teaspoon curry powder,
2 tablespoons flour,	¼ teaspoon salt,

1 cup hot soup stock.

Melt butter, add flour, then the seasoning, then ⅔ cup and gradually the rest of the hot soup stock. Let cook until thick and smooth and serve with hot left over meat.

MUSTARD SAUCE

1 cup white sauce,
1 tablespoon vinegar,
1 tablespoon mustard,
½ teaspoon sugar,
1 teaspoon cold water.

Mix the mustard with the water, and stir into the White Sauce, page 87, two minutes before serving. Season to taste. More or less mustard may be added as desired. Served hot with meat or fish.

CUCUMBER SAUCE

No. 1

This sauce may be made with large pickled gherkins. Chop two or three cucumbers finely, with a small tender onion; add a light sprinkling of sugar, a tablespoon of tarragon vinegar, a few grains of mace, and salt, celery salt and cayenne to taste.

No. 2

½ cup double cream,
¼ teaspoon salt,
A few grains pepper,
3 tablespoons vinegar or lemon juice,
1 fresh cucumber.

Beat the cream until solid, add the salt and pepper and gradually the vinegar or lemon juice.

When ready to serve, fold in the cucumber, pared, chilled, chopped coarse and drained.

WHIPPED CREAM SAUCE

1 cup milk,
2 tablespoons flour,
½ teaspoon salt,
⅛ teaspoon white pepper,
1 cup whipped cream.

Wet the flour with a little of the cold milk, gradually add the rest of the milk. Cook until thick, season and when cold add the stiff cream lightly.

Serve cold with asparagus.

EGG SAUCE FOR BOILED FISH

2 yolks of eggs,
1 cup Brown Sauce,
1 tablespoon vinegar or lemon juice.

Follow recipe for Brown Sauce, page 89, using fish liquor. Stir the hot sauce gradually on the beaten yolks; let cook a moment, stirring constantly until thick. Remove from fire and add lemon juice. If wanted hot serve at once.

LEMON SAUCE FOR FISH OR MEAT

Juice of one large lemon, ½ cup butter, pepper and salt. Heat, but do not allow to boil. Then mix it with two well beaten yolks.

SAUCE FOR BOILED TONGUE OR FISH

2 whole eggs, and
1 yolk,
1 tablespoon mustard,
2 tablespoons vinegar,
¼ cup olive oil,
¼ teaspoon salt, pepper,
paprika to taste.

Mix dry ingredients, add and mix thoroughly with the eggs, very well beaten and the rest of the ingredients and cook until thick over boiling water, stirring constantly. Add cream to thin.

NEWBURG SAUCE FOR FISH OR LOBSTER

4 or 5 yolks,
3 tablespoons sherry,
Salt and pepper to taste,
1 cup milk,
1 cup cream.

Beat the yolks until very light, add the rest of the ingredients and cook over boiling water, until thick and smooth, stirring constantly.

HORSERADISH SAUCE

No. 1

2 tablespoons fat,
¼ onion, cut fine,
2 tablespoons flour or cracker meal,
3 tablespoons grated horseradish,
2 tablespoons vinegar,
2 cloves,
2 bay leaves,
½ teaspoon salt,
⅛ teaspoon pepper,
2 tablespoons sugar,
1 cup soup stock or water.

Fry the onion in the fat, until brown, add the cracker meal and horseradish and gradually the hot soup stock and when smooth the other ingredients. Cook 5 minutes more and if desired add more horseradish, sugar or vinegar. Or, add the horseradish, vinegar, salt, pepper and sugar to White Sauce, page 87.

Serve hot with soup meat.

No. 2

3 tablespoons grated horseradish,
1 tablespoon vinegar,
¼ teaspoon salt,
Pepper,
¼ cup rich cream.

Mix the first four ingredients and add the cream, beaten stiff. Serve cold with cold meat or whole tomatoes as a relish.

CHAPTER XI

COMPOSITION OF FISH

	Refuse	Proteid	Fat	Mineral Matter	Water
Black Bass	54.8	9.3	.8	.5	34.6
Whitefish	53.5	10.3	3.0	.7	32.5
Herring	42.6	10.9	3.9	.8	41.7
Trout	48.1	9.8	1.1	.6	40.4
Perch	62.5	7.2	1.5	.4	28.4
Pickerel	47.1	9.8	.2	.7	42.2

GENERAL RULE

Fish must be perfectly fresh and should be kept in a cool place until cooked. Do not put in refrigerator on account of odor. The flesh should be firm and the eyes bright, the gills, bright red.

Fish is less stimulating and nourishing than the meat of other animals, but is easier of digestion.

To Scale Fish—Use fish-scaler, ordinary grater or knife. Begin at the tail end and go toward head, slanting the knife toward you to prevent scales from flying. Rinse and cleanse thoroughly in cold water. Sprinkle fish with salt and pepper, to preserve it and improve the flavor.

The head and tail may be removed. Dry fish need butter rubbed over them before broiling.

When fish is cooked the flesh separates from the bone. It can be served hot or cold with a sauce or garnished with lemon, hard-cooked eggs or parsley.

Cold cooked fish may be used in various ways, as creamed, scalloped, etc.

TO BONE A FISH

Clean the fish thoroughly. Cut open and remove entrails. Beginning at the neck, on the inner side of fish, cut with a sharp knife, the bones on one side, close to the backbone. Cut down to the tail close to the backbone, so the fish will lay flat on the board.

Scrape flesh from bone with back of knife, removing in one piece the backbone and bones attached to one side. Remove bones from other side with knife and pick out remaining small bones. Take care not to break the outer skin.

FRIED FISH

Clean fish, wipe dry as possible, sprinkle with salt and pepper, dip in flour, crumbs, or cornmeal, then in egg and again in crumbs. Let stand a few moments. Then fry a golden brown in deep, hot fat.

SAUTED FISH

Clean fish, sprinkle with salt and pepper, dip in flour or cornmeal, and cook in spider with enough hot fat to prevent its sticking to the pan. Shake the pan occasionally. Brown well on under side, then turn and brown on the other side.

BROILED FISH

Clean the fish. Split a thin fish down the back, and if you prefer, cut off the head and tail. Cut thick fish into slices and remove skin and bone. Oily fish need only salt and pepper, but dry fish should be spread with a little butter before broiling. Use double wire broiler and grease it. Put the thickest edge of the fish next to the middle of the broiler and broil the flesh side first. Cook about eight to twelve minutes, or until a delicate brown. Move the broiler up and down, that all parts may be equally browned, and then turn and cook the other side to crisp the skin. Broil over a clean fire, or if gas stove is used, one inch from gas in hot broiling over. When done, the fish should be white and firm, and separate easily from the bone. Remove to a hot platter, flesh side up, first loosening fish from broiler. Spread with salt, pepper and butter, and garnish with slices of lemon and parsley.

BROILED SMELTS

Use only the largest smelts, split them down the backs, clean and remove the backbone. Rub each fish with a little olive oil, sprinkle with salt and pepper, lay them on a greased broiler, and hold them under the gas flame for two or three minutes on each side. Have ready a nicely browned slice of toast for each smelt, lay the fish on the toast, put a bit of butter on each and garnish with watercress and points of hard boiled eggs. Serve with Tartar Sauce, page 92.

BROILED SARDINES

Twelve large sardines broiled under the gas flame for a few minutes, (in a broiler). Serve on toast, 2 sardines for each person. Decorate with parsley and a slice of lemon.

HALIBUT STEAK

Light your burners three minutes before the steaks go on and have your dripping pan ready. Lay the steaks in salt and water for half an hour, then marinate them in a bath of salad oil and lemon juice for another half hour. Wipe dry and broil, turning twice carefully. Lay upon a hot dish, anoint with a green sauce of butter, lemon juice and minced parsley, beaten to a cream; set in the oven for a minute, and serve.

BAKED BLACK BASS

3 lbs. bass,
Salt and pepper,
¼ cup butter,
2 tablespoons flour,
½ cup strained tomato or,
1 fresh tomato, sliced.

Clean and wash fish. Sprinkle with salt inside and out and let stand several hours. Stuff and sew. Tie or skewer into the shape of the letter S. Put in a pan across which you have placed strips of cloth by which to lift out when cooked. Rub it over with soft butter, and a little pepper. Dredge with flour. Put in a hot oven without water in the pan. Baste when the flour is brown, and often afterwards; add a tomato. When done, remove carefully and place in a hot platter. Draw out the strings and skewers, wipe off the water or fat that runs from the fish, serve with drawn butter flavored with lemon or with Hollandaise Sauce, page 91, in a gravy boat. Garnish with parsley or cress.

Haddock, blue fish and shad are good, baked.

STUFFING FOR FISH

½ cup bread crumbs,
½ cup cracker crumbs,
¼ teaspoon salt,
¼ cup melted butter,
1 teaspoon chopped onion,
1 teaspoon chopped parsley,
1 teaspoon capers,
1 teaspoon chopped pickles.

This makes a dry, crumbly stuffing; if a moist stuffing be desired, use stale bread crumbs (not dried), and moisten with one beaten egg, or moisten the crackers with ¼ cup hot water.

BAKED TROUT

3½ lbs. trout,
1 can tomatoes,
1 onion, cut fine,
1 piece celery root,
1 tablespoon flour,
1 yolk of egg,
Cream,
Worcestershire sauce,
1 tablespoon butter.

Wet the flour with a little of the cold tomato. Salt fish and let stand several hours. Place fish in dripping pan with tomatoes, onion, celery and butter and bake ½ hour. Strain the sauce and just before sending to the table, thicken with the egg yolk and add the cream and Worcestershire sauce.

BAKED FISH WITH SARDELLES

Take a trout, split it as for broiling and remove center bone. Place on a buttered platter, skin side down, cover with ½ cup butter, 1 cup thick sour cream, ¼ lb. sardelles which have been soaked in water and chopped fine, cayenne pepper, a little cracker dust; and add 1 cup stale grated American cheese. Bake in a hot oven one-half hour. Serve on small platter.

PLANKED FISH

Fish is planked when baked on a board (Must be maple wood or it will make the food bitter) in the oven. Place the board in oven until very hot. Place the fish on board, season with salt and pepper and a little butter, or split it and place it skin down on the board; brush with butter and dust with salt and pepper. Baste often with melted butter, and bake until a golden brown, then reduce the heat and finish cooking. Serve with parsley, lemon or pickles sliced.

White fish and trout is best served in this style.

FILLET DE SOLE

Two pounds flounder, boned and skinned and boiled in water, with salt, cayenne, onion, celery and carrot. Boil only a few minutes, drain, place in two long pieces on a well buttered platter with a space between. In this space put oysters or clams, some mushrooms, tomatoes strained, and plenty of butter and a little cracker dust. Bake twenty minutes in moderate oven.

BOILED FISH

3 lbs. fish, cut in slices and sprinkled with salt,
1 qt. water,
¼ teaspoon whole pepper,
1 tablespoon onion, cut fine,
1 tablespoon celery, cut fine,
1 tablespoon carrot, cut fine.

Clean fish and let stand in salt several hours. Let the water, pepper and vegetables boil until the water is well flavored. Add the fish, a few slices at a time, and let simmer until the flesh is firm and leaves the bones, no matter how long the time. Place on platter. Strain and reserve the fish stock, if wanted.

"SHARFE" FISH

3 lb. pike, or other fish,
1 tablespoon butter,
1 tablespoon flour,
1 cup hot fish stock,
1 egg (yolk).

Clean and salt the fish and cook, following recipe for Boiled Fish, above. Reserve 1 cup of the fish stock.

Melt the butter, add the flour and the hot fish stock. Take from fire and pour very gradually on the beaten yolk. Pour while hot over the boiled fish. Garnish with parsley.

SALMON TROUT, BROILED

3½ lbs. salmon trout,
¼ of a cabbage, cut fine,
1 carrot, cut fine,
1 onion, cut fine,
1 celery root, cut fine,
2 potatoes,
½ can tomatoes,
5 bay leaves,
1 qt. boiling water,
2 or 3 yolks of eggs,
½ cup cream,
1 tablespoon sherry,
¼ teaspoon peppercorns.

Salt the fish and let stand several hours. Cook the vegetables in boiling water, add the peppercorns and boil until the water is well flavored, about 1 hour; add fish and boil until the flesh separates from the bones. Place fish or platter. Strain the fish liquid. Beat yolk well, add cream and flavor with the sherry. Pour the hot fish liquid over the egg mixture, gradually, stirring constantly.

Then pour over the fish; set in the oven with oven door open, to keep hot and serve garnished with parsley. It will curdle if left too long in stove or if stove is too hot.

CREAMED SALMON

1 cup cold cooked or canned salmon,
½ cup White Sauce.

Remove skin and bone from canned salmon, shred, and add 1 teaspoon lemon juice to White Sauce, page 87. serve hot on toast.

Or, cook fresh fish after recipe for Boiled Fish, page 100, and add 1 teaspoon lemon juice to White Sauce. serve hot.

SALMON PUDDING

1 small can steak salmon,
1 tablespoon butter,
1 cup bread crumbs,
1 cup hot milk,
½ teaspoon salt,
⅛ teaspoon pepper,
2 eggs.

Remove skin and bones from salmon, and rub fish fine with potato masher. Melt butter in milk and add bread crumbs and seasonings. Combine with the fish. Last add the well beaten eggs. Put into a buttered deep baking dish and steam one hour.

When pudding is done, turn out on to platter and pour the following sauce around it. serve hot.

SAUCE

1 tablespoon butter,
1½ tablespoon flour,
1 cup milk,
Liquid from salmon,
½ teaspoon salt,
Few grains of cayenne.

Melt butter, add flour and slowly pour on hot milk, then add salmon liquid and seasonings.

SALMON MOULD

1 one pound can salmon,
½ teaspoon salt,
1½ tablespoons sugar,
1 teaspoon mustard,
¾ cup scalded milk,
1½ tablespoons melted butter,
2 yolks of eggs, beaten,
¼ cup hot vinegar,
¾ tablespoon granulated gelatine,
2 tablespoons cold water.

Rinse the salmon in a can with hot water, and drain thoroughly. Remove skin and bone, and pick the flesh fine with a silver fork, then set aside. Mix the dry ingredients. Pour over, gradually, the scalded milk, and, when well mixed, place in double boiler, and stir and cook 5 minutes. Then add the melted butter, the beaten yolks, with a tablespoon of cold water added, and the hot vinegar. Stir and cook a moment. Then add the granulated gelatine, softened in two tablespoons of cold water. Stir until melted, then add the salmon, and turn into small moulds to harden. Serve with Cucumber Sauce, No. 2, page 94.

FILLED FISH

3 lb. fish,
1 onion, juice or cut fine,
Salt,
2 eggs,
Pepper,
½ cup soft bread crumbs or ¼ cup cracker crumbs,
1 tablespoon almonds, chopped.

Clean the fish thoroughly, remove the skin without breaking, and the flesh by scraping it from the bones. Begin at the neck. With care, the backbone may be removed with all of the small bones attached. Chop the flesh fine. Mix these ingredients well. Wash fish-skin, and fill with the mixture. Sew up with coarse thread; shape, and place in gently boiling vegetable stock, as other Boiled Fish, page 100. Boil slowly until the stock is nearly absorbed.

FISH BALLS

½ lb. raw fish,
½ cup fine stale bread crumbs,
½ cup milk,
1 egg,
1 teaspoon grated onion,
1 teaspoon salt,
¼ teaspoon pepper.

Remove skin and bone from fish and chop fine. Cook bread and milk to a paste. Remove from stove, add egg, seasoning and fish and shape into balls, size of a walnut.

Drop into boiling, salted water and cook slowly 20 minutes. Serve with "Sharfe" Fish Sauce, page 100.

FISH CAKES

1 cup cold boiled fish,
1 cup cold mashed potatoes,
Salt and pepper,
Celery salt,
1 egg, beaten.

Equal quantities of cold mashed potatoes and shredded cold fish. Mix, season to taste, add the beaten egg, shape in rounds, cook in spider with 2 tablespoons hot butter until nicely browned.

BOILED FISH WITH LEMON SAUCE

3½ lbs. Pike or Salmon Trout,
2 lemons, juice and rind,
2 yolks of eggs,
1 cup of hot fish stock,
1 teaspoon sugar,
Salt to taste,
Chopped parsley.

Stir the grated rind of the lemons with the well beaten yolks, add the juice and very gradually pour on the hot fish stock. Cook until thick, stirring constantly. Add the sugar and parsley. Serve with fish, cooked in boiling water, to which salt, onion, whole pepper, parsley and a tablespoon of lemon juice has been added. Bone the fish.

The sauce may be made thicker by cooking a teaspoon of cornstarch (wet in cold water) with the strained fish stock, or more yolks of eggs may be added.

HALIBUT IN TOMATO SAUCE

1½ lbs. Halibut,
1 cup White Sauce,
1 red pepper,
½ teaspoon onion, chopped,
1 cut strained tomatoes.

Boil and shred the fish following recipe, page 100. Make White Sauce, page 87. Add stewed and strained tomatoes and the onion and the pepper, chopped.

Pour this sauce over the fish and serve hot on toast.

HALIBUT AND SHRIMP A LA NEWBURG

Part 1
1½ lbs. halibut,
2 slices onion,
1 cup White Sauce,
3 whites of eggs, beaten stiff,

Part 2
1½ lb. shrimp,
1 cup White Sauce,
¼ cup sherry wine,
3 yolks, beaten.

Cook fish in salted, boiling water with onion until tender (1 teaspoon salt to 1 qt. boiling water). Drain and shred. To one cup of the hot White Sauce, page 87, add the shredded fish and then the stiffly beaten whites. Place in center of hot platter and set in oven with oven door open. Take the boiled shrimp, remove the shell and break in small pieces. Add the wine to the remaining cup of White Sauce, and pour the hot sauce gradually on the beaten yolks. Mix the beaten yolks with a little cold water. Add the shrimp, heat thoroughly and place as border around the halibut and serve at once.

HALIBUT WITH LOBSTER A LA NEWBURG

One and one-half pound halibut boned and picked raw, chop fine, add salt, cayenne and beaten whites of five eggs, one cup of cream, whipped. Pack into a mould and boil thirty minutes. Serve in the center of a platter with Lobster a la Newburg, page 232, around it, substituting lobster in place of shrimp in the recipe above.

FISH PUDDING

2 lbs. raw Halibut,
1 cup cream,
1 cup butter,
3 yolks,
2 tablespoons flour,
3 whites, beaten stiff.

Shred fish from skin and bone, chop fine, add cream slowly and pass through a fine sieve. Add other ingredients, whites last. Butter pudding mould, sprinkle with chopped parsley. Boil one and one-half hours and serve hot with Sauce Hollandaise, page 91.

FISH WITH HORSERADISH SAUCE

3 lbs. fresh Salmon,
Salt,
1 tablespoon parsley,
1 pt. cream, beaten stiff,
½ lb. horseradish root,
¼ cup melted butter.

Clean fish, bone, salt and let stand several hours.

Place in fish kettle with boiling, salt water (1 teaspoon salt to 1 qt. water), and let boil ½ hour or until well cooked.

Lift out carefully, place on hot platter and pour over the melted butter and sprinkle well with the parsley.

Serve in a separate bowl the following sauce, a large spoonful with each portion of fish.

Peel horseradish root, grate and mix well with the pint of cream beaten stiff. The fish must be hot and the sauce cold.

SWEET AND SOUR FISH

3½ lbs. Pike, Trout or other fish,
4 gingersnaps,
½ cup brown sugar,
¼ cup vinegar,
½ teaspoon onion juice,
1 cup hot fish liquid,
¼ cup seeded raisins,
1 lemon, sliced and seeded.

Clean, slice and salt fish and let stand over night or several hours. Cook, following recipe for Boiled Fish, page 100. Drain and bone, reserving 1 cup of the fish liquid. Mix the rest of the ingredients and cook until smooth and thick. It must taste strong of vinegar and sugar, and more of either may be added to taste. Serve cold. Gingerbread for Fillings, page 33, is used in place of the gingersnaps.

TROUT WITH MAYONNAISE

3 lbs. salmon, trout or pike,	4 yolks of eggs,
2 cups water,	2 tablespoons sugar,
2 tablespoons chopped almonds (blanched),	1 tablespoon flour or cornstarch,
2 lemons (juice),	1 teaspoon salt,
2 tablespoons seeded raisins,	¼ cup Mayonnaise.

Clean, salt and slice fish and cook following recipe for Boiled Fish, page 100; skin and bone.

Boil water, lemon juice, chopped almonds and raisins until almonds are soft; add gradually the sugar and cornstarch wet in a little cold water and boil; add very gradually to the well beaten yolks of four eggs, stirred with 1 tablespoon cold water. Take from stove and when cold, add Mayonnaise Dressing, page 190, to taste. Serve cold garnished with capers, olives or chopped pickles and hard cooked eggs.

FISH A LA TARTARE

3½ lbs. fish, pike or trout,	1 teaspoon mustard,
4 hard cooked yolks of eggs,	¼ cup Mayonnaise dressing,
4 hard cooked whites of eggs, chopped,	1 tablespoon catsup,
	1 tablespoon powdered sugar,
1 tablespoon capers,	1 tablespoon vinegar,
1 tablespoon pickles, finely chopped,	1 teaspoon chopped parsley,
	1 cup strained fish liquid,
1 tablespoon onion, finely chopped,	Salt and pepper to taste,
	1 tablespoon salad oil.

Boil, page 100, and bone the fish, leaving it whole or cut in portions for serving. Rub the yolks smooth with the mustard and the oil, add the rest of the ingredients, the chopped ingredients last. Season to taste.

FISH A LA MACEDOINE

2 lbs. fresh salmon or halibut,	1 can Macedoine (fine mixed vegetables).
French dressing,	

Boil fish, page 100, in salt water, cool, surround with Macedoine, and while still hot add a French salad dressing, page 188. Serve cold.

FISH SALAD FOR 12 PEOPLE

2 lbs. halibut,
1 pint Mayonnaise,
4 hard boiled eggs,
½ pint bottle Cross & Blackwell's chow-chow.

Boil, page 100, cool and shred fish. Mix with the Mayonnaise, page 190, add boiled eggs, chopped—and the pickles chopped fine. Delmonico Pickles, page 436, may be used in place of the chow-chow.

Serve ice cold in head lettuce leaves.

FISH SALAD IN JELLY

2 cups cold boiled fish, cut in dice,
½ cup celery, cut in small pieces, or finely shredded cabbage,
½ cup pickle or cucumber, cut in slices,
½ cup apple or pear, cut in dice,
½ package granulated gelatine,
½ cup cold water,
½ cup vinegar,
Juice of one lemon,
1 pint of boiling water,
½ cup sugar,
1 teaspoon salt.

Soak gelatine in cold water 2 minutes; add vinegar, lemon juice, boiling water, sugar and salt. Strain and when beginning to set, add remaining ingredients. Turn into mould or small moulds and chill. Serve on lettuce leaves with Mayonnaise Dressing, page 190, if desired.

MOULDED FISH SALAD WITH CUCUMBERS

2 tablespoons granulated
1½ lbs. cold boiled halibut,
¾ cup Mayonnaise,
1 tablespoon granulated gelatine,
½ cup cold fish stock or water,
1½ cup boiling fish stock,
1 pint cream, whipped,
1 large fresh cucumber,
French dressing.

Follow recipe for Boiled Fish, page 100. Bone and cut or break into ½ inch cubes. Make ¾ cup of any desired Mayonnaise, page 180. Soak gelatine in the cold fish stock or water, add the boiling hot fish stock, water or milk, and stir until dissolved. Let cool. When mixture begins to thicken add the Mayonnaise. Beat, using an egg beater, until frothy, then fold in the cream, beaten stiff, and lastly stir in lightly the halibut or any desired fish. Turn into fish mould and set aside to harden. Serve cold, surrounded with shredded lettuce leaves and the cucumber, pared, chopped and drained and mixed with French dressing, page 188, or with Cucumber Sauce, No. 2, page 94.

FISH GLACE

1 to 1½ lbs. halibut or red snapper,
1 tablespoon granulated gelatine,
¼ cup cold water,
1 cup boiling water (scant),
1 tablespoon lemon juice,
¼ cup sherry or port wine,
1 tablespoon each of carrots and beets cut in fancy shape
1 tablespoon each of pimolas, and pickles cut in thin slices,
1 tablespoon capers,
1 cup Mayonnaise or Cream dressing,
Lettuce leaves,
French dressing,

Boil fish, following recipe on page 100, leaving the carrot whole. Slice and cut beets (pickled) and carrot in fancy shapes with small vegetable cutters. When fish is tender remove from liquid; bone, and shred.

Soak gelatine in cold water a few minutes with one tablespoon lemon juice to soften, then add the boiling water and wine, and stir until dissolved. Let dissolved gelatine stand one hour or longer to partially harden. Rinse fish or any other mould or moulds in very cold water, add a few tablespoons of the gelatine mixture, put in a layer of the shredded fish, a sprinkling of the mixed vegetables and spread over this a thin layer of Cream Dressing, page 189, or Mayonnaise, page 190. Add a few spoonfuls of the gelatine mixture to cover, that the designs may not be disturbed.

Add another layer of fish, cut vegetables, Mayonnaise and jelly mixture and continue in the same manner until mould is nearly filled and leaving the jelly mixture on top. Set aside over night or several hours to harden. Invert and turn out on serving dish. If fish mould is used, place caper in eye cavity and make a border of shredded lettuce mixed lightly with the dressing.

BOILED SALT MACKEREL

Soak mackerel over night in cold water, with the skin side up, that the salt may be drawn out, change the water often, and less time is required. Drain. Place mackerel in shallow kettle, pour water over to cover and boil 10 to 15 minutes or until flesh separates from the bone. Remove to platter and pour hot, melted butter over and serve with hot potatoes.

They may also be boiled and served with a White Sauce, page 87.

BROILED SALT MACKEREL

Freshen the fish by soaking it over night in cold water, with the skin uppermost. Drain and wipe dry, remove the head and tail, place it upon a butter broiler, and slowly broil to a light brown. Place upon a hot dish, add pepper, bits of butter, a sprinkling of parsley and a little lemon juice.

SALT HERRING

Soak salt herring over night in cold water, that the salt may be drawn out. Drain and serve with boiled potatoes, or bone and place in kettle of cold water, let come to a boil and let simmer a few minutes until tender, drain and pour melted butter over them and serve hot with boiled or fried potatoes.

For Pickled Herring, see page 62.

CREAMED CODFISH

Cut salt codfish in ¼ in. slices across the grain, and soak in lukewarm water, to draw out the salt and soften the fish. Drain and add 1 cup Thin White Sauce, page 87. Add 1 beaten egg just before sending to the table. Garnish with hard boiled eggs. Salted codfish is very nourishing.

CODFISH BALLS

2½ cups potatoes,
1 cup salt codfish,
½ tablespoon butter.
1 egg,
⅛ teaspoon pepper,

Wash in cold water and shred the fish. Wash, pare and cut the potatoes in pieces, cook the fish and potatoes together in boiling water until the potatoes are soft. Drain very dry over fire, mash fine, add butter, seasoning and beaten egg. Beat well, shape on a spoon, and drop into deep hot fat. Fry until brown and drain on brown paper. If they break apart add a little more egg.

SHELLFISH

OYSTERS

Oysters have about the same composition as milk, containing carbohydrate matter which most flesh foods lack. Since they cost at least five times as much as milk, they are clearly not an economical food; but their flavor and ease of digestibility are highly prized. Large oysters are, generally speaking, more nutritious than small ones.

Take up each oyster separately in the fingers and remove all bits of shell and seaweed. Pour cold water over them to cleanse them, and drain them in a strainer.

Oyster liquid is seldom used, as enough comes from the oysters in cooking, but if desired it should be strained through clean cheese-cloth before using.

Oysters are very easily digested, especially when eaten raw.

BROILED OYSTERS

1 pint selected oysters, 1/4 cup melted butter,
2/3 cup seasoned cracker crumbs.

Clean oysters and dry between towels. Lift with fork by the tough muscles and dip in butter, then in cracker crumbs which have been seasoned with salt and pepper. Place in a buttered wire broiler and broil over a clear fire until juices flow, turning while broiling. Serve with or without Maitre d'Hotel butter, page 91.

FRICASSEED OYSTERS

2 tablespoons butter, 1 teaspoon salt,
1/8 teaspoon white pepper, cayenne,
1 pint or 38 oysters.

Place all the ingredients, except the oysters, in a chafing dish or covered saucepan. When hot, add the oysters, cover and shake the pan occasionally. When the oysters are plump, drain them and place them where they will keep hot.

Add enough cream to the liquid to make 1 cup.

FRIED OYSTERS

24 large oysters,
1 teaspoon salt,
⅛ teaspoon pepper,
½ cup bread crumbs,
1 egg.

Clean and drain select oysters. Roll in bread crumbs, seasoned with salt and pepper. Let stand 15 minutes or more, then dip in beaten egg, roll in crumbs again, let stand again 15 minutes or more in a cool place, and fry one minute or until golden brown in deep hot fat. Drain on paper, serve on hot platter and garnish with parsley, sliced pickle or lemon. Serve with French Fried Potatoes, page 174.

OYSTERS ON TOAST

Clean oysters and drain from their liquor. Put in a stew-pan and cook until oysters are plump and edges begin to curl. Shake the pan or stir oysters with a fork as they cook to prevent sticking. Season with salt, pepper, and a few tablespoons butter, and pour on small slices buttered toast. Garnish with parsley and toast points.

ESCALLOPED OYSTERS

1 pint oysters,
2 tablespoons oyster liquor,
2 tablespoons milk or cream,
½ cup stale bread crumbs,
1 cup cracker crumbs,
½ cup melted butter,
Salt,
Pepper.

Mix bread and cracker crumbs and stir in butter. Put a thin layer in bottom of buttered, shallow baking dish, cover with oysters and sprinkle with salt and pepper; add ½ each of oyster liquid and cream. Repeat, cover top with remaining crumbs. Bake 30 minutes in hot oven. Never allow more than 2 layers for scalloped oysters; if 3 layers are used, the middle layer will be underdone.

OYSTERS AU GRATIN (FOR 6 PEOPLE)

18 oysters,
18 mushrooms,
2 tablespoons butter,
½ teaspoon salt,
⅛ teaspoon red pepper,
1 cup white sauce.

Cook the mushrooms a few minutes in hot butter. Place 3 oysters on an oyster shell, then the mushroom, some White Sauce, page 87, and seasoning. Sprinkle with cracker crumbs and butter and bake until brown.

OYSTERS AND MUSHROOMS

12 large mushrooms,	Salt,
12 large oysters,	Pepper,
3 tablespoons butter,	1 cup Brown Sauce.

Wash, remove stems, peel caps of mushrooms. Cook 5 minutes in a hot spider with 2 tablespoons butter.

Place in dripping pan, cap side up, place an oyster on each cap, season with salt, pepper and bits of butter and cook until oysters are plump and serve in Brown Sauce, page 89.

OYSTERS IN BLANKETS

12 firm oysters,	12 slices bacon (thin)
Red pepper,	Chopped parsley.

Drain well and wipe oysters dry and lay each oyster on a thin slice of bacon. Add a little red pepper, sprinkle with chopped parsley, fold bacon around oysters, fasten with a wooden tooth pick. Brown slowly in a frying pan and serve very hot.

OYSTERS, MANHATTAN STYLE

24 oysters,	½ teaspoon paprika,
1½ tablespoons butter,	½ teaspoon salt,
1 tablespoon parsley, finely chopped.	

Allow 3 to 6 oysters for each person. Have oysters freshly opened and on deep part of shell. Cream the butter, add the rest of the ingredients. Divide this mixture and put a bit on each oyster. Then cover each oyster with a slice of bacon. Set shells on baking tin, in a hot oven; cook about 12 minutes, or until bacon is crisp. Serve at once with a quarter of lemon.

FROGS' LEGS, FRIED

Scald the frogs' legs for just a moment; drain and dry; dust with salt and pepper, dip in beaten egg, then in rolled cracker, let stand 10 minutes, and fry quickly in deep hot fat.

CLAMS A LA ST. LOUIS

30 clams,	1 onion,
12 fresh mushrooms,	2 tablespoons butter,
4 eggs (yolks),	1 tablespoon flour,
1 teaspoon white pepper,	parsley and truffles,
½ teaspoon mustard,	½ teaspoon salt.
½ teaspoon red pepper,	

Fry the finely chopped onion in the butter, adding flour, stirring well, then add clams, chopped. Season with salt, red and white pepper and mustard. Cook for 30 minutes, remove from fire, add yolks of eggs, slightly beaten, with 2 tablespoons cold water. Reheat a moment, stir again. Serve.

STEWED LOBSTER

Cut the lobster fine; put in a stewpan, with a little milk or cream. Boil up once; add one tablespoonful of butter, a little pepper, and serve plain or on toasted crackers. Cook lobster just long enough to heat it, as a longer cooking renders it tough.

BROILED LIVE LOBSTER

Split the lobster and glaze with olive oil, broil on hot fire, with the meat side to the fire. When well broiled, season with salt, cayenne and plenty of melted butter, or place in spider, season, place in oven and baste.

LOBSTER RISSOLES

Mince the lobster meat, pound the coral and add grated onion, salt, cayenne. Add grated yolks of three hard cooked eggs. Make a batter of one egg, one tablespoon flour and two tablespoons milk. Beat well together and mix the above with it. Roll into balls and fry in deep hot fat.

LOBSTER A LA BORDELAISE

1½ lbs. lobster, cut in pieces,
1 cup white sauce,
¼ cup red wine,
1 small onion, chopped fine,
1 small piece carrot,
Salt,
Cayenne pepper.

Cook the onion and carrot chopped fine in the cup of milk, used in making the White Sauce, page 87, add the rest of the ingredients, the red wine last. Serve hot.

CHAPTER XII

MEAT

DIVISION AND WAYS OF COOKING A SIDE OF BEEF

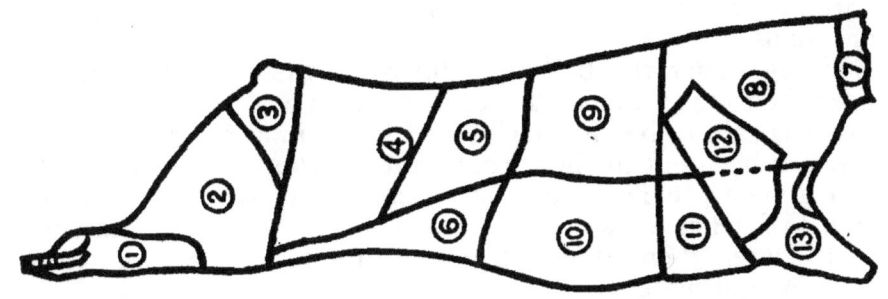

BEEF

Hind Quarter
- 1. Hind Shank
- 2. Round
- 3. Rump
- 4. Loin
- 5. Porterhouse
- 6. Flank

Fore Quarter
- 7. Neck
- 8. Chuck
- 9. Prime Ribs
- 10. Plate
- 11. Brisket
- 12. Shoulder
- 13. Fore Shank

Tough Cuts Used for
- Soup: Hind Shank, Fore Shank, Neck, Tail
- Stews: Brisket, Chuck, Shoulder, Neck, Flank, Plate

Tender Cuts
- Roasts: Prime Ribs, Porterhouse
- Pot Roasts: Chuck Ribs, Rump
- Steaks: Porterhouse, Loin, Round

GENERAL RULES

Meat should be removed from the paper in which it is wrapped and kept in a cool place.

The fibres of the meat contain nearly all the proteids (albumen).

Soaking meat in cold water draws out the blood, dissolves part of the organic salts, the soluble albumen and the extractive or flavoring matters.

Boiling water hardens albumen on the outside, keeping in the juice.

Intense heat, as in boiling, roasting or pan broiling, does the same thing.

Cooking under the boiling point after the first ten minutes, causes the toughest meat to become tender.

Meat is said to be "kosher" when the animal from which it is taken has been cut in the throat (not knocked in the head), the blood allowed to flow out that it may not coagulate. Before using, to further draw out the blood, it is soaked one-half hour in cold water, then allowed to stand one hour in salt, and then rinsed in cold water.

BROILED STEAK

Wipe, trim off extra fat. Grease the broiler with some of the fat. Broil over a clear fire, turning every 10 seconds. Cook 4 or 5 minutes if liked rare; longer if well done.

Place on a hot platter and season, serve with Maitre d'Hotel Sauce, page 91.

Beef steak should be tender and cut 1 inch thick.

Porterhouse steak may be served with Mushroom Sauce, page 89.

TO BROIL STEAK ON GAS STOVE

Wipe steak with a damp cloth. Trim off the surplus fat. When the oven has been heated for from five to seven minutes, lay steak on a rack, greased, as near the flame as possible, the position of the rack depending on the thickness of the steak. Let the steak sear on each side, thereby retaining the juice. Then lower the rack somewhat, and allow the steak to broil to the degree required. Just before taking from the oven, salt and pepper and spread with butter or melted fat.

You can get just as good results in preparing chops, fish, ham and bacon in the broiling oven.

BROILED TENDERLOIN

Three pounds tenderloin cut into three or four pieces. Flatten a little, season with salt, pepper, a little sweet oil and broil. Serve with sauce Bearnaise, page 92, or if preferred, melted butter. Follow directions above for broiling.

PAN-BROILING STEAK

Remove from the steak extra fat. Heat a frying pan very hot, and grease it with the fat scraps. Put in the meat and cook 1 minute; turn it and sear the other side; then cook more slowly until done, 5 minutes, if liked rare. Season and serve on a hot dish.

ROUND STEAK—PAN-BROILED

Have a slice of round steak ¾ of an inch thick. Wipe and trim off extra fat. Heat an iron frying pan blue hot, grease lightly with the fat scraps and put steak into it. Count 60, turn and let brown on under side; when brown on both sides half cover with boiling water, cover frying pan closely with a heavy cover and let simmer for from 20 to 30 minutes. Uncover, season with 2 tablespoons butter or fat, salt and pepper, and serve on a hot platter.

BEEFSTEAK AND ONIONS

Slice onions thin. Place in spider with a little fat and season with salt and pepper, brown slightly, add steaks, cover tightly. When meat is brown on one side turn and brown on the other. When ready to serve spread onions on top. A nice way to warm over steak.

STEAK FOR THE OVEN

Sirloin steak about two inches thick. Put in pan, salt it, add two tablespoons Worcestershire sauce, and three tablespoons catsup and little lumps of butter over the top. Put in hot oven for twenty minutes.

STEAK IN CASSEROLE

Broil a thick steak a few minutes; then put it into a casserole. Add one carrot, one onion, one parsley sprig, one bay leaf, one-half turnip, one teaspoon catsup, six mushrooms, one wineglass Madeira wine. Let cook slowly until vegetables are tender.

HAMBURG STEAK

1 lb. round steak,	1 teaspoon chopped onions,
1 tablespoon drippings,	Salt and pepper.

Take one pound of raw flank or round steak. Salt and prepare as desired. Cut off fat, bone and stringy pieces. Chop it very fine. Chop onions very fine and mix with meat. Season to taste. Make into round cakes a little less than one-half inch thick.

Heat pan blue hot, grease lightly; add cakes, count 60, then turn and cook on the other side until brown. When well browned they are done if liked rare. Cook 10 minutes if liked well done. Serve hot on hot platter, and garnish with celery tops or parsley, and two or three slices of lemon on meat. Pour the fat that the steak was cooked in over the meat.

BEEF LOAF

1 lb. raw beef, chopped,	Salt and pepper,
1 teaspoon chopped onions,	½ cup bread crumbs,
½ cup cold water.	

Mix all the ingredients together, then form into a roll about six inches long; lay strips of bacon over the top or cover with buttered paper; place in a baking pan and bake in a quick oven about 30 minutes; if the bacon is omitted baste every 5 minutes with ¼ of a cup of fat drippings melted in one cup of boiling water; serve plain or with brown mushroom sauce poured around it.

HOW TO ROAST MEATS WITH GAS

Meat is much better when roasted below the flame, than baked in the oven. Lay the roast on the broiling pan, placing it as near the flame as possible, till the meat is thoroughly seared outside. Then remove the roast to a medium distance from the flame, depending, of course, on its size. When the bake oven is not in use, you can finish roasting your meat there more quickly than in the broiling oven, if you are in a hurry. The advantage of the broiling oven for roasting, however, lies in the fact that it is heated by the same flame that heats the bake oven.

ROAST BEEF

Prepare and season meat as desired. Dredge with flour. Place on rack, in dripping pan, with two or three tablespoons of fat, in a hot oven, that the surface may be quickly seared, thus preventing escape of its juice. Reduce the heat and baste every ten minutes with the fat that has fried out. When meat is about half done, turn it over, dredge with flour, finish browning. If necessary, add a small quantity of water. Allow fifteen to twenty minutes for each pound of meat.

Three pounds is the smallest roast practicable.

ROAST BEEF GRAVY

Remove some of the fat from pan, leaving three tablespoons. Place on front of range, add 3 tablespoons of flour and stir until brown. Add gradually 1½ cups boiling water, cook 5 minutes, season and strain.

FILLET OF BEEF

Lard a 4 pound fillet, season with salt and pepper, put it into a roasting pan and roast thirty minutes in hot oven. Garnish with vegetables. Serve with Mushroom Sauce, page 89.

BRAISED BEEF

A piece of rump weighing three pounds, larded. Season with salt, pepper, chopped parsley and a little garlic minced fine if desired. Add one carrot, cut into round pieces; one slice onion, one bay leaf. Cover and brown well on both sides. Baste it often and add a little soup stock. Brown and strain the gravy over the meat. Serve with Horse-radish Sauce, page 95.

BEEF STEW

3½ lbs. beef,
½ onion,
¼ cup turnip, cut up,
¼ cup carrots, cut up,
2 tablespoons beef drippings,
2 potatoes,
Salt and pepper,
¼ cup flour,
Water to cover dumplings.

Wipe the meat, remove all the small pieces of bone, and cut into small pieces. Put the larger bones and tough meat into the kettle and cover with cold water. Dredge the rest of the meat with flour, pepper and salt, and brown it in the melted fat in the frying pan. Brown the onions also. Then put the meat and onions into the kettle and let it simmer 2 or 3 hours or until the meat is tender. Half an hour before serving add the other vegetables; 15 minutes before serving add the Dumplings, page 180. Cook 15 minutes. When done take out the dumpling, remove the pieces of bone and fat. If necessary thicken the gravy with flour and add some pepper and salt. One-half cup strained tomatoes can be added, if liked.

BRISKET OF BEEF WITH CELERY SAUCE

2 lbs. brisket of beef,	1 large celery root,
Salt and pepper to taste,	1 cup White Sauce.

Season the meat, let stand several hours, cover with boiling water and cook until well done, then slice. Scrub the celery root, cook in boiling, salted water until tender, peel and cut in one inch pieces.

Make a White Sauce, page 87, add the celery, boil 5 minutes, add the sliced meat, cook a few minutes longer and serve hot.

BRISKET OF BEEF WITH CARROTS

2 lbs. fat brisket of beef,	2 tablespoons fat,
2 bunches of carrots,	2 tablespoons flour,
Salt and pepper to taste,	1 cup carrot liquid.

Salt and pepper the meat and let stand several hours. Wash, scrape and cut carrot in small cubes. Place in kettle with meat, cover with boiling water and cook several hours or until meat and carrots are tender, and the water is half boiled away. Heat the fat in a spider, let brown slightly, add the flour and gradually 1 cup of carrot and meat liquid. Place in kettle with meat and carrots and boil until carrots become browned.

BRISKET OF BEEF WITH BEANS

2 lbs. brisket of beef,	2 tablespoons fat,
1 pint navy beans,	2 tablespoons flour,
Salt and pepper to taste,	1 cup bean liquid.

Salt and pepper the meat and let stand one hour or longer. Soak beans over night in cold water. Drain, cover with fresh water, heat slowly, keeping water below the boiling point, add meat and cook until meat and beans are tender. Heat the fat in a spider, add flour and gradually a cup of hot bean liquid. Pour this sauce over the meat and beans and cook until the beans are browned.

BRISKET OF BEEF WITH CABBAGE

2 or 3 lbs. brisket of beef,	2 tablespoons fat,
1 head cabbage,	2 tablespoons vinegar,
1 small onion,	2 tablespoons sugar,
Salt and pepper to taste.	

Shred the cabbage and brown with the onion, chopped fine, in a well greased pan. Season with salt and pepper to taste.

Cover the meat with cold water and let boil, then add the browned cabbage, and simmer until both are tender. Add vinegar and sugar to make it sweet and sour, and if too watery thicken with a sprinkling of flour and let cook until smooth. See Sauerkraut with Brisket of Beef, page 158.

POT ROAST

2½ lbs. of beef (chuck or rump),
1 tablespoon drippings,
1 pint boiling water,
1 tablespooon flour,
1 onion, chopped fine,
Salt and pepper.

Season and prepare meat as desired, and sprinkle over with flour. Heat the fat and fry the onion in it until light brown; add the meat, brown on all sides to harden the albumen to keep in the juices. Pour on the boiling water, and then let simmer slowly until tender. Add a little boiling water to prevent burning. Sliced or stewed tomato laid on top of the meat one-half hour before serving makes a fine flavor. Thicken gravy with 1 tablespoon flour. Serve with Franconia Potatoes, page 174.

BEEF EN CASSEROLE

2½ lbs. beef, chuck or round,
2 tablespoons beef drippings,
1 small carrot, cut in dice,
1 tablespoon flour,
1 small onion, sliced,
Salt and pepper to taste,
1 cup strained tomatoes,
1 bay leaf.

Salt and pepper the meat and dust with the flour. Heat the fat in a frying pan and brown the meat in it on all sides. Place meat in casserole, add other ingredients, cover and let simmer at a low temperature until tender, keeping the casserole well covered so as not to allow the steam and juices to escape. Serve hot with mashed or baked potatoes.

MOCK BIRDS OR BEEF ROLLS

1 lb. round steak or
Veal steak, ¼ inch thick,
1 teaspoon salt,
¼ teaspoon prepared mustard,
1 tablespoon chopped fat bacon,
1 teaspoon onion, chopped,
1 tablespoon pickle, chopped,
2 tablespoons fat drippings,
1 pint boiling water,
1 bay leaf,

Cut 1 pound of round steak ¼ of an inch thick in four pieces. Flatten each piece, sprinkle with salt and pepper, and spread with bacon, mustard, onion and a speck of paprika. Roll each slice and fasten with either string or toothpicks. Sprinkle each roll with flour and brown in fat or butter and add enough boiling water to cover. Simmer until nearly tender, then add salt according to taste and continue simmering until tender, and remove strings. Time required, 2½ to 3 hours.

Before serving, remove fat and sprinkle ½ tablespoon of flour over beef rolls. Allow to cook a few minutes; strain gravy, and serve very hot. Veal may be used in the same way. It does not require as long cooking as beef. Add 2 tablespoons Sherry if desired. Poultry Dressing, No. 1, page 134, may be used to spread on the slices, in place of the bacon and mustard dressing.

MOCK ROAST DUCK

2 small slices rump steak, or a flank steak,
1 teaspoon salt,
⅛ teaspoon pepper,
⅛ teaspoon ginger,
2 tablespoons fat drippings,
1 cup bread crumbs,
1 tablespoon grated onion,
1 teaspoon chopped parsley,
1 slice chopped boiled ham,
1 pint boiling water.

Have meat about 1 inch thick and see that it has no seams, openings or muscle tissues running through it. Season with salt, pepper and ginger.

Heat fat in spider, add bread crumbs and the rest of the ingredients and spread evenly over one of the steaks. Cover with the other steak and sew the edges together with coarse thread. Place the "duck" in spider or iron kettle with a little fat. Sprinkle well with flour, let brown, add 1 pint boiling water, cover closely and let simmer several hours or until tender. Remove strings, let brown nicely and serve hot in its own sauce.

BEEF A LA MODE

4 lbs. beef (shoulder),
1 onion, sliced,
8 cloves,
2 bay leaves,
Salt.
1 tablespoon sugar,
Vinegar,
¼ cup celery root (diced),
2 tablespoons fat,
3 gingersnaps.

Place meat, onion, bay leaves, cloves in an earthen dish; cover meat half with vinegar and cover dish closely. Let stand 12 hours. Turn on the other side and let stand 12 hours longer.

Heat the fat in the spider, or casserole, add the celery and meat, brown nicely on all sides; add some of the spiced vinegar or simply boiling water; cover closely, set in the oven and let simmer and bake several hours or until tender. Add salt, cook a little longer.

Take out meat, strain gravy; skin off the fat. Add the gingersnaps, gingerbread for Fillings, page 33, and sugar to taste. If you wish the gravy more tart, add lemon, sliced.

Return meat and gravy to kettle, heat and serve the meat hot, in the gravy.

SWEET AND SOUR BEEF

3 lbs. brisket of beef,
1 onion, sliced,
1 lemon (juice),
Small piece bay leaf,
3 tablespoons sugar,
1 cup boiling water,
Salt and Pepper.

Place the meat in a stew pan. Add the onion sliced thin and also the boiling water. Stew meat until tender—adding salt, pepper and a bit of bay leaf for seasoning. Add lemon juice and sugar until sweet and sour.

PICKLED BEEF

10 lbs. beef,
1 cup brown sugar,
¼ tablespoon soda,
¾ tablespoon saltpetre,
Salt and pepper to taste,
Ginger and a little garlic if desired.

Place in a stone jar, cover with large soup plate and allow to draw juice over night. Then cover with cold water and leave in this brine ten days. Tongue or goose-meat may be pickled in the same manner.

BEEF'S TONGUE, A LA JARDINIERE

Boil fresh beef's tongue one hour; skin and lay in your roaster upon a layer of vegetables cut into dice—carrots, turnips, celery, potatoes, peas, beans, and, if you can get them, button onions and small round tomatoes. Pour about the tongue some of the water in which it was boiled; cover and cook slowly, for two hours if the tongue be large.

Remove the tongue, keep it closely covered and hot while you take out the vegetables with a skimmer. Thicken the gravy with browned flour. Dish the tongue; arrange the vegetables in sorted heaps about it, and pour some of the gravy over all, sending the rest to table in a sauce-boat.

TO BOIL SMOKED TONGUE

1 smoked tongue,
Cold water to cover,
6 bay leaves,
1 teaspoon whole pepper,
1 teaspoon cloves,
1 onion, sliced.

Wash the tongue and if dried out, soak in cold water over night. Place in kettle with seasonings and let simmer slowly until tender from 2 to 4 hours.

Then remove from the brine, pull off the outer skin, cut off root and let cool in the brine. May be sliced cold or serve hot with Sweet and Sour Sauce, No. 2, page 89.

FRIED LIVER

1 lb. calf's liver, sliced,
Salt and pepper,
2 tablespoons flour,
1 large onion, sliced,
2 tablespoons goose or bacon fat.

Salt and pepper the liver to taste, then dredge with the flour. Heat the fat in a spider. Fry the slices until brown on both sides. Push the liver aside, add the onions, and let brown slightly, cover and let cook 10 to 15 minutes and serve with or without the onion—or pour over a Brown Sauce, page 89, using the gravy in the spider with hot water in place of other liquid and serve hot with Dumplings, pages 179 or 180.

BRAISED CALF'S LIVER

2½ lbs. calf liver (whole),
⅛ lb. of bacon for larding,
¼ cup each of carrots, onions and celery, sliced,
2 tablespoons goose fat or butter,
1 bay leaf,
6 peppercorns,
3 cloves,
2 cups soup stock or water,
Salt and pepper.

The liver is skinned, larded; seasoned with salt, pepper and if desired a little mace, fried in the hot fat; flour, vegetables and spices are added and then the 2 cups of soup stock or water. Cover closely and bake two hours, uncovering the last 20 minutes. When ready to serve, strain the liquor, season with lemon juice, and parsley, chopped fine and pour over the liver. Serve on hot platter, or thicken the liquid with 2 tablespoons flour made smooth with a little cold water, cook 5 minutes and pour around liver.

CALF'S HEART

Wash, remove the veins and arteries and stuff with bread crumbs, onion juice, melted fat, salt, pepper and chopped parsley. Sprinkle with salt and pepper, dredge with flour and brown in hot fat. Place in deep pan, half cover with boiling water, cover closely and bake slowly 2 hours, basting every 15 minutes. Add more water if necessary. Strain the liquid, add lemon juice and parsley.

STEWED TRIPE

Wash carefully 1 lb. of tripe that has not been pickled, and cut into inch squares. Put it into a stew pan with ¼ teaspoon each of salt, sugar and prepared mustard, with water enough to cover, about 1 pint. Boil up and skim carefully, then set back to simmer for 3 hours, watching closely lest it stick to the bottom of the pan and skim if necessary. Mix a tablespoon flour with a little cold water, stir it in, simmer ½ hour longer, and serve with more seasoning, if desired.

Or, one hour before serving, cook 6 medium sized onions ½ hour. Drain and slice them, and put them into a dry frying pan with 2 tablespoons of fat. Season with 1 teaspoon each of salt, sugar, dry mustard, a little white pepper and nutmeg; cook until golden brown and pour over the tripe; thicken with the flour.

LYONNAISE TRIPE

Cut honeycomb tripe in pieces 2 by 1½ inches, having 3 cupfuls. Put in a pan and place in oven that water may be drawn out. Cook 1 tablespoon onions, finely chopped, in 2 tablespoons fat, until golden brown, add tripe drained from water and cook 5 minutes. Sprinkle with salt and pepper and finely chopped parsley.

LAMB AND MUTTON

BROILED LAMB CHOPS

Season chops, remove extra fat. Grease wire broiler with some of it—and follow directions for Broiling Beefsteak on page 114.

PAN-BROILED CHOPS

Prepare meat and salt as desired. Have a frying pan very hot, without any fat, put in the chops and cook one minute, turn and sear the other side, to harden the albumen, and keep in the juices; then cook more slowly until done. Stand them up on the fat edge to brown the fat, without overcooking the meat. Serve hot, either plain, with Tomato Sauce, page 93, or with peas.

LAMB CUTLETS

Trim, season with salt and pepper, dredge with flour, dip in egg, then in bread or cracker crumbs and fry in fat from 5 to 8 minutes, until nicely browned on top of stove or place in oven 4 or 5 minutes to finish.

STEWED MUTTON

Prepare and season to taste, remove the pink skin and extra fat, and put into boiling water. Boil fifteen minutes, push kettle back, and allow the meat to cook slowly until tender fifteen minutes for each pound. A carrot diced and cooked with the meat, improves the flavor. Serve meat with a border of Baking Powder Biscuits, page 39, split in halves, and pour all over the top the following gravy: (Any tough meat is nice prepared in this way.)

Gravy for Mutton: To each cup of meat stock, add two tablespoons flour, moistened with a little cold water, and stir until smooth and thick like cream, pour it slowly into the boiling stock, stirring all the time. Boil until thoroughly cooked. Add salt and pepper to taste, and just before serving, add one teaspoon chopped parsley.

CROWN OF LAMB

Select parts from two loins containing ribs, scrape flesh from bone between ribs, as far as lean meat and trim off backbone. Shape each piece in a semicircle, having ribs outside and sew pieces together to form a crown. Trim ends of bones evenly and rather short and wrap each bone in a thin strip of the fat scraps to prevent bone from burning. Roast 1¼ hours or until tender, covering bones with buttered paper. Remove fat from bones before serving and fill center with peas, Puree of Chestnut, page 160, or mashed potatoes.

ROAST LAMB

Salt and pepper and dredge with flour, place on rake of dripping pan with 1 cup water in hot oven. When brown baste every 15 minutes. It will take about 2 hours to roast a medium sized roast.

Leg of lamb may be boned and stuffed with Bread Dressing No. 2, page 134. Serve with Mint Sauce, page 93, or Mint Sherbet, page 292.

PORK

PORK CHOPS

Wipe chops, sprinkle with salt and pepper, place in a hot frying pan and cook slowly until tender and well browned on each side.

BACON

Place thin slices of bacon (from which the rind has been removed) closely together in a fine wire broiler; place broiler over dripping pan and bake in hot oven until bacon is crisp and brown turning once, or

Place bacon in a cold frying pan, cook very slowly. When bacon is light yellow, it is done. If bacon is too salty, it should be freshened by covering with cold water and bringing quickly to the boiling point. Drain water off and broil.

LIVER AND BACON

Cover with boiling water slices of liver cut ½ in. thick, let stand 5 minutes to draw out the blood; drain, and flour, and remove thin outside skin and veins. Sprinkle with salt and pepper, place in frying pan with hot bacon fat and fry until brown on both sides. Remove to hot platter. Serve with bacon.

FRIED HAM AND EGGS

Have ham sliced ¼ inch thick. Place slices in boiling water and cook until tender. Put in frying pan with fat and fry until brown; place on hot platter; slip eggs in frying pan and fry gently by dripping hot ham fat over them until done. Take up carefully and lay them on the slices of ham.

FRIED SAUSAGE

Prick the sausage with a fork, put in a pan, pour on boiling water and cook 1 or 2 minutes. Remove the sausage and dry it. have ready a frypan with enough hot fat to cover the bottom. Put in sausage and turn it while cooking, to brown both sides and keep it from bursting open. It requires about 10 minutes to cook.

BOILED SAUSAGE

Place smoked sausage in kettle, pour boiling water over to cover and cook 5 to 10 minutes. Serve hot with Potato Salad, page 198.

BOILED HAM

1 fat ham, 10 lbs.,
1 medium onion, sliced,
1 dozen cloves,
Carrot, celery, diced,
Cold water,
10 pepper corns,
2 bay leaves,
½ cup brown sugar,
3 cups rye bread crumbs.

Soak ham several hours or over night in cold water to cover. Wash thoroughly, trim off hard skin near end of bone, put in a kettle with the onion, carrot, celery (twice as much as you would for flavoring soups), and spices, cover with cold water, heat to the boiling point, skim, and cook slowly until tender, 5 or more hours, ½ hour to a pound. Remove from stove, let cool in brine, remove from water and take off the skin. Place in dripping pan, sprinkle with the sugar and a thick layer of the bread crumbs. Stick with cloves ½ inch apart. Place in oven to brown about 1 hour.

BAKED HAM

Soak and scrub the ham. When ready to cook make a dough or thick paste of rye flour and water and spread over the ham, encasing it completely. Set on the rack in a baking pan into a hot oven to cook the paste, then lower the temperature and let cook about 5 hours. About 1 hour before done make a hole in the paste and pour in a cup of hot cider, repeat this twice if needed, or in place of cider, use liquid in the pan. When tender remove crust and skin. Brush with beaten yolk of egg, sprinkle with brown sugar and rye bread crumbs and return to the oven to brown. The crust may be reserved intact and used to preserve the left over ham.

VEAL

Veal is meat from the calf, and is less nourishing than beef or mutton. The muscle should be pink or flesh colored, and the fat white and clear. Veal should be thoroughly cooked, to make it digestible. Spring is the season for veal. It is cooked and served the same as the other meats.

ROAST VEAL

Take a thick piece of veal from the upper part of the leg, dredge with salt and pepper, ginger and flour. Put in dripping pan in a very hot oven, with three tablespoons of beef or poultry drippings. When the meat is all browned over baste with the fat and reduce the heat; add a little water and baste often until tender.

ROAST VEAL BREAST, STUFFED

Select a piece of veal breast and have the butcher make an opening on the underside and stuff with Bread Dressing No. 1, page 134, or Potato Stuffing, page 135. Sew up ends, dredge with salt, pepper, ginger and flour; place in hot oven, in roasting pan, with two tablespoons beef or poultry fat, an onion cut fine and a little boiling water. Turn and baste roast often until brown and tender. A little allspice and bay leaf may be added for seasoning. Lamb breast may be prepared the same way.

VEAL FRICASSEE

Cut in pieces, 2 lbs. of veal from loin. Cook slowly in boiling water to cover. Add 1 small onion, 2 stalks celery and 6 slices carrot. Remove the meat. Season with salt and pepper, dredge with flour and brown in butter. Serve with Brown Sauce, page 89.

VEAL CUTLETS

Use slices of veal from the ribs or from the leg cut ½ inch thick; season them, dip in crumbs, then dip in egg, then again in cracker or bread crumbs. Fry slowly until well browned in salt pork, fat or butter, or finish cooking in oven in dripping pan with plenty of fat.

VEAL POT PIE

Ends of the ribs, the neck or the knuckle may be used for a stew. Cut the meat in small pieces and remove the fine bones. Cover the meat with boiling water; skin as it begins to boil; add 1 onion, 1 teaspoon salt, ¼ teaspoon pepper for each lb. of meat. Simmer till thoroughly tender. Cut 2 potatoes in quarters, soak in cold water and parboil 5 minutes before adding the stew. Thicken with 1 tablespoon flour rubbed smooth in cold water, adding more seasoning if liked. Just before serving add ½ cup cream, water or milk with 1 tablespoon butter or fat. Serve with Dumplings, page 180.

HUNGARIAN GOULASH

1 lb. lean beef,
1 lb. lean veal,
1 tablespoon fat,
1 large onion, diced,
1 teaspoon paprika,
1 cup strained tomatoes.

Veal and beef mixed. Cut into one inch squares and brown in hot fat with the onion, salt and paprika. When the meat is brown, add the tomatoes, and one-half hour before serving, add some small potatoes. Let cook slowly closely covered.

VEAL ROLLS OR MOCK BIRDS

Take veal steak, cut thin, three by five inches in size. Spread with any desired Bread Dressing, page 134, or fill with chopped boiled ham, a small lump of butter or other fat, salt, pepper, chopped parsley and a little chopped onion. Make little rolls of them and tie or pin with a tooth pick. Brown them well in hot butter. Add a little soup stock and flour and cook until tender. Add one cup sour cream shortly before serving.

VEAL LOAF

| 4 lb. knuckle of veal, | 4 hard cooked eggs, |
| 1 small onion, | 1 T. chopped parsley, |

Salt and pepper to taste.

Wipe meat, put in kettle with onion and cover with boiling water. Cook gently until meat is tender. Remove from liquid, cool and put meat through chopper. Garnish bottom of mould with slices of hard cooked egg and parsley, put in half of meat, cover with slices of egg and sprinkle with parsley. Cover with remaining meat. Reduce liquor to 1 cup and pour over meat. Press and chill, turn on a dish, garnish with parsley and serve.

SWEETBREADS

BOILED SWEETBREADS

| 1 lb. sweetbreads, | ½ teaspoon salt, |
| 1 pt. boiling water, | 1 tablespoon vinegar or lemon juice. |

Soak the sweetbreads in cold water 20 minutes to extract blood, remove the pipes and membranes. Cook in boiling, salted water about 20 minutes or until tender with the lemon juice or vinegar, plunge into cold water to harden, and cut or break into small pieces and serve in White Sauce, page 87, on toast, in pattie shells, or ramikins. They may be combined with chicken, mushrooms, peas or Boiled Noodles, page 183.

CALF'S BRAINS

Soak calf's brains in cold water to cover for 1 hour. Remove membrane and parboil 20 minutes in boiling salted water with 1 tablespoon of vinegar. Drain, put in cold water as soon as cold, drain and separate in small pieces. Use same as Sweetbreads.

BAKED SWEETBREADS

1 lb. sweetbreads, 2 tablespoons fat or butter,
Salt and pepper.

Pour melted fat or butter over the parboiled sweetbreads and bake in oven until brown, basting frequently. Serve with green peas or Tomato Sauce, page 93.

BROILED SWEETBREAD

1 lb. sweetbreads,   Salt and pepper,
Maitre de Hotel butter.

Parboiled sweetbreads, split crosswise; sprinkle with salt and pepper and broil five minutes. Serve with Maitre de Hotel butter, page 91.

FRIED SWEETBREADS

1 lb. sweetbreads,
¼ cup bread crumbs,
1 egg,
½ teaspoon salt,
⅛ teaspoon pepper,
⅛ teaspoon ginger.

Parboil sweetbreads; roll in fine bread crumbs, then egg and again in crumbs. Fry a nice brown in deep, hot fat or in the frying pan with a little fat.

SWEETBREADS WITH MUSHROOMS

1½ cup boiled sweetbreads (cut in cubes),
1 scant cup stewed mushrooms, (cut in quarters),
1 cup cream,
1 tablespoon butter,
2 eggs, (yolks),
Salt and pepper to taste.

Heat cream in a sauce pan, add sweetbreads and mushrooms, the butter, pepper and salt and beaten yolks. Cook until thick, stirring constantly, and serve at once on buttered toast.

WARMED OVER MEATS

ROAST BEEF WITH GRAVY

Cut cold roast beef in thin slices, place on a warm platter, and pour over some of the gravy reheated to the boiling point. If the meat is allowed to stand in gravy on the range, it becomes hard and tough.

DRIED BEEF IN WHITE OR BROWN SAUCE

Chip dried beef very fine. If it is very dry or salty, pour boiling water over it, let it stand 5 minutes and press it dry in a strainer. Prepare a White Sauce, page 87, or Brown Sauce, page 89, and pour over the beef. Stir well and serve. Omit the salt from the sauce in this recipe.

½ lb. dried beef is sufficient for 1 cup brown or white sauce.

HASH

Remove bones and gristle and chop the meat. To each cup of meat, add 2 cups potatoes (mashed or chopped), ½ teaspoon salt and a speck of pepper. Mix thoroughly. Put 2 tablespoons butter or dripping into a fry pan, add the hash and let it cook slowly, until browned on the bottom.

A little stewed tomato or onion juice may be added.

MINCED MEAT ON TOAST

Chop cold meat (not very fine), season, add gravy or broth, or water to moisten. Heat in a frying pan. Serve hot on toast.

MEAT PIE WITH POTATO CRUST

Chop cold roast beef, removing all fat and gristle; cover the bones and trimmings with cold water; add a few slices of onion and carrot and a stalk of celery, if at hand; let simmer 1 hour; strain off the broth and simmer it in the slices of beef until they are tender. Season with salt and pepper, and pour into a baking-dish; shake in a little flour from the dredger, and, if at hand, add 4 or 5 mushrooms peeled; broken in pieces and sauted 5 minutes in a little butter; cover closely with a round of potato crust in which there is an opening; bake until the crust is done (about 15 minutes).

Potato Crust

2 cups of flour,
½ teaspoon of salt,
2 level teaspoons of baking powder,
½ cup of shortening,
1 cup of cold mashed potato,
Milk or water.

Sift together the flour, salt and baking powder, cut in the shortening, add the cold mashed potato and lastly the milk. Put on a floured board and roll gently.

POTATO AND MEAT PIE

Chop cold meat fine, removing the bones, fat and gristle. Put the meat in a pudding dish. To each cup of meat, pour in one-third cup of gravy or one-fourth cup water. Taste, and stir in, if needed, one-fourth teaspoon salt, one speck pepper, and a few drops of onion juice or a little chopped parsley. Spread mashed potatoes as a crust over the meat, bake on the grate of the oven, until golden brown.

SCALLOPED MEAT

2 cups cold meat (cooked),	3 tablespoons fat,
1½ teaspoons salt,	3 tablespoons flour,
¼ teaspoon pepper,	1½ cups hot meat stock,
¼ teaspoon onion juice, or parsley,	2 cups bread or cracker crumbs.

Make sauce with the fat, flour and seasoning, and add ⅓ cup of the hot stock and the rest gradually. Put one-half of the crumbs in a baking dish. Pour sauce mixed with meat (cut in small pieces) in dish, cover with crumbs and brown in oven twenty minutes.

RISSOULES

2 cups cooked meat,	1 teaspoon onion (chopped),
¼ cup hot water or meat stock,	¼ teaspoon celery salt,
1 teaspoon salt,	⅛ teaspoon pepper,
2 tablespoons cracker crumbs,	1 egg.

Can use any cold cooked meats. Cut the meat off the bones, remove fat, gristle and skin; put the meat in a chopping bowl and chop very fine, season it with salt, pepper, and a little chopped onion or celery salt. Add half as much bread crumbs as you have meat, moisten with a well beaten egg or eggs, or use a little thickened gravy, form into small cakes or a loaf. Put into shallow pans with a little beef drippings over the top; bake in a moderate oven about thirty minutes, a delicate brown. Serve with Tomato Sauce, page 93, or a thickened gravy.

CROQUETTES

Chop cold cooked meat into small pieces, add seasoning to taste—salt, cayenne pepper, chopped parsley; add a Thick White Sauce, page 88, and cool. Shape into cylinders and cover with crumbs, egg, and again with crumbs. Cook in deep, hot fat until brown.

CASSEROLE OF RICE AND MEAT

Steam
- 1 cup rice,
- 3 cups boiling water,
- 1 teaspoon salt,

2 cups cold cooked meat,	1 teaspoon chopped onions,
½ teaspoon salt,	2 tablespoons cracker crumbs,
¼ teaspoon celery salt,	1 egg,
⅛ teaspoon pepper,	1 cup hot water or stock,
⅛ teaspoon poultry seasoning.	

Steam the rice twenty minutes. Chop the meat very fine, add all seasonings, then the beaten egg, cracker crumbs, and stock, or hot water enough to pack it easily. Line the bottom and sides of a greased mould or small bread tin one-half inch thick with the cooked rice, pack in the meat, cover closely with rice, then cover with greased paper and steam forty-five minutes. Loosen around the edge of mould, turn out upon a hot platter and pour Tomato Sauce, page 93, around it. Garnish top with parsley.

CHICKEN A LA WALDORF

Cut white meat of boiled chicken into dice. Two truffles cut into dice, put into a sauce pan with one pint cream, salt, pepper, and cook twelve minutes. Pour gradually on two beaten yolks diluted in two large spoons of Madeira wine. Cook until it thickens, stirring constantly and serve at once.

DRIED BEEF WITH EGGS, No. 1

½ lb. dried beef, shredded,   3 eggs,
1 tablespoon fat or butter.

If beef is too salty, pour over boiling water and press dry. Heat the fat in a spider, add the meat, let soak a few minutes, add eggs slightly beaten; mix or scramble with the meat and let cook until the eggs are set and serve immediately.

DRIED BEEF WITH EGGS, No. 2

1 lb. thinly shaved dried beef,   ½ cup milk or water,
3 eggs,   Butter size of walnut.

Tear beef into small pieces, pour boiling water over it, allowing it to remain a moment, then drain, place in sauce pan with luke warm water to simmer about 10 minutes. If the water has not evaporated pour most of it off, add milk, and butter, and the eggs unbeaten. Stir back and forth as you would scrambled eggs. Season with salt and pepper. Serve hot.

SAUSAGE AND EGGS

1 lb. sausage,   2 tablespoons fat,
3 eggs.

Take cold, boiled sausage, skin and slice in half inch pieces. Place in frying pan with hot fat; brown on both sides a few minutes and just before serving add the eggs, beaten slightly; mix and cook until the eggs are set and serve immediately.

CHAPTER XIII

STUFFINGS FOR MEAT AND POULTRY

BREAD STUFFING FOR MEAT OR POULTRY

No. 1

1 qt. stale bread in pieces,
1 teaspoon salt,
⅛ teaspoon pepper,
2 tablespoons fat drippings, melted.
⅛ teaspoon ginger,
¼ teaspoon poultry seasoning,
1 egg,
½ teaspoon onion, chopped fine,
Heart, liver and gizzard.

Soak bread in cold water and squeeze dry. Season to taste and add the melted fat. Mix thoroughly, add the egg, slightly beaten and the onion if you wish. Add heart, liver and tender parts of gizzard, chopped fine, and partially boiled.

No. 2

Heart, liver and gizzard, chopped fine,
1 qt. stale bread, diced,
1 teaspoon salt,
2 tablespoons fat,
⅛ teaspoon ginger,
⅛ teaspoon pepper,
1 egg,
¼ teaspoon poultry seasoning,
½ small onion, cut fine,
1 teaspoon chopped parsley.

Soak bread in cold water and squeeze dry. Heat fat in a spider, add the soaked bread, stir until fat is absorbed. Season to taste, add the egg, slightly beaten, and the onion cut fine.

No. 3

1 qt. stale bread, diced,
1 egg,
¼ lb. liver sausage,
1 teaspoon salt.

Soak bread in cold water. Drain and press dry. Remove skin of sausage, mix with the rest of the ingredients and use in stuffing duck or goose.

BREAD DRESSING FOR GOOSE OR DUCK

1 qt. stale bread, diced,	2 tablespoons fat,
Liver, gizzard and heart, chopped fine,	1 teaspoon salt,
¼ onion, chopped fine,	⅛ teaspoon pepper,
¼ cup celery root, diced,	⅛ teaspoon ginger,
½ cup strained tomatoes,	⅛ teaspoon nutmeg,
	1 egg.

Soak the bread in water and squeeze dry. Heat the fat in a spider, add the bread crumbs and fry just a little, add the other ingredients and mix well. Nice for goose or duck.

POTATO STUFFING

Add 2 cups of hot, mashed Irish or sweet potatoes to Bread Stuffing, No. 1, page 134. Mix well and stuff in goose, stuffed veal or lamb breast, or in beef casings, cleaned and dressed.

OYSTER DRESSING FOR TURKEY

Follow recipe for Bread Dressing, No. 2, page 134, substituting 12 or more large oysters chopped coarsely and a little of the oyster liquor in place of the liver, heart and gizzard.

CHESTNUT STUFFING FOR TURKEY

1 qt. large chestnuts,	1 pt. bread crumbs or hot mashed sweet potatoes,
¼ cup butter,	
1 teaspoon salt,	½ teaspoon parsley, chopped,
1 egg,	The liver, chopped fine.

Shake chestnuts, in each of which a gash has been cut in the shell, in a tablespoon of melted butter, then set in the oven five or ten minutes. Remove the shells and inner skin together, and cook until tender in boiling, salted water. Drain and pass through a ricer. Add the rest of the ingredients and mix well, and additional seasonings, as onion or lemon juice and chopped parsley, according to taste. If a moist dressing be preferred, add cream or stock.

STUFFING FOR SQUABS

If the squabs or pigeons are stuffed with a bread stuffing, add to it a few spoonfuls of sherry. It gives a dainty taste to the forcemeat, quite unlike anything else.

An orange sauce is delicious with fried or roasted squabs. In the pan in which they were roasted, make a plain gravy with flour and water. Then add a tablespoonful of chopped parsley, two tablespoonfuls of orange juice, the grated rind of an orange, and salt and pepper as necessary. Strain, and serve hot. If the squabs are broiled, make a gravy the same way in a saucepan, and add a tablespoonful of meat essence, and flavor the same way.

PRUNE OR APPLE STUFFING

5 sour apples, or
¼ lb. prunes,
1 cup bread crumbs, or
1 cup cold boiled rice,
½ teaspoon poultry seasoning,
½ teaspoon salt,
1/16 teaspoon pepper.

Follow directions for Stewing Prunes, page 399, remove stones and cut in quarters.

Peel, quarter and core the apples, and stew until half done. Add the rest of the ingredients, mix, stuff and roast.

APPLE STUFFING FOR GOOSE OR DUCK

10 sweet sour apples,
1 cup currants.

Apples are peeled, quartered and mixed with the currants, and used as a stuffing.

STUFFING FOR GAME

1 German roll, soaked in milk,
2 German rolls, grated,
1 onion, chopped fine, with 3 or 4 slices bacon,
1 tablespoon butter, melted,
3 eggs, beaten,
1 piece of lemon and orange rind,
3 apples, cut in cubes,
Salt and pepper to taste,
A little thyme and marjoram.

Mix all together and fill the night before using.

CHAPTER XIV

Poultry

TO DRESS AND CLEAN POULTRY

Singe by holding the chicken over a flame from gas, alcohol or burning paper.

Cut off the head, turn back the skin, and cut the neck off quite close; take out wind-pipe and crop, cutting off close to the body. Cut through the skin around the leg 1 inch below the leg joint; take out the tendons and break the leg at the joint; in old birds each tendon must be removed separately by using a skewer.

Remove pin feathers with the point of a knife. Remove oil bag from the tail.

The internal organs are not always removed before the chicken is sold. If they have not been removed, make an opening under one of the legs, or at the vent, and remove them carefully, leaving a strip of skin above the vent. The intestines, gizzard, heart and liver should all be removed together; care must be taken that the gall bladder, which lies under the liver, be not broken; it must be carefully cut away from the liver. The lungs and the kidneys lying in the hollows of the backbone must be carefully removed. Cut off tip of heart and cut open to extract any blood. Cut gizzard through to the inner coat, half way around, take off the outer coat and throw the inner bag away. The gizzard, heart and liver, constitutes the giblets, and are prepared in numerous ways and may be used in making gravies and dressings for roasted poultry. Wash the giblets, put into cold water, heat quickly and cook until tender. The liver requires only a short time for cooking.

Clean the chicken by wiping thoroughly inside and out with a damp cloth. Stuff and truss for roasting, or cut into pieces for stew or fricassee.

TO CUT A CHICKEN INTO PIECES

Cut off the leg and separate at the joint into drumstick and second joint. Cut off the wing and remove the tip; separate wing at middle joint. Remove leg and wing from other side. Separate the wish-bone, with the meat which is on it, from the breast; cut through the ribs on either side and separate the breast from the back; cut the breast in half lengthwise, and the back through the middle crosswise. The side bones may be cut apart lengthwise with a cleaver. There should be twelve pieces. The neck and the tips of the wings may be cooked with the giblets, and used for making gravy.

ROAST CHICKEN

Dress, clean and season chicken. Place it on its back in a dripping pan, with two tablespoons fat. Dredge with flour and place in hot oven. When the flour is well browned reduce the heat, then baste every ten minutes, adding a little water when necessary to prevent burning. Turn chicken frequently. When the breast meat is tender, it is done. A four-pound chicken requires one and one-half hours.

GRAVY FOR ROAST CHICKEN

4 tablespoons fat,
4 tablespoons flour,
2 cups stock or boiling water,
Salt and pepper to season.

Pour off liquid from pan in which chicken has been roasted. Skim off 4 tablespoons fat; return fat to pan and brown with 4 tablespoons flour; add 2 cups stock in which giblets, neck and tip of wings have been cooked. Cook 5 minutes; season with salt and pepper, add giblets chopped, and serve hot with the chicken.

BROILED SPRING CHICKEN

Take a very young spring chicken of about 1 to 1½ lbs. Clean and split down the back, break the joints and remove the breast bone. Remove internal organs and clean thoroughly. Sprinkle with salt and pepper and rub well with soft butter. Place in broiler and broil 20 minutes over a clear fire, or under the flame in broiling oven of gas stove, being careful to turn broiler that all parts may be equally browned. The flesh side must be exposed to the fire the greater part of the time as the skin side will brown quickly. Remove to hot platter and spread with hot butter.

Or chicken may be placed in dripping pan, skin side down, seasoned with salt and pepper and spread with soft butter and bake 15 minutes in a hot oven and then broiled to finish.

FRIED SPRING CHICKEN

No. 1

1½ lb. spring chicken, Salt and pepper,
¼ cup butter, or poultry fat, Flour and ginger.

Season chicken with salt, pepper and ginger. Dredge with flour and fry them in plenty of hot fat in a frying pan until tender and brown, being careful not to burn.

No. 2

1½ lb. spring chicken, 1 egg,
Salt, pepper and cracker crumbs.

Dress, clean and cut for serving at the joints or in half, through back and breast bone, and season with salt and pepper. Let stand several hours. Dip each piece in cracker crumbs, let stand 10 minutes, then in egg (slightly beaten), again in crumbs and fry in deep, hot fat, or in a frying pan with butter, until a golden brown.

No. 3

1½ lb. chicken, ¼ cup butter or poultry fat,
Salt, pepper, bread crumbs.

Season chicken and rub well with softened fat, cover with fine bread crumbs, place in a pan and bake in hot oven ½ hour.

CHICKEN FRICASSEE

3½ lbs. chicken,
3 qts. boiling water,
½ cup each onion, celery and carrot, diced,
3 tablespoons chicken fat or butter,
4 tablespoons flour,
2 cups chicken stock,
Salt, pepper and ginger.

Dress, clean and cut the chicken at the joints, in pieces ready to serve. Add salt, pepper and ginger and allow to stand several hours or over night. Cover chicken with the boiling water, simmer 3 hours, add vegetables, cook until tender. Melt fat or butter in frying pan, add the flour, and gradually pour on the chicken stock or liquor. Stir to prevent lumps, season to taste and pour over chicken. Let cook a few minutes and serve with dumplings or biscuits. A good way to prepare old chicken or fowl, as they are always made tender by long, slow cooking.

OR, season chicken with salt and pepper, add red pepper (seeds removed), a sliced onion, ½ clove of garlic, minced, if desired, ¼ cup diced celery, 2 bay leaves. Cover with boiling water and let simmer until tender. Drain and serve with Cream Sauce, page 88, and boiled rice.

CHICKEN WITH MADEIRA SAUCE

3½ lbs. chicken,
1 cup water,
1 teaspoon paprika,
¼ lb. mushrooms,
¼ cup butter,
1 small onion,
1 teaspoon salt,
¼ cup Madeira wine.

Cut the chicken at joints, brown in the butter, add water, the onion, salt, pepper, mushrooms, and a few minutes before serving the wine. Cook two and one-half (2½) hours or until tender.

CHICKEN AND RICE

3½ lbs. chicken,
3 qts. boiling water,
1 cup rice,
Salt and pepper.

Select a fat, yellow skinned chicken. Clean and joint. Season with salt and pepper and let stand several hours. Place chicken in kettle, pour boiling water over and cook slowly several hours, until almost tender; add the rice and boil all together ½ hour longer or until tender. Serve hot on large platter.

CHICKEN EN CASSEROLE

3½ lbs. chicken,
Salt, pepper and ginger,
2 tablespoons flour.
¼ cup strained tomatoes,
2 tablespoons fat or butter,

Dress, clean and cut chicken at the joints in pieces for serving. Season with salt, pepper and ginger to taste and let stand over night. Dredge chicken with flour and fry in hot fat until brown. Place in porcelain or iron casserole, covered, and put in oven over a pan of hot water or on top of stove under very small flame. Add if you wish a little sliced onion and a piece of celery and carrot and the strained tomato. Simmer one hour or until tender and slightly browned. Add a little hot water if porcelain casserole is used to avoided cracking. Serve hot.

CHICKEN A LA MARYLAND

Dress, clean and joint chicken for serving. Season with salt, pepper and ginger, dip in flour, egg, and crumbs, place in a well greased dripping pan, and bake 20 minutes in a hot oven, basting after first 5 minutes of cooking with ⅓ cup melted butter. Arrange on platter and pour over two cups White Sauce, page 87.

PRESSED OR JELLIED CHICKEN

Dress, clean and cut up and salt a 4 lb. fowl. Put in a stewpan with 2 slices of onion, a little celery root, a small carrot and cover with boiling water; cook slowly until meat falls from bones. Remove chicken, reduce stock to one cupful. Strain and skim off fat. Butter a mould or take small individual moulds, decorate bottom and sides with slices of hard cooked eggs and parsley and the carrot cut in fancy shapes. Pack in the meat freed from skin and bone and sprinkle with salt and pepper. Pour on stock and set away to cool with weight on top of meat. In summer add 1 teaspoon granulated gelatine softened in 1 tablespoon cold water and stirred in 1 cup of the boiling chicken broth until dissolved. When ready to serve, dip mould in warm water one minute, turn out and decorate with parsley.

CHICKEN CREAM

1 tablespoon granulated gelatine,
¼ cup cold chicken stock,
¾ cup hot chicken stock, highly seasoned,
1 cup heavy cream,
1 cup cold cooked chicken, cut in dice,
Salt and pepper.

Soak the gelatine in cold soup stock, dissolve in hot stock, and strain. When mixture begins to thicken, beat, using an egg beater, until frothy; then add cream beaten until stiff, and chicken dice. Season with salt and pepper. Turn into ¼ lb. baking powder tins, first dipped in cold water, and chill, or in any desired mould or moulds.

ROAST TURKEY

Dress and clean turkey as for Roast Chicken, page 138, and follow any desired recipe for stuffing, page 135. Tie down the legs and rub entire surface with salt and let stand over night. Next morning place in large dripping or roasting pan on rack and spread breast, legs and wings with ⅓ cup butter or fat creamed and mixed with ¼ cup of flour. Dredge bottom of pan with flour. Place in a hot oven, and when flour on the turkey begins to brown, reduce the heat and add 2 cups of boiling water and baste with ¼ cup of fat in ¾ cup of boiling water. When this is used up baste with the fat in the pan. Baste every 15 minutes until tender; do not prick with a fork; press with the fingers; if the breast meat and leg are soft to the touch the turkey is done. If the oven is too hot, cover the pan; turn the turkey often, that it may brown nicely. Remove strings and skewers and serve on hot platter with Cranberry Sauce, or Cranberry Jelly.

BIRDS EN CASSEROLE

6 squabs,
1 sprig parsley,
1 bay leaf,
½ carrot,
1 pt. soup stock, or water,
1 onion,
4 cloves,
12 mushrooms,
½ wineglass sherry,
1 tablespoon catsup.

Place in the casserole, parsley, bay leaf, onion; then the squabs or chicken; add soup, salt, pepper or paprika; cover the dish and put into the oven one and one-half hours. When tender, make a sauce as follows: Heat one tablespoon butter, add one tablespoon flour, when light brown, add the sauce from the birds; when boiling, remove from the fire and add wine, mushrooms and catsup. Pour all over the birds, return to the fire, and when hot, serve in the casserole.

BROILED SQUABS

Remove feathers and pin feathers, insert a small, sharp knife between shoulders and backbone, being careful not to cut the entrails. Remove contents of body without breaking lungs, kidneys, crop and windpipe. Wet cloth in warm water to which a little soda has been added (½ teaspoon to 1 quart) and wipe skin and inside and then wipe dry. Season with salt and pepper. Flatten breast bone and place bird in wire broiler; place over fire skin side down. Turn and broil 12 to 15 minutes until well done. Serve on buttered toast.

GOOSE

ROAST GOOSE OR DUCK

Clean, singe, draw goose or duck and prepare same as for Roast Chicken. Cut open the gizzard, clean well and pull off the inner skin. Lay liver in salt water. Cut off top point of heart, squeeze out the blood and cut open on one side. Season all with salt, pepper, ginger and rub over with a little garlic if desired. Stuff goose with Dressing No. 3, page 134. Place in a roasting pan on a rack, and set in hot oven with 2 tablespoons fat drippings in the pan.

If fowl is young and fat, have no water in the pan; if old, add a little water while basting. Cover pan and brown fowl on one side, turn and brown on the other. Keep turning and basting every 15 minutes until fowl is tender, keeping pan closely covered all the time. Prick the fat skin with a fork from time to time to let the fat try out. Roast from 1 to 4 hours or until the meat on breast and legs are tender to the touch. Skim most of the fat from pan, add 2 tablespoons flour and 1 cup of hot water to form a gravy. Cover and keep hot. Serve hot with Apple Sauce. If goose is fat stuff with Apple Stuffing, page 136.

GOOSE GREBEN—CRACKLINGS

The fat skin of goose cut in square and fried.

Take goose that is too fat to roast; clean thoroughly, and wash in cold water. Remove wings and legs at the joints.

Cut the skin into 2 inch (or larger) scraps, together with the fat that lays loosely over the entrails. Scrape the fat carefully from the intestines and place in salt water over night, separately. Sprinkle salt over all and let lay over night. Next morning wash and drain; place in deep kettle with several cups of cold water, on a hot stove, and let cook gently for one or two hours, keeping it well covered. If you don't want the scraps or "Greben" brittle, take them out of the fat before they are browned. Place strainer over your fat crock, to catch the clear fat and let greben drain. If greben are too greasy place in baking pan in oven a few minutes to try out a little more. Serve at Lunch with Rye Bread.

TO RENDER GOOSE, DUCK OR BEEF FAT

Cut the fat into small pieces. Put in a deep, iron kettle and cover with cold water. Place on the stove uncovered; when the water has nearly all evaporated, set the kettle back and let the fat try out slowly. When the fat is still and scraps are shriveled and crisp at the bottom of the kettle, strain the fat through a cloth into a stone crock, cover and set it away in a cool place. The water may be omitted and the scraps slowly tried out on back of stove or in moderate oven. For beef fat take the fat from the top of the critter. When fat is tried out, pour in crock. To every 4 pounds of beef fat, allow 1 pound butter; let dissolve in the hot fat. The butter may be omitted.

GOOSE MEAT, PRESERVED IN FAT

If too fat to roast, render the fat of goose, remove and cut the skin into small pieces. The scraps, when brown, shriveled and crisp, are then "Greben," and are served hot or cold. When fat is nearly done or clear, add the breast and legs of goose, previously salted, and boil in the fat until tender and browned. Place meat in crock and pour the clear, hot fat over it to cover. Cool. Cover crock with plate and stone and keep in a cool, dry place. Will keep for months. When ready to serve, take out meat, heat, and drain off fat.

BRAISED BREAST AND LEGS OF GOOSE

Sew the skin of the neck of a goose over the breast, having removed original skin to use for Greben, page 144, and for rendered fat. Place breast and legs of goose in spider with hot fat; when nicely browned add a little boiling water, cover closely and let simmer until tender and adding water when evaporated. The skin of neck may be omitted if desired for any other purpose. Serve hot with apple sauce.

GANSEKLEIN OR FRICASSEED GOOSE

Back, wings, neck, gizzard and heart of goose,
Salt, pepper, ginger,
½ onion, sliced,
A clove of garlic, minced,
2 tablespoons fat,
2 tablespoons flour,
1 cup goose broth,
1 teaspoon chopped parsley,
A piece of celery root.

Season meat well with salt, pepper, ginger and if desired rub over with a little garlic. Let stand over night. Then place in a kettle with boiling water to cover, let simmer slowly several hours, add onion and celery, let boil 2 hours and when meat is tender remove from kettle, reheat and pour over the following sauce. Heat the fat, add flour and then 1 cup of the hot goose broth, let boil until smooth, season to taste, add the chopped parsley and serve hot, with Dumpling or Spatzen, page 81.

KISCHTKE, Russian Style

Buy beef casings of butcher. Make a filling of fat, flour (using ⅓ cup fat to 1 cup flour) and chopped onions. Season well with salt and pepper and fill the casing. Slice two large onions in a roasting pan and 1 cup of boiling water. Place stuffed casing in pan and roast slowly until well done and well browned. Baste frequently with liquid in pan.

STUFFED GOOSE, Russian Style

Remove skin from neck of goose, duck or chicken in one piece. Wash and clean well and stuff with same mixture as for Kischtke above. Sew at both ends and roast in hot over until well browned.

STUFFED GOOSE NECKS

Skin of Goose's neck or beef casings,	Bread dressing, 1 onion, sliced,

Scraps of raw goose meat.

Buy beef casings of the butcher or carefully remove skin from neck of goose. Tie up the small end and stuff with Bread Dressing, No. 2, page 134.

Using goose fat and adding scraps of raw goose meat ground fine. Sew up securely with coarse thread; place in an iron kettle, cover with a little water, add onion slices, set in the oven, baste occasionally—and bake until crisp and brown. Serve hot.

FRIED GOOSE LIVER

Goose liver,	Goose fat,
Salt,	¼ teaspoon sugar.

Remove gall bladder carefully from liver, then soak several hours in cold, salted water, drain and place a small amount of sugar where gall has lain. Place in sauce pan with very hot goose grease to cover. When browned on one side turn and brown on the other. Do not let them cook too long, or they will become dry.

SMOKED GOOSE

Breast and legs of goose,	⅜ lb. salt,
Filled neck,	1 teaspoon saltpetre,

1 tablespoon sugar.

Remove wings, legs, skin or fat of a goose. Separate breast and back, remove internal organs and clean thoroughly. Place breast, legs and skin of neck to one side.

Scrape the meat carefully from the bones of neck, back, etc., of the goose, remove all tendons and tissues and chop very fine.

Fill this in the skin of the neck and sew up with coarse thread on both ends. Place the filled neck with the legs and breast in a stone jar. Rub well with garlic. Season well with salt. Rub over with the sugar and saltpetre. Cover with a cloth and put weights on top—to form a brine. Put aside for 7 days, turning occasionally. Take out of the brine and cover with gauze and send to the butcher to smoke. When done, serve cold, sliced thin. Nice for sandwiches.

LIVER GOULASH

3 or 4 livers from chicken or other fowl,
1 onion cut up fine,
1 tablespoon butter,
½ teaspoon salt,
⅛ teaspoon paprika,
½ cup strong soup stock,
1 tablespoon claret or sherry.

Slice the livers and dredge well with flour. Fry the onion in the butter until light brown. Put in the liver and shake the pan over the fire to sear all sides. Add seasoning and stock. Allow it to boil up once. Add wine and serve immediately, on toast if desired.

GAME

BROILED QUAIL

Follow recipe for broiled Squab or Chicken; allow 8 minutes for cooking. Serve on pieces of toast and garnish with parsley and thin lemon slices. Serve with currant jelly.

ROAST QUAIL

Dress, clean and season Quail. Bake same as other poultry, allowing 15 to 20 minutes for cooking. If tough prepare as Birds en Casserole, page 142.

ROAST WILD DUCK

Duck,
Vinegar,
Salt,
Onion.

Clean well and draw. Fill with Stuffing for Game, page 136, or season with salt, pepper and add a tablespoon vinegar and an onion to remove the wild flavor. Let stand over night. If duck is tough steam or cook one hour, then place in roasting pan on rack in hot oven and roast same as chicken. When nearly done add a little sherry wine. Baste with the wine and let covered a little while and then serve with Currant Jelly Sauce, page 91.

VENISON

Prepare Venison roast as Roast Lamb, page 125, allowing less time that it may be cooked rare. Venison cutlets are prepared as other cutlets, rolled in bread crumbs and broiled 5 minutes in broiler or fried in a little hot fat in spider. Serve with Wine or Currant Jelly Sauce, page 91.

Saddle of Venison is prepared same as Hasen Pfeffer, recipe below, or as Beef a la Mode, page 120. The tougher parts may be stewed or braised.

BROILED VENISON STEAK

Follow recipe for Broiled Beef Steak, page 114. Serve with Maitre d'Hotel Sauce, page 91, using currant jelly instead of lemon juice; Venison should be cooked rare always.

RABBITS

Rabbits are cooked same as chicken—stewed, fricasseed or baked.

BELGIAN HARE

Fricassee—Skin and remove the fine skin from the meat. Cut in joints for serving and roll each in flour that has been seasoned with salt and pepper. Cook several slices of fat salt pork in a frying pan, removing them as soon as dry and laying aside.

Brown the joints of hare in the fat tried out from the pork, having it very hot, that they may brown quickly. Cover closely and set back to cook till tender in their own steam.

Pour off all the fat from the pan, and dissolve the glaze in a very little water; this to be served in the platter with the hare. Send to the table with gooseberry jelly or any very tart jelly and Horse Radish Sauce, No. 2, page 95.

HASEN PFEFFER

Lay the rabbit meat in a jar and cover with vinegar and water, equal parts; one sliced onion, salt, pepper, cloves and bay leaves. Allow this to soak two days. Remove the meat and brown it thoroughly in hot butter, turning it often, and gradually add the sauce in which it was pickled, as much as is required. Before serving, stir one cupful thick, sour cream into the sauce. Beef may be prepared the same way.

CHAPTER XV

TIME TABLE FOR COOKING VEGETABLES

Potatoes, white	20 to 30 m.	Parsnips	15 to 45 m.
Potatoes, sweet	15 to 25 m.	Green corn	10 to 20 m.
Asparagus	½ to 1 hr.	Cauliflower	20 to 25 m.
String beans	30 m. to 2 hr.	Tomatoes	15 to 20 m.
Beets	45 m. to 3 hr.	*Barley	1 to 3 hrs.
Cabbage	40 to 60 m.	*Boiled rice	20 m.
Turnips	30 to 40 m.	*Steamed rice	40 to 50 m.
Onions	30 to 60 m.	*Macaroni	30 to 50 m.
*Served same as vegetables.		*Noodles	10 to 20 m.

To avoid odor in cooking onions or cabbage, add ¼ teaspoon soda, leave kettle uncovered and change water twice.

GENERAL RULES FOR VEGETABLES

Wash vegetables thoroughly, pare and scrape, if skins must be removed. Keep in cold water until they are to be cooked, to keep them crisp and to prevent their being discolored. Cook in boiling water; the water must be kept at the boiling point. Use 1 teaspoon salt with 1 quart water; put the salt into the water when the vegetables are partially cooked. The water in which vegetables are cooked is called vegetable stock.

Fresh, green vegetables require less water than others.

Cabbage, cauliflower, onions and turnips should be cooked uncovered in a large amount of water.

All vegetables must be drained as soon as tender. Season with salt and pepper and serve hot with butter or sauce.

The color may be kept in green vegetables, as spinach, by pouring cold water through them after draining.

Cold vegetables may be used for salads, or may be placed in a baking dish with one-half the quantity of sauce (2 cups vegetable and 1 cup sauce) covered with buttered crumbs, and browned in a hot oven.

Parsnips, scrub till white, trim off the fine roots.

Carrots, scrub and scrape off the thin outer surface.

Turnips, scrub and scrape off the thin outer surface.

Turnips, scrub, cut in slices and pare.

Beets, wash carefully, for if the skin be broken, the sugar juices will escape.

Carrots, turnips, parsley and celery root may be kept all winter in a cool place in boxes or barrels buried in dry sand; cabbages in paper bags and hung in a cool place.

Cabbage and cauliflower, trim and soak top down to draw out and insects.

Green corn, husk with clean hands, but do not wash it.

Hard-shell squashes, wash, split, and cook in the shell.

FRESH ASPARAGUS

Cut asparagus on lower parts of stalks as far down as they will snap. Wash, remove scales and retie bunches. Cook in boiling, salted water fifteen minutes, or until tender, leaving tips out of water first ten minutes. To remove the bitter taste of white asparagus, parboil, drain and add fresh boiling water, then boil until tender. Drain, remove string and add tablespoon butter, browned, to each pound bunch of asparagus or serve in White Sauce, page 87, or Cream Sauce, page 88, or pour over them a few bread crumbs browned in hot butter or fat, allowing one tablespoon butter to one pound bunch asparagus. Serve on toast.

CANNED ASPARAGUS

Open one end of the can, as indicated on wrapper, so tips will be at opening. Pour off the liquid and allow cold water to run over gently and to rinse. Drain and pour boiling water over them in the can and set in a hot oven to heat thoroughly. When ready to serve, drain and arrange carefully on hot platter and serve same as fresh asparagus, hot on toast or cold with salad dressing, or with Hollandaise Sauce, page 91, poured over.

ARTICHOKES—French or Globe

French artichokes have a large scaly head, like the cone of a pine tree. The flower buds are used before they open.

The edible portion consists of the thickened portion at the base of the scales and the receptacle to which the leaf like scales are attached. These receptacles are the "bottoms." The parts of the flower in the center of the bud are called the choke and must be removed.

When the artichoke is very young and tender the edible parts may be eaten raw as a salad. When it becomes hard, as it does very quickly, it must be cooked. When boiled it may be eaten as a salad or with a sauce. The scales are pulled, with the fingers from the cooked head, the base of each leaf dipped in the sauce and then eaten.

The "bottoms" which is the most delicate part may be cut up and served as a salad or stewed and served with a sauce.

ARTICHOKES, STEWED

3 large or 6 small artichokes,
4 quarts water,
3 tablespoons salt,
2 tablespoons vinegar,
Any desired sauce.

With a sharp knife cut off the points of the artichoke about 1½ inches. Boil in the water, vinegar and salt. Remove from liquid, cut each artichoke in half and remove the white fuzzy fibre or "choke." Drain well. Serve in a dish with French Salad Dressing or Vinaigrette Sauce, page 188, or Tartare Sauce, page 92. The artichokes may be eaten either hot or cold. If eaten hot, serve with melted butter or Hollandaise Sauce, page 91.

ARTICHOKE SAUTES

Cut six fine, green artichokes into quarters and remove the chokes. Trim the leaves neatly and parboil them five minutes in salted water, drain. Lay them in a casserole, season with salt, pepper and ¼ cup butter; ¼ cup mushrooms, chopped fine, may be added. Cover and cook in a moderate oven twenty-five minutes. Serve with any desired sauce. Hollandaise, page 91, is best.

ARTICHOKES—Jerusalem

Jerusalem Artichokes look like small potatoes, but are not so mealy.

Wash and scrape them and throw them in cold water and a little vinegar and soak two hours. Then cover them with boiling, salted water and boil until tender. Watch closely and drain immediately or they will harden again. Or, boil with the skins on and when tender, peel. Serve with White Sauce, page 87, or use in salad, same as Potato Salad, page 198. Decorate with Endive.

FRIED BANANAS

6 Bananas,	2 tablespoons drippings.

Peel and remove the coarse threads from rather green bananas, cut the pulp in half inch slices on the bias—thus making longer slices than if cut directly across. Roll the slices in flour and cook in hot bacon fat drippings or olive oil, first on one side and then on the other, to a delicate brown color. Serve with bacon, sausage, lamb or pork chops in the place of potato. Or, use to garnish a mound of mashed potatoes against which the sausage are laid.

BAKED BEANS

1 qt. navy beans,	1 tablespoon salt,
½ lb. fat salt pork or	2 tablespoons molasses,
1½ lbs. brisket of beef,	3 tablespoons sugar,
½ tablespoon mustard,	1 cup boiling water.

Wash, pick beans over, cover with cold water and let soak over night. In the morning cover with fresh water, heat slowly and let cook just below the boiling point until the skins burst, which is best determined by taking a few on the tip of the spoon and blowing over them; if done, the skins will burst. When done, drain beans and put in pot with the brisket of beef. If pork is used scald it, cut through rind in ½ in. strips, bury in beans, leaving rind exposed. Mix mustard, salt, sugar, molasses and water, and pour over beans and add enough more water to cover them. Cover pot and bake slowly six or eight hours. Uncover pot the last hour so that pork will brown and crisp.

PEA PUREE

2 cups dried peas,
3 pints cold water,
1/8 lb. of bacon or other fat,
1/2 teaspoon sugar,
1 1/2 teaspoons salt,
1 speck white pepper,
1 large onion.

Pick over and wash the peas.

Soak over night, or for several hours in cold water.

Put them on to boil in three pints of fresh, cold water and let them simmer until dissolved. Keep well scraped from the sides of the kettle.

When soft, rub through a strainer, add a little boiling water or soup stock, add seasoning and beat.

Put bacon cut in small cubes into a frying pan and cook until light yellow, add onion cut in dice and continue cooking with the bacon until brown. Serve puree like mashed potatoes. Pour the bacon and onion over it before serving. Serve hot.

DRIED LIMA BEANS

Soak one pint of dried beans over night. Drain. Cover them with freshly boiling water; cook slowly one hour. Drain off this water. Cover again with boiling water, add 1/16 teaspoon of bicarbonate of soda, a sprig of mint if you have it, and 1 teaspoon salt. Cook until tender. Drain and season with salt, pepper, butter and one cup of hot cream or make a plain white sauce and pour over beans.

Cold lima beans may be mixed with other vegetables and used in salads. They may also be used in making cream soup.

LIMA BEANS

Soak one cup of dried Lima beans over night, drain and cook in boiling salted water until soft. Drain and serve seasoned with salt and pepper, add a little fat or butter and 3/4 cup soup stock, milk or cream.

BEANS AND BARLEY

2 qts. soup stock (poultry bones),
1/2 cup pearl barley,
1/2 cup navy beans,
1 teaspoon salt,
1/8 teaspoon pepper,
1 qt. boiling water.

Soak beans over night in cold water. Drain and cook in the boiling, salted water, let cook 1 hour or more, then add barley and cook until both are tender several hours more. As water evaporates add the soup stock strained, place in the oven, season to taste and bake until soup has just been absorbed by the grains, not browned. Use Turkey, Goose or any other soup stock made from the scraps of left over meat and bones of poultry.

STRING BEANS

Wash beans, remove strings and cut in one inch pieces. Cook in boiling water until tender, from one to three hours. Add salt last half hour of cooking. Drain and add White Sauce, page 87, or salt, pepper and butter, or make the following sauce: Two tablespoons butter, melt, and add two tablespoon flour; then one cup of hot liquid in which the beans were cooked; add salt and pepper to taste.

SWEET AND SOUR STRING BEANS

No. 1

1 qt. wax beans,
1 teaspoon salt,
1 tablespoon flour,
1 qt. boiling water,
2 tablespoons granulated sugar,
2 tablespoons vinegar,
Salt and pepper to taste.

Wash, string and cut beans in pieces. Cook in boiling water until tender, from 1 to 3 hours. Add salt when nearly done. Drain and reserve 1 cup of the bean water for following sauce: Melt butter, add flour, then the bean liquid or soup stock and bean water mixed; then the rest of the ingredients to taste. Add the boiled beans and serve hot.

No. 2

1 qt. wax beans,
1 teaspoon salt,
1 tablespoon flour,
1 qt. boiling water,
½ cup granulated sugar,
¼ cup vinegar,
Salt and pepper to taste.

Wash, string and cut beans in pieces. Cook in boiling water until tender from 1 to 3 hours. Add salt when nearly done. Drain and reserve 1 cup of the bean water for following sauce. Heat and melt the sugar in a dry, hot frying pan, stir in the flour and mix well, then add the hot bean water, vinegar, salt and pepper to taste. When sauce is smooth add the boiled beans, and let all come to a boil. Serve hot.

STRING BEANS AND TOMATOES

1 qt. string beans,
1 cup strained tomatoes,
2 tablespoons butter or fat,
1 teaspoon salt,
1 teaspoon sugar,
¼ teaspoon pepper,
2 tablespoons flour.

Cut off both ends of the beans, string them carefully and break into pieces about 1 inch in length and cook in boiling, salted water, 1 teaspoon salt to quart water. When tender reduce the liquor to about ½ cup.

Heat the butter, add the flour and seasoning and add the strained tomatoes; cook until smooth and pour this sauce over the beans; let cook slowly for about 15 minutes and serve hot.

BOILED BEETS

Wash beets, but do not cut them, as that destroys the sweetness and color. Cook in boiling water until tender. Young beets will cook in 1 hour, old beets from 3 to 4 hours. When cooked put them in a pan of cold water and rub off the skin. Young beets are cut in quarters and served hot with butter, salt, pepper and hot vinegar. Old beets are sliced and pickled in vinegar.

Can young beets for the winter, page 429.

PICKLED BEETS

1 qt. cold, boiled beets,
1 teaspoon salt,
⅛ teaspoon pepper,
1 pint vinegar.

Slice the beets, place in a stone jar and cover with the seasoning and vinegar; add a little caraway seed, if desired, or they may be preserved whole in air-tight cans, see page 429.

BRUSSELS SPROUTS

1 pt. Brussels sprouts,   1 cup White Sauce.

Pick over the little cabbage-like heads, remove wilted leaves, soak in cold water 15 minutes. Cook in boiling, salt water 20 minutes or until easily pierced with a fork. Drain and serve in White Sauce, page 87.

BOILED CAULIFLOWER

1 lb. head cauliflower,
2 qts. boiling water,
2 teaspoons salt.

Select cauliflower with white head and fresh, green leaves. Remove leaves, cut off stalk and soak (head down) in cold water. Separate flowerets and cook twenty minutes or until soft in the boiling salted water. Drain and reheat in one and one-half cups of White Sauce, page 87, or Cream Sauce, page 88. A little grated nutmeg may be added.

With Butter Sauce—Drain and place the hot boiled cauliflower in serving dish and pour over it ¼ cup of hot browned butter. Serve hot.

With Browned Crumbs—Drain and place the hot boiled cauliflower in serving dish and pour over it 2 tablespoons fine bread crumbs, browned in 1 tablespoon of hot butter or fat. Serve hot.

BAKED CAULIFLOWER

Place a whole cooked cauliflower on dish for serving, cover with buttered crumbs and place on oven grate to brown crumbs, remove from oven and pour 1 cup Thin White Sauce, page 87, around cauliflower.

CAULIFLOWER AU GRATIN

Put boiled cauliflower with White or Cream Sauce, pages 87 and 88, in buttered baking dish, cover with buttered crumbs, and if desired ½ cup grated cheese, and bake on center grate until crumbs are brown.

NEW CABBAGE

1 small cabbage,	1 teaspoon salt,
1 qt. boiling water,	1 cup White Sauce.

Cut a young cabbage in eight pieces, trimming off the limp outside leaves. Cook in the boiling, salted water ½ hour or until tender, leaving the kettle uncovered, that there will be very little of the cabbage odor in the house. Drain off the water and serve with White Sauce, page 87.

BOILED CABBAGE

1 qt. cabbage, chopped,	1 qt. boiling water,
1 onion, cut fine,	1 teaspoon salt,
2 tablespoons fat or butter,	⅛ teaspoon pepper,
2 tablespoon flour.	

Heat the fat, add the onion, brown nicely, then add the cabbage; cover and let steam for 10 minutes, then pour over the boiling water; salt and pepper, and let boil until tender from ½ to 2 hours. Sprinkle flour over to thicken, let boil a little longer and serve hot.

CABBAGE AU GRATIN

½ large cooked cabbage,
1 pt. White Sauce,
¾ cup grated cheese,
Salt and paprika,
½ cup cracker crumbs,
3 tablespoons melted butter.

Put a layer of the cabbage, coarse-chopped, into a buttered baking dish, sprinkle with grated cheese, paprika, and salt as needed, and cover with a layer of White Sauce, page 87. Repeat the layers until all the ingredients have been used, having the last layer of sauce. Cover with the cracker crumbs mixed with the butter. Let stay in the oven only long enough to make very hot and brown the crumbs.

SWEET AND SOUR CABBAGE

1 qt. cabbage,
  (red or white),
2 sour apples,
2 tablespoons fat,
4 tablespoons brown sugar,
2 tablespoons vinegar,
Salt and pepper,
2 tablespoons flour.

Shred the cabbage fine, salt and pepper to taste, add the apples cut in slices.

Heat the fat in a spider, add the cabbage and apples. Pour boiling water over them and let cook until tender; sprinkle over the flour, add sugar and vinegar. Cook a little longer and then serve hot with Potato Dumplings, page 181. If red cabbage is used pour boiling water over it 2 or 3 times to take out some of the color.

CABBAGE WITH SAUSAGE

6 sausages,
1 qt. minced cabbage,
½ teaspoon pepper,
Salt if necessary.

Fry the sausages crisp and brown. Take from the frying pan and pour off all but 3 tablespoons of the fat. Put the minced cabbage in the frying pan and cook 6 minutes. Arrange in a hot dish and garnish with the sausages. Serve mashed potatoes with this dish.

CABBAGE ROLLS

1 lb. lean raw beef, chopped,
Salt and pepper to taste,
1 small onion (juice),
½ cup cooked rice,
2 large tomatoes,
1 onion, chopped,
2 tablespoons vinegar,
2 tablespoons sugar,
8 large leaves of cabbage.

Season the meat highly with salt and pepper, add onion juice and rice.

Soak the cabbage leaves in hot water a few minutes to make them less brittle. Roll a portion of the meat mixture in each leaf. Place them in a kettle with the rest of the ingredients, add a little water and let simmer and stew until cabbage is tender and well browned.

SAUERKRAUT WITH BRISKET OF BEEF

1 qt. sauerkraut,
3 lbs. brisket of beef,
2 tablespoons flour,
2 tablespoons vinegar,
2 tablespoons brown sugar,
1 raw potato, grated,
1 onion,
1 teaspoon caraway seed.

Place one-half of the kraut in a large sauce pan, sprinkle with flour, add meat and a whole onion and cover with the rest of the kraut and sprinkle over a little more flour and add the potato. Cover with boiling water and cook until tender, about 2 hours. Remove onion, sprinkle a little flour over cabbage to thicken, add sugar and vinegar to make it sweet and sour. If boiled without meat add 2 tablespoons fat and a little soup stock.

CARROTS

1 qt. carrots, diced,
1 qt. boiling water,
1 teaspoon salt,
2 tablespoons butter or fat,
2 tablespoons flour,
Pepper,
Sugar to taste,
1 cup carrot liquid or soup chock.

Wash, scrape and cut the carrots in small cubes. Cook in boiling, salted water until tender and serve in a sauce made by heating the fat, adding the flour and gradually the hot carrot liquid. Season to taste and serve hot.

CARROTS—Sweet and Sour

Cook 1 quart of carrots, diced, in one quart of boiling water, with 1 teaspoon salt, drain and reserve the liquid. Make a Sweet and Sour Sauce, No. 1 or No. 2, page 88, using one cup of the carrot liquid.

COMPOTE OF CARROTS—Russian Style

1 cup sugar,	2 cups carrots, diced,
1 cup water,	2 tablespoons butter or fat.

Make a syrup of the sugar and water by boiling 10 minutes. To this syrup add the diced carrots which have previously been browned in hot fat or butter. Cook all together until carrots are tender.

LEMON CARROTS

Old carrots may be used for this dish, and are really better than the new ones. Pare and cut into dice, and simmer in salted water until tender, but not pulpy. Drain, return to the fire, and for one pint of carrots add a teaspoon of minced parsley, a grating of loaf sugar, ½ teaspoon paprika, one tablespoon of butter and the juice of half a lemon. Heat through, shaking the dish now and then, so that each piece of the vegetable will be well coated with the mixture or dressing.

FLEMISH CARROTS

1 qt. carrots,	1 teaspoon sugar,
1 qt. boiling water,	¼ teaspoon salt,
1 teaspoon salt,	⅛ teaspoon pepper (white),
2 tablespoons butter or fat,	1½ cup soup stock,
1 button onion,	1 teaspoon parsley (chopped).

Scrape, slice and cook the carrots in the boiling, salt water until tender; drain. Heat butter, add onion, brown lightly, add carrots and seasoning and shake well over the fire for 10 minutes, add the soup stock, cover and simmer for half hour, then add the parsley and serve hot.

CARROTS AND PEAS

1 pt. carrots,	1 pt. peas,
½ cup soup stock,	½ cup carrot water,
2 tablespoons butter or fat,	2 tablespoons flour.

Wash, scrape and cut carrots in small cubes, cook until tender, drain and reserve ½ cup carrot water. Mix carrots well with cooked green peas. Sprinkle with flour, salt, sugar and pepper to taste, add fat or butter, soup stock and carrot water, boil a little longer and serve. Can also be served with Sweet and Sour Sauce, Nos. 1 or 2, page 88.

CELERY STEWED

1 bunch stalk celery,
1 qt. boiling water,
1 cup White Sauce,
1 teaspoon salt.

Wash, scrape and cut the outer stalks of the celery into pieces 1½ inches long. Cook in boiling, salted water about ½ hour or until tender. Drain and serve with White Sauce, page 87.

Reserve the center stalks for table use.

CELERIAC OR GERMAN CELERY

In this vegetable the root and not the stalks are eaten. Scrub the turnip like roots well and cook in salted, boiling water until tender. Drain and rinse in cold water. Peel and slice. Serve with a White or Brown Sauce, pages 87–89, or as a salad, page 199.

TO SHELL AND BLANCH CHESTNUTS

Take French or Italian chestnuts. Make ½ inch slit on flat sides of chestnuts with sharp knife. To 1 pint chestnuts add 1 teaspoon butter, heat over fire, shaking all the time, until butter is melted. Let stand in oven 5 minutes. Then remove outside shell and inner at the same time.

CHESTNUT VEGETABLE

Remove shells from chestnuts and blanch as in the above recipe. Then boil very slowly in water until about half done, drain off any remaining water and add one cup of soup stock and one cup of brown sugar. Let this simmer until it is soft, adding also butter size of walnut. Serve in ramikins. Or cook in boiling, salted water; drain, mash, moisten with scalded milk. Season with salt and pepper and beat until light or riced. Pile lightly in center of dish and surround with meat.

CUCUMBERS

Cucumbers are usually served pickled or raw in slices, but when old may be pared, cut in pieces, cooked in boiling, salted water, drained, washed and seasoned with butter, salt and pepper or they may be cut lengthwise, in ⅓ inch slices, dipped in crumbs, salt and pepper, egg and crumbs again and fried in deep, hot fat.

DILL PICKLE VEGETABLE

6 large Dill pickles,   1 quart boiling water,
    Sweet and Sour Sauce.

Soak the pickles over night in cold water; drain, cut in ⅛ inch slices and cook in boiling water until tender. Drain and pour over Sweet and Sour Sauce, No. 3, page 89.

BOILED GREEN CORN

No. 1. Remove husks and silky threads, cover with boiling water and cook from 8 to 20 minutes according to number of cobs in the kettle. Remove from water and serve hot with fresh butter, salt and pepper.

No. 2. Pare off the outer leaves, but leave on enough to cover the corn. Fold remaining leaves down, remove silky threads, then turn back into place and tie at the tips to cover the corn. Cook in boiling water 10 to 20 minutes. Take out of water, remove the leaves and serve hot with fresh butter, salt and pepper.

No. 3. Grate the corn from the cobs, cook 5 to 10 minutes in their own juice and with butter, salt and pepper—add a little milk if necessary.

No. 4. Cut the cooked corn from the cobs and serve heated with butter, salt and pepper.

CANNED CORN

1 can corn,   ½ cup milk,
1 tablespoon flour,   Salt and pepper,
    1 tablespoon butter.

Sprinkle the flour over the corn and the butter and milk; stir and cook about 5 minutes, until thoroughly hot. Season to taste and serve hot.

ESCALLOPED CORN

6 ears of cooked corn or   1 teaspoon salt,
1 can of corn,   ⅛ teaspoon pepper,
½ cup corn liquid,   2 tablespoons flour,
3 tablespoons cream,   1 cup bread crumbs,
1 teaspoon sugar,   1 tablespoon butter.

Cut fresh boiled corn, too old to serve on cobs, from the cob; or use the pulp of 1 can of corn.

Mix corn with the salt, pepper, flour and sugar and add the liquids. Melt the butter, mix with the bread crumbs and cover bottom of a pudding dish with ½ of the crumbs, add the corn mixture and cover with the rest of the crumbs. Bake in a moderate oven about 20 minutes, and serve hot in pudding dish.

CORN—Southern Style

1 can corn, chopped,
2 eggs,
1 teaspoon salt,
⅛ teaspoon pepper,
1½ teaspoon melted butter,
1 pt. hot milk.

Beat eggs slightly, add rest of the ingredients and turn into a well buttered pudding dish. Bake until firm in a slow oven and serve hot.

CORN FRITTERS

No. 1

1 can corn, or
6 raw ears of corn,
2 eggs,
½ teaspoon salt,
3 tablespoon milk,
2 tablespoons flour.

Grate the corn off the cobs, or strain the canned corn. To the pulp add the yolks beaten, the rest of the ingredients and the beaten whites last.

Drop by teaspoonfuls in deep, hot fat and fry until nicely brown on a hot greased griddle or frying pan. Serve with hot syrup.

No. 2

1 pt. grated corn pulp,
Cracker crumbs,
½ teaspoon salt,
½ teaspoon baking powder,
A little pepper.

Add enough cracker crumbs, sifted, to the corn pulp to hold the mixture together. Mix and drop by spoonfuls in deep, hot fat and fry until brown. Serve hot.

SUCCOTASH

1 cup boiled corn,
1 cup boiled Lima beans,
Butter,
Salt,
Pepper,
¼ teaspoon milk.

Cut one cup of corn from cob, add the cooked beans and heat all together a few minutes and then serve.

DANDELIONS

Select dandelions early in the spring before they begin to blossom. Wash thoroughly, remove roots, drain and cook one hour or until tender in boiling, salted water. Allow two quarts of water to 1 peck of dandelions. Season with butter, salt and pepper. Serve with vinegar, or serve it raw as a salad with salt, pepper and vinegar.

ENDIVE OR CHICORY

Endive or Chicory is a vegetable that is used raw as lettuce, as a salad, or for decorations. The leaves are light colored and feathery.

BAKED EGG PLANT

Mashed egg plant,
2 tablespoons butter or fat,
¼ onion, cut fine,
2 tablespoons bread crumbs,
1 yolk of egg.

Parboil egg plant until tender, but not soft in boiling, salted water. Cut in half crosswise with a sharp knife. Scrape out the inside and do not break the skin.

Heat 1 tablespoon butter or fat, add the onion, brown, then scraped egg plant, bread crumbs, salt and pepper to taste and the egg yolk. Mix well together, refill shells, place in dripping pan, in oven—baste with butter or sprinkle cracker crumbs on top with bits of butter—baste often and brown nicely.

KOHLRABI

1 qt. Kohlrabi,
1 teaspoon salt,
2 tablespoons flour,
1 qt. boiling water,
2 tablespoons fat or butter,
Salt and pepper.

Wash, peel and cut the Kolhrabi root in dice and cook in salt water until tender. Cook the greens or tops in another pan of boiling water until tender, drain and chop with sharp edge of small empty baking powder can until very fine in a wooden bowl. Heat the butter or fat, add the flour, then the chopped greens, and 1 cup of liquor the Kohlrabi root cooked in or 1 cup soup stock. Add the Kohlrabi, cook altogether, and serve.

Turnips and Rutabagas may be cooked the same way, omitting the greens.

MUSHROOM SAUTES

1 lb. mushrooms,
2 tablespoons butter,
Juice of ½ lemon,
¼ teaspoon salt,
⅛ teaspoon pepper,
1 teaspoon parsley, chopped,
Toast.

Wash, remove stems, peel caps and break in pieces, the mushrooms. Place in spider with butter and seasoning. Cover and cook 10 minutes, tossing them. Add lemon juice and parsley and serve on hot slices of toast.

BROILED MUSHROOMS

12 large mushrooms,
¼ teaspoon salt,
⅛ teaspoon pepper,
2 tablespoons butter,
Toast.

Wash fine, large mushrooms, remove stems and place caps in a buttered broiler and broil 5 minutes, cap side down, during first half of broiling. Put a small piece of butter in each cap, sprinkle with salt and pepper and serve as soon as butter is melted. Keep mushrooms cap side up, to keep in the juices and serve on rounds of buttered dry toast.

BAKED MUSHROOMS

12 large mushrooms,
Salt and pepper,
2 tablespoons butter,
⅔ cup cream,
Toast.

Wash the mushrooms, remove stems, peel caps and place in buttered dripping pan, cap side up. Sprinkle with salt and pepper, dot over with the butter and add the cream. Bake 10 minutes in hot oven. Arrange on dry toast and pour over the remaining cream in pan and serve hot.

CANNED MUSHROOMS—(In Ramikins)

1 cup mushrooms,
2 tablespoons butter,
2 tablespoons flour,
1 cup milk or mushroom liquor,
10 drops onion juice,
¼ teaspoon salt,
⅛ teaspoon pepper,
1 teaspoon chopped parsley,
1 cup bread crumbs,
1 tablespoon butter.

Heat the butter, add the flour, then gradually the mushroom liquor or milk or equal parts of each; add mushrooms cut in pieces, boil up, add the parsley and serve; or place in individual or large pudding dish, with buttered crumbs on top, place in oven a few minutes to brown, placing ramikins in a pan of hot water so they will not crack. Serve hot with a sprig of parsley in center of each ramikin.

MACEDOINE

1 good sized carrot,
2 white turnips,
1 can or 1 pint of peas,
1 can or 1 pint of string beans.

Scrape the carrot, cut into cubes; pare the turnips and cut into cubes; put these in unsalted water and boil gently for three-quarters of an hour, or until tender, and drain. Drain, wash and cook the peas and beans and add them to the vegetables; reheat over water, and use with Brown Sauce, page 89, as a garnish to braised or stewed meats.

BOILED ONIONS

Peel onion under water. Put in sauce pan with boiling, salted water, 1 teaspoon salt to 1 qt. water. Boil 5 minutes, drain and again cover with boiling, salted water. Cook one hour or until soft. Drain, add a little milk, butter, salt and pepper to taste or cover with White Sauce, page 87.

ONIONS AU GRATIN

Peel the onions and remove the thick layer next the skin. Cook in salted water three minutes, drain them, cover with boiling water and cook until nearly done. Drain well, and place in a baking dish; make 1 cup White Sauce, page 87, and pour over the onions, add a layer of buttered cracker crumbs, and bake 10 minutes to heat through and to brown the crumbs. Serve hot.

BAKED ONIONS

Select even sized onions, wipe, but do not peel. Place in baking dish, roots down, and bake one hour, or until tender. Remove from fire, remove roots, peel carefully, return to dish, add pepper, salt, and a little melted butter or other fat; let stand five minutes in oven, and then serve hot.

OYSTER PLANT—Salsify

Wash, scrape and put at once in cold water with a little vinegar to keep from discoloring. Cut ½ inch slices and cook in boiling, salted water until soft. Drain and serve in White Sauce, page 87. Or boil in salted, boiling water until tender and cut in four pieces lengthwise, dredge with flour and sprinkle with a little salt and fry in hot butter or fat until nicely browned.

PARSNIPS

Wash, scrape, cut in pieces and cook young parsnips in salted, boiling water until tender. Drain and serve with hot butter, Drawn Butter, page 91, or White Sauce, page 87.

Or wash and cook in boiling, salted water until tender about 45 minutes. Drain and plunge in cold water and slip off skins. Cut in slices lengthwise and fry in butter or mash and season with butter, salt and pepper. Shape into flat, round balls, roll in flour, or dip in molasses and fry until crisp and nicely browned in butter or other fat.

CANNED PEAS

1 can peas,
Salt and pepper,
1 cup White Sauce,
Few grains sugar.

Drain liquid from can of peas into colander and rinse with cold water. Add milk or cream, a little butter, salt, sugar and pepper or White Sauce, page 87, or add a little meat gravy, or soup stock; serve hot.

GREEN PEAS

½ pk. green peas in pods,
1 qt. boiling water,
1 teaspoon salt,
A little pepper,
A few grains sugar,
2 tablespoons butter or fat,
2 tablespoons flour,
½ cup soup stock.

Remove peas from pods and let stand one half hour in cold water. Skim off undeveloped peas from top of water and then drain. Cook until soft in a small quantity of boiling water, add salt when nearly tender; let the water boil away, and without draining, add butter or any desired fat, sprinkle with the flour to thicken, add pepper and sugar if you wish, a little meat gravy or ½ cup soup stock or milk, boil a little longer and serve.

GREEN PEAS AND RICE

½ pk. fresh green peas or   ½ cup granulated sugar,
1 can peas,   ¼ cup butter or other fat,
½ teaspoon salt,   1 cup rice,
              1 qt. boiling water.

Shell the peas, and wash them well; if canned peas are used, pour off the liquid and rinse with cold water.

Heat butter in the spider, add the rice and let simmer, stirring constantly until rice is a golden brown, add the boiling water, then the drained peas and other ingredients. Place in pudding dish, set in the oven and bake until rice is tender and every kernel stands out separately. Serve hot.

GREEN PEAS AND EGG BARLEY

Egg Barley or   1 cup rice,
   Pfarvel,   ¼ cup butter or other fat,
½ pk. green peas or 1 can, 1 qt. boiling water,
½ cup sugar,   ½ teaspoon salt.

Make Pfarvel, page 86. Heat the butter, add the pfarvel and when a golden brown, add the boiling water and other ingredients and the peas strained. Set in moderate oven and bake ½ hour, or until every kernel stands out separately. Serve hot.

STUFFED PEPPERS

No. 1

1 onion,   1 egg,
8 green peppers,   1 teaspoon salt,
1 lb. lean raw beef,   ⅛ teaspoon pepper,
            ½ teaspoon onion juice.

Cut off stem end and remove seeds from green peppers. Mix meat with egg and seasonings. Fill peppers with meat mixture. Slice onions in a stew pan—cover slightly with water and stew peppers until well done.

No. 2

6 green peppers,   1 cup strained tomatoes,
2 cups boiled chicken, veal or   1 tablespoon grated onion,
   lamb, chopped,   2½ tablespoons melted
2 cups boiled rice,   butter,
                                    ¾ cup meat stock.
        2 tablespoons fresh bread crumbs.

Remove stem end and seeds of peppers, boil 8 to 10 minutes in boiling salt water; drain and fill with the next five ingredients well mixed. Place in baking dish, add crumbs, bake 25 minutes and baste with the meat stock.

STUFFED PEPPERS

No. 3

10 peppers,	3 cups stale bread crumbs,
40 oysters,	½ onion,

½ teaspoon salt.

Cut out the round piece of pepper with the stem on it—remove seeds, chop 1 pepper and ½ onion and saute in butter. Parboil oysters, drain, soak the crumbs in oyster liquor, season, add sauted onion and pepper and salt and fill peppers with this mixture. Sprinkle over with cracker crumbs, butter (melted). Bake until brown. Serve with Tomato Sauce, page 93.

No. 4

Green peppers,	Eggs,
1 onion (chopped),	½ cup bread crumbs,
½ cup butter,	Salt and Worcestershire sauce to taste.

Remove stem end and seeds of peppers. Boil 8 to 10 minutes in boiling salted water. Fry the onion in the butter, season with the salt and Worcestershire sauce. Put a tablespoonful of this mixture in each pepper, set in a buttered muffin tin. Break an egg in each mould over the mixture, cover with the buttered crumbs and bake 15 minutes. Serve on toast with Hollandaise Sauce, page 91.

RADISHES

There are many varieties of radishes, round and long, black, white and red. The small red radish may be obtained all year. They are served uncooked, merely for a relish. The large varieties are peeled, sliced and salted for the table.

To serve the small ones for table, remove tip end of root, remove the leaves and have only a small piece of stem on radish. They may be made to look like a tulip by cutting in to six equal parts from the root end, down ¾ of the length of the radish.

SPINACH

½ pk. spinach,
2 tablespoons butter or fat,
1 teaspoon chopped onion,
2 tablespoons bread crumbs or flour,
½ teaspoon salt,
⅛ teaspoon pepper,
$\frac{1}{16}$ teaspoon nutmeg,
1 cup soup stock or meat gravy and hot water.

Pick off the roots and the decayed leaves, wash in three or four waters. Put the spinach in a large kettle without water. Let cook slowly, until some of the juice is drawn out, then boil about 15 minutes or until tender.

Drain and chop very fine with empty baking powder can. If spinach is old, cook in 1 quart of boiling, salted water.

Heat the butter in a spider, add the onions and brown, then the bread crumbs or flour and the seasoning, and gradually the soup stock or gravy and hot water, then add the spinach. Heat through and if desired stir in 2 raw eggs and garnish with poached or hard cooked eggs, sliced.

SUMMER SQUASH

Squash, diced,
Boiling water,
2 tablespoons cream, or
2 tablespoons butter,
1 teaspoon salt,
speck pepper.

Summer squash are good only when young, fresh and tender. Wash, and cut into quarters or small pieces. Cook in boiling water 20 minutes or until tender. Drain thoroughly, mash and add the rest of the ingredients.

WINTER SQUASH, STEAMED

Squash, mashed,
½ cup milk,
1 tablespoon butter,
Salt and pepper.

Wash, cut in quarters or into 2 inch squares; peel and remove stringy portions and seeds and then steam until tender or cook in boiling, salted water 20 minutes or until tender. Drain and mash, adding the milk, butter and seasoning. The milk may be omitted and any beef or poultry fat may be used in place of the butter.

BAKED SQUASH

No. 1. Cut squash in 2 inch squares, remove seeds and strings, place in dripping pan with ½ teaspoon molasses and ½ teaspoon butter for each square. Bake 50 minutes or until soft. Serve in the shell.

No. 2. Cut squash in two crosswise, remove seed and strings; place in dripping pan, shell side up, and bake 2 hours or until soft, in a slow oven. Remove from shell, mash and season with butter, salt and pepper.

STUFFED SQUASH

1 qt. mashed squash,	1 egg,
2 tablespoons butter or fat,	½ tablespoon salt,
½ onion, chopped,	⅛ teaspoon pepper,
½ cup soaked bread,	½ cup cracker crumbs.

Bake squash following recipe No. 2. Scrape out the shells, being careful not to break the shells. Heat the butter or fat in a spider, add the onion, chopped fine, let brown lightly, add the soaked bread, mashed, and the squash. Fry all together 15 minutes, stirring occasionally. Remove from fire, add the salt, pepper and stir in the egg well. Place mixture back into shells; sprinkle cracker crumbs and bits of butter on top and return to oven to brown nicely.

TOMATOES

Take as many ripe, smooth tomatoes as you desire. Wash and wipe and serve with skin or plunge them into boiling water one minute; drain and remove skins and place on ice until wanted and serve whole with sugar or with sugar, salt and pepper to taste, or serve as salad, page 195.

STEWED TOMATOES

Wipe and cover tomatoes with boiling water. Let stand one minute, then skin. Cut in pieces, put in stewpan, and cook slowly twenty minutes, stirring occasionally. Season with butter, salt, pepper and a little sugar, if desired; add some bread crumbs.

STUFFED TOMATOES

No. 1

6 fine firm tomatoes,	1 tablespoonful chopped parsley,
1 cup grated rye bread,	
2 tablespoons butter,	¼ teaspoon grated onion,
2 yolks of eggs,	salt and pepper to taste.

Wash and dry tomatoes. Cut off tops. Remove pulp with small spoon, and rub through a fine sieve. Put butter in pan, add bread crumbs and onion juice, cook a few minutes, then add onion juice and the seasonings. Stir in the yolks of eggs, and fill the tomatoes with the mixture. Sprinkle tops with bread or cracker crumbs, buttered, and place in oven on buttered tin and bake ½ hour. Serve hot.

STUFFED TOMATOES

No. 2

8 fine, firm tomatoes,	1 medium sized onion,
½ oz. butter,	6 fresh mushrooms,
½ lb. chicken livers,	½ cup bread crumbs,
Salt and pepper to season,	Parsley.

Wash and dry tomatoes. Cut off top without detaching if possible so it will serve as a cover. Scoop out inside of each and place in cool place until later having seasoned inside with a little salt and pepper. Chop onion fine; place in sauce pan with butter and cook for 3 minutes to brown, being careful not to burn. Add mushrooms and the chicken livers chopped. Season with a little salt and pepper. Cook for 3 minutes stirring occasionally. Now add inside of tomatoes, bread crumbs and chopped parsley. Cook 2 minutes longer, and place in bowl to cool. Stuff emptied tomatoes with mixture, close down covers, and cook for 18 minutes. Serve hot. Sausage meat or chicken chopped may be used in place of the livers.

TURNIPS

Turnips are best in fall and winter. The rutabagas, a large yellow variety, the large white and the small flat purple top are all used. Wash and peel the turnips and cut into ¼ inch cubes. Cook 3 cups turnip cubes in boiling, salted water 20 minutes or until soft. Drain, mash, season with fat or butter, salt, a little sugar and pepper, or mix with an equal quantity of hot, mashed potatoes.

Or, after the turnips are drained, add 1 cup of White Sauce, page 87, or Brown Sauce, page 89.

CHAPTER XVI

POTATOES

COMPOSITION OF POTATOES

Water, 78.9%, Proteid, 2.1%,
Starch, 18%, Mineral matter, .9%,
Fat, .1%.

POTATOES—Give needed bulk to food rather than nourishment, and, lacking proteid, should be used in combination with meat, fish or eggs.

Potatoes are best in the fall when fully ripe. They keep best in a cool, dark, dry cellar. When sprouts appear they should be removed; receiving their nourishment from the starch, they deteriorate the potato.

BOILED POTATOES IN JACKETS

Scrub 6 potatoes well and let stand in cold water with a little salt ½ hour. Place in stew pan, pour boiling water over them to cover, about 1 qt., add 1 tablespoon salt and boil until fork will easily pierce them. Drain, shake gently over the fire to dry. Serve hot.

BOILED POTATOES

6 potatoes, 1 qt. boiling water,
1 tablespoon salt.

Scrub, pare and let stand in cold water ½ hour. Cook in boiling, salted water twenty to thirty minutes, or till tender. Drain and shake gently over the fire uncovered, till dry. Serve hot.

BOILED NEW POTATOES

Scrape new potatoes and let stand in cold water ½ hour. Boil until tender in salted, boiling water, tablespoon salt to 1 quart water, drain and dry; add 2 tablespoons melted butter and 1 tablespoon chopped parsley or if you desire 1 teaspoon caraway seed; shake well over fire and serve hot.

May also be served with White Sauce, page 87.

MASHED POTATOES

6 hot, boiled potatoes,	⅓ cup hot milk,
2 tablespoons butter,	1 teaspoon salt,

Pepper.

Rub the hot potatoes through a ricer, or mash and add the rest of the ingredients in their order. Beat with a fork until light and creamy. Serve hot.

With Onions—Any kind of fat may be used and the milk omitted. An onion may be chopped fine and browned in the fat and poured over the potatoes.

BAKED POTATOES

Take even sized potatoes. Scrub and cut out black portions. Place on floor of hot oven until soft, thirty to forty minutes. Break the skins to let the steam escape. Serve at once uncovered. Peel at once, any that may be left.

POTATOES ON THE HALF SHELL

6 baked potatoes,	1 cup American cheese, grated,
¼ cup hot milk,	
1 teaspoon salt,	2 tablespoons butter.

Cut the potatoes in half lengthwise, scoop out the inside. Mash and mix with the butter, salt and milk. Return to the shells and sprinkle with the cheese. Place in moderate oven and bake about 5 or 10 minutes and serve. The cheese may be omitted.

POTATO BALLS

1 pt. potato balls,	1 teaspoon salt,
2 tablespoons butter,	1 teaspoon chopped parsley.

Pare potato and throw into pan of cold water. With French vegetable cutter, cut balls, or cut into cubes and let stand in cold, salted water until wanted. Scraps may be used for soup or mashed potatoes. Heat butter in a sauce pan, add the potato balls, cover closely and cook slowly, shaking pan over fire to cook them evenly. Test with darning needle. When ready to serve, add salt, chopped parsley, or, they may be boiled, drained and Maitre d'Hotel Butter, page 91, added; or fry in deep hot fat, as French Fried Potatoes, page 174.

BOSTON BROWNED POTATOES

Wash and peel six medium sized potatoes. Cut in four equal parts. Place in a shallow tin, greased, and bake one-half to three-fourths of an hour in a hot oven. When done, pour over some meat gravy, and serve alone or around the meat on a hot platter. Serve at once.

FRANCONIA POTATOES

Wash, scrub and pare potatoes of uniform size. Put them in the dripping pan with the meat and baste when the meat is basted. Or place in a small tin pan beside the meat, or on the grate, and baste with the drippings.

SARATOGA POTATOES

Pare and slice potatoes very fine. Soak in cold, salted water, and drain dry between towels; fry only a handful at a time in deep, hot fat, until a delicate brown and crisp. Drain on unglazed paper. Sprinkle with salt and serve hot or cold.

Slightly stale chips may be made fresh and crisp by placing in hot oven, in shallow pan, a few moments before serving.

FRENCH FRIED POTATOES

Take long thin potatoes. Pare, wash and cut lengthwise into eighths. Soak in cold, salted water. Drain and dry, and fry in deep, hot fat, until tender and golden brown. Serve hot. Sprinkle with salt.

POTATO CROQUETTES

1 pt. mashed potatoes,
1/8 teaspoon white pepper,
1/4 teaspoon celery salt,
2 tablespoons butter,
1/2 teaspoon salt,
Yolk of 1 egg.

Mix together all the ingredients, except the egg, and beat until light; then add the yolk of the egg and mix well. Rub through a sieve and add 1 teaspoon chopped parsley. Shape into smooth balls, then into cylinders. Dip in bread crumbs, then in beaten egg, then in crumbs again. Fry in deep, hot fat. Drain on paper and serve on a hot dish.

POTATO PUFFS

2 cups grated, boiled potatoes,
Salt,
1 cup flour,
sour cream.

Sour cream enough to make it possible to knead the mixture. Roll it out thin as you can and cut with biscuit cutter. Fry in hot lard. Serve hot.

FRIED POTATOES

Cold, boiled potatoes,   Butter or other fat.

Cut cold, boiled potatoes into slices and chop. Have a frying pan hot and well greased with butter, bacon or other fat. Cook the potatoes in the fat until brown and serve hot.

LYONNAISE POTATOES

1 pt. cold, boiled potatoes,   1 teaspoon chopped onion,
½ teaspoon salt,   2 tablespoons beef dripping
speck pepper,   or butter,
2 tablespoons chopped parsley.

Cut the potatoes into slices, season with the salt and pepper. Fry the onions in the dripping till light brown, put in the potato and cook till it has taken up the fat. Add the chopped parsley and serve.

HASHED BROWNED POTATOES

Chop cold, boiled potatoes (new ones are best) into bits the size of a peanut. Season with salt and pepper, and for 1 qt. of potatoes allow 3 tablespoons butter. Heat the butter and toss the potatoes in it till they begin to show a little brown, then add ½ cup of cream and place in a very hot oven to brown. Serve in the baking dish.

POTATO CAKES

Take cold, mashed potatoes, make into rounds ½ inch thick. Put them in a hot, greased frying pan. Fry until well browned on one side, then turn and brown on the other and serve hot.

SURPRISE BALLS

Mashed potatoes,   Lean meat cooked (chopped).
Butter or fat.

Roll the potatoes into balls, press a hollow in the top with a teaspoon. Season meat and fill into the hollow ball. Place in greased pan, with a little fat on the top of each ball, brown in the oven and serve hot.

BAKED MASHED POTATOES

2 cups mashed potatoes,   2 eggs,
  (cold),   1 cup milk or cream,
2 tablespoons melted butter,   Salt and pepper.

Stir the butter well with the potatoes, add the eggs, beaten stiff and then the cream. Season to taste. Beat all together well, place in greased pudding dish and bake in a quick oven until brown and serve hot.

DUCHESSE POTATOES

Mashed potatoes,   1 egg.

Take freshly boiled and mashed potatoes or some that are left over, add to them the beaten yolk of egg, place in a greased tin and form in balls, hearts or flat cakes, brush with the beaten white and brown in oven.

CREAMED POTATOES

4 cold potatoes,   ½ teaspoon salt,
½ cup milk,   2 tablespoons butter,
spk. pepper,   1 tablespoon chopped parsley.

Cut the potatoes into cubes or thin slices. Put, with the milk, into a pan or double-boiler, and cook until they have absorbed nearly all the milk. Add the butter and seasoning, cook 5 minutes longer and serve hot. One tablespoon parsley, chopped fine, may be added with the seasoning. Another method is to heat the potatoes in a Thin White Sauce, page 87. Serve hot.

SCALLOPED POTATOES

No. 1

1 qt. cold potatoes,   1 tablespoonful chopped
1 teaspoon salt,   parsley,
¼ teaspoon pepper,   1 cup White Sauce,
  1 cup buttered cracker crumbs.

Cut the potatoes in slices and season with salt, pepper and parsley. Butter a baking-dish, put in the potatoes, pour on the White Sauce, page 87, cover with crumbs. Bake till brown.

No. 2

1 qt. parboiled potatoes,   ¼ cayenne pepper,
  sliced,   1 teaspoon salt,
2 tablespoons butter,   ¼ cup cracker crumbs,
¼ lb. stale, grated American 1 teaspoon chopped parsley,
  cheese,   1 cup milk.

Into a well buttered baking dish place a layer of the potatoes, a layer of grated cheese, bits of butter, salt and pepper, another layer of potatoes, cheese, bits of butter and so on until all of the potatoes are used up. Pour on milk. Sprinkle parsley and cracker crumbs over top with the cheese, butter and seasoning. Add milk just before placing in oven and bake in a moderate oven until potatoes are tender and nicely browned. Serve hot. The cheese may be omitted, and a sprinkling of flour may be used in place of the crumbs.

POTATOES AU GRATIN

Put Creamed Potatoes, page 176, in buttered baking dish, cover with buttered crumbs, a sprinkling of American cheese, if desired, and bake on center of oven until crumbs are brown.

SWEET POTATOES

BAKED SWEET POTATOES

Select 6 even sized sweet potatoes and place on the floor of a very hot oven ¾ hour or until done, then remove to the warmer to stand longer, to soften, or they may be parboiled in boiling, salted water and baked in the oven until soft.

BOILED SWEET POTATOES

Select potatoes of uniform size. Wash, pare and cook 20 minutes in boiling, salted water to cover. Sweet potatoes may be boiled with the skins.

MASHED SWEET POTATOES

4 cold, baked sweet potatoes,
1 tablespoon butter,
¼ cup milk or cream,
Salt and pepper.

Scoop out potatoes, add salt, pepper, cream and butter, a few grains of sugar, if desired, and mash and beat until creamy, or, when just done, mash with butter, milk and seasoning, and bake in a spring form, in a hot oven until brown. When done remove side of form and garnish top and sides with riced Irish potatoes.

GLAZED SWEET POTATOES

6 medium sized potatoes,
½ cup sugar,
¼ cup water,
3 tablespoons butter.

Wash and pare potatoes. Cook 10 minutes in boiling, salted water. Drain, cut in halves lengthwise, and put in a buttered pan. Make a syrup by boiling 3 minutes the sugar and water; add butter. Brush potatoes with syrup and bake 15 minutes, basting twice with remaining syrup.

SWEET POTATOES—Southern Style

4 boiled sweet potatoes,
¼ lb. butter,
¼ cup brown sugar.
1 tablespoon water,
Lemon juice,

Skin boiled potatoes and quarter. Place in baking dish, with butter on top, sprinkle with the brown sugar, add the water and a little lemon juice. Brown in oven and serve hot.

SWEET POTATO CROQUETTES

1 pt. mashed sweet potatoes,
⅛ teaspoon white pepper,
Yolk of 1 egg.
2 tablespoons butter,
½ teaspoon salt,

Mix together all the ingredients, except the egg, and beat until light; then add the yolk of the egg and mix well. Rub through a sieve and add 1 teaspoon chopped parsley. Shape into smooth balls, then into cylinders, or shape to resemble pears or apples. Dip in bread crumbs, then in beaten egg, then in crumbs again. Fry in deep, hot fat. Drain on paper and serve on a hot dish. For pear or apple shaped Croquettes use cloves for stems. When baked stick clove in at top, blossom side up, and at the other end stick blossom end in, having stem end show. Make day before using if desired, and warm in shallow pan with syrup used for Glazed Sweet Potatoes above.

CHAPTER XVII

MEHLSPEISE—(Flour Foods)

DUMPLINGS OR KLOESE

Kloese is the German for dumplings; they are shaped with a spoon or into small balls or oblongs and are cooked in boiling, salted water or soup stock. They are served in soups, or as an entree with Sauce—when they are—"Mehlspeise," or flour foods. Noodles, macaroni and the like are also used as "Mehlspeise."

GARNISHES FOR DUMPLINGS

The following garnishes are used with dumplings, noodles or macaroni when served in place of a vegetable:

Onions, cut fine and fried in butter or other fat are sprinkled over the top.

Scrambled eggs are mixed through the Kloese.

Cracker or stale ginger bread crumbs are sprinkled over the top.

Grated American cheese or cottage cheese with salt and pepper may be used.

Chopped walnuts or sugar and cinnamon mixed with cracker crumbs.

PLAIN DUMPLINGS (KLOESE)

No. 1

1½ cup flour,   ½ cup cold water,
1 teaspoon salt,   1 egg.

Beat egg well, add salt and water and stir this into the flour until you have a smooth batter.

Drop by teaspoonfuls or tablespoonfuls into boiling, salted water and let cook 15 minutes. Drain in colander. Pour hot fat over them and serve, or pour cold water over them in the colander that they shall not stick together, reheat in any desired meat or other sauce, or fat; garnish with fried onions, cracker crumbs or any desired dressing.

PLAIN DUMPLINGS

No. 2

3 eggs,	1 teaspoon baking powder,
1 cup water,	2 tablespoons fat,
2 teaspoons salt,	1 onion, cut fine.
3 cups flour,	

Beat 2 or 3 eggs well, add salt and water and then add the flour and stir to a smooth, stiff batter. Drop by tablespoonfuls into boiling, salted water and let cook 15 minutes. Drain in colander. Heat the fat in a spider, add the dumplings, heat through and just before serving add 2 or 3 eggs beaten slightly. Stir well with spoon and cook a few minutes until eggs are set or scrambled, or brown onion in hot fat and pour over the top. Cracker crumbs or chopped nuts may be used.

BAKING POWDER DUMPLINGS

1 pt. flour,	½ teaspoon salt,
4 teaspoons baking powder,	1 scant cup milk or water.

Mix the dry ingredients, stir in the milk or water gradually to make a soft dough. Drop quickly by the spoonful into the boiling water or stew, letting them rest on the meat and potatoes. Cover closely to keep in the steam, and cook just 10 minutes without lifting the cover. Serve at once with brown butter or any well seasoned meat sauce.

YEAST DUMPLINGS (HAFEN KLOESE)

1 pt. flour,	1 teaspoon sugar,
½ oz. compressed yeast,	2 eggs, beaten,
1 cup lukewarm water,	1 teaspoon salt.

Crumble the yeast in a cup with a little of the warm water, place in a mixing bowl with the rest of the ingredients, knead well to a smooth dough and set aside in a warm place to rise. When light, turn out on floured board and mould into large, round biscuits. Cover with a cloth and let rise in a warm place again. Then drop each biscuit or Kloese carefully into salted, boiling water (1 teaspoon salt to 1 quart water), and let boil 10 to 20 minutes, in a closely covered kettle. To test if done lift the cover just long enough to draw out one Kloese; then with two forks pull it apart and if doughy inside return to kettle, but if dry and spongy, serve at once. Removing each Kloese separately with a perforated skimmer; place on large, warm platter, cover with browned butter and sugar or any stewed fruit or sweet sauce.

MEHLSPEISE (FLOUR FOODS)

POTATO DUMPLINGS

No. 1

6 medium potatoes,
2 eggs,
1½ teaspoon salt,
½ cup flour,
½ cup butter or other fat,
½ teaspoon sugar,
⅛ teaspoon grated nutmeg,
⅛ teaspoon cinnamon.

Boil potatoes and when cold grate or mash. Add the eggs, salt, flour and seasonings. Mix and knead until smooth. Shape into one long, thick roll; cut roll into ½ inch pieces and roll into dumplings the shape and size of your finger.

Cook in boiling, salted water 10 minutes. Drain in colander, place in platter and pour hot fat over them that they shall not stick, keep hot, and serve with any desired dumpling garnish.

No. 2

2 lbs. cooked potatoes,
  (6 large potatoes),
2 eggs,
½ cup farina,
1 scant cup flour,
2 tablespoons salt,
⅛ teaspoon nutmeg, grated.

Boil potatoes in jackets. Peel, grate, or run through a ricer; cool and weigh.

Add the rest of the ingredients in the order given and form into balls, size of a walnut. Drop into boiling, salted water (1 teaspoon salt to 1 quart water), and let simmer 20 minutes. Drain and serve hot with browned butter or fat and garnished with browned cracker crumbs, or onions chopped fine and browned.

MOCK ASPARAGUS

2½ cups cold boiled potatoes,
  riced,
1 heaping cup flour,
¾ teaspoon baking powder,
½ teaspoon salt,
2 eggs.

Spread half of the flour over the potatoes, place egg in center and with fork beat and knead the mixture, gradually adding the rest of the flour with the salt and baking powder mixed. When smooth, shape into one long thick roll; cut roll into inch pieces and shape the size of your middle finger to resemble asparagus. Drop one at a time in boiling salted water (1 teaspoon salt to 1 quart water), let simmer 10 minutes. Drain and pour over them bread crumbs, browned in butter, or, they may be dipped in egg and then in cracker crumbs and fried like Potato Croquettes, page 174, in deep hot fat, or, the dumplings may be fried in deep hot fat without the eggs and crumbs. Serve hot.

LIVER DUMPLINGS

No. 1

½ lb. calf's liver,	½ teaspoon grated onion,
1 cup cracker or bread crumbs,	¼ teaspoon poultry seasoning,
1 cup milk or water,	⅛ teaspoon nutmeg, grated,
1 egg,	⅛ teaspoon pepper,
1 teaspoon salt,	Some grated lemon rind.

Skin the liver and remove every particle of tough fibre. Chop fine in meat chopper. Cook bread and water to a paste. Remove from stove, add egg, liver and seasonings and shape into balls size of a nutmeg and drop into boiling soup 10 minutes before serving time. Chicken liver may be used in place of the calf's liver. The heart and tender parts of gizzard may also be used.

No. 2

1 lb. calf's liver,	1 teaspoon parsley, chopped,
1 qt. wheat bread, diced, soaked and pressed dry,	1 teaspoon salt,
2 tablespoons flour,	⅛ teaspoon pepper,
6 eggs,	⅛ teaspoon nutmeg,
	2 tablespoons butter or fat,
1 onion, cut fine.	

Skin and grind or chop the liver very fine. Heat the fat in a spider, add the onion, brown a little, then add the liver and the rest of the ingredients; mix well and form into balls, size of a walnut and drop into salted, boiling water (1 teaspoon salt to 1 qt. water), and let simmer 10 minutes. Drain in colander and serve hot, in a well flavored meat gravy or simply reheat them in fat.

BEEF AND LIVER DUMPLINGS

½ lb. calf's liver,	1 teaspoon salt,
½ lb. round beef steak or veal,	1 egg,
1 cup cracker or stale bread crumbs,	1 teaspoon grated onion,
	¼ teaspoon pepper,
1 cup milk or water,	⅛ teaspoon nutmeg, grated,
	Some grated lemon rind.

Skin the liver and remove every particle of tough fibre from the meat and liver, chop or grind through meat chopper. Cook bread and milk to a paste, take from stove, add eggs and seasonings, and the chopped meat and shape into small balls, the size of a nutmeg. Drop into boiling soup 10 minutes before serving.

MATZOS KLOESE

6 matzos,	½ cup matzos meal,
2 tablespoons goose fat or butter,	½ teaspoon chopped parsley, Salt,
½ onion,	Pepper,
3 eggs,	Nutmeg.

Soak the matzos (unleavened bread) in water and squeeze dry. Heat the fat in the spider, add the onions, cut very fine, and fry a golden brown; then add the soaked matzos, stirring occasionally until it will not stick to the pan. Let cool, season, add the eggs and the matzo meal and shape into balls.

Drop in boiling, salt water and boil 15 minutes; drain and pour over them hot fat or butter with an onion, cut fine and browned.

BOILED BROAD NOODLES

4 eggs,	2⅔ cups flour (about).

Follow recipe for making Noodles, page 85, using four times the quantities. Divide into four portions and fold and cut one part into fine noodles, as for soup. Fold the other three parts, each into a long roll and cut into "broad" noodles 1 inch wide. When ready to serve drop broad and fine noodles in boiling, salted water, in separate kettles. Place broad noodles in deep covered kettle and boil 15 minutes. Drain in colander and pour cold water through them, that they do not stick together, or better, drain in colander, return to kettle and add 2 tablespoons hot butter or fat. Fry the fine boiled and drained noodles in hot butter or fat until brown and serve on platter, hot, as a garnish on top of broad noodles. These noodles may be used in place of macaroni.

BAKED NOODLES WITH CHEESE

Take the Broad Noodles, recipe above, cook them in boiling, salt water until they are soft. Drain through strainer, and pour cold water over them to prevent pieces from adhering. Make one and one-half cups White Sauce as follows:

2 tablespoons butter,	½ teaspoon salt,
2 tablespoons flour,	1½ cups hot milk.

Dissolve a speck of soda in a little hot water and add to the milk. Heat the butter, add the flour and seasoning, and then gradually the hot milk.

Put a layer of boiled noodles in a buttered baking dish, sprinkle with grated cheese; repeat, pour over white sauce, cover with buttered crumbs, and bake until crumbs are brown.

NOTE—Tomato Sauce, page 93, may be used in place of the white sauce and cheese.

EGG BARLEY

2 cups raw pfarvel,	3 cups soup stock or boiling
2 tablespoons fat or butter,	water with meat gravy,
¼ cup onions, cut fine.	

Make "Pfarvel," page 86. Heat the fat, add onions, fry until a golden brown, add the dried "pfarvel" and brown nicely. Place in pudding dish, add hot soup stock or water to more than cover. Bake in a moderate oven about 1 hour or until water has nearly evaporated and the "pfarvel" stand out like beads and are soft. The onion may be omitted. Serve hot in place of a vegetable.

FILLED DUMPLINGS

1 lb. chopped beef, raw,	A little pepper,
1 egg,	1½ teaspoon onion juice,
1 teaspoon salt,	Noodle dough.

Mix the first 5 ingredients. Make "Noodle Dough," page 85. Roll dough thin and cut into 1½ inch squares. Place a teaspoon of this mixture on each square and fold in three cornered shape, pressing the edges well together. Drop in boiling, salted water, (1 teaspoon salt to 1 quart water), or in soup stock and let cook 15 minutes. If used as a "Mehlspeise" drain in colander, place on platter and pour 2 tablespoons hot fat over them, with browned onions as a garnish. May be sprinkled with browned cracker crumbs, chopped walnuts, or ginger bread crumbs.

DUMPLINGS FILLED WITH CHEESE

1 pt. cottage cheese,
1 egg,
Salt and pepper to taste,
2 tablespoons sweet or sour cream,
Noodle dough.

Mix the first 5 ingredients. Make "Noodle Dough," page 85, roll thin and cut into 1½ inch squares. Place a tablespoon of this mixture on each square, fold in 3 cornered shape and cook until tender, in milk or sour cream mixed with water. Serve with browned butter. Sprinkle with chopped nuts, cracker crumbs or gingerbread crumbs.

BOILED MACARONI

Break one-quarter of a pound of macaroni in two three-inch pieces, and put into three pints of boiling, salted water. Boil twenty minutes, or until soft. Drain in a colander, and pour cold water through it to remove starchy water and prevent pieces adhering. Serve hot with browned butter or any meat gravy.

MACARONI AND CHEESE

Boil the macaroni and prepare White Sauce, page 87. Have ready 1 cup of good, grated cheese. Butter a pudding dish, put in a layer of macaroni, one of sauce and one of cheese, then another layer of each, ending with cheese on top. Dust the top with sifted bread or cracker crumbs, dot with bits of butter and bake 15 minutes in a hot oven. Serve in a pudding dish with a napkin or a paper frill around dish and place a platter under it.

MACARONI AND TOMATOES

¾ cup macaroni in one inch pieces,
2 qts. boiling water,
1 tablespoon salt,
2 cups hot, strained tomatoes,
¼ teaspoon onion, chopped,
⅛ teaspoon pepper,
2 tablespoons butter,
2 tablespoons flour.

Cook the macaroni in the boiling, salted water 20 minutes or until soft; drain in strainer, pour cold water over it to prevent pieces from adhering.

Heat the butter in a spider, add the flour and seasoning and gradually add the hot, strained tomatoes and onion. Cook until smooth and pour over the macaroni, reheat and serve or place in pudding dish and bake in a moderate oven 15 to 20 minutes. Sprinkle thickly with grated Swiss cheese.

Cover the bottom of a baking dish with about a tablespoonful of melted butter, then put over a layer of macaroni that has been cooked fifteen minutes and sprinkle lightly with bits of butter. Now put over a thick layer of washed mushrooms cut into slices, then another layer of macaroni, and so continue until the dish is full, having the last layer macaroni. Pour over one pint of cream. Cover with a lid or another pan and bake in a moderate oven one hour; then remove the cover and brown quickly.

MUSHROOM SAUCE FOR BOILED MACARONI

The following amount of sauce is enough for one pound of macaroni. Put into a saucepan one and one-half tablespoons butter. Add one small onion and a clove of garlic chopped fine.

Cook until all is browned, then add three tablespoons of strong beef soup stock and four dried mushrooms which have been soaked. Simmer all the ingredients for five minutes before pouring the sauce over the cooked macaroni.

MACARONI WITH TOMATOES AND MUSHROOMS

½ lb. Macaroni,
2 qts. boiling water,
2 teaspoons salt,
1 tablespoon butter,
1 small onion, cut fine,
1 teaspoon flour,
Cup of hot beef or chicken stock,
1 pt. of stewed tomatoes,
1 tablespoon finely chopped dried mushrooms,
1 teaspoon salt,
Cayenne pepper,
1 teaspoon parsley, chopped,
3 tablespoons grated Parmesan cheese.

Add salt and then the macaroni to the boiling water. Let boil 20 minutes, stirring to avoid sticking at the bottom of the kettle. Drain in colander; pour 1 cup of cold water through it; then return to cleared kettle.

If dried mushrooms are used, soak in warm water 1 or 2 hours, changing the water several times. Heat the butter, add the onion; when slightly browned, add the flour, then the soup stock. Stir until smooth; add the tomatoes, strained, and let simmer 20 minutes, then pour over the macaroni. Add mushrooms, season with salt and paprika; let heat through, add the parsley. Place on platter, sprinkle Parmesan cheese on top.

MACARONI WITH EGGS

To ¼ pound cooked Macaroni in a buttered dish, add salt, butter and pepper; grate over it 1 ounce cheese; stir two eggs in a cup of milk and pour over. Cover with bread crumbs and bake twenty minutes, until brown.

SPAGHETTI ITALIENNE

¾ lb. spaghetti,
3 quarts boiling water,
1 tablespoon salt,
2 tablespoons butter,
⅛ teaspoon salt,

⅛ teaspoon white pepper,
A little nutmeg,
1 cup tomato sauce,
2 oz. grated Parmesan or Swiss cheese or 1 oz. of each.

Slide Spaghetti without breaking it, in the boiling salted water gradually and boil 25 minutes. Drain, place butter in sauce pan, salt, pepper and nutmeg, let cook a few minutes add the hot Tomato Sauce, page 93, gently mix with a fork, then add cheese and mix well again with the fork for one minute or longer. Dress on a hot dish and serve.

CHAPTER XVIII

SALAD DRESSINGS

MIXED SEASONING

1 teaspoon salt,
¼ teaspoon mustard,
⅛ teaspoon red and white pepper or paprika.

FRENCH SALAD DRESSING

(For tomatoes, lettuce, etc.)

No. 1

1 teaspoon salt,
¼ teaspoon mustard,
⅛ teaspoon pepper,
2 tablespoons sugar,
1 tablespoon onion, chopped fine,
4 tablespoons vinegar,
¾ cup water.

Mix, set aside and keep very cold and pour over salad, just before serving.

No. 2

½ tablespoon salt,
¼ teaspoon white pepper,
1½ tablespoons vinegar,
½ tablespoon lemon juice,
3 or 4 tablespoons olive oil or any poultry fat,
½ teaspoon onion juice.

Mix the ingredients, and stir until well blended. Serve ice cold over lettuce, tomatoes, etc., and to marinate boiled meats and vegetables.

VINAIGRETTE DRESSING

¼ chopped onion,
2 branches parsley,
3 stalks chives, or
¼ green pepper, chopped,
3 teaspoons vinegar,
Salt and pepper,
4 tablespoons good oil.

Mix all together but the oil; put that in last, and slowly.

SWEET OR SOUR CREAM DRESSING

1 cup sweet or sour cream,
2 tablespoons lemon juice,
2 tablespoons vinegar,
1 tablespoon sugar,
1 teaspoon salt,
¼ teaspoon pepper,
1 teaspoon or more of mixed mustard.

Beat the cream with an egg beater until smooth, thick and light. Mix the other ingredients together and gradually add to the cream, beating all the while.

This dressing may be modified to suit different vegetables. Add and mix 2 tablespoons olive oil, salt, sugar and vinegar together, then beat in ½ cup tomato catsup and finally add the cream, beating it in gradually.

This dressing is very good for vegetables or for fish salads.

GERMAN SALAD DRESSING

2 tablespoons hot goose, chicken, bacon fat or butter,
½ cup hot vinegar,
1 teaspoon dry mustard,
1 tablespoon sugar,
1 teaspoon salt,
⅛ teaspoon pepper,
½ onion, cut fine,
½ cup sweet or sour cream, milk or water.

Dissolve the sugar in the cream. Mix with the rest of the ingredients. Mix while hot with any hot vegetable and serve with slightly warm salad.

CREAM MAYONNAISE DRESSING

5 yolks, beaten,
½ cup cream,
½ cup vinegar,
½ cup water,
⅛ teaspoon cayenne pepper,
1½ teaspoon salt,
1 teaspoon mustard,
1 tablespoon flour,
2 tablespoons sugar.

Beat the yolks well in a cup, fill up the cup with cream. Mix the dry ingredients, wet with a little water, add to the yolk and cream. Place in double boiler and let cook until thick and smooth, stirring constantly.

MAYONNAISE FOR COLD MEAT

No. 1

2½ tablespoons soup stock,
2½ tablespoons white wine,
2½ tablespoons melted butter,
1 teaspoon French mustard,
1 tablespoon lemon juice or vinegar,
1 teaspoon sugar,
3 yolks of eggs.

Mix dry ingredients, add the rest and place in double boiler. Cook 10 minutes or until thick and smooth, stirring constantly.

MAYONNAISE FOR COLD MEAT

No. 2

Yolks of 6 eggs,
¼ lb. butter,
1 cup hot soup stock
¾ teaspoon French mustard,
3 tablespoons vinegar,
½ teaspoon salt,
½ teaspoon sugar.

Mix and place in double boiler; stir rapidly until it comes to a boil. Remove from stove and when cool add lemon juice to taste.

Nice for mixed ham or tongue.

BOILED MAYONNAISE DRESSING

No. 1

2 teaspoons sugar,
½ teaspoon salt,
½ teaspoon mustard,
⅛ teaspoon pepper,
½ cup vinegar,
¼ cup butter,
1 teaspoon flour,
1 yolk of egg.

Mix the first four ingredients, stir in the vinegar and boil all together. Rub the butter and flour to a cream and pour on the boiling vinegar. Cook 5 minutes and then pour it gradually over the well beaten yolk. Mix while hot with cabbage or potatoes. For potato salad add 1 cup sweet or sour cream or butter milk.

No. 2

½ teaspoon mustard,
¼ teaspoon salt,
1 teaspoon sugar,
Speck of cayenne pepper,
2 tablespoons vinegar,
2 tablespoons lemon juice,
1 teaspoon butter,
Yolks of 2 eggs.

Mix the ingredients, add and stir well with beaten yolks, then add the vinegar. Boil in double boiler until thick. Take from the stove, and add the butter or fat and the juice of the lemon. Thin with cream or lemon juice just before serving.

No. 3

⅛ teaspoon pepper,
1 teaspoon salt,
½ teaspoon mustard,
¾ teaspoon sugar,
2 yolks of eggs, or
1 whole egg,
2½ tablespoons melted butter,
¾ cup milk or water,
¼ cup vinegar,
1 teaspoon flour.

Mix the salt, mustard, sugar and flour. Add the egg slightly beaten, the butter and milk or water. Dilute the vinegar if strong, and add it very slowly.

Cook in a double boiler until it thickens slightly. Strain and cool or bottle.

This dressing may be used with cabbage, lettuce or cold meat.

BOILED MAYONNAISE DRESSING

No. 4

Yolks of 4 eggs,
¾ cup vinegar,
¼ cup water,
3 tablespoons sugar,
1 tablespoon mustard,
⅛ teaspoon red pepper,
1 tablespoon flour,
1 teaspoon salt,
1 tablespoon butter.

Mix the dry ingredients, then add the butter, vinegar and water; boil over hot water until thick, then pour gradually to the beaten yolks. When ready to serve add a little cream or lemon juice to thin.

BOILED OIL MAYONNAISE

No. 1

4 whole eggs,
½ cup olive oil,
2 tablespoons vinegar,
1 tablespoon lemon juice,
1 teaspoon sugar,
½ teaspoon salt,
1/16 teaspoon cayenne pepper,
½ teaspoon dry mustard.

Mix dry ingredients, add and mix thoroughly with the eggs, well beaten, and place in double boiler over boiling water; add alternately oil, vinegar and lemon, stirring constantly.

When ready to serve add ½ cup thick cream, sour preferred.

No. 2

7 yolks,
2 whole eggs,
1 cup olive oil,
1 cup cream,
⅛ teaspoon red pepper,
3 tablespoons vinegar,
Juice of 1 lemon,
1 teaspoon salt,
1 teaspoon mustard.

Beat all together well and place in double boiler, over boiling water and cook until thick, stirring constantly. Remove from stove. If too thick when ready to use, add a little cream.

OIL MAYONNAISE DRESSING

No. 1

1 teaspoon mustard,	Yolk of 1 egg,
1 teaspoon powdered sugar,	1 cup olive oil,
¼ teaspoon salt,	1 tablespoon vinegar,
⅛ teaspoon cayenne pepper,	1 tablespoon lemon juice.

Mix the first four ingredients in a small bowl. Add the egg. Beat with Dover egg beater. Add oil gradually, at first drop by drop, and beat constantly. As mixture thickens thin with vinegar or lemon juice. Add oil and vinegar or lemon juice alternately, until all is used, beating constantly. If oil is added too rapidly, dressing will have a curdled appearance. Should be jellylike. Keep very cold.

NOTE—If dressing should separate, take a yolk of egg and pour mixture on it very slowly and beat well.

No. 2

3 hard cooked yolks,	1 tablespoon sugar,
1 raw yolk,	Juice of 1 lemon,
2 teaspoons prepared mustard,	2 tablespoons white wine vinegar,
1 teaspoon grated onion,	
⅛ teaspoon pepper,	3 teaspoons oil.

Mash and rub the cooked eggs smooth, add the dry seasonings, then the raw yolk and the rest of the ingredients, all but the oil, stir until smooth and add the oil drop by drop. Stir constantly and keep cool until wanted.

DELMONICO SALAD DRESSING

1 hard cooked egg, chopped fine,	2 tablespoons olive oil,
1 teaspoon tomato catsup,	¼ teaspoon chopped green peppers,
1 teaspoon Worcestershire Sauce,	Red pepper and salt to taste,
	Chopped truffles if desired,
2 tablespoons tarragon vinegar.	

Mix and serve cold over lettuce, tomatoes, etc.

GARGOYLE SAUCE

Boiled oil mayonnaise,	¼ teaspoon paprika,
1 teaspoon Worcestershire Sauce,	1 teaspoon pearl onions,
3 tablespoons Chili Sauce,	½ teaspoon chopped green peppers.

Make ½ recipe of Boiled Oil Mayonnaise, No. 1, page 191, as a foundation for this salad dressing, stir in the rest of the ingredients and serve ice cold over fish or filled tomatoes. Will serve six people.

WHITE, GREEN OR RED MAYONNAISE

White Mayonnaise

One cup of cream, whipped stiff and added to Butter Mayonnaise Dressing No. 3. Serve ice cold over egg salad.

Green Mayonnaise

Finely chopped parsley leaves pounded with a small quantity of lemon juice, strained through a cheese-cloth and added to Mayonnaise, makes Green Mayonnaise. Spinach greens may be used if desired.

Red Mayonnaise

1 cup thick Tomato Sauce,   1 cup Whipped Cream.
1 cup Mayonnaise Dressing,

Prepare Mayonnaise, page 191, slightly flavored with ham, thick Tomato Sauce, page 93, and Whipped Cream. Have Tomato Sauce hot and pour it boiling over the Mayonnaise, beating vigorously, and then set in ice water. Add the beaten cream and serve with Fish.

Lobster Coral, rubbed through a fine sieve, added to Mayonnaise makes red Mayonnaise also.

CHAPTER XIX

GENERAL RULES FOR SALADS

Simple salads consist of fresh vegetables which require no cooking,—as lettuce, watercress, etc., with French or cream dressing. Cooked vegetables, meat, fish, eggs, cheese, apple, pineapple and other fruits are used for salads.

The salad plants are valuable for the water and potash salts they contain. Lettuce, Endive, Watercress and Cucumbers are examples. Salads are cooling, refreshing, and assist in stimulating the appetite. They should be served cold. An endless variety of salads are made of cooked meats (chicken, veal, sweetbreads, etc.), fish (canned or cold, boiled), eggs, vegetables, raw (celery, tomatoes, cucumbers, etc.), or cooked (peas, beans, potatoes, asparagus, etc.), fruits (bananas, oranges, apples, etc.) and nutmeats (English walnuts, pecans, boiled chestnuts, hickory nuts, etc.), alone or in combination—with the addition of a dressing. The salad greens should always be served crisp and cold, and the dressing added just before serving. Cooked vegetables and meats are best if marinated one hour before serving with salt and pepper, oil and vinegar, and Boiled or Mayonnaise dressing not added until ready to serve. All skin, bone and gristle should be freed from meat and fish, and cut in small cubes or flaked. Salads may be made very attractive by serving on lettuce leaves, in cups made by scooping out tomatoes, peppers, beets, cucumbers, oranges, lemons, apples, etc.

LETTUCE SALAD

Lettuce,
1 small onion, chopped fine,
French Dressing or
German Dressing.

Cut roots and coarse outside leaves of ordinary lettuce or head lettuce. Remove the outer leaves one at a time and place in cold water until wanted. Drain, shake off the water, add onion, if you desire and place in salad bowl or in individual dishes and pour over French Dressing, page 188, or German, page 189.

ENDIVE SALAD

1 head endive,
French Salad Dressing,
4 hard cooked eggs,
1 pt. boiled potatoes, sliced.

Wash, and dry endive pick off the green outer leaves and use only the light colored feathery leaves. Arrange on salad dish with white leaves in center. Place eggs, cut into quarters lengthwise, around carefully, and mix with potatoes and pour over all French Dressing, page 188.

CUCUMBER SALAD

1 large cucumber,
Ice water,
French Dressing,
Lettuce leaves.

Lay the cucumbers on the ice, or in ice water, until ½ hour before serving. Then pare and slice them into ice water. Just before serving drain off water. Drain, arrange on lettuce leaves and cover with French Dressing, page 188.

TOMATO SALAD, No. 1

6 firm red tomatoes,
1 small onion, sliced thin,
French Dressing,
Lettuce leaves.

Wash and wipe the tomatoes and slice thin with a very sharp knife. Line a salad bowl with lettuce leaves, lay the sliced tomatoes in, mixed with the sliced onion and pour over all a French Dressing, page 188. Serve cold.

TOMATO SALAD, No. 2

Wipe tomatoes, plunge in boiling water, one minute; drain and remove skins, place on ice to cool. Place on lettuce leaves and put about 1 tablespoon Mayonnaise, page 190, over each tomato. Serve cold. The tomato may be cut in half crosswise; or, into quarters, ⅔ down and let spread to form a flower with stem end up, placing olive in center and mayonnaise over top.

CUCUMBER AND TOMATO SALAD

Place a bed of crisp lettuce in a salad dish, then a layer of sliced cucumbers, then sliced tomatoes and pour a French dressing, page 188, or a Mayonnaise, pages 190 or 191, over the whole.

STUFFED TOMATO SALAD

6 ripe tomatoes,	2 cucumbers,
½ pint Cream Dressing, page 189,	Lettuce, Salt and pepper.

Scald the tomatoes so that the skins can be easily removed. Cut a slice from the top of each, and with a small spoon remove the seeds. Peel the cucumbers, and cut them into dice, season highly and mix with at least half the dressing. Fill the tomato cups with this, and put another spoon of the dressing on top. Sprinkle a very little finely chopped parsley over and serve on a bed of lettuce leaves.

TOMATO BASKETS

4 firm red tomatoes,	1 can asparagus tips,
1 large green pepper,	Salad Dressing.

Cut the peppers into slices crosswise to form ¼ inch rings.

Scald tomatoes, peel, chill and cut in half crosswise. Place on lettuce leaves, with the cut side up. Lay 4 or 5 asparagus tips side by side in center of each tomato half. Cut pepper rings at one end and lay across the top of asparagus to meet the sides of the tomato, thus forming a handle to the tomato basket. Serve ice cold with French Dressing, page 188, or Gargoyle Sauce, page 192. For eight people.

CABBAGE SALAD

2 cups shredded cabbage,   French Dressing No. 2, or
½ cup warm Salad Dressing.

Shave ½ cabbage in thin strips or chop fine and mix with French Dressing, No. 2, page 188, or German Salad Dressing, No. 2, page 189. Do not mix dressing with more cabbage than you wish to use, as it will turn dark.

RED AND WHITE CABBAGE SALAD

1 cup red cabbage (chopped fine),   1 cup white cabbage (chopped fine),
1 cup hot Boiled Dressing.

Select nice, firm red and white cabbage, wash, cut off wilted leaves, quarter and soak in cold water. Drain, cut into thin slices, and chop very fine, each kind separately. Divide the Boiled Dressing, No. 2, page 190, into two parts, mix with each part while hot. Take three-fourths of the white mixture pack it smoothly on platter one inch from the edge. Make wreath of the red all around the white, keeping lines distinct and smooth. Reserve one-fourth of the red to decorate the top of white and the remaining white to top the whole.

CABBAGE ROSE SALAD

Small solid white cabbage,   1 pt. celery, diced or
1 red pepper, shredded,   1 pt. boiled potatoes, sliced
Boiled Salad Dressing.

Remove the outside leaves of the cabbage and cut off stalks close to leaves. Cut out center with sharp knife. Place "Cabbage bowl" in cold or ice water for one hour, drain dry as possible. Shred remaining cabbage mix with equal parts of celery, moistened with Salad Dressing, page 188, or the potatoes and refill cabbage. Turn back outer leaves of cabbage to resemble open rose, lay the finely shredded bits of red peppers thickly over the top of leaves, and serve cold.

POTATO SALAD

No. 1

1 qt. hot, sliced potatoes,   French Dressing, hot,
1 medium sized onion (chopped fine),   Parsley or 1 teaspoon chives (schnittlauch) cut fine, to garnish.

Boil potatoes in their jackets and while hot, peel and slice; salt and pepper, add the onion, and mix with hot French dressing, page 188. Garnish with parsley or chives. Serve warm or cold. A little sour cream may be added.

POTATO SALAD

No. 2

1 qt. sliced potatoes,
1 medium onion, cut fine,
1 cup table celery, cut fine,
1 cup Boiled Mayonnaise Dressing.

Mix the ingredients together lightly and tossing the Boiled Mayonnaise Dressing, No. 2, page 190, gently through it. Garnish as desired with pickles, beets or hard cooked eggs.

NOTE—If celery cannot be had, use chopped cabbage, diced pickles or cucumbers.

No. 3

12 small potatoes,
3 tablespoons salad oil,
¼ cup red wine,
¼ cup vinegar,
1 teaspoon salt,
¼ teaspoon pepper,
1 teaspoon mustard,
1 tablespoon sugar,
¼ red or green pepper, chopped, or parsley, chopped.
½ cup celery, diced.

Mix the oil, wine, vinegar and the spices well together.

Boil potatoes in their jackets, peel and slice. Into a salad bowl place a layer of the potatoes and while hot, pour over a part of the Salad dressing, just mixed. Add another layer of potatoes, more of the dressing, and so on, with dressing for the top. Serve cold. Decorate with the peppers and parsley; chopped olives, cold beets cut in fancy shapes or any other way desired.

POTATO SALAD WITH BACON, (Hot)

1 quart boiled potatoes, sliced, (10 small potatoes),
¼ lb. bacon sliced and cut fine,
1 medium onion, cut fine,
1 teaspoon salt,
⅛ teaspoon pepper,
½ teaspoon sugar,
½ teaspoon flour,
½ cup vinegar,
½ cup water.

Scrub potatoes; boil in boiling salted water until tender. Drain and while hot skin and cut into ¼ inch slices; sprinkle with the salt, pepper, sugar and flour. Add water to vinegar and let heat thoroughly. Place bacon in spider, let fry light brown, add onion, brown slightly, add potatoes and over all pour the hot vinegar, let heat through to absorb the vinegar and water, place in serving dish and serve hot. The bits of fried bacon may be omitted. If the salad is too dry add a little hot water. It should have a glassy look, without being lumpy or greasy.

GERMAN CELERY SALAD

No. 1

3 or 4 celery roots or Celeriac,
1 onion, sliced,
Vinegar and water,
1 teaspoon salt,
1/8 teaspoon pepper.

Select small, firm roots; wash them well. Place in kettle of boiling, salted water and boil 2 hours or until tender. Drain, peel and slice; add salt and pepper, the onions, and cover with vinegar and water equal parts, more or less according to taste. Serve slightly warm or cold. Place in jars well covered.

No. 2

2 small heads celery root,
2 cups stalk celery, diced,
½ cup vinegar,
¼ cup sugar,
¼ teaspoon pepper,
1 teaspoon salt,
¼ lb. almonds, blanched and chopped,
½ cup thick, sour cream.

Scrub celery root well, and boil several hours until tender in salted water. Peel and slice, then measure and take an equal measure of stalk celery. Mix with the rest of the ingredients, adding the sour cream last. Place in salad bowl and serve cold.

CELERY AND CABBAGE SALAD IN GREEN PEPPERS

Hollow out green peppers and fill with chopped celery and chopped cabbage equal parts. Either Mayonnaise, page 191, or Vinaigrette dressing, page 188, can be used with it.

WAX BEAN SALAD

1 pint wax beans,
1 pint cut celery,
1 head lettuce,
French Salad Dressing, or
⅔ cup cream Mayonnaise.

Add celery and fold in cream Mayonnaise, page 189; serve on lettuce.

Mix the cooked cold beans with French dressing, page 188. Add 1 teaspoon finely-cut chives or onions. Pile in center of salad dish and arrange around base thin slices of radishes. Garnish top with radish cut to represent a tulip.

RUSSIAN VEGETABLE SALAD

1 cup peas,
1 cup carrots, diced,
1 cup turnips, diced,
1 cup string beans in ½ inch pieces,
French dressing,
Boiled Salad Dressing.

Cook each vegetable separately and drain. Marinate each with French Dressing, page 188, arrange in 4 sections on a dish upon a bed of lettuce. Potatoes may be used in place of turnips, or a combination of any two of the vegetables. Add Boiled Dressing, No. 1, page 190, and put small sprigs of parsley or finely chopped whites of hard cooked eggs and the yolks forced through a strainer, in lines, dividing sections.

WATER LILY SALAD

1 large or two small heads of lettuce,
3 or 6 hard cooked eggs.

Cook eggs one-half hour. When cold, remove the shell and cut the egg crosswise in small points to resemble leaves of a flower.

Carefully wash and wipe the lettuce; cut the large leaves into narrow shreds, but save the nicest small ones whole. Then make a Boiled Dressing, No. 1, page 190, arrange the finely shredded lettuce in the bottom of the platter, pour over the dressing, arrange the leaves on top of it, put half an egg in the center of each leaf. Garnish with radishes.

EGG SALAD

3 to 6 eggs, hard cooked,
Mayonnaise Dressing,
1 beet boiled,
Lettuce.

A pretty salad may be arranged upon small plates by bordering the plates with cress, parsley or lettuce leaves; dress with rich Mayonnaise, page 192, arrange thin slices of hard cooked egg and about the edge of each plate have small hearts cut from boiled beets. Cut beet in ¼ inch slices, then form with small vegetable cutter. The beets may be omitted.

STUFFED BEET SALAD

Beets,
Cold boiled potatoes,
Celery,
Mayonnaise.

Boil without peeling, medium sized beets until they are tender. Cut a slice off the bottom, so that they will stand upright, and scoop the inside out carefully, keeping the shell as whole as possible. Peel the shells, and when cold fill with a mixture of the beet centers, cold boiled potatoes and celery all cut in small pieces, and well moistened with good Mayonnaise, page 192. Serve on lettuce leaves, and place a slice of hard boiled egg on each portion of salad. Any other salad may be served in the beets.

CAULIFLOWER AND BEET SALAD

1 head cauliflower, boiled,	Salt and pepper,
1 large beet, boiled,	Oil,
A head of lettuce,	Vinegar or lemon juice.

Dress flowerets of cold cooked cauliflower with oil, salt, pepper, and vinegar, or lemon juice. Dress the shredded outside leaves of a head of lettuce, and a beet cut in slices and then in figures, and the chopped trimmings, each separately with the same ingredients. Dispose the lettuce on the centre of a serving-dish, and the carefully drained cauliflower above. Sprinkle with the figures cut from the beets, and dispose the chopped beets in points around the central mass. Serve mayonnaise in a dish apart.

CHESTNUT SALAD

Chestnut salad is much in favor, and great is the variety both in method of preparation and serving. The chestnuts should in any case be cooked until very tender, cooled and mixed with French Dressing, page 188, or Mayonnaise Dressing, page 192.

Equal parts of shredded celery and chestnuts is a popular combination.

Bananas, apples, celery and chestnuts go well together. The fruit is pared, cored and cut in slices and mixed with the chestnut meats. Dress with mayonnaise dressing and garnish with lettuce hearts.

ARTICHOKES SALAD

Boil the French artichokes from 30 to 40 minutes, until the leaves may be easily pulled out. Cool, and then put on ice. Serve with a thin Mayonnaise, page 191, or with a Vinaigrette Dressing, page 188.

ASPARAGUS SALAD

No. 1

Take boiled or canned asparagus, drain; season with salt and pepper and add 1 cup vinegar.

Serve cold on crisp lettuce leaf with 1 teaspoon Mayonnaise Dressing, page 191, on the side of the dish, or pour French Salad Dressing, page 188, over the drained, boiled or canned asparagus. Serve cold.

ASPARAGUS SALAD
No. 2

1 bunch asparagus,
2 hard cooked eggs,
Boiled dressing,
Lettuce leaves.

Cook asparagus until tender and cut into one inch pieces. Place with lettuce leaves, mix with Boiled Dressing, No. 2, page 191, and garnish with the eggs cut lengthwise in quarters.

SHERRY'S SALAD

4 small red peppers,
8 green peppers,
½ small Bermuda onion,
Chopped parsley,
½ cup olive oil,
5 tablespoons vinegar,
½ teaspoon powdered sugar,
1 teaspoon salt,
Lettuce leaves.

Chop onion very fine and add twice as much chopped parsley as onion. Chop peppers and mix all together and let stand in covered glass fruit can one hour. Shake hard for five minutes and serve very cold on a bed of tender lettuce leaves.

BIRD'S NEST SALAD

½ lb. cream cheese,
¼ lb. nut meats, chopped,
1 head lettuce,
1 cup Mayonnaise Dressing,
1 teaspoon chopped parsley.

Mix nut meats and parsley with any good cream cheese, form into balls size of a hickory nut. Take the center crisp leaves of head lettuce, form 3 or 4 for each plate into a nest. Place balls in nest, add Mayonnaise Dressing, page 190, and serve cold.

CELERY AND NUT SALAD

1½ cup celery, diced,
½ cup pecans, shelled,
½ cup olives, pitted,
½ red or green pepper, chopped,
Mayonnaise Dressing,
Cress or lettuce.

Mix the first four ingredients and serve cold with Mayonnaise Dressing, page 191, on lettuce leaves or in green or red peppers, tops off, and scooped out. If cress is used, wash and dry well. Arrange on outside edge of platter.

CELERY, APPLE AND NUT SALAD (Waldorf)

2 cups celery, cut,
2 cups apples, sliced and diced,
1 cup pecan and walnut meats, crumbled,
Mayonnaise dressing.

Clean the celery and lettuce and keep them crisp in a wet napkin on the ice. When ready to serve, cut the celery in thin crescent shaped pieces; cut the apples in eighths, remove core and skin and slice crosswise in thin pieces, then crumble the pecans and walnuts. Take equal parts of celery and apple and ¼ part of nuts. Mix with Mayonnaise, pages 190 to 192, to hold together. Arrange the mixture on a platter in a mound with lettuce around the edge, and cover with Mayonnaise, and garnish with thin rings or crescents of red skinned apple and the celery tips. Two figs cut in small pieces may be added.

PINEAPPLE SALAD

1 can pineapple, sliced,
½ lb. English walnuts, shelled,
2 cups celery, diced,
Cream Mayonnaise Dressing.

Drain the pineapple; halve the walnuts, wash and cut the celery in small pieces.

Just before serving mix all together and add a Cream Mayonnaise Dressing, page 189. Serve cold on lettuce leaves; or,

Just before serving hollow out and peel apples, as many as you need; fill with the celery and pineapple, and cover with Mayonnaise. Serve ice cold.

CHERRY SALAD

1 can large California cherries, red or white,
Filbert nutmeats,
French dressing,
Lettuce leaves or
Squares of lemon jelly.

Drain and pit the cherries and fill them with the nut meats, whole or chopped. Add to French Dressing, page 188, the juice of the cherries. Pour over cherries and serve very cold on crisp lettuce leaves or on squares of Lemon Jelly, page 210, using the hot cherry juice in place of the boiling water to dissolve the gelatine. Appropriate for Washington's Birthday parties.

ORANGE OR GRAPE FRUIT SALAD

Carefully remove the pulp from the grape fruit or oranges. Have large pieces. Have an equal amount of celery cut in dice and lettuce or endive for decoration. Dress with French Dressing, page 188, or with Mayonnaise, page 190, whitened with whipped cream, and serve very cold.

COMQUARD SALAD

Dress on a plate, Chicory or Endive Salad, (selecting the sweet bleached leaves), curled celery and sliced comquards, (small orange-like fruit). Cover with a thin Mayonnaise, page 191, and serve very cold.

BANANA CROQUETTES SALAD

4 bananas,	¼ teaspoon fine salt,
3/4 cup pecan nuts,	2/3 cup Mayonnaise,
1 head lettuce.	

Chop nuts in bowl until fine, add salt. Peel bananas and cut in halves crosswise, removing the round ends, so they are as uniform as may be, dip each in Cream Mayonnaise, page 189, diluted with 1 tablespoon of milk or cream (if too thick to drain well), roll bananas in nuts and serve on lettuce with a teaspoon of Mayonnaise beside it.

OYSTER SALAD

1 pint oysters,	1 teaspoon Worcestershire
1 pint celery,	Sauce,
Lemon slices,	Lettuce,
French Dressing,	Parsley.

Wash and drain oysters. Place in stew pan with a little water and cook until oysters are plump and edges begin to curl. If oysters are large, cut into quarters. Add celery to oyster and pour over French Dressing, page 188, with a scant teaspoon Worcestershire added. Serve on lettuce leaves and decorate with lemon slices and sprigs of parsley.

SHRIMP AND CUCUMBER SALAD

Shrimp,	Mayonnaise,
A fresh cucumber,	Lettuce.
French Dressing,	

Break shrimps in pieces and pour over it a French Dressing, page 188. Let stand until serving time, then add to it an equal amount of chilled cubes of cucumber, and mix with a little Mayonnaise, page 192. Place on serving dish, on crisp lettuce leaves, decorate with whole shrimps and sliced cucumbers, dressed with some of the French Dressing.

SHAD ROE AND CUCUMBER SALAD

A Shad Roe,
1 slice onion,
1 bay leaf,
1 tablespoon vinegar,
1 fresh cucumber,
French Dressing,
Mayonnaise,
Lettuce.

Let shad roe simmer 20 minutes in salted water with the vinegar added. Cool, cut in slices and cubes and pour over it a French Dressing, page 188; add cucumber, peeled, cut in cubes, and Mayonnaise, page 191, to moisten. Place salad on a bed of crisp lettuce leaves; garnish with sliced cucumbers.

SALMON SALAD

1 lb. can salmon,
1½ cups celery,
Lettuce,
1 cup Mayonnaise Dressing.

Free the salmon from skin, bones and oil; pick the fish apart and add the celery (which has been cut fine) and Mayonnaise Dressing, page 190, tossing lightly. Season to taste. Save a little Mayonnaise to pour over the top. Arrange in salad dish and garnish with curled lettuce and drops of red jelly, or serve on fresh, crisp lettuce leaves.

LAMB AND MINT SALAD

2 cups cold lamb, in
   ½ inch cubes,
1 cup cold potatoes, sliced,
2 hard cooked eggs,
Mayonnaise,
1 tablespoon gelatine,
⅓ cup cold water,
½ cup mint leaves,
1 cup boiling water,
Salt and cayenne pepper,
Green vegetable coloring.

Soak the granulated gelatine in the cold water a few minutes to soften; steep the mint in the boiling water, then strain it while boiling over the gelatine; if desired, color green with a few drops of green vegetable coloring, seasoning with salt and cayenne pepper. Stir and cool, then place on ice to harden. Cut the cold lamb in small cubes, mix with half its bulk of sliced cold potatoes, season with salt and pepper, mix with Mayonnaise, page 190, and garnish with slices of hard cooked eggs and the mint jelly cut in fancy shapes.

LIVER AND EGG SALAD

6 chicken livers, or	4 hard cooked eggs,
Some calf's liver,	3 small onions,

French Dressing, No. 1.

Bake or fry the liver; chop eggs and liver not too fine, chop onion very fine. Mix with French Dressing, No. 1, page 188, using chicken or goose fat in place of the olive oil. Serve cold on lettuce leaves.

TONGUE SALAD

Fresh tomatoes,	2 cups celery, diced,
1 cup cold, boiled, pickled tongue,	½ cup Mayonnaise, Lettuce leaves.

Cut tops of sound round tomatoes, but do not peel. Scoop out the juice and pulp and set aside to keep cool. Add some of the firm pulp to tongue and celery and mix with some of the Mayonnaise, page 189, thinned with cream or lemon juice. Keep cool, at serving time fill the tomato cups, place on lettuce, add a tablespoon of the Mayonnaise on the top of each tomato.

HAM OR TONGUE SALAD FOR 12 PEOPLE

2 lbs. cold boiled ham or tongue,	Mayonnaise, ½ cup capers,
½ teaspoon paprika,	Red radishes.

Chop ham or tongue very fine. Sprinkle with paprika and mix with Mayonnaise for Cold Meat, No. 2, page 190. Place on platter. Garnish, dividing the meat in sections and fill dividing lines with capers. Make a circle of red radishes cut to resemble tulips, and place around the meat; add a border of Saratoga Chips, page 174.

CHICKEN SALAD

1 pt. chicken, diced,	½ spk. pepper,
½ pt. cut celery,	1 tablespoon vinegar,
2 tablespoons salad oil,	2 tablespoons Mayonnaise,
¼ teaspoon salt,	1 tablespoon capers.

Mayonnaise, olives, celery leaves or white lettuce for garnishing. Cut the cold chicken into one-half inch cubes. Cut the cleaned celery into pieces about twice as large. Mix these together and pour over the oil. Mix well, then sprinkle with the salt and pepper; add the vinegar. Mix well and set in a cold place for 2 or 3 hours. Then add the Mayonnaise, pages 189–192, and put on a bed of lettuce.

NOTE—Veal may be used in place of the chicken, or use half chicken and half veal.

CHICKEN SALAD IN TOMATOES

Cut a slice from the top of as many ripe, smooth tomatoes as you wish to serve. Scoop the inside out carefully, keeping the shell as whole as possible. Make chicken salad after foregoing recipe and fill in the tomato shells. Place on lettuce leaves on small plates and dress the top of each tomato with a teaspoon of Mayonnaise, page 190.

MUSHROOM SALAD

2 cans mushrooms,
½ can peas,
⅓ teaspoon salt,
1 tablespoon butter,
2 times (bulk of other ingredients), celery,
1 head lettuce,
¾ cup Cream Mayonnaise.

Drain, then fry mushrooms until delicate brown, using butter and salt; cool, drain peas quite dry, add to mushrooms. Cut celery enough to measure twice the bulk. Fold in with Mayonnaise, page 189. Serve on lettuce. For six people.

CHICKEN, SWEETBREADS AND MUSHROOM SALAD

1 pt. cooked chicken cut in small pieces,
1 cup sweetbreads in small pieces,
1 cup mushrooms,
1 cup Mayonnaise,
Lettuce leaves.

Have everything very cold. Mix the first three ingredients with the Mayonnaise, page 192, and place on lettuce leaves on small plates.

NOTE—Chicken and sweetbreads, dressed with Mayonnaise is also a good combination.

SWEETBREADS AND MUSHROOM SALAD

3 lbs. sweetbreads,
2 cans mushrooms,
1 cup walnuts, blanched,
4 large stalks celery, diced,
Whites of 6 hard cooked eggs, cut in ½ inch dice,
2 cups boiled Mayonnaise,
Yolks of 6 hard cooked eggs.

Follow directions for Boiled Sweetbreads, page 129, adding a small onion, carrot and celery to water for flavor. When tender and cool, trim and cut into ½ inch dice. Break walnuts into large pieces. Drain mushrooms and cut each mushroom in half. Double the recipe for Boiled Mayonnaise, No. 3, page 190, and thin with plain or whipped cream. Have all the ingredients ice cold; when ready to serve, mix the first five, with the Mayonnaise. Serve on lettuce leaves and garnish with the yolks, riced, lightly over the top. This serves 24 people.

SWEETBREAD AND PEA SALAD

2 cups sweetbreads, cut in dice,
2 cups celery, diced,
1 cup cooked or canned peas, drained,
1 cup Mayonnaise.

Follow recipe for boiling sweetbreads, page 129. Have all the ingredients very cold, and just before serving mix with the Mayonnaise, page 191, and place on crisp lettuce leaves. May also be served in tomato or green peppers, scooped out.

NOTE—Chicken may be used in place of the sweetbreads. Canned corn, drained, may be used in place of the peas.

SWEETBREAD, CUCUMBER AND TOMATO SALAD

¾ cup sweetbreads, in cubes,
Sliced cucumbers,
Sliced tomatoes,
French Dressing,
Mayonnaise,
Whipped cream.

Pour French Dressing, page 188, over the Sweetbreads, that are boiled, cooled and diced. Drain and mix with sliced cucumbers and Mayonnaise Dressing, page 192, whitened with whipped cream. Arrange in a salad dish, with a circle of sliced, chilled tomatoes on lettuce leaves, dressed with French Dressing. On the tomato place slices of sweetbread capped with stars of Mayonnaise.

ASPIC JELLY, No. 1

3 pints clear strong soup stock,
Whites and shells of 2 eggs,
2 oz. (1 package) granulated gelatine,
1 cup cold water.

Take fish or meat stock, enough stock to fill the mould. Season highly with salt, pepper, celery seed, herbs, lemon, vinegar or wine. If ½ cup of wine is used for flavoring, take that much less of soup stock. Place gelatine in large sauce pan, add the cold water and let stand a few minutes to soften. Have the soup stock cold and carefully remove every particle of fat and do not use the sediment at the bottom. Add to this the crushed shell and white of egg or eggs, slightly beaten, whisk well together and set over the fire to heat, stirring all the time, until the liquid boils. Let boil 5 minutes, set on back of stove for 5 minutes. Shim carefully and then strain through a fine napkin. Pour into moulds and set aside several hours or over night to chill and harden.

If the mould is to be decorated, pack it in a pan of snow or broken ice and pour in jelly to the depth of ½ inch. When hard, garnish with fancy vegetables of different colors, slices of hard cooked eggs and the like. Fasten each ornament in place with liquid jelly and when hard add enough jelly to cover all. When this is hard, place the meat or whatever you have to mould in the center, being careful not to let it break the jelly. Keep the meat in place with some of the liquid jelly, and when hard add enough jelly to fill the mould. Keep in cool place until ready to serve. To remove it, dip the mould quickly in warm water, put the dish over it and invert dish and mould together and serve, garnished to suit taste. Tongue, boned turkey or chicken, fish and meat may be served in the jelly.

ASPIC JELLY, No. 2

1 teaspoon extract of beef,
1 oz. (½ package) granulated gelatine,
½ cup cold water,
1 pint hot water, or cleared soup stock,
2 teaspoons sugar,
½ cup Sherry wine.

Cover gelatine with cold water, let stand 5 minutes. Add hot soup stock or beef extract, dissolved in a little hot water; add sugar and wine. Stir until dissolved. Strain and put into mould until cold. To clear soup, add shell and white of egg. See recipe above.

For garnishing Salads, Game, and Entrees, and for the Invalid and Convalescent.

HOME MADE RING MOULD

Place a coffee cup within a quart bowl; or a small pail within a larger pail, if you have no regular ring mould. Fill the smaller dish with ice, or ice water. Pour the gelatine pudding or jelly between the two dishes or pails. When the jelly is all firm, remove the ice and add warm and not hot water to the smaller dish; take it out carefully and you have a ring or border of jelly. Fill with any desired cream or salad.

TOMATO ASPIC WITH SALAD

1 can tomatoes, or	2 tablespoons vinegar,
8 medium tomatoes,	2 tablespoons granulated gelatine (1 oz.),
6 cloves,	
2 small onions, chopped fine,	1 lemon, grated rind and juice,
1 bay leaf,	
1 teaspoon salt,	½ cup cold water.
1 teaspoon whole black pepper,	

Boil the first 7 ingredients until the tomatoes are soft, then strain; reserve 2 cups, reheat to the boiling point. Soften the gelatine in ½ cup water a few minutes; then pour on the boiling, strained and well flavored tomato juice and lemon rind and juice and stir until dissolved. Strain and pour in small cups and set aside in cool place over night to harden. Invert and serve as fresh tomatoes on lettuce leaves with Mayonnaise Dressing, page 191. Or cut in cubes and use as a garnish for cold meats. Or pour in ring mould and serve as a border to sweetbread or chicken salad.

LEMON JELLY

¼ box of strip gelatine, or	3 tablespoons lemon juice,
1¼ tablespoons granulated gelatine,	½ cup sugar,
	1 cup boiling water.
¼ cup cold water,	

Soak the gelatine in the cold water 15 minutes for strip gelatine; 1 minute for granulated gelatine; dissolve in the boiling water. Add the sugar and lemon juice. When the sugar is dissolved, strain through a cheese cloth into moulds or glasses which have been wet in cold water. Chill and serve; cut in cubes, or pour into lemon shells, cut in half lengthwise; when hard cut in half lengthwise again, to represent lemons cut into quarters, or pour into ring moulds and serve as a border to any salad.

WINE JELLY

1⅛ tablespoon granulated gelatine,	1 cup boiling water,
	⅓ cup sugar,
1 tablespoon lemon juice,	¼ cup Sherry, or Port wine,
¼ cup cold water,	Or equal parts of each.

Soak the gelatine in the cold water, let stand 2 minutes, add the boiling water and sugar and stir until dissolved, then add wine; strain and pour into moulds. Set aside in cool place several hours, or over night, to harden. Serve cold. In warm weather use less water.

MOULDED SALAD JELLY

½ package (1 oz.) granulated gelatine,
½ cup cold water,
½ cup vinegar,
Juice of 1 lemon,
1 pint of boiling water,
½ cup sugar,
1 teaspoon salt,
3 cups of any mixed salad food, diced.

Soak gelatine in cold water 2 minutes, add vinegar, lemon juice, boiling water, sugar and salt. Strain and when beginning to set add remaining ingredients. Turn into a mold and chill. Serve on lettuce leaves with Mayonnaise Dressing.

MIXED MOULDED SALAD COMBINATION

No. 1

Two cups celery cut in small pieces, 1 cup finely shredded cabbage, ¼ can sweet red peppers, finely cut. Add Moulded Salad Jelly above.

No. 2

One cup apples, diced, 1 cup celery, cut in small pieces, ½ cup broken nutmeats (boiled chestnuts are good), ½ cup bananas, sliced. Mix with Moulded Salad Jelly above.

No. 3

Two cups cold cooked halibut, diced, 1 cup mixed and finely diced or sliced, stuffed olives, pickle or cucumber, celery capers, sweet red peppers, red beets, alone or in any desired combination.

No. 4

Two cups cold cooked sweetbreads, or chicken, or veal, diced; ½ cup celery, cut in small pieces; ½ cup olives, cut in rings; capers; slices of fresh pear and broken nut meats, mixed. Asparagus tips may be used, but they must be carefully placed in the jelly just when it hardens.

MOULDED SWEETBREAD AND CUCUMBER SALAD

¼ cup sweetbreads, in cubes,
1 slice onion,
A bit of bay leaf,
A blade of mace,
¾ cup cucumber, cubes,
½ cup boiling water,
1 teaspoon granulated gelatine,
1 tablespoon cold water,
1½ tablespoons vinegar,
Lettuce leaves,
French Dressing.

Parboil a pair of sweetbreads, page 129, adding to the boiling, salted water the onion, bay leaf and mace. Cool and cut into cubes.

Soak the gelatine in cold water a few minutes, add the boiling water, and stir until dissolved. Let stand to slightly harden. Rinse a ring or other mould in very cold water, place a few spoonfuls in bottom of mould, add a layer of sweetbread and cucumber dices, then a layer of gelatine mixture, again the cucumber and sweetbread cubes and so on until all is used; leaving the layer of jelly on top. Serve on large platter with a border of lettuce leaves on which is arranged a circle of chilled, sliced tomatoes; cover with French Dressing, page 188. If ring mould is used fill center with Sweetbread Salad, page 208, and Mayonnaise Dressing, page 192.

TOMATO ASPIC SALAD

2½ cups Tomato Aspic,
2 cups English celery, diced,
½ cup Mayonnaise Dressing.

Make Tomato Aspic, page 210. Pour in mould or shallow pan, to harden over night or for several hours—dependent on the weather. Cut in slices, mix in the celery, and cover with Mayonnaise, page 189, or pour in ring mould and serve with center filled with chicken or sweetbread salad.

JELLIED CUCUMBER SALAD

¾ cup fresh cucumbers, cut in dice,
3 tablespoons tarragon vinegar,
2 tablespoons pickled nasturtium seeds, chopped fine,
1 tablespoon granulated gelatine,
¼ cup cold water,
1 cup boiling cleared chicken or veal broth,
Salt and pepper to taste.

Peel the cucumber and chop rather fine, add the nasturtium seeds and the vinegar. Soak the gelatine in cold water a few minutes, stir in the boiling broth and stir until dissolved, season with salt and pepper to taste. Let cool, then add to the cucumber mixture. Pour into mould and set aside several hours or over night to harden in a cool place. Serve, cut in tiny cubes in tomato cups with Mayonnaise or a Boiled Dressing, pages 189 to 192, on lettuce leaves.

Wine or Lemon Jelly, page 210, may be used with the Cucumber and Nasturtium Mixture, if desired.

CHAPTER XX

ENTREES

BATTER FOR FRITTERS

No. 1

1⅓ cups flour,	¼ teaspoon salt,
2 teaspoons baking powder,	⅔ cup milk,
1 egg.	

Mix and sift the dry ingredients, add milk gradually and the egg well beaten.

No. 2

1 egg,	⅛ teaspoon salt,
¼ cup water or milk,	½ cup flour,
1 tablespoon melted butter.	

Beat the yolk and the white of the egg separately. To the yoke add the butter and salt and one-half of the liquid, and stir in the flour to make a smooth dough. Add the remainder of the liquid gradually to make a batter, and beat in the stiff white of the egg.

DIRECTIONS FOR FRYING

Frying is cooking in deep hot fat.

Cooking in Deep Fat—General Rules

The fat used for cooking may be olive oil, cottonseed oil, cottolene, beef drippings, lard, or a mixture of several fats.

The food must be covered with crumbs and egg, or a batter, to keep it from absorbing fat.

Place the articles to be cooked in a bath of the fat, deep enough to float them. The kettle should be of iron; a frying basket may be used.

Foods already cooked or needing little cooking require a higher temperature than batters. The temperature of the fat for oysters, croquettes, fish balls, etc., may be tested by browning a cube of bread while counting forty. Counting sixty, while the bread browns, gives the right temperature for all other batters.

All the articles cooked must be drained on unglazed, brown paper.

When one quantity of food has been taken from the fat, it must be reheated and tested before adding a second set.

In the absence of a frying basket, a wire spoon may be used to remove the food from the fat.

Fat which has been used for frying should be cooled and clarified by cooking with a few slices of raw potato in it for 10 minutes; strain through muslin, and when cold cover. Fat may be used several times for frying and then be made into soap.

APPLE FRITTERS

2 medium sized sour apples, Powder sugar,
Batter No. 1 or 2, Lemon juice.

Core, pare and cut apples in ⅓ inch rounds or slices, sprinkle with powdered sugar and a few drops of lemon juice, cover and let stand ½ hour. Drain, dip pieces in batter No. 1 or No. 2, page 213, fry in deep hot fat and drain. Sprinkle with sugar and cinnamon.

PINEAPPLE FRITTERS

Soak slices of pineapple in Sherry or white wine, with a little sugar and let stand one hour. Drain and dip slices in Batter No. 1 or 2, page 213, and fry in deep hot fat. Drain on brown paper and sprinkle with powdered sugar.

FRUIT FRITTERS

Fresh peaches, apricots or pears may be cut in pieces, dipped in batter and fried same as other fritters.

Canned fruits may be used after being drained.

QUEEN FRITTERS

½ cup boiling milk or water, 2 tablespoons powdered sugar,
¼ cup butter, 2 eggs,
½ cup flour, Pinch of salt,
Fruit Preserves.

Put butter in small saucepan and pour on water. Heat to boiling point, add flour all at once and stir until mixture leaves sides of sauce pan and cleaves to spoon. Remove from fire, add eggs, one at a time, beating constantly. Drop by spoonfuls and fry in deep fat until well puffed and browned.

Drain, make an opening, fill with preserves and sprinkle with powdered sugar.

TO PREPARE BREAD CRUMBS

Dry pieces of bread thoroughly, either in the open air or in a slow oven. Crush them fine and even with a rolling pin or run them through a food chopper. If two grades are desired, sift them, keeping the finer crumbs in one jar and the coarser in another.

HOW TO EGG AND CRUMB CROQUETTES

Break an egg in a plate, beat slightly with a fork and add 1 tablespoon water. Place a fork and tablespoon in this mixture.

Fill another plate with crumbs.

Roll the croquette in crumbs to dry it. Place it upon the fork and dip the egg over it with the spoon, carefully covering every part. Drain and slip from the fork into the crumbs. Cover croquette well with crumbs before handling it.

Be careful not to get the fork and spoon into the crumbs.

RICE CROQUETTES

1 pt. cold, cooked rice,
2 or 3 tablespoons milk,
1 egg,
2 tablespoons butter,
½ teaspoon salt,
little white pepper,
Cayenne,
2 tablespoons chopped parsley.

Warm the rice in a double boiler, with enough of the milk to soften it. Add the butter, seasoning and beaten egg, and cook until the egg thickens. Spread the mixture on a shallow plate to cool, then shape into rolls. Roll in fine bread crumbs which have been seasoned with salt and pepper; dip in beaten egg, and roll in crumbs again. Cook in deep hot fat until brown.

CHICKEN CROQUETTES

3½ cups chopped chicken,
Onion juice,
1 tablespoon parsley,
2 teaspoons lemon juice.

Make 1 pint of very Thick White Sauce, page 88.

Chop the chicken very fine, and add sauce to make it as soft as can be handled. Cool as in making rice croquettes, and shape and cook in the same way.

Sometimes a beaten egg is added to the sauce before mixing it with the meat.

LOBSTER CHOPS

2 large lobsters, boiled,	1 teaspoon chopped parsley,
½ teaspoon grated onion,	1 cup thick white sauce.

Chop the lobster meat, make a Thick White Sauce, page 88. Add the boiled lobster meat, then the onion and parsley. Cook thoroughly, add salt and cayenne pepper to taste. Remove from stove. Divide in heaps, about ten, on a piece of clean paper, and cool thoroughly. Form into chop shape, and roll in egg and then in grated bread crumbs. Fry in deep hot fat. Serve with a claw in each, to represent the bone. Serve very hot, with Tartare Sauce, page 92.

CRAB MEAT CHOPS

2 cupfuls crab meat, boiled and picked,	1 teaspoon chopped parsley,
1 cup thick white sauce,	½ teaspoon chopped onion,
	½ teaspoon salt,

Cayenne pepper.

Make Thick White Sauce, page 88, mix with the rest of the ingredients.

Cook all together and cool. Make 8 separate heaps of this and let stand an hour. Take each heap and form into a chop shape, dip in beaten egg, dredge in cracker dust and fry in hot, deep fat. Serve with hot Tartare Sauce, page 92, or Hollandaise Sauce, page 91.

SALMON CROQUETTES

1 lb. can salmon,	¼ cup cracker crumbs,
½ teaspoon salt,	½ teaspoon grated onion,
cayenne pepper,	1 well beaten egg,

1 tablespoon chopped parsley.

From a can of salmon, opened neatly, take the fish and mince it fine; add salt and pepper, and a tablespoonful of chopped parsley or celery tops and cracker crumbs; moisten it with a raw egg and mix well, turn it out upon a dish; then roll it into cones, dip these in beaten egg seasoned with salt and pepper, roll them in bread crumbs, drop into deep, hot fat and fry a delicate brown, drain them a moment, arrange neatly on a hot dish and serve with Tartare Sauce, page 92.

CHESTNUT CROQUETTES

1 cup mashed French chestnuts,	2 yolks of eggs,
2 tablespoons thick cream,	1 teaspoon sugar,
	¼ teaspoon vanilla.

Mix ingredients in order given. Shape in balls, dip in crumbs again, fry in deep hot fat and drain. See Chestnuts, page 160.

EGG CUTLETS

6 hard cooked eggs,	½ teaspoon paprika,
1 cup Thick White Sauce,	1 teaspoon onion juice,
1 tablespoon chopped parsley.	

Chop eggs rather coarsely, and add the parsley. Make a Thick White Sauce, page 88. Season to taste with onion juice, paprika and salt. Take from the fire and add the eggs and parsley.

Spread out on a buttered dish and set away until cold. Dust the hands lightly with flour and shape spoonfuls of mixture in small cutlets, being careful to pat them out until of an even thickness; use as little flour as possible, or the creamy consistency will be lost. When all are shaped, dip each cutlet into slightly beaten egg, then in fine, dried bread crumbs, and immerse in hot deep fat until golden brown. Drain on unglazed paper and serve with Tomato, page 93, or Cream Sauce, page 88.

SWEDISH TIMBALE CASES

¾ cup flour,	½ cup milk,
½ teaspoon salt,	1 egg,
1 teaspoon sugar,	1 tablespoon olive oil.

Mix dry ingredients, add milk gradually and beaten egg; then oil. Put timbale iron deep enough into hot fat to more than cover it and let heat. Turn timbale into a cup. Lower hot iron into cup to only ¾ its depth. Then immerse iron in the deep, hot fat again, the mixture will rise to top of iron and when crisp and brown, may be easily slipped off. If the cases are not crisp the batter is too thick and must be diluted with milk.

Fill cases with creamed chicken, sweetbreads, oyster or chicken and sweetbreads in combination with mushrooms or with peas.

FISH AND CHEESE IN TIMBALES OR RAMIKINS

1½ lbs. cold, cooked halibut, chopped fine,
2 cups cream sauce,
1 teaspoon Worcestershire sauce,
½ cup soup stock,
¼ lb. Parmesan Cheese.

Follow recipe for Cream Sauce, page 88, add the Worcestershire sauce and soup stock, mix with the chopped halibut, place on stove and heat. Fill in well buttered ramikins or timbale forms. Sprinkle plentifully with grated parmesan cheese and bake 15 minutes in a moderate oven, in a pan half filled with warm water. This serves 9 people.

CANNED CORN TIMBALES

1 cup corn pulp,
2 yolks, beaten,
1 teaspoon salt,
⅛ teaspoon white pepper,
Cayenne,
1 tablespoon melted butter,
1 teaspoon sugar,
½ cup soft bread crumbs,
2 whites of eggs.

Chop, mash and sift enough corn to make 1 cup of the pulp. Add well beaten egg yolks, salt, white pepper and a few grains of cayenne, melted butter, sugar and fine, soft white bread crumbs. Mix them, then add the stiffly beaten whites. It should be stiff enough to just drop from the spoon.

If too stiff, add cream; if too thin, add more crumbs. Turn it into well buttered, small tin timbale moulds till ⅔ full. Place them in a pan of hot water, cover with buttered paper and bake about 20 minutes, or till puffed up all over. Turn out on a shallow dish and garnish with parsley.

EGG TIMBALES—FOR 6 PEOPLE

5 eggs,
1 cup milk,
1 large pinch white pepper,
1 teaspoon chopped parsley,
⅛ teaspoon salt.

Beat the whole eggs till lemon colored, then add rest of the ingredients.

Butter the timbale forms, fill with mixture and place forms in a pan half filled with water and bake 15 minutes in moderate oven. Serve with Cream Sauce, page 88.

SALMON TIMBALES

1 lb. fresh salmon,
¼ lb. blanched almonds, chopped,
⅛ teaspoon salt,
1 pinch white pepper,
1 teaspoon Worcestershire sauce,
1 teaspoon onion juice,
1 egg,
1 cup whipped cream.

Chop salmon very fine, add almonds, seasoning, the egg yolks and the white, beaten stiff; then whipped cream and fill into buttered timbale forms, bake in pan half filled with cold water 15 minutes.

Turn them out in warm plates, and serve at once with Cream Sauce, page 88, colored with a pinch of pistachio coloring.

HALIBUT TIMBALE

½ lb. halibut, cut fine,
1 cup grated bread crumbs,
½ cup milk,
1 teaspoon salt,
A dash of white pepper,
Beaten whites of 5 eggs.

Take uncooked halibut, cut it into fine pieces, pound it, put it through a strainer; heat bread crumbs with milk, stir to a smooth paste. Remove from fire, add the fish pulp, salt and white pepper; beat it lightly in the stiff froth of five eggs. Fill the mould or moulds, place in a pan of hot water in the oven for twenty minutes. Serve with a Tartare, page 92, or Hollandaise Sauce, page 91.

SWEETBREAD TIMBALES

1½ lb. sweetbreads,
1 teaspoon salt,
⅛ loaf stale wheat bread,
6 mushrooms,
¼ teaspoon grated onion,
1 pinch white pepper,
3 eggs,
6 truffles.

Parboil sweetbreads, and chop, add grated onion, salt and pepper. Soak bread in cold water, squeeze dry and mash through colander. Mix sweetbreads, bread, beaten yolks of eggs, mushrooms, then the stiffly beaten whites of eggs. Butter small timbale forms, put in a few pieces of truffles, cover with the sweetbread mixture, place forms in pan of boiling water. Cover with another pan and bake from ½ to ¾ hours. Serve with Cream Sauce, page 88. Truffles and mushrooms may be omitted.

CHICKEN TIMBALES

½ lb. raw white chicken meat, Whites of 5 eggs,
1 pint cold cream, Salt and white pepper.

Chop fine, and then pound the raw, white meat of a chicken from which the skin and sinews have been removed, add to this, while pounding, a rather scant pint of very cold cream, 1 teaspoon salt, white pepper, and the whites of 5 eggs, press through a sieve and then refill little tin moulds which have been well buttered, place them in a sauce pan in which you have put water about the depth of an inch. Cover the sauce pan, put into oven for twenty minutes, then turn out of moulds on to a round platter, or serve individually with Cream Sauce, page 88.

CHICKEN LIVER TIMBALES, No. 2

12 chicken livers, ½ teaspoon salt,
1 teaspoon butter, Speck white pepper,
¼ teaspoon chopped onion, 1 teaspoon chopped parsley,
5 eggs, 1 tablespoon bread crumbs.

Chop the raw livers and rub through a sieve. Place them in a pan and add butter and onion, cook 5 minutes and remove from stove to cool, add the seasonings, 5 egg yolks, bread crumbs and mix. Beat the whites to a stiff froth and add to the mixture. Grease the timbale forms and sprinkle with bread crumbs and bake, at once in pan half filled with water 15 minutes.

Serve hot with the following sauce:

1 tablespoon butter, ¼ teaspoon salt,
1 tablespoon flour, Pepper and parsley to taste,
½ cup cream, ¼ can mushrooms.

Heat butter, stir in flour, then cream, seasoning and mushrooms and cook until smooth.

CHEESE

CHEESE—General Rules

Cheese should not be tightly covered.

When it becomes dry and hard, grate and keep covered until ready to use. It may be added to starchy foods.

Soda, in cheese dishes which are cooked, makes the casein more digestible.

A soft, crumbly cheese is best for cooking.

Cheese is sufficiently cooked when melted, if cooked longer, it becomes tough and leathery.

COTTAGE CHEESE

Heat sour milk slowly until the whey rises to the top; pour it off, put the curd in a bag, and let it dry for six hours without squeezing it. Pour it into a bowl, and break it fine with a wooden spoon. Season with salt. Mould into balls and keep in a cool place. It is best when fresh.

BOILED CHEESE (Koch Kase)

Cottage cheese,
A little caraway seed,
A little salt,
Piece of butter,
1 egg, beaten.

Take fresh cottage cheese, press dry enough to grate, add caraway seed and only a little salt.

Spread in earthen dish, but do not press it down. Cover with plate. Put in a warm place, stir every day with a fork, until ripe and clear. Place butter in spider, add cheese and let come to a boil slowly, stirring constantly.

When melted take from stove and add the beaten egg. Put in china cups, well rinsed with cold water, and serve, when cold.

PREPARED CHEESE

1 tablespoon butter,
¼ lb. American cheese, cut fine or grated,
⅛ teaspoon cayenne pepper,
Yolk of 1 egg, beaten,
¼ cup cream.

Melt the butter, add cheese and pepper. Stir until melted, then beat in gradually the yolk of egg, diluted with cream, and cook, stirring constantly until thick and smooth. When smooth, set aside to become cold in small jars.

CHEESE BALLS

No. 1

1 cup creamery cheese, mild,
½ cup fine grated bread crumbs,
5 drops Worcestershire sauce,
1 egg, well beaten.

Mix well and roll into small balls; place in wire basket, and just before serving fry in deep hot lard a delicate brown.

No. 2

1 cup grated cheese,
1 teaspoon flour,
1 white of egg,
½ teaspoon salt,
Speck pepper.

Mix seasoning and flour with grated cheese, then beat into the stiffly beaten white of egg. Fry in deep, hot fat.

CHEESE BALLS

No. 3

1 cake Neufchatel cheese,
Piece of butter half the size of cheese,
6 dashes Tabasco sauce,
1 tablespoon cream,
¼ teaspoon salt.

Mix all well together in a bowl and form one large ball or small ones for each person, and roll in chopped pecan nuts.

CREAMED CHEESE

1 tablespoon butter,
1 cup milk,
2 tablespoons flour,
¼ cup grated cheese,
¼ teaspoon salt,
1 egg.

Melt butter in a sauce pan, stir in flour; when smooth add milk slowly and stir constantly, until mixture boils. Then place mixture over hot water, add the cheese and cook until it melts, stirring all the time.

Add beaten egg and cook 2 minutes. Serve on toast or crackers.

CHEESE FONDUE

No. 1

½ lb. grated cheese,
1 tablespoon butter,
1 teaspoon corn starch or
1 egg,
¼ teaspoon salt,
¼ teaspoon mustard,
Few grains cayenne pepper,
½ cup cream or milk.

Melt butter, remove from fire, add corn starch, stir until well mixed, then add cream gradually and cook 2 minutes. Add cheese and stir until cheese is melted. Season, and serve on crackers.

Either a double boiler or chafing dish may be used.

No. 2

½ cup bread crumbs,
1 scant cup milk,
1 egg, yolk and white beaten separately,
½ cup dry cheese, grated,
1 tablespoonful butter,
A speck of soda,
Salt and pepper to taste.

Soak crumbs in the milk, dissolve soda in a drop of hot water, and add to milk. Add rest of ingredients, beat well, pour into a well buttered baking-dish, strew dry crumbs moistened with butter over top, and bake in a hot oven until light brown. Serve at once in the dish in which it is baked.

OYSTER AND MACARONI

1 pint oysters,	1 cup White sauce,
1 pint boiled macaroni,	½ cup crackers, rolled.

Break and boil Macaroni, page 185, in salt water. Into a well greased pudding dish place drained oysters, and add macaroni, cover with White Sauce, page 87, which has some of the oyster liquor in it. Sprinkle with cracker crumbs and bits of butter. Bake until the crumbs are browned.

TOASTED CRACKERS AND CHEESE

Prepare grated cheese, moisten with cream, season with salt and cayenne pepper. Butter and cover each cracker with the mixture and return it to the oven. When cheese is melted the crackers are ready for use.

SCALLOPED FISH
(In Ramikins)

2 lbs. boiled fish, in ½ inch cubes,	¼ cup almonds, cut fine, Tomato Sauce,
1 cup bread crumbs,	Parsley.
2 tablespoons butter,	

Butter the crumbs. Butter the ramikins, sprinkle with the buttered bread crumbs, put in a layer of the shredded fish, sprinkle with the almonds and add another layer of fish. Cover with hot Tomato Sauce, page 93, and sprinkle bread crumbs on top. Place ramikins in a pan of hot water and bake from fifteen to twenty minutes or until the crumbs are slightly browned. Serve hot, decorated with parsley.

CHICKEN OR SWEETBREADS WITH MUSHROOMS
(In Ramikins)

½ cup mushrooms,	½ cup milk, cream or Mushroom liquid,
2 cups chicken or Sweetbreads, diced,	½ cup chicken or Sweetbread liquid,
2 tablespoons butter,	
2 tablespoons flour,	Salt, pepper and ginger,
2 tablespoons chopped almonds,	1 teaspoon chopped parsley.

Blanch the almonds, drain the mushrooms. Take equal parts of cold, boiled chicken or sweetbreads, diced and mushrooms. Heat butter, add flour and gradually one cup of hot liquid, milk or cream with mushrooms and chicken or sweetbread liquid. Boil until smooth, add seasoning and almonds and parsley.

Place in ramikins or in large pudding dish with buttered crumbs on top and brown in the oven.

If ramikins are used set them in a dish of hot water to prevent cracking.

SHRIMP SPANISH

(In Ramikins)

1 pint shrimp,	1 tablespoon cream,
1 tablespoon flour,	1 cup hot soup stock,
1 tablespoon butter,	2 yolks,
1 tablespoon catsup,	Salt, cayenne and grated onion.

Heat butter, add flour, add other ingredients in order given. Cook until smooth and add the shrimps. Fill this mixture into ramikins and cover with cracker dust and butter, and bake six minutes. Serve at once.

CHEESE RAMIKINS

4 tablespoons grated cheese,	Pepper and salt,
4 tablespoons grated bread,	½ cup cream,
2 tablespoons butter,	3 yolks,

3 whites beaten stiff.

Cook in a sauce pan until smooth, bread, cheese, butter and seasoning. Add yolk, then whites of egg. Grease the ramikins, fill three-fourths full and bake six minutes. Serve at once.

CHEESE SOUFFLE

2 tablespoons flour,	½ cup grated cheese,
2 tablespoons butter,	4 eggs,

1 pint of milk.

Rub butter and flour together over the fire, when they bubble, add gradually hot milk; season with pepper and salt. Add slowly the grated cheese. Remove from fire. Add the beaten yolks, cool the mixture, then add the beaten whites, stirring all together thoroughly. Put in pudding dish which has been well buttered, and bake in a moderately hot oven from fifteen to twenty minutes, until it is set—like custard. Serve at once.

TOMATO SOUFFLE

1 can tomatoes,	1 slice onion,
1 bay leaf,	2 tablespoons butter,
Bit of mace,	2 tablespoons flour,
1 teaspoon salt,	3 yolks beaten,
6 peppercorns,	3 whites beaten.

Cook the first six ingredients 20 minutes. Strain and reserve 1 cup of the strained tomato mixture. Melt butter, add flour, and pour in slowly the tomatoes. When smooth, pour this over 3 well beaten egg yolks, and set aside to cool. Beat three whites very stiff and mix gently with tomato sauce, and bake in a moderate oven about 20 minutes. Grated cheese may be sprinkled over the top thickly before baking. Serve immediately.

SHRIMP A LA CREOLE IN CASSEROLE

1 quart shrimps (boiled),	3 cloves,
½ can mushrooms,	1 bay leaf,
½ can French peas,	2 tablespoons catsup,
¼ can tomatoes,	Salt and cayenne pepper.
1 onion,	

Stew all the above ingredients together, but the shrimp, one hour in a casserole, add the boiled shrimp, cut into dice. Serve very hot.

LOBSTER IN SHELLS OR RAMIKINS, No. 1

Cut into dice lobster (boiled) and mushrooms, add yellow Cream Sauce, page 88, red pepper and salt. Put in shells or ramikins, cover with cracker crumbs and butter, bake light brown. Or chop the boiled lobster and season with salt, red pepper, grated onion. Add one cup White Sauce, page 87, and cook together three minutes. Fill the tail shell of the lobster with the above mixture, cover lightly with cracker dust and a little melted butter, and bake fifteen minutes.

SHRIMPS IN TOMATO CASES

1½ cups shrimps in small pieces,	1 cup soft bread crumbs,
2 tablespoons butter,	¼ cup cream,
2 slices onion,	Salt and paprika,
	Buttered crumbs.

Cut the tomatoes in halves, removing the pulp and inverting on sieve to drain.

Melt butter in saucepan, and cook in this, slowly, the onion until slightly browned, then remove onion and add the tomato pulp. Cook this for fifteen minutes, and add enough soft bread crumbs and cream to make a soft paste, about one-fourth a cup. When well blended, add the shrimps, also high seasoning of salt and paprika, place in tomatoes, cover with buttered crumbs, and bake quickly until browned. Serve on lettuce leaves or on rounds of bread, either toasted or fried.

MACARONI IN TOMATO CASES

8 tomatoes,
1 cup boiled macaroni,
1 cup White Sauce,
½ teaspoon salt,
½ teaspoon paprika,
½ cup grated cheese,
1 tablespoon chopped ham.

Cut top off tomatoes, and scoop them out, fill with macaroni, White Sauce, page 87, salt and pepper, and some of the scooped out tomato and the ham. Cover with cracker crumbs, butter, the cheese. Bake in hot oven 15 minutes, and serve at once.

PATTIES

Patty shells are made of very rich and light pastry, Puff Paste, page 301, in rounds, with a cavity in the center. They are baked crisp. They may be filled with creamed oysters, chicken and sweetbreads, sweetbreads and peas, chicken and mushrooms. They are served as a course for dinner or luncheon. The meat is cooked and cut in small pieces and heated in a thick, highly seasoned White or Cream Sauce, pages 87–88. Heat patty shells in oven; fill with hot mixture and serve. Rounds or squares of stale bread, cut very thick may be used in place of the patty shells. Scoop out the centers, or use small scooped out biscuits. Brush with melted butter and brown in the oven or fry in deep hot fat.

GOOSE LIVER PATTIES

Place several goose livers in milk and allow to remain one day. Drain. Some sliced truffles, salt and pepper. Smother in goose fat or butter, or both, until very tender. When cold, chop; add the butter which they were cooked in, and a little Madeira wine; heat the mixture, fill into patties which have been heated and serve at once.

SHRIMP WIGGLE—Patties

1 cup shrimps,
1 cup canned peas,
4 tablespoonfuls butter,
2 tablespoonfuls flour,
½ teaspoonful salt,
⅛ teaspoonful paprika,
1½ cups milk.

Melt the butter and add flour, with salt and paprika, stirring constantly; then pour on gradually the milk as soon as sauce thickens. Add shrimps broken in pieces, and the peas drained from their liquor. Fill into patties which have been heated and serve at once.

FILLET OF BEEF WITH ARTICHOKE

6 slices tenderloin of beef,
6 slices artichoke, the heart,
6 large mushrooms,
1 tablespoon chopped parsley,
6 tablespoons Bearnaise sauce.

Broil steak, page 114, place on the heated artichoke, and on top of this place sauted mushroom, parsley and Bearnaise sauce, page 92, serve very hot. This serves 6 persons.

BRUNSWICK STEW

1 lb. brisket of beef,
3 lbs. (young chicken),
1 pint Lima beans,
1 pint soup stock or water,
4 ears corn (cut from cob),
3 potatoes (sliced),
2 tomatoes (quartered),
1 small onion,
1 teaspoon paprika,
1 teaspoon salt.

Cook all together until tender and before serving remove the meat and any visible chicken bones.

CHOP SUEY—FOR 4 PERSONS

2 chicken livers, cut in chunks,
2 chicken gizzards, cut in chunks,
1 lb. pork, in pieces,
½ oz. green root ginger,
2 stalks celery,
4 tablespoons olive oil,
1 tablespoon vinegar,
½ cup boiling water,
1 tablespoon Worcester Sauce,
½ teaspoon salt,
Black and red pepper, cloves and cinnamon to taste,
1 can mushrooms,
½ cup string beans,
See-Yu Sauce.

Fry the first five ingredients in the olive oil, add the next four ingredients and the seasoning to taste and cook. When nearly done, add a small can of mushrooms, half a cup of either bean sprouts or French green peas, or string beans, chopped fine, or asparagus tips. The see-yu sauce, which is eaten with this dish, can be procured at any Chinese grocery.

SPANISH RICE

Put up 1 cup unwashed rice in frying pan with 4 or 5 tablespoons lard, 5 onions and 2 pieces garlic, minced fine. Fry for ten minutes; add 3 ripe tomatoes or 1 can tomatoes. Add salt and 1 teaspoon paprika. Add water. Cook 1 hour or until done.

CHILI CON CARNE

Take suet size of an egg and 2 onions; put through meat chopper. Set on stove till slightly brown. Add ½ can tomatoes and 1 can beans and 1 lb. steak or chopped meat, tablespoon salt and paprika to suit taste.

HOT TAMALES

Cut small about 1½ lbs. beef or small chicken; cook until tender in just enough water to cover; add salt and one tablespoon paprika. Add 1 or 2 tablespoons corn meal to chicken. Stir gradually 1 quart corn meal in 2 quarts boiling water and 1 tablespoon salt. Add 1 cup lard, and stir 10 minutes. Wash 4½ dozen corn husks. Use three husks to each tamale. Spread thin layer of corn meal in center of each. On one husk place spoonful of meat and add 3 or 4 olives and 2 or 3 raisins. Cover the meat with two other husks and tie at ends. When all are made, place in kettle with husks in the bottom and boil for one hour. Will make 1½ dozen.

CHAPTER XXI

CHAFING DISH RECIPES

CHAFING DISHES

The chafing dish is king, and everyone is looking for new recipes with which to regale and surprise his friends at the evening lunch.

It is said that the chafing dish originated with the Israelitish women, and that it has been used through each succeeding generation by both men and women.

A tray should always be used under the chafing dish, as there is so much danger of setting fire to the tablecloth from the overflow of the alcohol, when no tray is used.

When a recipe calls for milk or cream, the hot water pan should be used in all cases, to avoid all possibility of burning; but when something is to be sauted or fried, this pan is omitted and the dish is placed directly over the flame; constant watching and turning and shaking is necessary, however, as the alcohol flame is hot and comes in direct contact with the metal pan. Oysters are usually cooked in the blazer only, at first, and then, when they are plump, if a sauce is to be added to them, the hot water pan is introduced underneath.

Use Davy Toaster over chafing dish for toasting bread and broiling.

NOTE—Chafing dish may be used in preparing eggs and omelets, following the recipes in Chapter VI, pages 47 to 57.

CHEESE ON TOAST

¾ to 1 cup stale bread crumbs,
1 tablespoon butter,
1 egg,
½ teaspoon salt,
1 cup milk,
½ to 1 cup soft, mild cheese cut in small pieces,
Few grains cayenne.

Soak bread crumbs fifteen minutes in milk. Melt butter, add cheese, and when cheese has melted, add soaked crumbs, egg slightly beaten and seasonings. Cook three minutes and pour over toasted crackers.

MACARONI WITH TOMATO SAUCE

To one cup of stewed tomatoes which has been strained through a colander and seasoned with salt, paprika and one tablespoonful of butter, add a cup of chopped French mushrooms and olives mixed; pour over ½ lb. cook Macaroni, pour in a chafing dish and serve.

WELSH RAREBIT

No. 1

1 tablespoon butter,	1 egg,
½ lb. cheese,	⅛ teaspoon salt,
¼ cup milk,	⅛ teaspoon mustard,

Speck of cayenne pepper.

Melt the butter, break the cheese into small pieces, and add with the seasoning to the butter. When the cheese melts, add the egg, beaten with the milk, and cook one minute. Serve at once on toast or wafers.

No. 2

1 lb. cheese, cut into dice,	1½ teaspoons butter,
½ glass stale ale, or beer,	¼ teaspoon dry mustard,

Salt and cayenne.

Put butter into the chafing dish; when melted, add cheese, mustard, salt and pepper, and gradually the ale or beer. Stir constantly. If desired, add teaspoon of Worcestershire sauce.

No. 3

1 lb. fresh cheese, cut in dice,	½ glass stale beer,
1 tablespoon butter,	1 egg yolk,
1 teaspoon dry mustard,	½ teaspoon salt,

$\frac{1}{16}$ teaspoon cayenne.

Melt butter in chafing dish, stir in cheese and dry ingredients. As cheese melts, add beer gradually, then the slightly beaten yolk of egg. Stir well and serve on toast.

CREAMED CRAB MEAT

2 tablespoons butter,	1 pt. crab meat,
½ cup bread crumbs,	2 yolks, beaten,
1 cup cream,	Salt,
½ teaspoon dry mustard,	Cayenne pepper, or
	Tabasco sauce.

Put the first four ingredients into chafing dish; when it boils, stir in the rest.

MOCK CRAB ON TOAST

2 tablespoons butter,
½ lb. cheese,
1 tablespoon anchovy paste,
½ cup cream,
½ teaspoon salt,
½ teaspoon dry mustard,
$\frac{1}{16}$ cayenne pepper,
2 yolks.

Melt butter in the blazer (over hot water pan), add cheese, anchovy seasoning. Then stir the yolks in the cream and add to the mixture, stirring constantly; when smooth serve on toast.

FRESH CRAB MEAT AND GREEN PEPPERS

1 pt. crab meat,
2 green peppers,
½ pt. White sauce.

Cook the crab meat in the White Sauce, page 87, and add the green peppers, cut in small pieces. Cook in a chafing dish.

LOBSTER A LA THACKERAY

Meat of 2 lobsters, inch pieces,
½ cup butter,
¼ teaspoon salt,
3 dashes cayenne pepper,
1 tablespoon walnut catsup,
1 teaspoon paprika.

Put into the sauce pan (or chafing dish) the green part of the lobster, and add butter, salt, cayenne, walnut catsup, and paprika. Cook this five minutes, then add the meat of two lobsters cut into one inch pieces.

OYSTERS A LA POULETTE

30 oysters,
1 tablespoon butter,
1 tablespoon flour,
1 cup bouillon,
4 yolks,
½ pint cream,
Salt, cayenne,
Juice of ½ lemon.

Heat butter, add flour, then bouillon, or oyster liquid and when well cooked and smooth, add seasoning and four yolks beaten with the cream. Steam thirty large oysters, pour sauce over them and cook two minutes; add chopped parsley.

OYSTER RAREBIT

1 cup oysters,
2 tablespoons butter,
½ lb. soft, mild cheese, cut in small pieces,
¼ teaspoon salt,
Few grains cayenne pepper,
2 eggs.

Clean, parboil and drain oysters, reserving liquor; then remove and discard tough muscle. Melt butter, add cheese and seasonings; as cheese melts add gradually oyster liquor and eggs, slightly beaten; when smooth add oysters. Serve at once.

SCOTCH WOODCOCK

4 chicken livers, boiled and mashed,
2 tablespoons anchovy paste,
2 tablespoons butter,
1 yolk,
1/16 teaspoon cayenne pepper,
2 yolks,
1 cup cream,
1/2 teaspoon salt,
Toast.

Mix a paste of livers and anchovy, butter, 1 yolk, salt and pepper; spread this on toast and put in the oven, then make a sauce (in the double boiler), of 2 yolks, slightly stirred with 1 cup cream, cook together, and pour over the spread toast.

RICTUM—DITY

1 can tomatoes,
1 cup grated cheese,
1/2 small grated onion,
1 green pepper, chopped,
2 tablespoons butter,
2 eggs,
1 teaspoon salt.

Mix tomatoes, cheese, onion juice and the pepper, chopped. Melt the butter, in chafing dish, add the mixture, and when heated add the eggs well beaten. Cook until eggs are of creamy consistency, stirring and scraping from bottom of pan. Serve at once.

ENGLISH MONKEY

1 cup stale bread crumbs,
1 cup milk,
1/2 cup soft, mild cheese in small pieces,
1 tablespoon butter,
1 egg,
1/2 teaspoon salt,
Few grains cayenne.

Soak bread crumbs in milk 15 minutes. Melt the butter, add the cheese and when melted add soaked bread, egg slightly beaten and seasonings. Cook three minutes and pour over toasted crackers.

CHICKEN A LA NEWBURG

1 pint cooked chicken, in large dice,
2 tablespoons butter,
1 tablespoon flour,
1 teaspoon salt,
1/8 teaspoon pepper,
1 cup cream,
Yolks of 3 eggs,
1/4 cup sherry wine.

Melt butter in chafing dish, add flour; cook 1 minute, then add cream; cook 3 minutes, add chicken, warm through; add Sherry or Madeira wine. Mix a little cold water with the slightly beaten yolks, pour them gradually into the cooking mixture and stir constantly until thickened, about 1½ minutes. Serve at once with toast.

CHICKEN A LA KING

½ boiled chicken, (1 pint in thick pieces),
2 tablespoons butter,
2 fresh mushrooms,
1 cup cream,
½ cup Sherry wine,
Yolks of 2 eggs,
1 teaspoon salt,
1 green pepper and 1 red pepper, cut in long thin strips.

Melt butter, add mushrooms, cook 5 minutes. Add chicken, heat through, add salt, wine and the strips of peppers. (The chicken should be removed from bone in long thick pieces.) Beat the yolks until light, add the cream, cook over boiling water or in chafing dish, stirring constantly until thickened, about 1½ minutes; then pour over the hot chicken mixture and serve at once on toast.

FROG LEGS A LA NEWBURG

Boil the frog legs in salt water and drain. Prepare sauce as follows:
2 tablespoons butter,   ½ cup Madeira,
Salt and cayenne pepper.

Boil three minutes. Add one-half pint cream and three yolks, slightly beaten. Cook two minutes, stirring constantly, and pour over the frog legs.

NOTE—Frog legs are nice dipped in egg and cracker crumbs and fried a golden brown in hot fat.

LOBSTER A LA NEWBURG

1 large lobster,
1 dash cayenne pepper,
¼ cup Sherry or Madeira wine,
1 teaspoon sweet cream,
1 tablespoon salt,
2 tablespoons butter,
1 teaspoon sugar,
Yolks of 3 eggs.

Remove boiled lobster meat from shell and cut in inch pieces. Season with salt and pepper; melt butter, add lobster, allow to simmer 5 minutes, then add wine and sugar. Allow this to cook 3 minutes. In the meanwhile beat yolks of eggs light with cream, add to mixture and cook until thickened, stirring constantly. Serve hot on toast.

MINCED MEAT WITH JELLY SAUCE

1 cup chopped, cooked mutton,
Or shredded ham,
½ tablespoon butter,
⅓ cup currant jelly,
Few grains cayenne,
¼ cup Sherry wine.

Put butter and currant jelly in chafing dish; as soon as melted add pepper, wine and the meat, simmer 5 minutes and serve.

GRILLED SARDINES

Drain 12 sardines and cook in a chafing dish until heated, turning frequently. Place on small oblong pieces of dry toast and serve with Maitre d'Hotel Butter, page 91.

SARDINES ON TOAST

6 medium sized sardines,
1 teaspoon butter,
½ wine glass White wine,
1 teaspoon anchovy paste,
Pinch of white pepper.

Cook butter, anchovy paste and wine together, in a chafing dish, add the sardines, heat and place each sardine on buttered toast size of same. Serve very hot.

HOT SAM SANDWICHES

½ lb. cold boiled ham,
Prepared English mustard,
8 slices stale bread,
2 eggs,
¾ cup milk,
2 tablespoons butter.

Chop the ham very fine, or put through meat grinder, and moisten thoroughly with the prepared mustard. Spread a layer of this mixture between thin slices of stale bread and press firmly together. Beat the eggs slightly, add milk and beat again, dip sandwich in this egg mixture and saute in well greased frying pan until a golden brown on both sides. Cut the sandwiches diagonally, serving two persons at one time.

CAKE CANOPES

Fry circular pieces of sponge cake in butter until delicately browned. Drain any canned fruit, as peaches, add powdered sugar, few drops lemon juice, nutmeg grating, if desired. Melt 1 tablespoon butter, add drained fruit and when heated serve on cake.

DEVILED ALMONDS OR CHESTNUTS

Fry until brown blanched almonds or chestnuts, cut in thin slices in enough butter to prevent nuts from burning. Season with Tabasco sauce or few grains paprika. To the almonds add Worcestershire sauce and chopped pickles to taste, and serve with oysters.

CHAPTER XXII

SANDWICHES

SANDWICHES

Wheat, Rye or Boston Brown Bread may be used.

Bread for sandwiches cuts better when a day old. Wrap them in paraffine paper to keep moist, or place in a tin box. Cream or wash the butter before spreading. Cut bread the shape as desired before spreading.

ROLLED BREAD

Cut fresh bread, while still warm, in as thin slices as possible, using a very sharp knife. Spread evenly with butter which has been washed and creamed. Roll slices separately, and tie each with baby ribbon.

BREAD AND BUTTER SANDWICHES

Take wheat, rye, entire wheat, graham or brown bread. Remove end slice of bread. Spread end of loaf evenly with creamed butter. Cut off a slice as thin as possible. Repeat until the number of slices required are prepared. Put together in pairs, cut in squares, oblongs, triangles or rounds (with biscuit cutter), and remove crust if you desire.

CHEESE SANDWICHES

Cut thin slices of American, Brick or Swiss cheese and place between thin slices of buttered rye or wheat bread.

CHEESE SANDWICHES, HOT

Grated American or   Bread,
New York Cream Cheese,   Butter.

Butter thin slices of bread very lightly, sprinkle generously with the cheese; press two slices firmly together, cut in half and toast quickly. Serve at once, with coffee.

Or, toast circular pieces of bread, sprinkle with a thick layer of grated cheese, seasoned with salt and cayenne. Place in shallow pan and set in oven to bake until cheese is melted. Serve at once.

CHEESE AND ANCHOVY SANDWICHES

2 tablespoons butter,	1 teaspoon vinegar,
¼ cup grated American cheese,	Salt, paprika, mustard, Anchovy essence.

Cream the butter, add the cheese and vinegar. Season and spread between thin slices of bread.

CHEESE MIXTURE FOR SANDWICHES

1 small jar prepared cheese, 1 small jar peanut butter,
6 finely chopped olives.

Follow recipe for Prepared Cheese, page 221. Mix all together thoroughly; if too hard or stiff add enough butter or fresh cream to make smooth enough to spread between thin slices of bread.

COTTAGE CHEESE SANDWICHES

¼ cup pimentoes or stuffed olives, chopped,	½ cup cottage or Neufchatel cheese, riced.

Add salt to cheese and mix to a smooth paste with a little cream or milk; then gently stir in the pimentoes. One-half cup walnuts, chopped or shredded cocoanut may be added. Spread between thin slices of bread.

SWISS CHEESE SANDWICHES

¼ lb. Swiss cheese,	¼ lb. English walnut meats,
Salt, paprika,	¼ cup butter, creamed.

Grate cheese, chop nut meats, season with salt and paprika. Mix well and spread between thin slices of bread or on crisp crackers.

CHICKEN SANDWICHES

Cut cold, boiled or roasted chicken in thin slices and place between thin slices of buttered bread, or

Chop chicken and moisten with Mayonnaise, page 189 or 190, or season with salt and pepper and moisten with cream or chicken gravy. Sprinkle with finely minced sweet green peppers.

CHICKEN-AND-NUT FILLING

Chop fine cold roast chicken (use bits that are too small or shapeless for other use). Mix with a little chicken sauce. Add some chopped nuts, a few drops of lemon juice and celery salt. Spread between slices of buttered bread.

CHECKER BOARD SANDWICHES

1 inch slice Brown Bread,   Butter,
1 inch slice Wheat Bread,   Mayonnaise, or
          Any preferred sandwich paste.

Bake brown bread or graham bread in ordinary bread pans, same size and shape as wheat bread. Cut in 1 inch slices. Butter thickly one slice of brown and one of wheat and press the buttered sides together. Cut this thick sandwich in 1 inch slices, crosswise. Spread each of these slices again thickly with butter or any desired sandwich paste on cut side showing the brown and white layers; then press the slices together in pairs to form long blocks 2 inches square, the brown and white alternating each other as in a checker board. Then cut each block in thin slices and arrange sandwiches on serving plate to show checks.

DATE, FIG OR PRUNE SANDWICHES

Remove stems and stones and chop fine. Moisten with lemon juice and place between thin slices of buttered bread. Finely chopped nuts may be mixed with the fruit. Spread between thin buttered slices of brown bread. See Spanish Sweets, page 394, for the proportions.

EGG SANDWICHES

4 hard cooked eggs,   1 tablespoon mayonnaise,
Salt and pepper to taste,   Slices of buttered bread.

Chop finely the whites of hard boiled eggs; force the yolks through a potato ricer. Mix yolks and whites, season with salt and pepper, and moisten with Mayonnaise, pages 189 to 192. Spread mixture between thin slices of buttered bread.

EGG AND SARDINE SANDWICHES

Sardines,   Yolks of 6 hard cooked eggs,
Salt, pepper,   Dry mustard,
Lemon juice,   Round slices of bread.

Take equal quantities of egg yolks and sardines, the latter drained, skinned and boned. Season with salt, cayenne pepper and mustard. Rub until smooth and add lemon juice or olive oil to make a paste. Spread between thin slices of buttered bread or on fresh wafers, or use Mayonnaise, pages 189 to 192, in place of the lemon juice and other seasoning.

HAM SANDWICHES

½ lb. cold boiled ham,   Thin slices of bread,
¼ cup mayonnaise.

Chop the ham very fine, without taking off the fat. Make Mayonnaise, pages 189 to 192, mix with the ham and spread between layers of thinly sliced bread.

JELLY SANDWICHES

Spread any desired jelly or preserves on a thin slice of buttered bread. Cover with a slice of buttered bread.

LETTUCE SANDWICHES

Wash and dry fresh crisp lettuce leaves, place between thin slices of buttered bread and spread a teaspoon of Mayonnaise Dressing, pages 189 to 192, on each leaf.

LOBSTER SANDWICHES

Remove lobster meat from shell and chop. Season with salt, pepper, prepared mustard and lemon juice or moisten with any Salad Dressing, pages 188 to 193. Spread on crisp lettuce leaf and place between thin slices of buttered bread.

PATE DE FOIE GRAS SANDWICHES

Small goose livers,   3 hard cooked eggs,
2 tablespoons goose fat,   Salt and pepper,
A little grated onion.

Smother goose livers until soft in goose fat, mash into a paste, with the eggs, add salt, red pepper and onion, spread on small, thin slices of toast.

RIBBON SANDWICHES

5 large slices bread, cut thin,   ¼ cup red radish skins,
1 cup thick cream   chopped fine,
   mayonnaise,   ¼ cup cucumber, chopped
¼ cup green pepper,   fine,
   chopped fine,   ¼ cup stuffed olives,
      chopped fine.

Butter 4 slices of the bread slightly, spread the peppers on one slice, the radish on the next, the cucumber on the third and on the fourth the olives. Put a thick layer of Cream Mayonnaise, page 189, on each mixture. Pile one slice on top of another, layer cake fashion, with the remaining ungarnished slice for the top layer. Cut in thin slices and arrange on serving plate to show the green, red, white and olive layers.

SWEETBREAD SANDWICHES

Boiled sweetbreads, Mayonnaise.

Follow recipe for Boiled Sweetbreads, page 129, and when cold chop fine. Mix with Mayonnaise Dressing, pages 189 to 192, and spread between bread for sandwiches.

STUFFED OLIVE SANDWICHES

Deviled olives, Mayonnaise.

Chop olives fine in a wooden bowl, mix with a little Mayonnaise Dressing, page 192, and spread between thin slices of brown or wheat bread. Cut in triangles or circles.

VEAL MIXTURE FOR SANDWICH

½ lb. finely chopped roast veal,
1 chopped apple,
1 celery heart, chopped fine,
6 walnuts, chopped fine,
Enough mayonnaise to make smooth paste.

Mix and spread between thin slices of bread.

NUT BUTTERS FOR SANDWICHES

Peanut

No. 1. Crush the shelled peanuts, divested of skins, or pass them through a food-chopper. Season with salt and mix to a paste with cream, or omit the salt and add to creamed butter. Spread between slices of bread.

Peanut

No. 2. Add one cup of boiling water to half a cup of crushed peanuts, or peanut meal. Dilute a teaspoonful of cornstarch with a little cold water and stir into the boiling mixture. Stir and simmer eight or ten minutes. Season to taste with salt, and spiced poultry seasoning. Spread between slices of bread.

NUT BUTTERS FOR SANDWICHES

Almond

Shell almonds, throw into boiling water and allow to stand just a moment; rub off the brown skins. Put in baking pans in moderate oven to dry, but not to brown. Grind at once. Pack in glasses, cover and keep in cool place.

Brazil Nut

Crack the nuts, and with a sharp, thin knife trim off all the brown skins, being careful not to soil the nuts. Cut them into slices, grind, pack in glasses, cover and keep in a cool place.

Vegetarian

¼ lb. almonds,
½ lb. pecan nuts,
½ lb. hazel nuts or filberts,
½ lb. roasted peanuts.

Shell and blanch the nuts. Mix all together and put them through a grinder, knead until it becomes a little soft, pack closely into tumblers or baking powder cans and stand at once in a cool place. When ready to use dip can in hot water, until the mixture slips out easily. Cut the "cheese" into slices and serve in place of meat.

CHAPTER XXIII

PUDDING SAUCES

BRANDY SAUCE

1 egg, well beaten,   1 cup sugar,
½ cup butter,   Brandy.

Stir mixture to a cream and add 1 tablespoon boiling water, put in double boiler and stir until sauce boils, then add brandy to suit taste. Serve with Plum Pudding, page 260.

Or, beat into the yolks of three eggs enough pulverized sugar to thicken them, add tablespoon brandy and stir in the whites of the eggs, beaten to a stiff froth the last thing.

CARAMEL SAUCE

Put ⅓ cup sugar in a spider, stir over the fire until melted and light brown; add very gradually ½ cup of boiling water and simmer 10 minutes; or, melt sugar in sauce pan, add 1 pint cream and set over hot water until the caramel liquefies.

CHOCOLATE SAUCE

2 cups milk,   2 tablespoons hot water,
1½ tablespoons cornstarch,   2 eggs,
2 oz. bitter chocolate,   ⅔ cup powdered sugar,
1 teaspoon vanilla.

Add cornstarch to a little of the cold milk and mix with the rest of the milk and cook in double boiler until thick, 8 minutes. Melt chocolate over hot water, add to the hot milk mixture. Beat white of eggs stiff, add powdered sugar, then add the unbeaten yolks and stir well into the cooked mixture. Cook 1 minute, add vanilla and cool before serving.

COFFEE SAUCE

2 eggs,   ½ cup black coffee,
¼ cup sugar,   ½ cup thick cream.

Strain the coffee and while hot add the sugar and a few grains of salt, and pour very gradually on the slightly beaten eggs. Place in double boiler and cook, stirring constantly until mixture coats the spoon. Strain into cold dish, and when cold and ready to serve, fold in the cream, beaten stiff.

CREAM SAUCE

1 cup cream,
⅓ cup powdered sugar,
½ teaspoon vanilla.

Have cream ice cold, beat until stiff with egg beater or cream churn; add sugar and vanilla.

CREAMY SAUCE No. 1

2 tablespoons butter,
⅜ cup powdered sugar,
1½ tablespoons cream or milk,
¼ teaspoon vanilla.

Cream butter; add sugar slowly and then cream and vanilla very slowly.

CREAMY SAUCE No. 2

1 cup sugar,
½ cup water,
White of 1 egg,
1 cup whipped cream.

Boil sugar and water to a thick syrup and pour in a fine stream into the white of an egg, beaten until foamy, but not dry. Set the sauce into a dish of ice water, and beat until cold, then fold in the whipped cream. Flavor to taste.

CUSTARD SAUCE, No. 1

1½ cups scalded milk,
⅛ teaspoon salt,
¼ cup sugar,
½ teaspoon vanilla,
Yolks of eggs.

Beat eggs slightly, add sugar and salt; stir constantly while adding gradually the hot milk. Cook in a double boiler until mixture thickens; chill and flavor.

CUSTARD SAUCE, No. 2

Vanilla bean,
1 pint milk,
2 yolks of eggs, beaten,
2 whites of eggs, beaten.

Soak the bean in the milk, let cook, then pour on the beaten yolks slowly, stirring all the time; add the beaten whites and heat through and cool.

HARD SAUCE

⅓ cup butter,
⅓ cup powdered sugar,
⅓ teaspoon lemon extract,
⅔ teaspoon vanilla.

Cream the butter, add sugar gradually, and flavoring.

JELLY SAUCE

1 glass jelly,
¼ cup hot water,
1 tablespoon butter,
1 tablespoon flour.

Add hot water to jelly and let melt on stove. Heat butter in sauce pan, add flour and gradually the hot jelly liquid. Cook until smooth and serve hot over any pudding.

Or the jelly may be placed on stove and melted with the hot water.

KIRSCH SAUCE

1 pt. cold water,
1 cup sugar,
2 tablespoons cornstarch,
½ cup cold water,
1 cup Kirsch wine.

Place sugar and water on stove. Mix cornstarch in cold water, and when the water in sauce pan is boiling, add cornstarch and stir for two minutes. Remove from fire and add Kirsch and stir again. Strain and serve with pudding.

LEMON SAUCE

2 cups hot water,
1 cup sugar,
1 lemon rind and juice,
2 tablespoons cornstarch,
2 tablespoons butter.

Mix the sugar and cornstarch, add the boiling water gradually, stirring all the time. Cook 8 to 10 minutes, add lemon juice and butter. Serve hot.

SAUCE FOR MATZOS PUDDING

1 cup white wine,
½ cup water,
3 slices lemon,
⅛ teaspoon cinnamon,
¼ cup sugar,
1 teaspoon potato flour,
4 yolks, beaten,
4 beaten whites of eggs.

Mix the first 5 ingredients and boil until well flavored. Moisten the potato flour with a little water and add to the wine mixture, stirring to avoid lumping. Then pour the hot wine gradually on the beaten yolks, stirring constantly to avoid curdling. Return to sauce pan, add part of the beaten whites, heat through, and continue the beating. Remove to sauce bowl, place remaining whites on top sweetened with sugar.

SAUCE FOR STEAMED PUDDINGS

½ cup butter,
1½ cups sugar,
¾ cup hot milk,
1 tablespoon sherry.

Cream butter and sugar, add sherry and just before serving add hot milk.

STRAWBERRY SAUCE

½ cup strawberry juice,
1 cup whipped cream,
1 tablespoon Maraschino wine,
Sugar to taste.

Mix and serve cold over any pudding.

STRAWBERRY HARD SAUCE

⅓ cup butter,
⅔ cup strawberries,
1 cup powdered sugar.

Cream the butter, add the sugar gradually and then the strawberries and beat until berries are well mashed. Serve with custards.

VANILLA SAUCE

1 tablespoon butter,
2 tablespoons flour,
2 cups boiling water,
¼ cup sugar,
1 teaspoon vanilla.

Melt the butter, add flour and stir until smooth; add the boiling water and sugar. Boil until thoroughly cooked. Add flavoring, strain and serve hot.

WINE SAUCE, No. 1

1½ cup sugar,
1 teaspoon lemon or
Vanilla extract or
3 tablespoons brandy or wine
1 tablespoon butter,
½ cup water.

Cook sugar and water together 6 minutes. Remove from fire. Add flavoring and butter. Serve over Date Pudding, page 260.

WINE SAUCE, No. 2

1 cup wine, (sherry or Madeira),   2 eggs,   ¾ cup sugar.

Heat wine to the boiling point and pour slowly into the eggs that have been beaten light with the sugar, stirring all the time. Cook until thick, pour in sauce dish and keep warm until ready to serve.

CHAPTER XXIV

PUDDINGS

HOT PUDDINGS

STALE BREAD DESSERT

Slices of stale bread, 1 cup milk,
1 egg, 2 tablespoons butter,
1 tablespoon sugar.

Cut bread in ½ inch slices. Beat the egg slightly, add milk and sugar. Dip bread in this mixture, moistening both sides.

Heat the butter in a spider and fry bread, on both sides, a nice golden brown. Serve hot, with a little jelly spread on each piece.

BREAD AND FRUIT PUDDING

Slices of buttered bread, Hot stewed fruit.

Lay bread in a pudding dish. Pour over each slice boiling hot stewed fruit made very sweet.

Care should be taken to have more syrup than the bread can absorb or the pudding will seen dry. Cherries or berries are the most suitable, but peaches or other high-flavored fruit can be used. Serve ice cold with cream, either plain or whipped.

BREAD PUDDING

No. 1

1½ cups stale bread crumbs, 2 eggs,
1 pt. milk, ¼ teaspoon salt,
2 tablespoons sugar, 1 teaspoon vanilla, or
1 tablespoon melted butter, ¼ teaspoon spice.

Soak bread crumbs in milk; add sugar, butter and eggs slightly beaten, salt, and flavoring. Put into a buttered pudding dish and set dish in a pan of hot water. Bake in moderate oven about ½ hour. Try with knife. If the knife comes out clean, the pudding is done.

BREAD PUDDING

No. 2

2 cups bread crumbs,	1 pt. milk,
4 eggs,	1½ cups powdered sugar,
Grated peel of 1 lemon,	½ cup seeded raisins.

Soak the bread crumbs in the milk ½ hour, add the yolks of eggs well beaten with 1 cup of the sugar, the lemon rind and raisins. Pour into well buttered pudding dish and bake in moderate oven ½ hour. Beat whites of eggs to stiff froth with ½ cupful sugar. Cover pudding with thin coating of jelly, then the whites of eggs and return to oven to brown. Serve hot, with whipped cream.

No. 3

1 cup of bread cubes,	3 eggs,
1 pt. of milk,	1 teaspoon of vanilla,
¼ cup of sugar,	1 cup stewed apples.

Cut the bread into ½ in. cubes; beat the yolks of the eggs and 1 white together, add the sugar and vanilla, and beat until well mixed; add the milk, and stir until the sugar is dissolved. Pour this custard over the bread and bake in a moderate oven until set; take from the oven and cover with stewed apples. Make a meringue of the remaining 2 whites and 2 rounding tablespoons of granulated sugar; add a few drops of vanilla, spread over the apples, and place in a cool oven until a delicate brown. Serve hot with or without cream. Any kind of preserve or jelly may be used in place of the apple.

CHOCOLATE BREAD PUDDING

1 oz. bitter chocolate,	⅓ cup sugar,
¾ cup stale bread crumbs,	1 egg,
2 cups scalded milk,	⅛ teaspoon salt,
½ teaspoon vanilla.	

Soak bread in 1¾ cups milk ½ hour; melt chocolate over hot water, add sugar and the remaining ¼ cup milk to make smooth paste. Add to bread with salt, vanilla and egg, slightly beaten. Place in well buttered pudding dish and bake ½ hour until set. Serve with cream or Creamy Sauce, page 242.

SCALLOPED APPLES (Brown Betty Pudding)

3 cups apples, chopped,	¼ teaspoon cinnamon,
2 cups soft bread crumbs,	¼ teaspoon nutmeg,
½ cup sugar,	2 tablespoons butter,
¼ cup water.	

Melt the butter and add the crumbs; mix the sugar, spice and lemon rind. Put one-fourth of the crumbs in the bottom of a buttered dish. Then one-half of the apples. Sprinkle with one-half of the sugar and spice, then add another quarter of the crumbs, the remainder of the apples, and the sugar and spice. Sprinkle the lemon juice over this and the water, and put the rest of the crumbs over the top. Cover closely, cook 45 minutes in the oven, uncover, brown quickly. To be eaten plain or with sweetened cream.

SCALLOPED RHUBARB

Rinse quickly, wipe clean and remove skin or shreds from larger stalks. Flavor sugar with orange peel. Follow directions of Scalloped Apples, recipe above, using 1 cup of sugar and 3 cups of rhubarb cut in short lengths. Flavor with grated yellow rind of orange.

APPLE PUDDING

2 quarts stewed apples, Lemon juice,
4 eggs, Sugar.

Take two quarts tart apples, stewed, strained and sweetened to taste. Cool and add one tablespoonful lemon juice and four yolks, well beaten. Turn this into a buttered dish and bake half an hour in hot oven. Cool, then spread with the whites of egg, beaten stiff, with four tablespoonfuls powdered sugar and one teaspoon lemon juice. Dust with sugar and return to the oven to brown. Serve either hot or cold.

RICE PUDDING

No. 1

½ cup of well-washed rice, ⅛ teaspoon salt,
½ cup sugar, 1 quart milk.

Soak ½ hour. Bake 2 hours, slowly at first, till the rice has softened and thickened the milk; then let it brown slightly. This is creamy and delicious, though often called "Poor Man's Pudding." Serve with milk and sugar or with strawberry jam.

No. 2

1 cup rice, ⅓ cup sugar,
4 cups boiling water, 1 tablespoon butter,
1 teaspoon salt, 1 egg (well beaten).

Steam the rice in the boiling, salted water until tender, and while hot add the rest of the ingredients. Cook 5 minutes and bake twenty minutes in a buttered baking dish, with bread crumbs at the top and bottom. If desired, fruit may be added in layers to the rice.

BAKED INDIAN PUDDING

5 cups milk, scalded,
⅓ cup yellow cornmeal,
½ cup molasses,
1 teaspoon salt,
1 teaspoon ginger or grated lemon rind.

Pour milk slowly on the corn meal, cook in double boiler 20 minutes, add molasses, salt and ginger or lemon rind as desired. Pour into buttered pudding dish and bake two hours in a slow oven. Serve with cream or butter.

GRANT THOMAS PUDDING

2 eggs, beaten,
1 cup sugar,
3 tablespoons flour,
1 teaspoon baking powder,
1 cup walnuts, quartered,
1 cup chopped figs.

Beat eggs and sugar until very light, add flour sifted 3 times and the rest of the ingredients. Stir well and bake in a slow oven 25 minutes, in shallow pan. Serve hot or cold with whipped cream.

ICE CREAM PUDDING

1½ cups butter,
½ cup sugar,
6 yolks, beaten,
1 pt. milk,
1 cup flour,
6 whites of eggs, beaten,
¼ cup sugar.

Cream butter, add sugar, then stir in the beaten yolks, add the flour and lastly the beaten whites.

Bake in deep, buttered pudding dish and when done, make 6 or 7 slashes in cake, pour in the milk sweetened with the ¼ cup sugar and bake again until milk is absorbed. Serve warm with cold Custard Sauce, No. 2, page 242.

ROLY POLY

Make a dough either of Plain Pie Crust, page 300, or Biscuit Dough, page 39. Roll out ½ inch thick. Spread with chopped apples, raisins, sugar and cinnamon, or with jam; roll. Shape it into a small baking pan, spread the butter over all and add 2 cups of cold water and bake in a hot oven, basting often, with the sauce in the pan, until done. Serve hot.

Or it may be placed in a greased pudding dish and set in boiling water for an hour or longer until apples and dough are well cooked and serve hot with any desired sweet sauce.

POTATO PUDDING FOR EASTER

4 yolks, beaten,
½ cup sugar,
2 tablespoons almonds, blanched and grated,
½ lemon juice and rind,
¼ lb. cold, boiled potato, grated,
¼ teaspoon salt,
4 whites of eggs, beaten stiff.

Add sugar to the beaten yolks and stir well, add almonds, lemon rind and juice, then the grated potatoes and salt, and lastly the whites of the eggs. Place in well greased pudding dish and bake ½ hour, setting the dish in a pan half filled with boiling water. Serve on platter with wine or Chocolate Sauce, page 241.

GRANDMOTHER'S PUDDINGS

APPLE STRUDEL, No. 1

2 qts. sour apples, cut fine,
1 cup stoned raisins,
1 cup sugar,
1 teaspoon cinnamon,
1½ cups flour,
½ cup currants,
¼ teaspoon salt,
½ cup warm water,
1 egg,
½ cup butter, melted,
¼ lb. almonds, chopped and blanched.

Into a large mixing bowl, place the salt and flour. Beat the egg lightly and add it to the warm water, and combine the two mixtures. Mix the dough quickly with a knife; then knead it, place on board, stretching it up and down to make it elastic, until it leaves the board clean. Now toss it on a well floured board, cover with a hot bowl and keep in a warm place. Lay the dough in the center of a well floured tablecloth on table; roll out a little, brush well with some of the melted butter, and with hands under dough, palms down, pull and stretch the dough gently, until it is as large as the table and thin as paper and do not tear the dough. Spread the apples, raisins, currants and almonds, if desired, the sugar and cinnamon evenly over three-fourths of the dough, and drop over them a few tablespoons of melted butter. Trim edges. Roll the dough over apples on one side, then hold cloth high with both hands and the strudel will roll itself over and over into one big roll, trim edges again. Then twist the roll to fit the greased pan. Bake in a hot oven until brown and crisp and brush with melted butter. If juicy small fruits or berries are used, sprinkle bread crumbs over the stretched dough to absorb the juices. Serve slightly warm.

APPLE STRUDEL, No. 2

1 cup butter,
6 large apples,
2 cups sugar,
1 lemon,
½ cup raisins.

Roll out a Noodle Dough, page 85, as thin as possible. Cover with the butter, melted, sugar, apples chopped fine, raisins, lemon rind and juice. Roll like a jelly roll and bake well in a buttered pan 1½ hours. Baste often with sugar water.

RAHM STRUDEL

1 qt. thick, sour milk,
2 cups granulated sugar,
1 cup grated bread crumbs,
1 cup chopped almonds,
1 cup raisins,
1 teaspoon cinnamon.

Make Strudel Dough, No. 1, page 250, drip sour milk on it lightly, with a large spoon, put bread crumbs over milk, now add other ingredients, roll and put in well buttered pan, put small pieces of butter over top, basting frequently. Serve warm with Vanilla Sauce, page 244.

CABBAGE STRUDEL

1 medium sized cabbage,
2 cups granulated sugar,
½ cup chopped almonds,
½ cup goose oil,
1 cup raisins and currants, mixed,
1 teaspoon cinnamon.

Heat the goose fat, add the kraut and let it simmer till done, stirring constantly to keep from burning. While cooling, prepare Strudel dough, No. 1, page 250, fill with kraut and other above ingredients, roll and put little pieces of butter or grease on top; bake in hot oven and baste frequently. Butter pans generously, and serve hot.

NOODLE PUDDING

No. 1

Fine noodles,
4 eggs,
1 cup powdered sugar,
2 tablespoons grated almonds.

Make fine Noodles after recipe on page 85. Boil in salted,

boiling water 10 minutes. Place in colander, pour cold water over them and drain.

Separate the eggs, beat the yolks light with the sugar, add the salt, almonds and drained noodles and lastly, stiffly beaten whites. Pour into a well greased pudding dish, set dish in boiling water and boil 1½ hours.

NOODLE PUDDING

No. 2

Noodles,
2 tablespoons fat or butter,
3 yolks,
1 cup sugar,
1½ teaspoons cinnamon,
2 apples, sliced,
¼ cup dried currants,
½ cup chopped nuts,
3 beaten whites.

Follow recipe for Noodles, page 85, using 3 eggs and salt and flour in proportion. Cut noodles fine. Boil in salt water (1 teaspoon salt to 1 qt. water), 5 minutes and drain in colander. Heat fat or butter in a spider, add the noodles and cook just long enough to absorb the fat. Add the beaten yolks, sugar and the rest of the ingredients in the order given. Place in well greased pudding dish and bake ½ hour in a moderate oven. Serve in the baking form, plain or with wine, jelly, or Creamy Sauce, page 242.

No. 3

Noodles,
2 tablespoons fat or butter,
1½ cups walnuts, grated,
1 cup sugar,
1 tablespoon cinnamon,
1 lb. plum butter.

Follow directions for making Noodles, page 85, using 3 eggs and salt and flour in proportion, cutting noodles ¼ by 3 inches. Cook in boiling, salt water (1 teaspoon salt to 1 qt. water), 5 minutes and drain through colander. Heat the fat in a spider, add the noodles and cook only long enough to absorb the fat. Mix 1¼ cups of the walnuts with the sugar and cinnamon.

Into a well greased baking dish place ½ of the noodles; spread the plum butter, thinned with hot water, over this, sprinkle with ½ of the nut mixture. Add the rest of the noodles, sprinkle with the rest of the nut mixture. Bake ½ hour in a moderate oven. Remove from form, strew with the remaining nut meats and serve hot.

DAMPF NOODLES

Kuchen Dough, ½ lb. stewed prunes,
¼ cup butter.

Make Kuchen Dough, No. 1, page 311. Let rise. Toss on floured board, and mould into small, thick noodles or biscuits; place them in a closely covered iron kettle, with plenty butter at the bottom and not too close together. Let rise in a warm place and then pour over a cup of cold water, milk or prune juice, cover and place in a moderately hot oven and let cook until you hear it fry and the steam or water has all evaporated. The noodles will then be brown on the bottom. Remove the cover and let them brown on the top.

Serve them with Caramel Sauce, page 241, stewed prunes, page 399, or any other dried fruit sauce.

STEAMED NOODLES

Kuchen Dough, Stewed prunes.

Kuchen dough raised twice, rolled and cut into round pieces and raised once more. Then put them into a buttered iron pot with a cover, pour some stewed prunes over them and bake an hour. Serve at once.

HUTZLE OR SNITZ KLOESS

½ loaf stale bread, grated,
½ lb. suet, chopped fine,
¾ cup brown sugar,
2 eggs,
½ teaspoon cinnamon,
Pinch of salt,
2 or 3 tablespoons flour,
¼ teaspoon baking powder.

Roll mixture in a ball and place on plate in kettle. Take 1 lb. dried pears which have been soaked over night, then boil with sugar, cinnamon until tender. Put pears around pudding, and boil 3 hours, covered. Serve hot.

AUF-LAUF

Stale cake or macaroons,
Fruit,
Sugar,
6 tablespoons sugar,
6 eggs,
Almonds.

Line a pudding dish with any stale cake you may have, or with macaroons if preferred. Cover this with fruit and sugar, and put on the back of the stove to heat. Cover with sponge made of six yolks, six tablespoonfuls sugar, six whites beaten to froth, and some chopped almonds. Bake quickly. Serve hot.

KUGEL

5 wheat rolls,
¾ lb. raw suet,
½ cup brown sugar,
1 tablespoon molasses,
1 teaspoon cinnamon,
1 grated lemon rind,
1 tablespoon water,
Salt,
½ lb. prunes, stewed.

Soak rolls in water, then press the bread quite dry. Knead it with suet, sugar, molasses, cinnamon, and lemon rind, one tablespoonful of water, a pinch of salt. Mix very well together. Line an iron pot with alternate layers of above dough, and stewed and stoned prunes. Bake two hours; baste often with prune juice.

RICE KUGEL

1 cup rice,
4 cups boiling water,
1 teaspoon salt,
4 eggs beaten,
¼ cup sugar,
¼ lb. Sultana raisins,
¼ cup fat, (chicken, goose or butter.)

Cook the rice in the boiling, salted water 30 minutes or until nearly done. Mix with the rest of the ingredients and place in well greased pudding dish and bake until top of Kugel is quite brown.

NOODLE KUGEL

3 cups broad noodles, 4 eggs,
(¾ cup fat, chicken, goose or butter.)

Cook Noodles, page 85, in salted boiling water, 10 minutes. Drain and add the fat and the eggs, well beaten. Place in a well greased pudding dish and bake in a hot oven until top of Kugel is well browned. Serve hot.

DIMPES DAMPES

½ cup sugar,
¼ teaspoon salt,
1 pint flour,
1 pint milk,
1 cup butter (scant),
1 quart apples, sliced.

Mix sugar, salt and flour and gradually add the milk to make a smooth batter.

Melt 1 cup or a little less of butter in a large shallow dripping pan and let it spread all over the pan to grease it well, then pour the remaining butter and the apples to the batter. Mix and pour into pan or pans not more than ¾ inch deep and bake in a moderate oven 30 to 45 minutes until a golden brown.

APPLE CHARLOTTE

2 qts. apples, diced,
1 cup sugar,
1 teaspoon cinnamon,
1 cup seeded raisins,
½ cup currants,
1 lemon rind and juice,
¼ cup of red or White wine.

Line a well greased pudding dish with Murberteig, page 301, ½ in. thick, fill with chopped apples, sugar, almonds, red wine, raisins, lemon juice and rind. Cover with pie crust ¼ inch thick and bake 30 to 60 minutes in hot oven.

MATZOS SCHALET

1½ matzos (unleavened bread),
1 tablespoon goose fat,
A pinch salt,
4 yolks, beaten,
½ cup sugar,
½ lemon, juice and rind,
4 whites, beaten.

Soak the matzos and press dry. Place in mixing bowl and stir and cream with the goose fat until very light, add beaten yolks and the other ingredients, the beaten whites last; pour into a well greased pudding dish and bake about ½ hour. Must be placed in oven immediately after mixed and served when done or it will fall. Serve with Wine Sauce or Jelly Sauce, page 243.

MATZOS CHARLOTTE WITH APPLES

1 matzos,
¼ lb. suet, chopped fine,
2 cups apples, sliced fine,
¼ cup sugar,
3 yolks, beaten,
2 tablespoons raisins, seeded,
1 tablespoon almonds, blanched and grated,
¼ teaspoon cinnamon,
3 whites of eggs, beaten stiff.

Soak matzos in water and press out dry; add the rest of the ingredients, mix thoroughly, fold in the beaten whites last. Bake about 1 hour in moderate oven.

MATZOS PUDDING

2 cups apples, grated,
4 yolks, beaten,
⅔ cup powdered sugar,
½ lemon rind,
¼ cup matzos meal,
4 whites, beaten.

Stir sugar with the beaten yolks, add the apples, grated lemon rind and the meal and lastly the beaten whites. Bake in spring form. Sprinkle 4 tablespoons almond blanched and cut fine on top and bake in moderate oven.

MATZOS CRIMSEL

No. 1

2 matzos,	3 eggs,
½ tablespoon salt,	½ cup sugar.

Soak matzos in water and press quite dry. Mix in the rest of the ingredients and stir well. Drop from tablespoon in hot deep fat and fry slowly until browned on both sides. Serve warm with stewed cherries or prunes.

No. 2

4 matzos,	¼ cup sugar,
4 eggs,	⅛ teaspoon salt,
Whites, beaten,	½ cup walnut or almond
½ cup matzos meal,	meats pounded.

Soak matzos in water. Drain and press quite dry. Mix smooth with sugar, yolks, etc., adding the beaten whites last. Drop by spoonsful in deep, hot goose or any other preferred fat, and fry, not too fast until brown on both sides. Serve warm surrounded with stewed prunes.

No. 3

1 cup matzos meal,	1 tablespoon chopped almond,
1 cup boiling water,	1 teaspoon sugar,
milk, soup stock or wine,	¼ teaspoon salt,
4 eggs.	

Scald the matzos meal with the hot water or other liquids, stir well and add the other ingredients, separating the eggs and adding the beaten whites last. Drop by tablespoonfuls in deep, hot goose or other fat and fry slowly until browned on both sides.

Serve hot, sprinkled with powdered sugar, wine sauce or stewed fruits.

No. 4

3 matzos, soaked and squeezed dry,	¾ cup sugar,
	⅛ teaspoon salt,
2 tablespoons seed raisins, chopped,	1 lemon, grated rind,
	1 tablespoon lemon juice,
2 tablespoons chopped almonds,	3 whites, beaten.
3 yolks of eggs,	

Mix in the order given and drop from tablespoon in deep, hot fat. Serve hot with stewed prunes flavored with orange juice.

MATZOS CRIMSEL—FILLED

1½ matzos,
1 tablespoon goose fat,
¼ cup matzos meal,
2 eggs,
⅛ teaspoon salt,
2 tablespoons sugar,
Stewed prunes, stoned.

Soak the matzos and press dry; heat the fat, add matzos, to dry a little more, add matzos meal, eggs, sugar and salt. Mix well and form into oblong cakes. Place a prune in the center of each cake and form into egg shaped balls.

Dip balls in beaten egg and fry in deep, hot goose fat until brown and thoroughly done. Serve hot with Jelly or Wine Sauce, page 244.

SPRITZ KRAPFEN

2 cups flour,
2 cups water,
1 tablespoon butter,
1 lemon, grated rind,
4 yolks,
4 whole eggs.

Add butter to water and when boiling, stir in the flour all at once and stir vigorously. Remove from fire, add sugar and lemon juice and the unbeaten eggs one at a time and beating constantly between each addition of eggs. Drop by spoonfuls or through Spritz Krapfen tube into deep, hot fat (butter) and bake a nice brown. Serve with Wine Sauce, page 244.

STEAMED PUDDINGS

GENERAL RULES FOR STEAMING

See that the water is boiling in the kettle or steamer when the food is ready for cooking. Keep the water boiling constantly. Refill when necessary with boiling water.

Do not jar the kettle.

A mould or tightly covered tin can may be used; it should be thoroughly greased, and if it has no cover, a strong piece of glazed paper may be tied over the top; this should also be greased. It should be put into a streamer over boiling water, or on a rack in a kettle of boiling water.

SUET PUDDING, No. 1

1 cup suet, chopped fine,
1 cup molasses,
1 cup bread crumbs,
½ cup sweet or sour milk,
1½ cup flour,
1 teaspoon cinnamon,
1 teaspoon salt,
1 teaspoon soda,
1 cup raisins, seeded currants, or any preserved fruit.

Add soda to milk, and mix well with the other ingredients. Turn in to well greased pudding mould, cups, or baking powder cans. Cover closely with greased paper or the fitted covers. Tie down the covers. Put into a kettle of boiling water on a rack or trivet; the water should half cover the cups. Cover kettle and steam 3 hours, if in a mould or 1 hour if in cups. Turn out of moulds and serve on a hot dish with any desired pudding sauce.

SUET PUDDING, No. 2

1 pint flour,
1 cup suet,
2 eggs,
4 tablespoons baking powder,
1 cup currants.
Cold water,
1 cup raisins,
¼ teaspoon salt,
1 cup brown sugar,

Mix the flour, baking powder and salt; add finely chopped suet and rub it into the flour with the tips of the fingers. Add the eggs, well beaten, and the sugar. Seed, and cut the raisins in halves, clean the currants by sprinkling them with flour and rubbing between the hands. Flour the fruit and add to other ingredients with enough water to form a dough. Grease a mould or several cups. Fill ¾ full and cover with greased paper. Put them into a kettle of boiling water on a trivet; the water should half cover the cups. Cover the kettle and steam 2 hours if in a mould, and 1 hour if in cups. Serve on a hot dish with a sauce. Baking powder boxes are convenient to use for moulds. Tie the covers on tightly.

WHOLE-WHEAT PUDDING

2 cups whole wheat flour,
½ teaspoon soda,
½ teaspoon salt,
1 cup milk,
½ cup molasses,
1 cup stoned and chopped raisins or dates,
Or 1 cup ripe berries.

Mix ingredients in order given. Steam 2½ hours and serve with whipped cream or any plain pudding sauce.

One cup of figs, stewed prunes or chopped apple or raisins makes a pleasing variety.

BREAD PUDDING

1½ cups stale bread crumbs,
1 pint milk,
2 tablespoons sugar,
1 tablespoon melted butter,
2 eggs,
¼ teaspoon salt,
1 teaspoon vanilla, or
¼ teaspoon spice.

Soak bread crumbs in milk. Add sugar, butter and eggs, slightly beaten, salt, butter and flavoring. Put into a buttered pudding dish and set dish in a pan of hot water. Bake in a slow oven about ½ hour. Try with knife. If the knife comes out clean the pudding is done.

RICE SNOW BALLS

3 cups cooked rice,
¼ cup sugar,
¼ lb. stewed prunes.

Wring small pudding cloths, one-third yard square, out of hot water, and lay them over a one-half pint bowl. Spread the rice one-third of an inch thick over cloth. Put the stewed prunes in center, draw the cloth around until prunes are covered smoothly with the rice. Tie tightly and steam ten minutes. Remove cloth carefully and turn the balls out on a platter, and serve with prunes. This amount makes six balls. They may be filled with steamed apples or any other fruit.

FRUIT DUMPLINGS

2 cups flour,
4 teaspoons baking powder,
½ teaspoon salt,
¾ or 1 cup milk,
or water,
5 tablespoons shortening.

Make the dough as for biscuit. Pat and roll out ¼ inch thick. Cut into 4 in. squares. Place in the center of each square an apple or other fruit, sprinkle with sugar and cinnamon or nutmeg. If the fruit is hard, first steam 5 to 10 minutes. Moisten the edges of the dough with cold water, fold so that the corners meet and the fruit is covered, press the edges together. Place in a greased pan and bake in a hot oven about 20 minutes.

The dumplings may be steamed by placing them in a buttered steamer and cooking over boiling water ½ hour. Serve with cream or a sweet sauce.

FIG PUDDING

½ lb. dried figs, chopped fine,
1 cup beef suet, chopped fine,
2⅓ cups stale bread crumbs,
½ cup milk,
2 eggs,
1 cup sugar,
¾ teaspoon salt.

Chop suet, and work with hands until creamy, then add figs. Soak bread in the milk, add egg well beaten, sugar and salt. Combine the two mixtures, place in buttered mould or in top of double boiler, buttered and steam three hours. Serve with Vanilla, Wine or Brandy Sauce, pages 241–244.

DATE PUDDING

1 lb. stoned dates,
½ cup sugar,
1 teaspoon ginger,
1 scant teaspoon salt,
½ cup milk,

½ lb. suet,
1 cup flour,
1 teaspoon cinnamon,
2 eggs,
1 cup soft bread crumbs.

Pass dates and suet together through a food chopper or grinder. Mix all ingredients well together, adding the well beaten eggs last. Turn into well buttered moulds, and steam 2 hours. To serve decorate with holly, and surround with Hard Sauce, page 243. Figs, stoned raisins, currants, candied peel, prunes or nuts, alone or in combination, may replace dates. Serve with Wine Sauce, No. 1, page 244.

STEAMED FRUIT PUDDING

3 cups flour,
3 teaspoons baking powder,
½ teaspoon salt,
1 cup suet, chopped finely,
1 cup milk,

1 cup molasses,
1 teaspoon soda,
½ cup currants,
½ cup raisins,
1 teaspoon mixed spices.

Mix dry ingredients together and add suet, mixing thoroughly. Lastly add the liquid. Put in moulds and steam 3 hours. Serve with Vanilla Sauce, page 244.

PLUM PUDDING

1½ cups stale bread crumbs,
1 cup suet, chopped fine,
½ cup sugar,
1 cup molasses,
3 eggs,
¼ cup flour,
1½ lb. seedless raisins,
2 oz. citron, cut fine,

½ cup chopped almonds,
2 cups sour apples, chopped fine,
1 teaspoon ground cinnamon,
½ teaspoon ground allspice,
½ teaspoon ground cloves,
1 teaspoon salt,
1 cup brandy,
Rind of a lemon.

Soak raisins, citron, almonds and apples in the brandy over night; then add the rest of the ingredients. Turn into a buttered mould and cover or place in a well floured bag and steam from 4 to 8 hours, the longer the better. Good warmed over. Serve with Brandy Sauce, page 241.

ENGLISH PLUM PUDDING

¾ lb. stale bread crumbs,
½ cup scalded milk,
½ cup sugar,
4 eggs,
½ lb. raisins, seeded, cut in pieces and floured,
½ lb. currants,
¼ lb. citron, cut fine,
1 cup suet,
¼ cup brandy,
½ grated nutmeg,
1 teaspoon salt.

Soak bread in milk, let stand until cool, add sugar, beaten yolks of eggs, raisins, currants and citron. Chop suet and work with hands until creamy. Combine the two mixtures, and add brandy or wine and brandy mixed, the spices, and then the stiffly beaten whites of eggs. Turn in buttered mould, cover and steam 5 or 6 hours. Serve hot with Brandy Sauce, page 241.

CHOCOLATE PUDDING

No. 1

6 eggs,
1 cup sugar,
1 cup chocolate, grated,
2 tablespoons bread crumbs,
1 teaspoon baking powder,
Vanilla, cinnamon and cloves.

Beat together yolks and sugar, add other ingredients, then beaten whites of eggs. Boil 1½ hours in air tight pudding form. Serve hot with Hard Sauce, page 243, or Vanilla Sauce, page 244.

No. 2

10 eggs, separated,
1½ cups sugar,
¾ cup grated chocolate,
¾ cup grated almonds,
½ cup flour,
2 teaspoons cinnamon,
½ teaspoon cloves.

Beat yolks until very light, add sugar and beat again, add chocolate, spices, almonds and flour, stir well, then gradually add some of the stiffly beaten whites of eggs and then fold in the rest. Place in buttered pudding mould, tightly cover, and boil 2 hours. Serve hot with cream sweetened and flavored with vanilla.

STEAMED CARAMEL PUDDING

6 tablespoons sugar,
1 tablespoon flour,
3 oz. ground almonds,
1 cup milk,
¼ cup butter,
6 eggs.

Melt the sugar in a spider until light brown. Add flour, and milk; stirring until it forms a paste. Cool, then add butter, almonds, the yolks of eggs well beaten, and lastly the whites that have been beaten stiff. Butter the form, cover butter with a little more sugar. Steam 1 hour. Serve with whipped cream.

SPONGE PUDDING

1 pint milk,
½ cup flour,
teaspoon salt,
¼ cup sugar,
¼ cup butter,
5 eggs, separated.

Stir flour, sugar and salt with a little of the milk until smooth, then add the rest of the milk, hot, and cook until it thickens, about 10 minutes; add the butter and when well mixed stir it into the well beaten yolks; then fold in the whites, beaten stiff. Bake in well buttered pudding dish, in a pan of hot water in a moderate oven, about 30 minutes. Serve hot with vanilla, wine or Cream Sauce, pages 242–244.

COFFEE SOUFFLE

3 tablespoons butter,
3 tablespoons flour,
1 cup black coffee,
⅛ teaspoon salt,
3 eggs, separated,
⅓ cup sugar.

Melt the butter, add the flour, cook until frothy, add ⅔ of the coffee, stir, then add the rest and cook until smooth. Remove from fire, add sugar, salt, and yolks of eggs, beaten until thick and smooth; then fold in the whites of eggs, beaten very stiff; pour into buttered baking dish, set in a pan of hot water, and bake 25 minutes in a moderate oven. Serve with Coffee Sauce, page 241.

MACAROON SOUFFLE

1 doz. macaroons,
1 cup milk,
3 eggs,
French fruit, chopped fine,
Whipped cream.

Scald the macaroons in the milk, pour over the beaten yolks of eggs and cook over hot water until thickened slightly; fold in the whites of eggs beaten stiff and bake in a buttered mould, set in a pan of hot water about 20 minutes. Turn from the mould, sprinkle top with the fruit and surround with the whipped cream.

CHESTNUT SOUFFLE

½ cup sugar,
2 tablespoons flour,
1 cup chestnut puree,
½ cup milk,
Whites of 3 eggs.

Boil chestnuts; drain and rice or mash. Mix sugar and flour, add chestnuts and milk gradually, cook 5 minutes, stirring constantly; beat whites of eggs until stiff and cut and fold into the mixture. Turn into buttered and sugared individual moulds, having them ¾ full. Set mould in hot water and bake in slow oven until firm. Serve with Cream Sauce, page 242.

CHOCOLATE SOUFFLE

6 eggs, yolks,
1 cup grated chocolate,
1 cup sugar,
6 whites of eggs, beaten.

Stir the yolks and sugar together, add the chocolate and six whites of eggs. Bake in a greased pudding dish set in a pan of hot water, about 15 to 20 minutes in a moderate oven.

WALNUT SOUFFLE

6 eggs, yolks,
6 whites of eggs, beaten,
1 cup grated walnut meats,
1 cup sugar.

Stir the yolks and sugar together, and then add the nuts and whites of eggs. Bake about 15 minutes in a greased pudding dish in moderate oven set in pan of hot water.

LEMON SOUFFLE

6 eggs, yolks beaten,
1 cup sugar,
6 whites of eggs, beaten very stiff,
1 lemon, grated rind and juice.

Beat yolks and sugar until lemon colored, add juice and rind of lemon, then fold in the beaten whites. Place in buttered pudding dish, set in pan of hot water and bake 35 to 40 minutes in slow oven. Serve with or without sauce.

CHAPTER XXV

COLD PUDDINGS

CUSTARDS

GENERAL RULES FOR CUSTARD

Eggs should be thoroughly mixed, but not beaten light, with sugar and salt, add the hot milk slowly, stirring all the time. Custards must be cooked over moderate heat—over water in the oven if baked, or in a double boiler if steamed. When thick enough, the custard coats on the spoon. It curdles if cooked a minute too long. If it curdles, put in a pan of cold water immediately and beat until smooth. Always strain custards. Use the yolks instead of the whole eggs to make a soft custard.

SOFT CUSTARD

1 pt. milk, scalded,
4 tablespoons sugar,
1 tablespoon cornstarch,
¼ teaspoon salt,
½ teaspoon flavoring,
1 egg or 2 yolks.

Mix sugar, cornstarch and salt; add egg slightly beaten. Add scalded milk, stirring constantly. Cook in double boiler until it thickens slightly. Strain, cool and flavor.

CHOCOLATE CUSTARD

Follow the recipe for soft custard, melting one-half ounce chocolate with the milk.

COCOANUT CUSTARD

1 pint milk,
½ cup sugar,
3 eggs, separated,
½ cup cream,
½ cup powdered sugar,
¾ cup cocoanut.

Heat milk with sugar, and when steaming add the yolks of the eggs beaten light, and a few grains of salt; remove from the fire, and while warm add cream. Beat until smooth and partly cool, pour into a serving dish, beat the whites of the eggs with the powdered sugar and cocoanut, spread upon the top of custard, and brown lightly in the oven.

FLOATING ISLAND

1 pt. milk,	¼ teaspoon spice, or
4 eggs,	¼ teaspoon salt,
4 tablespoons sugar,	½ teaspoon flavoring.

Scald the milk. Separate the eggs. Mix salt, sugar and cornstarch. Add to yolks and beat slightly. Beat the whites until very stiff, add 2 teaspoons sugar to them, beat slightly and spread mixture on top of the hot milk. Let cook 2 or 3 minutes until firm, lift out on a plate and pour the hot milk on the beaten yolks. Put this mixture into a double boiler and stir until it thickens. When nearly cool stir in flavoring, put the cooked whites on the top and serve cold as a pudding. A pretty way to serve it is to lay specks of jelly on the whites.

CUP CUSTARD OR BAKED CUSTARD

1 pt. milk,	4 tablespoons sugar,
2 eggs,	pinch salt.

Beat eggs slightly, add salt and sugar and stir until the sugar dissolves and pour the milk into the beaten eggs. If desired a little nutmeg or flavoring may be added. Pour into buttered cups or a pudding dish, place the cups in a pan of boiling water, put the pan in the oven and bake until the custards are firm in the center—20 to 30 minutes. Try with a knife. If the knife comes out clean the custard is done.

ORANGE CUSTARD

1 pt. milk,	¼ cup sugar,
3 eggs,	½ teaspoon vanilla,
⅛ teaspoon salt,	3 oranges or 6 bananas.

Separate the yolks and whites of eggs. Beat yolks lightly, add the salt and sugar, and beat well. Pour the hot milk slowly into the eggs. Stir constantly until smooth and thick, and strain. When cool, flavor with vanilla. Peel and slice oranges or bananas, and place in serving dish. Pour on the custard, and take whites of the three eggs (beaten very light), one-fourth cup powdered sugar and few drops of vanilla for the meringue, and drop in large spoonfuls on the custard. Any kind of fruit may be substituted for oranges or bananas.

COFFEE CUSTARD

1 cup very strong cold coffee,
4 eggs, beaten slightly,
1 cup thin cream,
4 tablespoons sugar.

Mix and strain into small cups and place them in a shallow pan. Put boiling hot water into the pan until it reaches half way up to the cups. Set into a moderate oven and cook very gently until the custard is firm. Serve ice cold with little cakes.

CARAMEL CUSTARD

¾ cup sugar,
¼ cup hot water,
4 eggs,
8 yolks of eggs,
½ teaspoon salt,
½ cup sugar,
1 quart milk.

Cook three-fourths a cup of sugar in a small sauce pan over the fire, until the sugar melts and becomes light brown in color. Lift the pan from the fire occasionally, to prevent burning. Add very carefully, as the mixture will steam up to some height, about one-fourth a cup of boiling water, and let stand in a hot place, until the caramel on the spoon and dish is melted. Beat four whole eggs and eight yolks with half a teaspoonful of salt. Add half a cup of sugar, and beat again. Then add one quart of milk and the caramel, and strain into a mould. Bake, standing in a pan of hot water on heavy asbestos paper, until a knife, cut down into the center, comes out holding no uncooked mixture. When cold, pass a knife between the mould and custard, and turn onto a serving-dish. Half instead of three-fourths a cup of sugar will give enough caramel flavor to suffice the taste of some.

CUSTARD WITH CARAMEL SAUCE

½ cup sugar,
3 whites of eggs,
4 eggs, or
2 whole eggs and 4 yolks.
½ teaspoon salt,
⅓ cup sugar,
1 pt. milk.

Melt ½ cup sugar in a spider until changed to a smooth liquid caramel. Turn quickly a little caramel into a timbale mould, keeping the rest hot, while the mould is turned round and round thus lining it with the caramel. Proceed in the same way with all the moulds, or if you prefer line a large pudding dish with the melted sugar or caramel. Set aside.

Make a custard of the remaining ingredients; add salt to sugar and beat with the eggs, then add the milk; stir well and pour into the caramel lined moulds or pudding dish. Cook, standing in hot water until custard is well set, testing with a knife, if knife comes out clean custard is done. When cold remove from moulds onto the serving dish. The caramel will form a sauce around the custard.

Two ounces of melted chocolate with a little melted sugar and water, may be added to the milk of which custard is made, or the caramel may be melted in a little boiling water and used in the custard instead of sugar, thus giving caramel custard.

BLANC-MANGE

⅓ cup Irish moss,
1 quart milk,
¼ cup sugar,
¼ teaspoon salt,
1½ teaspoon vanilla, or other flavoring.

Soak moss in cold water to cover. Let stand 15 minutes, drain and pick over. Put milk in double boiler, add moss, let cook 30 minutes. Add salt, strain; add sugar and flavoring; stir and strain again into individual moulds that have been dipped in cold water. Chill and turn on serving plate, and serve with cream and sugar or sliced bananas.

CHOCOLATE BLANC-MANGE

Blanc-mange,
⅓ cup boiling water.
1½ oz. bitter chocolate,

Follow directions for Blanc-mange, recipe above. Melt chocolate over boiling water when dissolved; add ⅓ cup boiling water and stir until smooth, and add to the milk just before taking from fire. Serve with sugar and cream.

TAPIOCA CREAM

⅓ cup pearl tapioca,
1 pint milk,
Yolks of 2 eggs,
A speck of salt,
Whites of 2 eggs,
½ teaspoon vanilla,
⅓ cup sugar.

Pick over the tapioca, put it in the top of a double boiler and cover with boiling water. Add the milk as soon as the water is absorbed, and cook until the tapioca is soft and clear. Beat the yolks of the eggs, add the salt and sugar and the hot milk, and cook until it thickens like soft custard. Remove from the fire, fold in the whites of the eggs beaten stiff. Flavor when cold. The whites may be mixed with 2 tablespoons powdered sugar, put on top of pudding, and browned in oven a few minutes.

APPLE TAPIOCA

¾ cup pearl tapioca,
cold water,
2½ cups boiling water,
½ teaspoon salt,
7 sour apples,
½ cup sugar.

Soak tapioca 1 hour in cold water to cover; drain, add boiling water and salt; cook in double boiler until transparent. Core and pare apples, arrange in buttered pudding dish, fill cavities with sugar, pour over tapioca, and bake in moderate oven until apples are soft. Serve with sugar and cream.

Pearl or minute tapioca requires no soaking.

BAKED TAPIOCA PUDDING

¼ cup tapioca,
1 pt. milk,
1 tablespoon butter,
½ cup sugar,
2 eggs,
Salt,
1 teaspoon vanilla,
3 or 4 macaroons.

Cook tapioca in milk until transparent. Add a few grains of salt, butter, sugar, and remove from the fire. Let cool a little, then pour over one or two beaten eggs. Add a teaspoonful of vanilla, and turn into a buttered baking-dish. Let bake in a very moderate oven until the egg is set. Three or four macaroons crumbled fine are an addition to this pudding. Serve hot or cold. If it be served cold, use from one-half to one whole cup of milk additional.

RENNET CUSTARD OR JUNKET

2 cups milk,
2 tablespoons sherry wine or
½ tablespoon vanilla,
¼ cup sugar,
2 tablespoons liquid rennet.

Heat milk until lukewarm, add sugar; add wine slowly; when sugar is dissolved add rennet. Turn into a small mould or put in glasses and let stand in a cool place until firm. If wine has been used grate a little nutmeg over the top when ready to serve, and serve with sugar and whipped cream. Junket tablets may be used in place of the liquid rennet.

CORN STARCH PUDDING

1 quart of milk,
½ cup cornstarch,
¼ cup sugar,
½ teaspoon salt,
Whites of 3 eggs,
1 teaspoon vanilla.

Scald the milk; mix the cornstarch with sugar and stir into the hot milk; and cook 15 minutes; then, before folding in the whites of the eggs, beaten stiff, add the vanilla. Turn into a mould which has been rinsed in cold water and set aside to become chilled and firm. Serve with currant jelly, cream and sugar, or with a soft custard.

For Chocolate Cornstarch Pudding, use ½ cup sugar and 2 ounces of chocolate.

PINEAPPLE CORNSTARCH PUDDING

1 cup water,
1 cup pineapple juice,
¼ cup cornstarch,
½ teaspoon salt,
Sugar to taste,
Whites of 3 eggs.

Boil water and fruit juice together, wet cornstarch in a little cold water and stir into the boiling syrup. Cook 20 minutes, add the salt and sugar, remove from fire, cool slightly, and add whites of eggs beaten until stiff. Pour into serving dish, and when cold serve with boiled custard.

ROTHE GRITSE

1 qt. red raspberries,
1 quart red currants,
2 cups cold water,
1½ cups sugar,
¼ cup cornstarch dissolved in cold water.

Boil berries and water; strain and add sugar. Let boil and add three heaping tablespoons cornstarch (which have been dissolved in cold water), when thick put in a melon and serve cold with cream.

APPLE SNOW

½ tablespoon lemon juice,
1 tablespoon powdered sugar,
White of 1 egg,
2 apples.

Cut 2 small apples into quarters and remove the cores. Cook them with a small amount of water until very soft. Drain and rub through a fine sieve. Beat the white of the egg, add the sugar gradually, and slowly beat in the strained apple. Serve with cream.

FRUIT DESSERT

1 pint raspberries,
1 cup white wine,
6 eggs,
1 lb. macaroons,
Sugar.

Sweeten the raspberries and set aside. Beat the yolks of six eggs until light, stir them into the wine, sweetened and heated. Cook a few moments and set aside to cool. Place in dish a layer of macaroons, raspberries and wine custard alternately, until dish is full. Beat whites to a stiff froth. Brown slightly in oven.

RICE WITH APPLES OR PINEAPPLE

2 cups rice (steamed), ½ cup sugar,
3 eggs, 2 apples (steamed),
½ cup milk.

Pare and core the apples, cut in eighths and cook until soft. To the Steamed Rice, page 19, add well beaten yolks of eggs, sugar and cooked apples. Fold in the stiffly beaten whites and bake 30 minutes in well-buttered baking dish. Serve with cream.

FIG AND PIEPLANT DESSERT

¼ lb. dried figs, Stale cake,
Rhubarb, Whites of 2 eggs,
Sugar.

Cut figs in small pieces and stew until partly soft; add twice their bulk of pieplant cut into small pieces. Put these into a baking dish lined with thin slices of stale cake, add sugar to taste and bake slowly, covered. A meringue made of the whites of eggs and sugar may be added, and slightly browned.

ALMOND DESSERT

9 eggs, separated, 2½ cups almonds, blanched
1½ cup sugar, and grated,
Pinch of salt, Grated rind of 1 lemon.

Place in spring form and bake in a moderate oven; serve cold with Wine Sauce, page 244, or bake in 3 layers with whipped cream between layers, and serve.

APPLE DESSERT

10 large apples (greenings), ¼ cup currants,
5 yolks of eggs, 1 tablespoon brandy,
¾ cup sugar, 1 teaspoon vanilla,
25 chopped almonds, ⅛ teaspoon cinnamon,
5 whites of eggs.

Chop the apples. Separate the eggs, beat the yolks until light with the sugar, add the chopped apples, then the rest of the ingredients, the beaten whites last.

Place in spring form and bake in moderate oven until well set and serve with cream.

BANANA WHIP

3 small bananas,
⅓ cup sugar,
1 tablespoon lemon juice,
1 teaspoon wine,
Little salt,
1 cup double cream.

Press the pulp of three bananas through a ricer, vegetable press or sieve; cook with sugar and lemon juice until scalded; cool and flavor with a few drops of vanilla or a little wine, add also a few grains of salt; then beat gradually into a cup of double cream beaten solid with a Dover egg beater. Set aside to become chilled, then serve piled high, in small glasses, with a sprinkling of fine-chopped pistachio nuts on the top. Line the glasses before filling with slices of banana. This makes a particularly good Charlotte Russe filling.

PRUNE OR DATE WHIP

⅓ lb. prunes,
½ cup sugar,
Whites 5 eggs,
½ teaspoon lemon juice.

Pick over and wash prunes or dates and soak in cold water. Cook in same water until soft; then remove stones and rub through strainer. Add sugar and cook 5 minutes or until the consistency of marmalade. Beat whites until stiff and add when cold, fruit mixture gradually, and lemon juice. Heap lightly in buttered dish, and bake 20 minutes in a slow oven. Serve cold with thin custard or cream.

SWISS RICE

1 cup rice,
3 to 3½ cups boiling milk,
1 teaspoon salt,
1 pint cream, whipped,
½ teaspoon vanilla,
Raspberry or cherry juice.

Add salt to milk. Steam rice in the milk over boiling water 30 to 45 minutes until tender. Add vanilla. When cool add and fold in all but ½ cup of the whipped cream; shape into any desired form with spoon.

Add enough fruit juice to the remaining whipped cream to color prettily and use it to garnish the top. Serve cold.

CHESTNUT FLAKE

1 lb. chestnuts,
2 cups sugar,
1 cup water,
1 pt. cream, whipped,
1 tablespoon maraschino.

Take fresh chestnuts. With a sharp-pointed knife, slit each chestnut shell across one side. Cook a minute in boiling water.

Drain and dry, add a teaspoon of butter to each pint of nuts and stir and shake over the fire, three or four minutes. Then remove the shell and skin together; keep nuts covered with thick cloth as they shell better when hot.

Boil chestnuts until half done in boiling water, drain and put them into a syrup (made by boiling 2 cups sugar with 1 cup water 10 minutes) and boil until soft. Put through a potato ricer and serve with whipped cream flavored with maraschino.

MARSHMALLOW DESSERT

½ lb. marshmallows,
¼ cup mlk,
1 cup cream, whipped stiff,
½ cup walnut meats.

Break marshmallows in pieces, add the milk and let cook over hot water until dissolved. Remove from fire, stir well and when cool, fold and whip in the stiffly beaten whipped cream. Place in mould that has been dipped in cold water and sprinkle the broken nut pieces all through the mixture. Chill and let stand 8 or more hours. Place in serving dish and serve ice cold, surrounded with lady fingers.

HEAVENLY HASH

1 pt. whipped cream,
25 best marshmallows,
Candied cherries,
1 cup chopped nuts.

Mix the marshmallows, broken in small pieces, with the whipped cream, let stand on ice several hours, then decorate with candied cherries and serve ice cold.

QUEEN OF TRIFLES

1 lb. lady fingers,
1 lb. macaroons,
½ lb. shelled almonds,
1 pint sherry wine,
½ lb. crystallized cherries,
  cut in halves,
1 quart cream, whipped stiff,
1 pint hot milk,
2 tablespoons flour,
1 egg,
½ cup sugar,

Soak the macaroons in the wine; blanch and chop almonds, not too fine. Make a custard by mixing sugar and flour with the egg until very light, add gradually to the hot milk and let cook in double boiler until very thick, stirring constantly. Cool, add almonds, cherries and the cream whipped very stiff. Line glass bowl with lady fingers, cut in half; add custard, macaroons, cream, putting cherries all through the bowl; have the cream on top decorated with the cherries.

BANANA PUDDING

1 doz. lady fingers, or
Slices of stale sponge cake,
6 bananas,
1 pt. whipped cream,
¼ cup powdered sugar,
½ teaspoon vanilla.

Cover bottom of serving dish with a layer of the cake, put on a layer of sliced bananas, then a layer of the sweetened and flavored whipped cream and so on until the dish is filled.

Place on ice for one hour and serve cold.

BOHEMIAN CREAM

1 pint double cream,
1 pint grape juice or jelly, melted.

Stir together and whip the whole to a froth. Drain if needed. Put in cups and set on ice for several hours. Serve with lady fingers.

WINE SYLLABUB

1 pint cream,
Juice of 1 lemon,
¾ cup sugar,
1 cup sherry, madeira or port
A grating of nutmeg, or
A little cinnamon.

Mix sugar with lemon juice and wine and when dissolved add the cream and whip to a froth. Drain if necessary. Serve very cold in glasses. Have wine soaked bit of cake in bottom of glass.

GELATINE PUDDINGS

ANGEL CHARLOTTE RUSSE

1 tablespoon granulated gelatine,
¼ cup cold water,
¼ cup boiling water,
1 cup sugar,
1 pint heavy cream,
6 rolled stale macaroons,
12 marshmallows in small pieces,
2 tablespoons chopped candied cherries and vanilla or sherry,
¼ lb. blanched and chopped almonds.

Soak gelatine in cold water, dissolve in boiling water, and add sugar. When mixture is cold, add cream, beaten until stiff, almonds, macaroons, marshmallows and candied cherries. Flavor with vanilla or sherry. Turn into a mould, first dipped in cold water, and chill. Remove from mould and serve with Angel Cake.

This dessert may be made more elaborate by cutting the top from an angel cake, and removing some of the inside, leaving a case with three-fourths inch walls, then filling case with mixture, replacing top of cake, covering with frosting, and garnishing with candied cherries and blanched almonds.

BANANA CREAM

1 cup of banana pulp,
The juice of one lemon,
¼ cup of sherry,
1 cup of cream,
½ cup of sugar,
⅓ package of gelatine,
⅓ cup of cold water.

Soak the gelatine in the cold water; add the banana pulp (pass the peeled bananas through a sieve) and let scald over hot water; remove from the fire, and add sugar, and when cool the wine and the lemon juice. Let stand in a cool place, and when it begins to thicken fold in the cream, beaten stiff. Mix and turn into mould and serve with sliced oranges or strawberries.

BANANA SPONGE

⅓ package of gelatine,
⅓ cup of cold water,
⅓ cup of boiling water,
1 cup of sugar,
Juice of 1 lemon,
1 cup of banana pulp,
Whites of 3 eggs,
Slices of banana.

Soften the gelatine in cold water, add the boiling water and sugar; when the sugar is dissolved strain over the banana pulp, heat to the scalding point, cool, add the lemon juice and beat over ice water until light and cold, then beat in, gradually, the stiffly beaten whites of the eggs. Turn the mixture into a mould lined with slices of banana. Serve cold, ornamented with whipped cream, sweetened and flavored.

CHOCOLATE CREAM

½ box granulated gelatine, (2 tablespoons),
1 quart sweet milk,
½ cup cold water,
1 cup sugar,
2 oz. grated chocolate.

Soak the gelatine in the cold water; boil the sweet milk with sugar and grated chocolate and a little salt, 5 minutes; then add dissolved gelatine, stirring constantly; flavor with vanilla, and pour into mould; serve with whipped cream and garnish cream with candied cherries, cut fine.

CHOCOLATE CHARLOTTE

¼ package granulated gelatine,
⅓ cup cold water,
½ oz. chocolate, scraped,
2 tablespoons sugar,
1 tablespoon boiling water,
½ cup hot milk,
½ cup powdered sugar,
1 pint cream, whipped.

Soak gelatine in cold water a few minutes to soften. Put chocolate in a small pan with two tablespoonfuls of sugar and one of boiling water, and stir over the hot fire until smooth and glossy. Add to this the hot milk and the soaked gelatine, and stir until the gelatine is dissolved. Whip cream to a froth, and put it in a bowl, which should be placed in a pan of ice water. Sprinkle a generous half cupful of powdered sugar over the cream. Now add the chocolate and gelatine mixture, and stir gently until it begins to thicken. Line a quart charlotte-mould with lady fingers, and when the cream is so thick that it will just pour, turn it gently into the mould. Place the charlotte in a cold place for an hour or more, and, at serving time, turn out on a flat dish.

COFFEE JELLY

½ box gelatine, or
2 tablespoons granulated gelatine,
½ cup cold water,
2 cups strong boiling coffee,
¾ cup sugar,
¾ cup boiling water,
¼ cup sherry wine.

Soak gelatine in cold water 2 minutes; add the boiling coffee; when dissolved stir in the sugar and boiling water and when cool the wine. Strain into mould and serve with cream and sugar or with whipped cream. If wine is omitted add more water.

CREAM PUDDING

½ cup powdered sugar,
5 yolks of eggs,
½ cup milk,
1 tablespoon granulated gelatine,
¼ cup cold water,
1 cup cream, whipped,
1 tablespoon vanilla.

Soften the gelatine in the water a few minutes. Stir yolks and sugar with Dover egg beater until very, very light; add milk, the softened gelatine. Cook over boiling water (in double boiler) until the mixture coats the spoon, add vanilla and fold in the cream, whipped stiff. Turn into a mould and let stand several hours to chill.

DANISH RICE PUDDING

½ cup rice,
1 pt. milk,
1 teaspoon butter,
¼ cup sugar,
½ box granulated gelatine,
¼ cup warm water,
1 pt. whipped cream,
1 tablespoon sherry.

Cook the first four ingredients until perfectly smooth; then put through a ricer.

Dissolve the gelatine in the warm water, add the strained rice. Let cool and fold in the whipped cream flavored with the sherry. Put in mould to harden. Serve with fresh fruit or fruit sauce.

DELMONICO DESSERT

Yolks of 2 eggs,
¼ cup sugar,
1 pint hot milk,
¼ teaspoon salt,
1½ tablespoons granulated gelatine,
¼ cup cold water,
½ cup boiling water,
2 tablespoons lemon juice,
Whites of 2 eggs,
½ teaspoon vanilla,
¼ lb. macaroons,
¼ cup sherry or vanilla water,
1 tablespoon candied cherries.

Part 1. Soak gelatine in cold water until soft, then dissolve in boiling water; add lemon juice. Make a custard with the yolks of eggs, beaten slightly and mixed with the sugar and salt; pour on the hot milk and cook in the double boiler until it thickens, stirring constantly. Then add the gelatine water, let cook a minute and stir. Strain, cool, add vanilla and the whites of eggs beaten stiff. Soak the macaroons in either sherry, milk or cream or water flavored with a little vanilla; place a candied cherry on top of each macaroon. Place a large melon mould in a pan of ice water; pour in jelly ½ inch deep. When it begins to thicken line the bottom of the mould with the soaked macaroons, cherry side downward. Pour the rest of the gelatine custard over the macaroons and proceed with the following Whipped Cream Layer:

1 pint cream, whipped stiff,
½ cup pulverized sugar,
1 teaspoon vanilla,
¼ lb. candied fruit, (cherries, pineapple, apricot, lime).

Part 2. Sprinkle sugar over cream, add vanilla, fold and place on top of gelatine. Spread the candied fruit, chopped fine, on top of this layer.

Part 3. Stale Sponge Cake. ¼ lb. almonds blanched and cut in thick slices lengthwise. Make Sponge Cake, No. 1, page 350, a day or two before using. Cake should be about 1 inch thick and cut to fit the top end of mould. Prick cake with fork and saturate well with sherry or the flavored vanilla water used to soak the macaroons. Stick almonds half way through top of cake at frequent intervals. Place in mould, almond side down, next the fruit, pressing the cake gently down so the almonds will extend down in the whipped cream layer.

Let stand 1½ hours in ice chest. Turn out of mould and serve with a border of whipped cream. Serves 12 to 15 people.

EASTER EGG DESSERT

2½ pts. lemon jelly, Empty egg shells.

Make a Lemon Jelly, page 278, using 4 tablespoons or the whole package of granulated gelatine. To 2 tablespoons gelatine add the pink vegetable coloring in package and set aside.

Break the top of the shell of an egg only large enough to allow the eggs to slip out. Rinse the shells in cold water. Set each shell upright in a narrow glass or cup; and pour as much of the white jelly into a ring mould as it will contain, and fill the rest, the pink and white jelly into the empty egg shells. Set aside in a cool place to harden over night. In serving, invert the ring on a large platter to form a nest. Roll and crumble the egg shells and the jelly will come out in perfect egg forms; place eggs in nest and serve cold with cream.

GELATINE PUDDING

½ oz. or ¼ box gelatine, or
1 tablespoon granulated
  gelatine,
¼ cup cold water,
Yolks of 3 eggs,

½ cup sugar,
½ teaspoon salt,
1 pint milk,
Whites of 3 eggs,
1 teaspoon vanilla.

Soak the gelatine in cold water until soft, then dissolve in boiling water. Make a custard with the yolks of the eggs, beaten slightly and mixed with the sugar and salt. Pour on the hot milk and cook in the double boiler till it thickens. Then add the gelatine water and strain and cool; add the vanilla, the whites of eggs, beaten stiff. Mix well, and turn into moulds wet in cold water. Place in ice water and when hard and ready to serve turn out on a dish. Varied by adding rolled macaroons, nuts, or fruit.

LEMON JELLY

1 oz. (½ box) gelatine, or	2½ cups boiling water,
2 tablespoons granulated gelatine,	1 cup sugar,
½ cup cold water,	½ cup lemon juice,
	Grated yellow rind of lemon.

Soak gelatine in cold water, 2 minutes for granulated gelatine, 15 minutes for strip gelatine. Steep the grated lemon rind in the boiling water a few minutes for flavor. Add to the softened gelatine and stir until dissolved. Strain through cheese cloth, add sugar and when cool add the lemon juice.

Pour into any desired mould to harden, several hours or over night. Chill and serve. Reserve 1 cup of the warm gelatine mixture, add a little vegetable coloring (in package), use as garnish. In warm or damp weather use more gelatine.

MACAROON AND CHOCOLATE PUDDING

1 pt. cream,	¼ cup boiling water,
1 tablespoon granulated gelatine,	6 macaroons,
2 tablespoons cold water,	¼ lb. sweet chocolate.

Dissolve gelatine in cold water, then add the boiling water and stir until dissolved. When cold add it to the cream whipped. Divide the cream in two parts and in one-half stir the grated chocolate, and in the other half, the broken macaroons. Put in a dish in layers and put in the ice box for several hours to harden.

MACAROON DESSERT

1 pt. hot milk,	1 cup cold water,
5 yolks,	5 beaten whites of eggs,
1 cup sugar,	½ cup sherry or other wine,
½ box granulated gelatine, (2 tablespoons),	¼ lb. macaroons.

Beat the yolks with the sugar until light. Soak the gelatine in the cold water, add the milk boiling hot. Stir until dissolved; pour this onto the yolks and sugar mixture gradually and stir constantly. Place on stove to reheat for about 2 minutes, fold in the beaten whites and pour into mould which has been rinsed with the wine and lined with the macaroons.

NESSELRODE PUDDING

½ cup cold water,
½ box granulated gelatine,
2 cups hot milk,
5 eggs,

⅔ cup raisins,
3 tablespoons blanched almonds,
Small piece of citron, cut fine
½ cup sugar.

Beat yolks of eggs with sugar and add to the hot milk. Cook one minute or until it coats the spoon, stirring constantly. Dissolve gelatine in the cold water. Add to hot milk mixture and stir until dissolved; then add the chopped nuts, raisins, citron and a little salt. Set in a pan of cold water for five minutes. Then add the beaten whites of the five eggs. Also one tablespoon brandy and one teaspoon vanilla. Put in a mould until stiff. Serve with plain or whipped cream.

ORANGE JELLY

½ package (1 oz.) granulated gelatine,
½ cup cold water,
1 cup boiling water,

1 cup sugar,
2 cups orange juice,
3 tablespoons lemon juice.

Soak the gelatine in the cold water, add the boiling water, sugar and juice; strain. 1½ cups of any other fruit juice may be used.

A pretty dish, resembling whole oranges, cut in quarters, is made as follows:

Cut oranges in halves lengthwise. Score with knife, extract and strain juice, without destroying the orange shell. Scrape out clean; set each shell upright in a cup and when the gelatine has partially hardened fill in orange cups. Let stand over night to harden and when ready to serve, cut each piece in two equal parts lengthwise. Arrange in fruit dish and serve.

ORANGE, OR STRAWBERRY CHARLOTTE

2 tablespoons granulated gelatine,
⅓ cup cold water,
⅓ cup boiling water,

1 cup sugar,
1 cup fruit juice and pulp,
3 tablespoons lemon juice,
Whites of 3 eggs,
½ pint whipped cream.

Soak the gelatine in cold water, then dissolve in boiling water. Add sugar, cool, then add lemon juice, fruit juice and pulp. When cold whisk until frothy, then add whites of eggs beaten stiffly and fold in cream. Line a mould with sections of orange or fresh ripe strawberries, turn in the mixture and chill.

PINEAPPLE JELLY

Soak 1 box granulated gelatine in 1 pint cold water, set on stove in double boiler to dissolve; when gelatine is cold and beginning to set, beat into it pineapple juice and pineapple, and place on ice to harden. Be sure you follow the above, for if you mix pineapple and its syrup with the gelatine when you first make it, the acid in it will digest the gelatine so it will not harden.

PRUNE PUDDING

½ box granulated gelatine,
½ cup cold water,
½ pound prunes,
¾ cup of sugar,
¾ cup of lemon juice,
Boiling water.

Wash prunes, then soak over night in 1 quart water; then cook in same water until tender. Drain, remove the stones and cut in pieces. Soak the gelatine in the cold water; add enough boiling water to the hot prune liquid to make one pint and pour over the soaked gelatine. Stir until dissolved and strain. Cool, then add the sugar, lemon juice, pieces of prunes, and a little wine, if approved; stir until the sugar is dissolved. Turn into a mould and set aside to chill and become firm. Serve with whipped cream. Stir twice while cooling to prevent prunes from settling.

RICE A LA DRESDEN

¼ cup rice,
¾ cup sugar,
1 pt. cream, (whipped),
¼ box granulated gelatine,
(1 tablespoon, 1½ oz.),
½ cup cold water,
1 inch vanilla bean.

Dissolve the gelatine in cold water a few minutes. Steam rice in 1 cup boiling water until half done; drain off water and add milk in its place and cook until the rice is soft. Add sugar, dissolved gelatine and vanilla and cool, then add whipped cream, pack in a mould and put on ice 2 hours. Decorate the pudding with maraschino cherries, or Glaced orange, page 395. Serve with either fruit or Chocolate Sauce, page 241.

SNOW PUDDING

½ box of granulated gelatine,
½ cup cold water,
1½ cups sugar,
1 pt. boiling water,
½ cup or juice 3 lemons,
Whites of 3 eggs.

Soak the gelatine in cold water 5 minutes, add boiling water, sugar and lemon juice. Stir until gelatine and sugar are dissolved. Strain. When the mixture begins to stiffen, beat until smooth and add the beaten egg whites. Beat until white and foamy all through and like a drop batter. Pour into a mould which has been rinsed in cold water. Let stand several hours. Serve with Custard Sauce, No. 1, page 242. Color half of the mixture with the fruit red, for variety.

WINE JELLY

1 oz. (½ pkge.) of gelatine,
½ cup cold water,
2 cups boiling water,
1 cup wine (claret, madeira, sherry or port),
3 tablespoons lemon juice,
1 cup of sugar.

If granulated gelatine is used, take 2 tablespoons; add the cold water and let stand 2 minutes to soften. Add the boiling water, stir until dissolved; strain, add sugar and when cool add the wine and lemon juice. Pour into moulds. Set aside in cool place several hours, or over night to harden. Serve cold. In warm weather use less water. One-third cup of orange juice may be added for flavor in place of water or liquor. If a stronger jelly is desired add more wine and less water. One-half cup sherry and ½ cup port is a good combination. One-half cup sherry, 2 tablespoons brandy and enough Kirsch to make one cup of liquor is another combination used.

CHAPTER XXVI

Ices

ICE CREAMS, ICES AND FROZEN PUDDINGS

ICE CREAM

GENERAL RULES

Scald and then chill can, cover and dasher of freezer before using. Adjust can in tub, put in the mixture, then the dasher and cover; adjust the crank, and pack with finely chopped ice and rock salt; this must be higher around than the mixture is inside.

Use three parts of ice to one part of rock salt for freezing, and use four parts ice to one part rock salt for packing afterwards.

Ice cream must be frozen slow and steadily; water ices steadily five minutes. Let stand five minutes, turn again five minutes; repeat until frozen.

When mixture is frozen, remove ice and salt from top of can; wipe top and the cover; uncover and remove dasher, scrape it, beat the frozen mixture with a wooden spoon. Place heavy paper over it, put on cover and place a cork in the hole. Do not strain off the water until the mixture is frozen. Repack the freezer, putting ice on the top, cover with carpet or newspaper, and stand in cool place several hours.

A tightly covered tin can and a wooden pail may be substituted for an ice cream freezer, using a wooden spoon to scrape the mixture from sides and bottom of can as it freezes.

The ice must be finely crushed. Place ice in a burlap bag and give a few blows with the broad side of an ax or hatchet to crush easily.

In preparing ice cream with fruit, the sugar and crushed fruit should stand 1 hour in a cool place, or until the sugar is dissolved, then add cream and freeze; in preparing ice creams without fruit, the cream should be scalded and the sugar dissolved in it; cool, add flavoring and freeze.

Either juice or crushed fruit may be used for ice cream; it is preferable to use only the juice of very seedy fruits.

APRICOT OR PEACH ICE CREAM

1 qt. can apricots or peaches,   1 quart cream,
2 cups sugar.

Scald the cream and melt in it one cup of the sugar, then set away to cool or freeze. Drain off the apricot or peach juice and save it for pudding sauce. Rub the pulp through a puree sieve. When the cream is partly frozen add the fruit pulp and freeze as usual.

BANANA ICE CREAM

1 qt. thin cream, scalded,   1 cup banana pulp,
1½ cups sugar,   ¼ cup lemon juice,
1 pint thin cream.

Scald the quart of thin cream, dissolve in this one cup and a half of sugar; when cold add a pint of thin cream unscalded and begin to freeze. When the cream is rather more than half frozen, add a cup of ripe banana pulp (measured after being pressed through a ricer), mix with the lemon juice, and finish freezing. Let stand an hour to ripen. Serve with banana slices and garnish with pistachio nuts blanched and chopped fine.

BROWN BREAD ICE CREAM No. 1

1 quart hot cream,
1 cup dried brown bread crumbs,
¾ cup sugar,
¼ teaspoon salt.

Dry some stale brown bread in the oven, pound and roll it fine; sift through a fine strainer. Mix the sifted crumbs with the hot cream, add salt and sugar and when cold freeze as usual. Stale sponge corn cake may be dried and used in the same way.

CARAMEL ICE CREAM

No. 1

1 cup sugar,
2 tablespoons cornstarch or flour,
2 cups scalded milk,
1 egg,
1 scant cup sugar, melted to a brown liquid,
½ teaspoon vanilla,
1 quart cream.

Make a custard of first four ingredients, as in Vanilla Ice Cream, No. 2, page 288. Then melt one scant cup of sugar in an iron spider, until it is a brown liquid, and pour it very gradually into the hot custard. Cool, add cream and flavoring, stir and freeze.

No. 2

¼ lb. maple and chocolate, caramels, mixed,
2 whole eggs,
¾ cup sugar,
1½ pints cream.

Melt the caramels with ¼ cup of the cream. Add sugar to eggs, beat well and stir into the melted candy. Fold in the cream, beaten slightly. Freeze.

COFFEE ICE CREAM

1 quart cream,
1½ cups scalded milk,
⅛ cup ground mocha coffee,
1¼ cups sugar,
Yolks of 4 eggs,
¼ teaspoon salt,
A little vanilla.

Pour the hot milk over the coffee, add 1 cup sugar. Mix the eggs slightly beaten with the remaining sugar; combine the two mixtures and cook over hot water until thickened, add 1 cup of cream, let stand where it will keep hot ½ hour. Cool, add remaining cream then strain through double cheese cloth. Add vanilla to taste and freeze. Garnish with maraschino cherries. More eggs may be added, if desired, or they may be omitted entirely.

ICE CREAMS, ICES, ETC.

CHESTNUT ICE CREAM

3 cups chestnuts, cooked in milk and riced,
A little vanilla,
1½ pints cream,
3 cups sugar and 1½ cups water, cooked to a syrup,
6 yolks,
½ lb. candied fruit, cut fine.

Add chestnuts to syrup and when boiling, add gradually to six well beaten yolks, stirring well. Remove from stove, stir until cold, and add cream, and candied fruit, cut fine, dipped in maraschino. Freeze.

CHOCOLATE ICE CREAM

No. 1

Add from 2 to 4 oz. of bitter chocolate melted over teakettle, to Vanilla Ice Cream, No. 2, page 288, stirring until smooth by the gradual addition of a little of the hot milk or cream. Mix and freeze.

No. 2

1½ oz. chocolate,
Or ¼ cup cocoa,
1 cup sugar,
¼ cup hot water,
1 tablespoon vanilla,
1 quart cream.

Melt the chocolate, add the sugar gradually, and then the hot water slowly. Cool, add cream and flavoring, and then freeze.

No. 3

6 yolks,
¾ cup sugar,
6 sticks Maillard's chocolate, grated,
1 cup hot milk,
1 quart cream,
1 teaspoon vanilla.

Stir egg and sugar, add grated chocolate melted in the hot milk, then add cream and vanilla, and freeze.

FANCY ICE CREAM

4 eggs,
1 cup powdered sugar,
1 quart cream,
1 teaspoon vanilla,
¼ lb. stale macaroons,
¼ lb. marshmallows,
¼ lb. walnut meats,
12 candied cherries.

Separate the eggs. Beat the yolks very light with the sugar; then add the whites beaten very stiff and the cream and freeze. When about half frozen add the macaroons, rolled, the marshmallows each cut in 8 pieces; the walnut meats and the cherries cut fine. Freeze.

FROZEN EGG NOG

1 qt. rich cream,
1 cup powdered sugar,
1 gill brandy,
½ gill rum,
Mix all and freeze.

GRAPE ICE CREAM

1 qt. grape juice,
1 quart cream.
Juice of 1 lemon,

If juice is unsweetened add 1 lb. of sugar. Mix and freeze.

MACAROON ICE CREAM

12 stale macaroons,
1 quart cream,
¾ cup sugar,
2 tablespoons sherry wine, or
1 teaspoon almond extract.

Dry macaroons, roll or pound them fine, and sift through a fine gravy strainer. Add them to cream and sugar and flavor with extract of almond or sherry wine. Stir them in when the cream is partly frozen.

MAPLE ICE CREAM

1 cup rich maple syrup,
1 pint cream,
4 yolks of eggs,
1 white of egg.

Heat syrup to the boiling point and pour gradually on the well beaten yolk. Cook in double boiler until thick and when cool, add to the cream, whipped with the white of the egg; freeze.

ORANGE ICE CREAM

Vanilla ice cream,
Grated rind of 2 oranges,
Grated rind of ½ lemon,
Juice of 4 oranges.

Follow recipe for Vanilla Ice Cream, page 288, adding the grated rind of lemon and orange to the custard, before boiling. Strain and cool and in place of the vanilla flavoring add the orange juice, more or less juice and rind to suit taste.

PEACH ICE CREAM

No. 1

2 quarts ripe peaches,
1 cup sugar,
A few peach stone meats,
1 quart cream,
1 teaspoon vanilla,

Pare peaches, cut them fine and mash quickly with a wooden masher; then add one cup of sugar and a few of the peach-stone meats, and keep it closely covered until the sugar is dissolved.

Add cream and vanilla, freeze and when the cream is half frozen strain the peach pulp through coarse cheese-cloth and stir it into the cream. Freeze as usual.

PEACH ICE CREAM

No. 2

6 yolks,
1¼ cups sugar,
1 cup hot milk,
6 ripe peaches,
1 quart cream.

Stir yolks and sugar together, add milk, the peaches cut fine and mashed and cream. Freeze.

PEACHES MELBA ICE CREAM

1½ pt. of cream,
1 vanilla bean,
6 eggs (yolk),
½ lb. powdered sugar.

Put the cream in a double boiler, with the vanilla bean split in half. Beat the yolks of the eggs and the sugar together until light, add to the hot cream, stir until the eggs begin to thicken. Strain through a sieve; when cool, freeze.

Take ½ cup strawberry syrup, ½ cup raspberry syrup.

Put on stove—when it begins to boil add a scant teaspoon cornstarch dissolved in a little water. Take from fire and put in cool place.

Peel fresh peaches and place on ice, then pour the above syrup and peaches over the ice cream.

Whole preserved, sweet peaches are used, out of season.

PISTACHIO ICE CREAM

Vanilla Ice Cream,
4 oz. pistachio nuts,
A few drops of rose water,
¼ cup sugar,
¼ cup cream,
1 teaspoon vanilla,
½ teaspoon almond extract.

Shell and blanch pistachio nuts. Pound them in a mortar, with a few drops of rose water, add the sugar and cream, till like a fine paste. Make any vanilla ice cream, and scant the proportion of sugar. Flavor it with a delicate flavor of vanilla and almond and add the pistachio paste. Color it a pale green with Burnett's Leaf Green.

RASPBERRY OR STRAWBERRY ICE CREAM

1 quart berries,
1 quart cream,
1 cup hot milk,
6 yolks,
2 cups sugar.

Press and strain the fruit. Beat eggs and sugar well together add fruit juice, then hot milk, and lastly the cream. Freeze.

STRAWBERRY ICE CREAM

1 qt. thin cream,
1 box strawberries,
⅞ cup sugar.

Wash and hull berries. Sprinkle with sugar. Let stand one hour; mash and rub through a strainer. Add the cream and freeze.

TO USE VANILLA BEAN FOR ICE CREAM

Split a vanilla bean, or a portion of one, and heat it with the milk and sugar. Then remove it, and scrape out the seeds and soft part. Mix them with a little sugar and add them to the cream.

VANILLA ICE CREAM

No. 1, Cornstarch

1 pint milk,
2 tablespoons cornstarch or flour,
1 cup sugar,
⅛ teaspoon salt,
1 egg,
2 teaspoons vanilla,
1 quart cream,

Mix flour, sugar, salt, and the milk gradually. Cook over hot water twenty minutes, stirring well; take from stove, add the well-beaten egg gradually. Cool. Add cream and flavoring. Strain and freeze. If cream cannot be obtained, more eggs and flour should be used.

No. 2, Philadelphia

1 quart cream,
1 cup sugar,
1 teaspoon vanilla.

Mix sugar and cream, add flavoring, and freeze.

No. 3, Neopolitan

4 whole eggs, or
8 yolks,
1 cup sugar,
1 quart cream,
2 teaspoons vanilla.

Scald over hot water, but do not boil the cream. Beat the yolks till thick and creamy, add the sugar and beat again. Beat the whites stiff, and beat them well into the yolks. Pour the hot cream into the eggs, and when well mixed, turn back into the double boiler and cook like boiled custard. Stir constantly until the foam disappears and the custard has thickened enough to coat the spoon. Strain at once, and when cold add the flavoring and freeze.

CHOCOLATE SAUCE FOR ICE CREAM

No. 1

2 oz. chocolate, ½ cup boiling water,
1 cup powdered sugar.

Stir and cook in double boiler to the consistency of molasses and serve hot with Vanilla ice cream.

No. 2

1 oz. chocolate, 2¾ cups sugar,
3 tablespoons sugar, 2 in. stick cinnamon,
1 cup boiling water, 1 teaspoon vanilla.

Melt chocolate over hot water; add 3 tablespoons sugar and gradually the boiling water; stir until smooth and glossy; add the remaining sugar and cinnamon and stir until boiling begins; let boil 5 minutes; strain, cool and add vanilla.

CLARET SAUCE FOR ICE CREAM

2 cups sugar, ½ cup hot water,
½ cup claret wine.

Melt the sugar with the water. Stir until dissolved and then boil without stirring until it forms a soft ball in cold water.

Remove from stove and add the claret, cool and serve with ice cream.

MAPLE SAUCE FOR ICE CREAM

1 pint maple syrup, ¼ cup butter.

Boil the syrup and butter until it forms a thread, when dropped from tip of spoon.

Pour while hot over Vanilla or Lemon Ice Cream.

STRAWBERRY SAUCE FOR ICE CREAM

1 pint strawberries,   ¾ cup sugar,
½ cup water.

Boil sugar and water 10 minutes; cool and when ready to serve add to the chilled and crushed juice and pulp of berries.
For Vanilla or Lemon Ice Cream.

WATER ICES AND SHERBETS

In freezing sherbets or water ices, freeze steadily five minutes, let stand five minutes, turn again five minutes. Repeat until frozen.

In preparing frozen fruit or water ice the sugar and water should be made into a syrup, which should be boiled 5 minutes, then strained.

Fruit juice is used for water ice; the fruit is pressed through a colander or cut in small pieces with a silver knife for frozen fruit.

CAFE PARFAIT

1 quart cream,   3 tablespoons Crosse & Blackwell's Mocha Essence,
2 whole eggs,
Sugar to taste.

Freeze quite soft shortly before using and serve in glasses with whipped cream and maraschino cherries.

CHAMPAGNE SHERBET

1 quart water,   ½ pint orange juice,
1 pint water,   ½ pint champagne.

Boil water and sugar 15 minutes; cool, add other ingredients and freeze.

CRANBERRY FRAPPE

1 quart cranberries,   2 cups water,
2 cups sugar,   Juice of 2 lemons.

Cook the berries in the water eight minutes, strain; add sugar and bring to the boiling point. Cool, add lemon juice and freeze to a mush, using equal quantities of salt and ice. One cup of crabapples boiled with the cranberries, make a pleasing variety.

CREME DE MENTHE ICE

4 cups water,
1 cup sugar,
⅓ cup creme de menthe,
Burnett's leaf-green coloring.

Make a syrup of sugar and water, boil twenty minutes and add creme de menthe and coloring; strain and freeze.

FRUIT ICE

1 quart water,
2 cups fruit juice or crushed fruit,
2 cups sugar,
Lemon juice to taste.

Boil water and sugar to a syrup five minutes, cool, add fruit juice and lemon to taste; freeze.

NOTE—Orange, raspberry, strawberry, grape, currant, apricot, pineapple, etc., juice or fruit crushed, may be used alone, or in combination.

VANILLA SAUCE FOR ICE CREAM

1 cup sugar,
½ cup water,
1 pint cream,
1 teaspoon vanilla.

Boil sugar and water 8 minutes; let cool and add cream and vanilla. Serve with Chocolate or Strawberry Ice Cream.

GRAPE FRAPPE

4 cups water,
2 cups sugar,
¼ cup lemon juice,
2 cups grape juice,
⅔ cup orange juice.

Make a syrup of boiling water and sugar 15 minutes; add grape, lemon and orange juice; cool, strain and freeze to a mush, using equal parts of ice and salt.

LEMON ICE

No. 1

1 quart water,
2 cups sugar,
¾ cup lemon juice.

Boil water and sugar to a syrup five minutes. Cool, add juice, and freeze.

No. 2

1 quart water,
1 pint sugar.
¾ cup lemon juice,

Make a syrup of sugar and water, boiled twenty minutes; cool, add juice. Freeze and serve with creme de menthe.

LEMON MILK SHERBET

2 cups sugar,
Juice of 3 lemons, or ½ cup lemon juice,
1 quart milk.

Mix in the order given, and freeze.

MINT SHERBET

6 lemons,
2 oranges,
2 cups sugar,
2 cups water,
1 large bunch of fresh mint,
1 white of egg,
1 piece of green leaf,
½ size of a pea,
(Burnett's).

Squeeze out the juice of the lemons and oranges. Over the peelings pour the cold water and put on the stove, allowing it to come to just the boiling point. Pour quickly over the sugar and mint, cut up fine. Cover and allow it to steep for one hour. Then strain over the fruit juice. Take the leaf green and add a little of the above mixture to it, stirring until dissolved and clear. Then put all together and when cold put into the freezer with the well beaten egg and freeze.

To be served in sherbet glasses, using sprigs of mint and maraschino cherries for garnishing. Serve with lamb.

ORANGE FRAPPE

1 quart water,
1 pint sugar,
1 pint orange juice,
2 lemons, juice only.

Make a syrup of water and sugar, boiling it twenty minutes. Add other ingredients, strain and freeze.

PINEAPPLE SHERBET

1 can grated pineapple,
1 quart milk,
1 cup sugar,
Juice of 1 lemon.

Add sugar to the pineapple and lemon juice; add milk, and freeze.

RASPBERRY OR CURRANT ICE

4 cups water,
2 cups sugar,
1¼ cup raspberry juice or raspberry and currant juice mixed,
Juice ½ lemon.

Let sugar and water boil 6 minutes. When cool add raspberry and lemon juice. Freeze.

ICE CREAMS, ICES, ETC.

STRAWBERRY ICE

4 cups water,
1½ cups sugar,
2 cups strawberry juice,
1 tablespoon lemon juice.

Make a syrup of sugar and water and boil 20 minutes; cool, add strawberries crushed and squeezed through double cheesecloth; add lemon juice; strain and freeze.

FROZEN PUDDINGS

TO MOULD FROZEN MIXTURES

Mixtures to be moulded must not be frozen hard, but should be solidly packed in the moulds and covered with buttered paper, butter side up. Fill moulds to overflowing. Repack in ice and salt, four parts ice to one part salt. Let stand several hours. At serving time remove mould, wipe carefully, and place in a vessel of cold water one minute. Remove cover, run knife around edges of cream, invert can on serving dish, and the frozen mixture will slip out. If necessary, wring cloth out of hot water and pass over the mould.

ICE PUDDING

1 pt. whipped cream,
¼ lb. crystallized cherries,
1 doz. crushed stale macaroons;
½ slice candied pineapple, cut fine.
Powdered sugar and vanilla or Maraschino to taste.

Place in mould. Pack in salt and ice and let stand 3 or 4 hours.

FROZEN PUDDING

No. 1

3 yolks, beaten,
3 tablespoons sugar,
1 pint whipped cream,
4 oz. chopped hazelnuts,
Vanilla.

Mix in order given, and place in a mould and pack in 4 parts ice to 1 salt. Let stand three hours.

No. 2

1 cup sugar,
5 eggs, beaten very light,
1 doz. stale crushed macaroons,
¼ lb. assorted crystallized fruit,
1 pt. whipped cream,
Vanilla to taste.

When thoroughly mixed put in mould, pack in 4 parts of ice to 1 of salt and let stand 3 or 4 hours.

ANGEL MOUSSE

1 cup sugar,	1 cup English walnuts,
½ cup water,	candied pineapple and
3 whites of eggs,	cherries, chopped fine,
½ teaspoon vanilla,	1 pt. cream, whipped stiff,

Boil sugar and water, stirring only until sugar is dissolved and then boil until it spins a thread, then pour it on the well beaten whites, beat until cool, flavor when cold, stir in gently 1 pt. of cream well whipped and drained, add the chopped nuts and cherries and put in a mould. Pack in ice and salt for about 4 hours. When ready to serve, turn out on platter and cut with a knife. One-quarter cup of very strong coffee in place of the fruit makes a good Coffee Mousse.

BAKED ALASKA

Whites 6 eggs,	¾ teaspoon vanilla,
6 tablespoons powdered sugar,	2 quarts of ice cream, Thin sheet sponge cake.

Make two quarts of ice cream after any recipe and when frozen remove the beater and pack it well in the freezer can. Let it stand till hard. Just before serving make a meringue by beating the whites of six eggs till stiff, then beating in, gradually, six rounding tablespoonfuls of sifted powdered sugar. Put a thin, round sheet of sponge cake on a plate suitable for serving, and turn out the mould of cream on the cake. Pile the meringue thickly round the edge and top of the cream, but do not smooth it. Place the dish on a wooden box cover and brown the meringue quickly in a hot oven. Serve at once. The plate should be larger than the cake, and the cake larger than the bottom of the can. The cream will not melt, for the wood and the meringue serve as non-conductors of the heat. This is recommended chiefly for its novelty.

CRANBERRY PARASADE

1 qt. cranberries,	3 cups sugar,
1 cup boiling water,	½ cup orange juice,
	3 whites of eggs.

Wash and pick over the berries. Put on to boil with water. Cover and let cook until tender. Strain, reheat and add the sugar and stir until dissolved; add the orange juice and the whites of eggs beaten stiff, fold in gently and pack into mould, cover with buttered paper, butter side up, and then with mould cover. Pack mould in ice and salt; 4 cups ice to 1 of salt, let stand 3 to 4 hours, remove from mould and serve.

FROZEN CHESTNUT PUDDING

1 cup chestnuts,
1 pt. cream, whipped,
½ cup sugar,
1 teaspoon vanilla,
2 tablespoons sherry.

The chestnuts must measure 1 cupful after boiling and put through a press, see Chestnut Vegetable, page 160; add cream, sugar, vanilla and sherry. Put in a mould and pack in ice and salt 3 hours. Decorate with maraschino cherries and marrons.

FROZEN COFFEE PUDDING

6 yolks,
1½ cups sugar,
1 cup hot milk,
1 cup strong coffee,
2 tablespoons granulated gelatine,
½ cup cold milk,
1½ cups cream,
6 whites, beaten.

Add coffee to hot milk and sugar to beaten yolks, mix all together, add cream and cook in double boiler until thick. Remove from stove. Soak the gelatine in cold milk, add to the hot mixture and stir until dissolved. Cool slightly, add six beaten whites and place in mould to freeze. Cover mould, pack in salt and ice and let stand 3 or 4 hours. Serve with whipped cream sweetened with powdered sugar and flavored with vanilla.

FROZEN CHOCOLATE PUDDING

No. 1

3 sticks or ¼ lb. Maillard's chocolate,
½ cup sugar,
½ cup hot water,
6 eggs, separated,
1 pt. cream.

Cook the water and sugar to a thin syrup, add chocolate, grated. Pour this gradually on to the 6 beaten yolks, add the 6 whites, beaten stiff; cool, then add the cream whipped stiff. Pour in a mould, and pack in ice and salt from 4 to 6 hours. Use 3 cups of ice to 1 cup salt. This serves 12 persons.

No. 2

3 yolks,
2 oz. chocolate, grated,
½ cup milk,
¼ cup sugar,
1 pint whipped cream.

Stir eggs slightly with sugar, add the milk, and the chocolate, shaved; place over boiling water, let cook until it coats the spoon. Cool, then add the whipped cream. Place in mould and pack in ice, 4 parts ice to 1 of salt. Let stand 3 or 4 hours.

FROZEN DESSERT

1 qt. cream, whipped stiff,
1/3 cup powdered sugar,
1 tablespoon maraschino,
1 tablespoon granulated gelatine,
1/4 cup cold water,
1/3 cup hot, scalded cream.

Soak gelatine in cold water a few minutes, add scalded cream and stir until dissolved. Let cool and fold in the whipped cream, stirring 1/3 at a time; if gelatine thickens too much, melt over hot water and cool again and mix with the cream. Place in mould and pack in ice 3 to 4 hours.

FROZEN DIPLOMAT

6 yolks,
1 cup sugar,
1 pint cream,
6 lady fingers,
Sherry wine to moisten the lady fingers,
2 tablespoons maraschino,
1/8 lb. candied cherries,
1 pint whipped cream.

Separate the lady fingers and sprinkle with the sherry, cut the cherries in half, soak in maraschino. In a double boiler, scald one pint cream, add it to the beaten yolks and sugar. When thick, strain and cool. Flavor with vanilla, add one pint whipped cream, and freeze very firmly. Stand a mould in a pan of ice and fill with alternate layers of frozen cream and lady fingers and candied fruit. Have the last layer cream. Bury the mould, well closed, in salt and ice for three hours.

FROZEN KISS PUDDING

1 quart whipped cream,
1/2 lb. ground Kisses,
1 teaspoon vanilla,
1 tablespoon Maraschino,
2 tablespoons sherry.

Mix and put into a mould and pack in salt and chopped ice three or four hours. Add a few candied cherries, chopped fine.

FROZEN NESSELRODE

1 1/2 cups sugar,
3/4 cup water,
1/2 lb. candied fruit, cut fine,
1 wine glass sherry,
4 yolks,
1 1/2 cups chestnuts (boiled and put through a ricer),
1 qt. whipped cream.

Boil sugar and water to a syrup, cool, add yolks, and put on stove in a double boiler; cook until smooth, stirring constantly; cool again, add the chestnuts, page 160, after straining through a ricer, add all other ingredients and fill in a mould. Pack in ice and salt for 4 hours.

FROZEN STRAWBERRY PUDDING

1 qt. strawberries,
½ lb. macaroons,
1 cup sugar,
4 yolks,
1 cup white wine.

Alternate sugared strawberries and macaroons in a pudding dish. Heat wine and pour gradually over the beaten yolks. When slightly cooled pour over the berries and macaroons and mix. Fill into an air tight mould and pack in ice and salt six hours. Serve with sweetened whipped cream.

LALLA ROOKH CREAM

5 yolks of eggs,
1 cup sugar,
1 cup cream,
5 whites of eggs,
2 tablespoons granulated gelatine,
1 pint whipped cream,
2 tablespoons rum.

Make a boiled custard of yolks and sugar and one cup cream, add gelatine (dissolved in a little cold milk), and stir until dissolved, remove from fire, cool, add rum, five whites of eggs beaten stiff, and whipped cream. Mix all well together and pack in a mould. Place the mould in ice and salt three hours. When serving, decorate with maraschino cherries and some of the cherry juice.

MAPLE MOUSSE

1 cup maple syrup,
5 eggs,
1 pt. cream, whipped stiff,
1 teaspoon vanilla.

Beat eggs till very light, add syrup and cook until it thickens, stirring constantly. Place the dish in a pan of ice and stir until creamy; add vanilla and whipped cream. Fill mould and pack in ice and salt, 4 parts of ice to 1 of salt. Let stand 4 hours.

RASPBERRY BOMBE GLACE

Raspberry ice,
1 cup double cream,
½ teaspoon vanilla.
White of 1 egg,
¼ cup powdered sugar,

Line a 3 pint melon mould with Raspberry Ice, page 292. Fill the center with whipped cream, white of egg beaten stiff, powdered sugar and vanilla added before whipping. Let stand packed in equal parts of ice and salt for 3 hours.

STRAWBERRY PARFAIT

1 quart cream,
1 cup sugar,
½ pint strawberry juice.

Whip the cream, add sugar and fruit juice. Put into a mould and freeze three hours, using 4 parts ice to 1 of salt.

CHAPTER XXVII

PASTRY AND PIES

GENERAL RULES

All of the materials must be as cool as possible.

The shortening should not be cut very fine, if a flaky crust is desired.

The dough should be mixed with a knife and not touched with the hands. It should be rolled on one side, using but little flour. The dough is rolled thin and baked until brown.

Meat and oyster pies should be made without an undercrust. The crust should be cut in several places to allow the steam to escape.

If an undercrust is used, this crust may be baked on the outside of a tin plate, then filled. In this case, the crust must be pricked all over with a fork, so that it may keep its shape.

If two crusts are used, the lower one should be moistened around the edge with cold water, then a ½ inch strip of paste may be placed around the edge of the undercrust. This strip should also be moistened, and the uppercrust placed over the pie and pressed slightly around the edge.

The paste may be made the day before using, then covered and placed on ice. It rolls more easily if placed on ice after mixing.

PLAIN PASTRY OR PIE DOUGH

1¼ cups flour (pastry),
¼ teaspoon baking powder,
¼ teaspoon salt,
⅓ to ½ cup shortening,
(butter or other fat),
⅓ to ½ cup cold water.

Use butter, beef drippings, lard or any other desired fat, alone or mixed. Sift flour, salt and baking powder into a chopping bowl. Flour the blade of a chopping knife or a small empty baking powder can and chop the shortening into the flour until the mixture looks like meal; or rub the shortening into the flour with the tips of the fingers. Use knife to mix the dough, adding the cold water gradually and use only enough water to make a paste that is not crumbly, but sticks together without adhering to the knife or bowl. Take up all the particles of dough or flour on the sides of the bowl and with aid of knife turn on to a board lightly dredged with flour, pat with rolling pin and roll out. Use no more flour than is absolutely necessary. Roll in 2 circular pieces ⅛ inch thick; have one a little larger than the other and place it on the pie tin or plate loosely without stretching. Brush over top of this dough, with white of egg, slightly beaten, or sprinkle with a tablespoon of bread crumbs to prevent the dough from becoming soggy. Put in the filling, brush over the edge of pastry with cold water, and lay the second round of paste loosely over the filling; press the edges together lightly, and trim, if needed. Cut several slits in the top crust, or prick it with a fork before putting it in place. Bake in a slow oven from 35 to 45 minutes. Brown well.

SHORT OR FLAKY PASTRY

1 heaping cup flour,
¼ teaspoon salt,
¼ cup lard,
¼ cup butter,
Ice water.

Have all the material ice cold. Chop the shortening in the flour till the size of peas and beans. Toss lightly with a knife, adding enough ice water to about half wet the flour. Turn out on a smooth, cold board. Gather with the knife into a square pile. Then pound lightly with rolling pin till well flattened. Roll in an oblong piece ½ in. thick; fold in thirds and roll again; repeat, and after the third rolling it will usually be sufficiently compact to roll thin enough to line a plate. This paste improves by standing half an hour or more on the ice. Sufficient for 1 pie.

COOKIE DOUGH FOR PIES

1 tablespoon butter,
1 cup flour,
½ teaspoon baking powder,
¼ cup sugar,
1 egg.

Mix dry ingredients. Work in butter with the finger tips; add egg; mix. Toss on slightly floured board and roll ¼ inch thick. This makes enough dough for a large oblong pan; used for apple, cheese, blueberry or any other fresh fruit open pie.

PUFF PASTE

1 lb. flour,
1 lb. butter,
A little ice water.

All the utensils used should be ice cold. Chill the flour; divide the butter into three parts; wash and pat each into a thin oblong pat; wrap two of the butter pats in a napkin and place them between pans of cracked ice; with the tips of the fingers work the other butter pat into the flour, keeping plenty of flour between the butter and the fingers; add ice water, using as little as possible to make a smooth paste; toss the paste on floured board, knead just enough to form a ball; shape pat and roll out one-fourth inch thick, keeping paste a little wider than long and corners square; lay one pat of the butter on the paste, dredge very lightly with flour; fold over the paste so as to enclose the butter; roll up like a jelly roll; pat and roll out one-fourth inch thick; add butter and roll out as above. After all of the butter has been added, fold and roll out four or five times; the more times it is folded and rolled out the more air will be enclosed. The more air retained in the paste the more puffy it will be. The rolling should be done with gentle stroke from center out. As often as the paste becomes a little soft, place it in a napkin between two pans of cracked ice and let it stand until thoroughly chilled. Puff paste requires a hot oven, greatest heat coming from the bottom; turn frequently that it may rise evenly; when well risen, decrease temperature of oven.

Puff paste should be used for pies, patties, vol-au-vents, rissoles, cheese straws, tarts, turnovers, etc.

MURBERTEIG FOR PIES OR FILLED TORTES

No. 1

3 cups flour (¾ lb.),
1 cup butter (½ lb.),
¼ cup sugar,
Yolks of 2 eggs,
1 tablespoon brandy,
¼ cup cold water.

Beat eggs with the water. Mix butter and flour. Combine the mixtures, adding the other ingredients. Put in cool place to harden. Grated rind and piece of lemon may be used in place of the brandy.

MURBERTEIG

No. 2

1 cup butter,	1 yolk of egg,
1/2 cup sugar,	1 teaspoon rum,
1 whole egg,	1 teaspoon baking powder,

2 cups flour.

Cream the butter, add the sugar, then the eggs, stir well, add the rest of the ingredients. Place dough in cool place to harden and when cool enough to handle, roll or press into shape to fit form. Fill with any desired fruit or torte mixture and bake. Juice and rind of lemon may be used in place of rum.

No. 3

1 1/2 cups butter,	1 whole raw egg,
1 cup sugar,	3 cups flour,
5 hard boiled yolks of eggs,	3/4 lemon (juice)

A little mace.

Rub the cooked yolks to a paste, add the raw egg. Mix all ingredients and press dough on to pie plates very thin with fingers, since it will be impossible to roll it.

MATZOS PIE CRUST

1 1/2 matzos,	2 eggs,
1 tablespoon fat,	1/8 teaspoon salt,
1/4 cup matzos meal,	2 tablespoons sugar.

Soak matzos and press dry; heat fat and add the soaked matzos. When dry add the matzos meal, eggs, sugar and salt. Mix well and press into pie plate with hands as it is possible to roll this dough. Have dough 1/4 inch thick.

APPLE PIE

| 4 apples, medium size, | 1/2 cup sugar, |
| Flavor with cinnamon, nutmeg or lemon juice, | 1 or 2 tablespoons water, if apples are not juicy. |

Pare, core and slice the apples. Line a pie plate with Plain Pastry, page 300. Sprinkle with bread crumbs. Lay in the apples, sprinkle with sugar and spices if wanted. Cover with upper crust, slash and prick, and bake in moderate oven until the crust is brown and the fruit is soft.

APPLE PIE (Chopped)

4 large apples, chopped,	¼ cup raisins, seeded,
¼ lb. almonds, blanched and chopped,	¼ teaspoon cinnamon,
	1 lemon juice and rind, or
¾ cup sugar,	¼ cup wine.

Mix all together and stew 5 minutes. Cool. Line a pie plate with Matzos Pie Crust, page 302, or Murberteig, page 301. Place mixture on dough and bake in moderate oven. Beat white of egg very stiff, sweeten to taste and spread on top. Return to oven and brown slightly. Or, vary the amount of sugar according to the acidity of the apples, using 2 tablespoons or more for an apple. If the apples are not juicy, add from ½ tablespoon to 1 tablespoon water, according to the size of the apple.

The apples may be flavored with lemon juice, cinnamon or nutmeg, and should be dotted with bits of butter.

Or, thick apple sauce may be used on a baked crust.

APPLE, PEACH OR PLUM PIE OR KUCHEN

Cover a well greased oblong tin as thin as possible with raised Kuchen Dough, page 311, or with Cookie Dough, page 301. Core, pare and cut four or five apples in eighths. Lay them in parallel rows on top of the dough and sprinkle with sugar and cinnamon. Beat the yolk of an egg, add three tablespoons cream, and drip around apples. Bake twenty or thirty minutes in hot oven, or until crust is well baked and apples are soft. Peaches or plums may be used in place of the apples; pare the peaches, cut in halves and remove the stones. If plums are used, wipe carefully, cut in halves and remove the stones. Place in parallel rows and proceed as for Apple Kuchen.

Or dip each piece of apple, peach or plum in melted butter, before placing in rows on the dough. Sprinkle plentifully with sugar, add a little cinnamon and bake in hot oven until fruit is soft and crust well browned underneath.

BLUEBERRY PIE OR KUCHEN

No. 1

1 qt. blueberries,	3 tablespoons cream,
¼ cup sugar,	Yolk of 1 egg,
2 tablespoons lemon juice,	Cinnamon.

Wash and pick over blueberries, line pie plate with a thin layer of Kuchen Dough, page 311, or Cookie Dough, page 301, sprinkle with bread crumbs. Add the berries, sprinkle with sugar, not too much, and cinnamon, lemon juice, and over all the yolks of an egg beaten with cream. If green grapes or currants can be obtained, strew around in place of the lemon juice.

BLUEBERRY PIE OR KUCHEN

No. 2

1 qt. blueberries,	1 teaspoon butter,
1 cup milk,	1 teaspoon cornstarch,
¼ cup sugar,	¼ teaspoon vanilla.

Mix sugar and cornstarch; wet with a little of the milk, add butter and the rest of the milk. Cook until it coats the spoon. Remove from fire and add the vanilla.

Line a pie plate or oblong shallow pan with thin layer of Kuchen Dough, page 311, or Cookie Dough, page 301. Sprinkle top with a few bread crumbs. Wash and carefully pick over the blueberries, add a tablespoon of lemon juice or a little vinegar, sprinkle with a little sugar and cinnamon. Place on dough, add the cooked custard. Place in hot oven, and bake until the bottom is well browned.

CHEESE PIE OR KUCHEN

No. 1

2 tablespoons butter (melt and add to cheese),	1 cup sugar,
	1 cup cream, beaten stiff,
1 lb. (1 pt.) cheese (press dry and put through colander),	Lemon rind for vanilla,
	3 eggs beaten, separately,
1 heaping tablespoon cornstarch,	Juice of ½ lemon.

Mix well and bake on Plain Pie Crust, page 300, or Kuchen Dough, page 311, until a golden brown and well set in moderate oven from ¾ to 1 hour.

No. 2

¼ cup butter (melt and add to cheese),	1 cup cream, beaten,
	Rind of lemon, grated,
1½ pints cheese (press dry and put through colander),	3 eggs beaten separately,
	¼ cup washed currants,
¾ cup sugar,	¼ lb. blanched almonds, cut fine.
1 tablespoon cornstarch,	

Line a pie plate with pastry or Kuchen Dough, page 311, pour in the mixture and bake in moderate oven until a golden brown and well set.

CHEESE PIE OR KUCHEN

No. 3

1½ cups cottage cheese,	¼ cup sugar,
2 tablespoons flour,	1 tablespoon butter (melted),
2 tablespoons cream,	½ teaspoon vanilla,
3 eggs,	¼ cup currants

Line a pie plate or shallow pan with Cookie Dough, page 301, or Kuchen Dough, page 311.

Rub cheese through colander, add pinch of salt, the flour and cream, mix well. Separate the eggs. Beat yolks, light, add sugar and butter, stir well and mix with the cheese. Add currants, vanilla and lemon rind and the beaten whites lastly. Place mixture on dough and bake in a moderate oven until well set and the crust well browned at the bottom.

No. 4

2 tablespoons butter,	1 qt. cottage cheese,
2 cups sugar,	1½ tablespoons flour,
5 yolks,	Grated rind of 1 lemon,
5 whites of eggs.	

Line a spring form with a small portion of Kuchen Dough, No. 1, page 311. Fill with the following: Cream butter and sugar, add yolks and beat until light; add cheese which has been pressed through colander. Add flour and lastly the beaten whites of eggs. Sprinkle top with finely grated almonds, sugar and cinnamon.

CHERRY PIE OR KUCHEN

1 qt. ripe cherries,	3 tablespoons cream,
1 yolk of egg,	½ cup sugar.

Wash cherries, stem and then place in colander over dish to catch the juice. Take a new steel hairpin, insert bent end in the stem end of cherry, loosen, and draw out the stone.

Place thin layer of Kuchen Dough, page 311, or Cookie Dough, page 301, on shallow pan, sprinkle top with bread crumbs. Spread cherries over evenly. Sprinkle with sugar and cinnamon. Beat yoke well, add the cream and cherry juice and pour over all. Bake in a hot oven until well browned at the bottom.

CHOCOLATE PIE

3 eggs,	1 cup cream, whipped stiff,
1 cup sugar,	2 tablespoons powdered
2 oz. bitter chocolate,	sugar,
2 tablespoons browned	¼ teaspoon vanilla.
bread crumbs,	

Melt the chocolate over hot water, and mix with the eggs, sugar and bread crumbs.

Place on Plain Pastry, page 300, and bake 20 minutes in a moderate oven. When cool and ready to serve spread the whipped cream flavored and sweetened on top.

CUSTARD PIE

No. 1

1½ cups scalded milk,	Speck salt,
2 eggs,	3 tablespoons sugar,
A little nutmeg.	

Line a deep pie plate with pastry, page 300, pinch down the edges, and fill in the custard made as follows. Scald the milk and add it to the beaten eggs and sugar, and seasoning. Bake in a quick oven at first, then decrease the heat or it will curdle.

No. 2

3 eggs,	Speck salt,
¼ cup sugar,	2½ cups milk, scalded,
A little grated nutmeg.	

Beat the eggs, add the sugar, nutmeg and salt and then stir in the scalded milk. Line the plate with Pastry, page 300, rolled thin, having it extend over the edge of the plate about ¼ of an inch. Pinch this up around the edge and pour in the custard. Bake in a quick oven at first, then decrease the heat. When the knife blade comes out clean the custard is cooked.

CURRANT PIE

1 cup fresh, ripe currants,	2 yolks,
1 cup sugar,	1 tablespoon flour,
½ cup water,	2 whites eggs,
4 tablespoons sugar.	

Line pie plate with Plain Pie Dough, page 300. Mash the currants, add sugar and water, beat yolks slightly, add flour and combine the mixtures. Pour on top of pie dough and bake in moderate oven until set. Mix the beaten whites with the remaining sugar and spread over the top. Return to oven to brown slightly.

LEMON PIE

No. 1

¼ cup flour or cornstarch,
1 cup sugar,
1 cup boiling water,
2 eggs,
1 tablespoon butter,
Juice and rind of a lemon.

Mix sugar and flour, add the boiling water slowly and boil until clear, stir frequently. Add butter, the yolks of eggs beaten lightly and lemon. When the mixture is cool, place on a baked crust, Plain Pastry, page 300. The whites of eggs may be beaten stiff and stirred with the custard when taken from the stove, or it may be mixed with four tablespoons powdered sugar, spread on top and baked a delicate brown.

No. 2

6 eggs, separated,
¾ cup sugar,
2 lemons, juice.

Beat yolk and sugar until light, add the lemon juice, and cook in double boiler until thick; while warm add the beaten whites and put on baked crust. See general rules for Pastry, page 299. Place in oven to brown slightly.

MINCE MEAT FOR PIES

No. 1

3 lbs. meat, chopped,
1½ lb. beef suet, chopped,
6 lbs. apples, chopped,
3 lbs. raisins, seeded,
2 lbs. currants,
1 lb. citron, chopped fine,
½ each of lemon and orange peel.
1 oz. cinnamon, ground,
½ oz. cloves,
1 nutmeg, grated,
3 lbs. brown sugar,
1 qt. boiled cider,
1 qt. molasses,
Salt to taste.

Cook all together 2 hours and seal in glass cans.

Mince pies should always be baked with two crusts. Usually made between Thanksgiving and New Year.

No. 2

2½ lbs. fresh, boiled tongue, skinned, chopped fine or
2½ lbs. beef rump, chopped,
2 lbs. sugar,
1 orange peel, cut fine,
1 nutmeg, grated,
½ lb. suet,
2 lbs. raisins,
½ lb. currants,
1 lb. citron, cut fine,
⅛ oz. cloves, mace and allspice,
½ oz. cinnamon,
⅛ oz. cloves,
1 qt. sour wine,
1 pt. of brandy, whisky or a little cider.

After all the ingredients are put together except the wine and brandy or cider, put in a preserving kettle with a little cider and cook enough to make the suet look clear. Then add liquors; put away in glass jars and it will keep for years. When ready to bake pies, add an equal measure of chopped apples to the mince meat. Pecan nut meats may also be added.

MOCK CHERRY PIE

1 cup cranberries,
½ cup raisins, seeded,
1 teaspoon butter, melted,
¾ cup sugar,
1 tablespoon flour.

Cut cranberries in halves; raisins, in pieces. Add the rest and bake in moderate oven between crusts.

PUMPKIN PIE

No. 1

1½ cups strained and mashed, pumpkin,
¼ cup syrup,
¼ cup brown sugar,
1 beaten egg,
½ teaspoon salt,
⅓ teaspoon ginger,
2 cups milk.

Mix in order given and bake until firm, in a tin lined with Plain Pastry, page 300. Have pumpkin dry and mealy, steaming or baking slowly.

No. 2

1 cup steamed or baked and strained pumpkin,
¼ cup sugar,
½ teaspoon salt,
¼ teaspoon cinnamon,
⅛ teaspoon mace,
½ teaspoon vanilla,
1 egg and 1 yolk,
½ cup milk,
½ cup cream,
Grated lemon juice and rind.

Mix dry ingredients, add pumpkin and lightly beaten eggs, and the milk and cream gradually. Bake until firm in a tin lined with Plain Pastry, page 300.

To Bake Pumpkin or Squash. Wash and cut in half crosswise. Scrape out seeds and stringy parts. Place in dripping pan, shell side up and bake until it begins to fall in and is tender. Scrape pulp from shell, strain. If wanted more dry, finish by turning, being careful not to have fire too hot.

GINGER BREAD FILLING FOR KUCHEN

1 cup stale ginger bread, grated,
Sugar to taste,
Rind of ½ lemon,
2 tablespoons melted butter,
1 teaspoon molasses or syrup,
Sprinkling of cinnamon,
Pinch of salt.

Grated Leb Kuchen may be used in place of the ginger bread. Recipe for Gingerbread for Fillings, page 33. One cup each of seeded raisins and currants may be added, if desired, also a little citron and a few almonds, each cut fine.

Spread thick on thin layer of Kuchen Dough, page 311, and use for Spice Roll, page 318, or as a garnish for Boiled Noodles, page 183.

POPPY SEED FILLING FOR PIE OR KUCHEN

No. 1

1 cup black poppy seed,
2 tablespoons butter,
2 tablespoons molasses or syrup,
½ cup chopped almonds,
½ teaspoon vanilla or lemon rind,
1 tablespoon chopped citron,
¼ cup seedless raisins,
Sugar to taste,
1 cup milk.

Grind poppy seed and boil with milk and other ingredients until thick. If not sweet enough, add sugar. When cool add vanilla. The raisins, nuts and citron may be omitted. Use mixture of Kuchen Roll, page 318, Pie or Turnovers, page 313.

No. 2

1 cup ground poppy seed,
6 eggs,
¾ cup sugar,
6 bitter almonds, pounded,
1 lemon rind grated,
¼ cup almonds, blanched and pounded.

Separate eggs, mix ingredients in order given, beaten whites of eggs last; use for Kipfel, Turnovers, page 311, Pie or Kuchen, page 313, in place of fruit or preserves.

PRUNE FILLING FOR PIE OR KUCHEN

½ lb. prunes,
½ cup sugar,
1 tablespoon lemon juice.

Boil prunes, following directions, page 399. Stone and rub through colander. Mix and mash well with juice, add sugar to taste and flavor with lemon juice or rind or cinnamon. Use mixture for Pie or Kuchen fillings and in place of preserves in Turnovers or Kipfel, page 313. If used for pie, have upper crust or add whipped cream sweetened and flavored.

CUSTARD FOR KUCHEN

1 yolk of egg,
3 tablespoons cream,
Sugar and cinnamon,
2 tablespoons almonds, sliced or ground.

Beat the yolks slightly, add the cream, mix well, spread well over top of Coffee Kuchen, page 312, sprinkle thickly with sugar and cinnamon, and add the almonds if desired. Let raise and bake. Use also with fruit Kuchens, page 303, dripping it over the fresh fruit before baking.

STREUSEL FOR TOP OF COFFEE KUCHEN

1 teaspoon flour,
1 teaspoon sugar,
1 teaspoon butter.

Mix together, by rubbing well with the hollow of the hands, until small grains are formed. Add a few pounded almonds.

Sprinkle over top of Coffee Kuchen, page 312, that has been brushed with melted butter.

CHAPTER XXVIII

KUCHEN

KUCHEN DOUGH, No. 1

1 pint scalded milk,
½ cup butter,
½ cup sugar,
1 teaspoon salt,
5½ to 6 cups flour,
Yolks of 2 eggs, or
1 whole egg,
½ oz. yeast,
Grated nutmeg.

Warm bowl and flour. Crumble the yeast in a cup with a teaspoon of sugar, and one-half cup of the scalded, cooled milk. Set in a warm place to rise. To the rest of the scalded milk add the butter, sugar, salt, nutmeg, and when lukewarm, the beaten yolks of the two eggs. Use flat, wooden spoon and stir in the yeast and the rest of the flour, less or enough more to knead, mix and knead until the dough is smooth and elastic. Cover closely and let rise double its bulk. Form into any desired shape, place in pans, let rise again and bake.

KUCHEN DOUGH, No. 2

½ cup butter,
½ cup sugar,
2 yolks or one whole egg,
4½ cups flour,
1 oz. compressed yeast,
1 cup lukewarm milk,
Grated rind of ½ lemon.

Crumble yeast in the bowl, add the lukewarm milk, and a cup of the flour and set aside to rise in a warm place. Cream the butter, add the sugar and the egg, stir well, then add the rest of the flour and the yeast mixture alternately. Mix well, add enough more flour to knead and knead until the dough is smooth and elastic. Set aside in a warm place to double its bulk and form into any desired shapes, let rise again and bake.

KUCHEN DOUGH, No. 3

2 quarts (2 lbs.) flour,
1 oz. (2 cakes) yeast,
1 teaspoon salt,
1 cup (½ lb.) butter,
1 cup (½ lb.) sugar,
1 pint milk,
4 eggs,
1 lemon, juice and grated rind.

Scald the milk, add the sugar and salt; when lukewarm, add yeast cake, crumbled, with a teaspoon of sugar; let stand 5 minutes, add 3 cups flour; beat well, cover and let rise in a warm place until light. Add eggs, beat well; the butter softened, lemon juice and rind and just enough more flour to knead. Knead ½ hour or until the dough is smooth and elastic and blisters. Cover and let rise again in a warm place. Form into any desired shape, place into pans, well greased with butter, let rise again and bake.

COFFEE KUCHEN

1 cup milk,
⅓ cup butter, or butter and lard,
¼ cup sugar,
½ teaspoon salt,
1 egg,
¾ yeast cake dssolved in ¼ cup lukewarm milk,
½ cup raisins, stoned and cut in halves,
2¾ cup flour.

Add butter, sugar and salt to the milk; when lukewarm add dissolved yeast cake, egg, well beaten, flour to make a stiff batter, add raisins; cover and let rise; spread in buttered dripping pan ½ in. thick. Cover and let rise again. Before baking melt 2 tablespoons butter and spread over the coffee cake; also sprinkle with sugar and cinnamon. If set at night use ½ the quantity of yeast, or,

Flour the board and take ¼ part of the raised Kuchen Dough, No. 1. Roll one-half inch thick and place in well greased, oblong shallow pans. Brush melted butter over the top and sprinkle with sugar and a little cinnamon, and a few chopped almonds if desired. See Streusel, page 310. Let rise until light and bake a golden brown in a hot oven fifteen to twenty minutes.

NOTE—To freshen Kuchen, place in a hot oven a few minutes before using; or it may be cut into slices one-half inch thick and dried or toasted in the oven.

CINNAMON ROLLS OR SCHNECKEN

1 cup milk,
1 yeast cake,
Flour,
¼ cup sugar,
1 teaspoon salt,
1 egg,
Yolk of one egg,
¼ cup melted butter.

Scald the milk, when lukewarm, add sugar, salt and yeast cake, let stand 5 minutes and add 1½ cups flour; beat well, cover, and let rise until light. Add eggs well beaten, butter, and enough more flour to knead; knead and let rise again. Roll all the dough ½ inch thick, brush with melted butter, sprinkle with brown sugar and cinnamon mixed. Roll up like jelly roll and cut in 1 inch pieces. Place pieces in pan close together with butter between, flat side down. Brush tops with butter; sprinkle with sugar and cinnamon. When light, bake in moderate oven, or

Use the above proportions, or take ½ of the raised Kuchen Dough, No. 1, page 311. Roll one-half inch thick and spread well with melted butter. Sprinkle generously with scraped maple, brown or granulated sugar and cinnamon, then roll. Cut the roll into equal parts about one inch thick, place close together endwise, in a spider, generously buttered, spread with one-quarter inch layer of brown or maple sugar. Let rise until light, and bake ten to twenty minutes in a hot oven, a golden brown. Invert the spider, remove rolls, and serve caramel side up.

KUCHEN TARTS

Roll a piece of raised Kuchen Dough, Nos. 2 or 3, page 311, one inch thick on floured board, cut with biscuit cutter, and place close together in a buttered pan. Let rise until very light. Dip fingers in flour and make a cavity in center of each biscuit, and drop in a bit of jelly or preserves. Bake 15 to 20 minutes in hot oven.

TURNOVERS, KIPFEL OR POCKETBOOKS

Make a Kuchen Dough, page 311, and when raised, or Plain Pastry, page 300, or Cookie Dough, page 301. Roll out ¼ in. thick, cut into 3 inch squares and place 1 tablespoon preserves or jam or any desired Pie or Kuchen Filling, page 309 to 310, in center of each square. Wet fingers with cold water. Catch the four corners of each square, lift up over the filling and pinch together on top and at corners that the juice shall not escape or wet top edges of the squares, take hold of one corner and fold and pinch it to the opposite corner, thus forming a three cornered little pie, or place filling on lower half of square and fold over the other half, pinch the edges well together.

Lay in greased pan and if Kuchen Dough is used let stand in warm place to raise and then bake in a moderately hot oven until well done and browned.

FILLED WALNUT KIPFEL

1½ cups (¾ lb.) fresh butter,
4 cups (1 lb.) flour,
1 cake yeast,
1 teaspoon vanilla,
½ cup cream or milk,
5 eggs, separated,
½ cup sugar.

Add to the beaten yolks, the sugar, vanilla and one-half of the cream. Dissolve the yeast with the rest of the cream (lukewarm). Add a little flour, let stand to raise. Rub the butter into the flour, combine the three mixtures, add more flour if necessary. Roll the dough quite thin, cut into small squares, place a small portion of filling, below, in each square. Roll, beginning at one corner, and form into crescent shape; place in pan and frost with the beaten whites of the 5 eggs. Let rise two or more hours, bake thirty minutes in a moderate oven.

Filling—One pound chopped walnuts, the juice of one lemon and sugar to taste, or grind the nuts, add cream to make a paste, sugar to taste and flavor with vanilla.

SOUR CREAM KIPFEL

4 cups (1 lb.) flour,
1 cup (½ lb.) sweet butter,
¾ cup sour cream,
⅓ teaspoon cinnamon,
2 eggs (raw),
¼ lb. almonds, (chopped),
2 tablespoons sugar.

Mix flour, butter, sour cream and 2 raw yolks together and put in ice box over night. Then roll it out and fold it at least four times, then roll it out as thin as pie crust, cut into 2 inch squares. Put a teaspoon of jam on each, fold over the corners, press edges together, spread top with the beaten white of the 2 eggs, sprinkle with sugar, cinnamon and chopped almonds.

VIENNA KIPFEL (Cheese Squares)

¼ lb. (½ cup) cottage cheese,
½ cup butter,
½ cup flour.

Mix all together. Roll quite thin. Cut in 2 inch squares. In center of each square place one teaspoon of jelly or preserves. Pick up the four corners, press together to form a square turnover or fold into any desired shape. Bake in a quick oven.

RUSSIAN TEA CAKES

1 cup sugar,
1 cup eggs (about 5),
1 cup sour cream,
Flour to roll,
¾ lb. brick butter, sliced,
1 cup chopped almonds.

Mix eggs, sugar and cream with enough flour to roll. Toss on board, roll out ¼ inch thick, spread with a thin layer of the butter, fold the dough over, roll and spread again with butter; fold, roll and spread again; repeat three or four times. Then place dough in a bowl, cover, and let stand on ice to harden. Then roll as thin as possible, strew with chopped almonds, sugar and cinnamon, and cut into 7 inch strips. Roll each strip separately into a roll, cut into squares and strew top with chopped almonds, sugar and cinnamon. Bake in a hot oven.

BOHEMIAN KOLATCHEN

Make Kuchen Dough, No. 1, 2 or 3, pages 311 and 312. Add a little cinnamon and mace and 1 teaspoon anise, seed well pounded, or flavor to taste. Let rise till very light, then take out on mixing board, and roll out to about half inch. Cut in rounds, 3 inches in diameter, and lay on a well-buttered pan, pressing down the centre of each so as to raise a ridge around the edge. When well risen, brush the top over with stiffly beaten white of an egg and sprinkle with granulated sugar.

SOUR CREAM KOLATCHEN

½ cup butter,
5 yolks,
2 tablespoons sugar,
Grated rind of a lemon,
1 cup thick sour cream,
1 oz. (2 cakes) yeast dissolved in 2 tablespoons lukewarm milk,
3 cups flour,
¼ lb. raisins or candied cherries.

Cream the butter, add eggs, sugar, lemon rind and sour cream and the yeast dissolved with a little sugar in the lukewarm milk. Stir all together and add the flour; mix and drop from end of teaspoon on well greased pans. Let rise until light in a warm place. Place a raisin or cherry on the top of each cake, spread with beaten white of egg, sprinkle with sugar and bake 10 minutes in a hot oven.

ICE KOLATCHEN

1 cup (¼ lb.) flour,   1⅛ cups (9 oz.) butter.

Dough No. 1 (Rich Pastry). Have all materials and utensils ice cold.

Chop or rub the butter in the flour, then work into a dough. Set in a cool place to harden. Then prepare the following:

2 cups (½ lb.) flour,   Rind of ½ lemon,
½ cup lukewarm cream,   1 cake (½ oz.) yeast,
2 yolks of eggs and   ½ teaspoon salt,
1 whole egg,   A nutmeg grating,
1 tablespoon (½ oz.) sugar,   Whites of 2 eggs,
              Raspberry jam.

Dough No. 2 (Rich Kuchen Dough). Dissolve the yeast in the lukewarm cream, add sugar, eggs and the rest of the ingredients and beat until smooth.

Roll out Dough No. 1 and Dough No. 2, ¼ inch thick each separately and then place Dough No. 2 on top of Dough No. 1. Pat and roll out together keeping the paste a little wider than long and corners square. Now fold the ends of dough towards the center, making 3 layers; pat and roll. Repeat twice, turning the paste half way around each time before rolling.

Now fold in a dampened napkin and set in a cool place, over night to chill but not to freeze.

Next morning, roll the dough again, cut into rounds with biscuit cutter 3 inches in diameter, place on floured board and let rise in a warm place until light several hours. Place a teaspoon of raspberry jam on lower half of each piece, then fold over the other half and press edges together.

Brush the stiffly beaten whites of 2 eggs all over top and sides of Kolatchen and roll in granulated sugar. Bake in a moderate oven.

RAISED DOUGHNUTS

Let Kuchen Dough, No. 1, 2 or 3, pages 311 and 312, rise until doubled in bulk, then roll into a thin sheet, and cut into rings. Let stand until nearly doubled in bulk, then fry in deep hot fat. Drain on soft paper, and roll in powdered sugar.

BERLINGER PFANN KUCHEN

Make a Kuchen Dough, No. 1, 2 or 3, pages 311, 312, roll one inch thick, cut into rounds with biscuit cutter. Place a piece of jelly or preserves in the center of one-half of them. Brush edges with white of egg and cover with the other half. Press edges neatly. Place on well floured board, let raise very light and fry in deep fat until brown. When done they will have a white strip around center. Sprinkle with powdered sugar.

STOLLA

2 lbs. (2 quarts) flour,
1 pint milk,
1 teaspoon salt,
1 oz. (2 cakes) yeast,
1 cup sugar,
4 whole eggs,
1 lb. butter, softened,
¾ lb. raisins,
½ lb. chopped almonds,
A little nutmeg,
Grated rind of 1 lemon.

Scald milk, add sugar and salt, when lukewarm, add yeast cake, let stand 5 minutes, then add 2 cups flour, beat well. Cover and let rise in a warm place, until light. Add the eggs, well beaten, then the butter and the rest of the ingredients with the remaining flour, and only enough more flour to knead. Knead until the dough blisters and is smooth and elastic.

Toss the dough on floured board. Divide into 2 or 3 loaves. Knead each loaf, and roll it slightly. Spread top with melted butter, sprinkle lightly with chopped almonds, sugar and cinnamon. Press down the center and fold over double into long loaf, narrow at the ends. Brush melted butter over the top, let rise again to double its bulk, and bake in a moderate oven about 45 minutes, or until brown and well done. When baked brush the top with Plain Frosting, page 325, flavored with rum.

YEAST KRANTZ

1 cup lukewarm milk,
1 oz. compressed yeast,
1 cup butter,
½ cup sugar,
Yolks of 4 eggs,
4 cups flour,
Grated rind of 1 lemon.

Set the yeast with the lukewarm milk and stir in one cup of the flour, let stand in a warm place to raise. Cream the butter with the sugar, add the eggs one at a time and beat well; add flavoring, combine the two mixtures, add the remaining flour.

Place in a well greased, round form, with tube in center; let rise in a warm place and bake until well done and browned; or,

Make Kuchen Dough, No. 1 or 2, page 311, add ¼ cup washed currants. Let rise in warm place; then toss on floured board. Divide into 3 or 4 equal parts, roll each part into a long strand and work the strands together to form one large braid. Place braid in form of a circle in greased baking pan or twist the braid to resemble the figure 8, pretzel shape. Let rise again in a warm place and bake in a moderate oven ½ hour or until thoroughly done. Brush with beaten egg and sugar, sprinkle with a few chopped almonds. Return to oven to brown slightly.

KUCHEN ROLL OR KUGELHOPF

Kuchen Dough, No. 1 or 2,
¼ cup seeded raisins,
¼ cup melted butter,
Sugar and cinnamon.

Roll a piece of raised Kuchen Dough, page 311, quite thin, on floured board; brush well with melted butter, sprinkle well with sugar, add a little cinnamon and the raisins. Begin at one end and roll over and over into a long roll. Place in a well greased long, or round form with tube in center. Let rise to double its bulk and bake in a moderate oven until browned and thoroughly done. When baked brush top and sides with melted butter and sprinkle with sugar.

POPPY SEED ROLL OR MOHN KUCHEN

Kuchen Dough, No. 1 or 2,   Poppy seed filling.

Take about ½ of the recipe for Kuchen Dough, No. 1 or 2, page 311. When raised, roll quite thin and spread the Poppy Seed Filling, No. 1 or 2, page 309, evenly over the top; start at one side and roll over and over, into a long roll. Place in long or round form with tube in center, let raise twice its bulk. Spread top with melted butter, and bake slowly until well browned and thoroughly done. Serve, cut in slices.

SPICE ROLL

Make same as Poppy Seed Roll, using Gingerbread Filling, page 309, in place of the poppy seed mixture.

BUNDT KUCHEN, No. 1

1 cake of yeast (½ oz.),   1 cup lukewarm milk,
1 cup flour.

No. 1—Set the yeast with a cup of the flour and the milk, and let rise in warm place, and then proceed with the following:

½ cup butter,   2 cups flour,
1 cup sugar,   4 eggs,
Rind of lemon.

No. 2—Beat the butter to a cream, add the sugar, eggs, one at a time, rind of a lemon, a little grated nutmeg. Now mix part 1 and 2, and add the remaining flour, a little more if desired. Have pan well greased. Place dough in pan, let rise very light, and bake 45 to 60 minutes in a moderately hot oven.

BUNDT KUCHEN, No. 2

1 cup butter,   1 cup lukewarm milk,
1 cup sugar,   4 cups flour,
8 eggs, beaten separately,   1 oz. compressed yeast,
⅛ tablespoon salt,   Raisins, seeded.

Scald the milk and when lukewarm add the salt and yeast and one cup of the flour, set aside to rise. Grease Bundt form (a heavy round fluted pan with tube in center) well, and flour lightly. Cream, butter and sugar well, add beaten yolks and beat, then the raised mixture and the rest of the flour, and lastly the beaten whites. Pour in pan, let rise until very light, and bake until well done and brown in a moderately hot oven, about forty-five minutes.

SAVARIN (French Coffee Cake)

4 cups flour,   1 teaspoon salt,
1 cup milk,   5 eggs,
1 tablespoon sugar,   ½ oz. compressed yeast,
1½ cups butter,   Rind of 1 lemon,
2 tablespoons maraschino.

Stir milk, yeast and 1 cup of flour, and let it raise. Then add the other ingredients, beat until very smooth and light. Butter several large ring forms or moulds, sprinkle with chopped almonds and half fill with the dough. Let rise to the top of the mould and bake in a moderate oven. When baked, turn from the mould and pour over the following syrup: Cook two tablespoons sugar, one tablespoon water, when boiled add one tablespoon maraschino.

CHAPTER XXIX

TARTLETS AND FRIED CAKES

TARTS

Roll Plain Pastry or Puff Paste, page 301, one-eighth inch thick. Shape with a fluted, round cutter, first dipped in flour; with a smaller cutter remove centers from half the pieces, leaving rings ½ inch wide. Brush with cold water the larger pieces near the edge; fit on rings and press lightly. Chill thoroughly and bake 15 minutes in hot oven. Brush top with beaten yolk of egg and teaspoon of water. Cool and fill with jelly or jam.

LADY LOCKS

Cut puff or other Rich Pastry, page 301, rolled into a thin sheet, into strips about three-fourths of an inch wide. Wind this around round wooden forms or lady lock sticks, having edges overlap, but keeping the space between the paste quite narrow. Dispose on a baking-sheet, and bake in a moderate oven. Remove the pastry from the sticks, and fill the hollow centres with heavy cream, sweetened and flavored before whipping.

LEMON OR ORANGE TARTS

Cut Pie Dough, page 300, rolled ⅛ inch thick in strips 5 inches long by one inch wide, and bake in hot oven. Put together in pairs with Orange or Lemon Filling, page 333.

STRAWBERRY TARTLETS

Line gem or muffin pans with Cookie Dough or Murberteig, No. 1, page 301. Prick dough with fork to avoid blisters. When baked fill centers with fresh strawberries, sugared, cover top with whipped cream.

MACAROON TARTS

Rich Pie Dough,
Jam or marmalade,
½ lb. grated almonds.
Whites of 3 eggs,
½ lb. powdered sugar,

Line a gem or muffin pan with Rich Pastry, page 301; half fill each tart with any desired preserve, and bake in a quick oven. Beat the whites of eggs to a stiff froth, add the powdered sugar and stir about 10 minutes or until very light, and gradually add the grated almonds. Divide this macaroon paste into equal portions. Roll and shape into strips, dusting hands with powdered sugar in place of flour. Place these strips on the baked tarts in parallel rows to cross each other diagonally. Return to oven and bake in a slow oven about 15 minutes. Let remain in pans until almost cold.

CHEESE FINGERS

Roll Flaky Pie Dough, page 300, out thin, brush lightly with ice water, cut into strips half an inch wide and four inches long. Scatter grated cheese on half of the strips, put on the others, press together lightly, lay on buttered paper and bake in a quick oven. Serve with salad.

CHEESE STRAWS

No. 1

2 tablespoons butter,
½ cup flour,
3 tablespoons bread crumbs,
Pinch cayenne pepper,
¼ cup grated cheese,
⅛ teaspoon salt,
1 egg.

Cream the butter, add the dry ingredients, and mix all together with the egg. Roll thin, cut in long, narrow strips and bake in a quick, hot oven. If desired a variety of shapes may be made. The strips may be twisted in corkscrew fashion, or into rings with doughnut cutter.

No. 2

4 cups flour,
2 teaspoons baking powder,
1 teaspoon salt,
1½ cups butter,
2 tablespoons lard,
2 yolks of eggs,
2 cups milk,
1 lb. grated cheese, parmesan or Edam.

Mix dry ingredients, rub in butter, add egg and milk. Roll; sprinkle cheese over one-half of dough, fold, press edges together, fold again; pat and roll out ¼ inch thick. Sprinkle with cheese and proceed as before. Cut in strips ¼ inch wide and 5 inches long, or in round with doughnut cutter. Bake 8 minutes in a hot oven. Pile the sticks log cabin fashion and serve with salad course.

FRIED CAKES

TO RENDER BUTTER

Any butter that is unfit for table use may be made sweet and good for cooking purposes and will last for months, if prepared in the following manner: Place the butter in a deep, iron kettle, filling only half full to prevent boiling over. Set it on the fire where it will simmer slowly for several hours. Watch carefully that it does not boil over, and when the fat is clear, and the sediment at the bottom is just browning, take it from the fire gently, so as not to distrub the sediment. Let cool a little, strain through cloth into crock, cover, and keep in a cool place.

To Render Beef Fat, see page 144.

DOUGHNUTS

No. 1

1 pint flour,
½ cup sugar,
1 teaspoon salt,
4 teaspoons baking powder,
¼ teaspoon cinnamon,
A little grated nutmeg,
2 tablespoons melted butter,
½ cup milk,
1 egg.

Sift dry ingredients. Add the milk to the beaten egg, and combine the mixtures. Roll on well floured board, cut with form, or roll into small balls, and fry in deep hot fat. Dust with powdered sugar.

No. 2

3 eggs,
1 cup sour cream,
1 cup sugar,
1 teaspoon soda,
4 cups flour,
A little grated nutmeg.

Beat eggs, add sugar gradually and stir again. Add soda to cream. Combine the two mixtures and add the flour. Roll quite thin, cut or shape into form and fry in deep hot fat. Dust with powdered sugar.

APPLE FRITTERS EN SURPRISE

7 or 8 greening apples,   Fritter batter.

Cut out the stems together with a round piece of apple, and clean out the core carefully. Cut out the little blossom end, but do not cut deep enough to meet the cavity in the center. Pare the apples, fill the centers with marmalade, dip the corresponding pieces of apple with stem adhering, into Fritter Batter, page 213, and press them into place. Dip the apples in fritter batter, covering every portion, and fry in deep fat. Cook six or eight minutes. Drain, and dust with powdered sugar.

ROSE TARTS

3 eggs,   Flour,

Beat eggs slightly, add a little salt, and flour enough to make a very stiff dough. Knead until elastic, then roll into a very thin sheet. Cut in rounds of three sizes. Pinch together at center. Let stand for 15 or 20 minutes. Drop in deep hot fat and fry to a delicate brown. Dust with powdered sugar and drop jelly into the scallops. For Lily Tarts, cut in stars of 3 sizes.

SNOWBALLS

1 egg,   1 tablespoon cream,
1 tablespoon sugar,   ¼ teaspoon salt,
1 teaspoon butter,   1 teaspoon brandy,
         Flour to roll.

Mix butter, salt and sugar with the egg. Add the cream and brandy and flour to make a stiff dough. Toss on a floured board and roll very thin, in pieces three inches long by two inches wide.

Make four one-inch gashes with a knife at equal intervals. Run fork in and out of gashes, lower into deep, hot fat. Fry until light brown and sprinkle with powdered sugar.

HESTERLISTE (Snowballs)

3 eggs, well beaten,
5 tablespoons melted butter,
1 pint milk,
2 teaspoons baking powder,
Flour to roll.

Flour enough to roll as thin as pie crust. Cut into strips, and slash as in above recipe and fry in deep hot lard. Sprinkle with sugar.

CHAPTER XXX

CAKE FROSTINGS AND FILLINGS

UNCOOKED FROSTINGS

WATER ICINGS

3 tablespoons water, or
3 tablespoons fruit juice,
1½ cups XXXX Confectioner's sugar,
Flavor to taste.

If the cake is cold, have liquid hot. Stir the liquid into the sifted sugar, adding more, a few drops at a time, as needed. A little lemon added to any fruit juice improves the flavor. The icing is of the proper consistency when it coats the spoon and conceals its color.

PLAIN ICING

1 cup confectioner's sugar,
2 tablespoons boiling water or milk,
¼ teaspoon vanilla, lemon, or other extract,
Or 1 teaspoon lemon juice.

To the sugar add the liquid, a little at a time, until thin enough to spread. Flavor, stir and spread with broad bladed knife.

LEMON ICING

1 cup confectioner's sugar,
Grated rind of ½ lemon,
1 tablespoon lemon juice,
1 tablespoon boiling water or milk,

Add lemon rind to juice and water to the sugar, a little at a time, until thin enough to spread.

ORANGE ICING

No. 1

1 cup confectioner's sugar,
2 tablespoons orange juice,
1 teaspoon lemon juice,
Grated rind of ½ orange.

Add orange juice and rind to the sugar, a little at a time, until thin enough to spread. Spread with broad bladed knife.

ORANGE ICING

No. 2

A little grated orange rind, ½ teaspoonful lemon juice,
1 tablespoonful orange juice, Yolk of 1 egg,
1 cup confectioner's sugar.

Mix in order given and add confectioner's sugar until the right consistency to spread.

CHOCOLATE FROSTING

1½ cup confectioner's sugar, About 6 tablespoons boiling water,
1 oz. chocolate, shaved, or cocoa, ⅓ teaspoon vanilla extract.

Melt chocolate over hot water, add boiling water and stir until smooth; add vanilla and stir in the sifted sugar, adding more hot water, if needed, to spread the mixture smoothly. If cocoa is used melt in the boiling water. A little cinnamon may be added.

FRUIT JUICE ICINGS

1 cup confectioner's sugar, Or fruit syrup,
2 tablespoons fresh fruit juice, 1 teaspoon lemon juice.

The strained juice of fruits, strawberries, cherries, grapes, etc., added to the sugar, a little at a time, until thin enough to spread.

EGG FROSTING

White of 1 egg, 1 cup powdered sugar,
1 tablespoon lemon juice or 1 teaspoon vanilla.

Put the unbeaten white of the egg into the bowl, add the sugar slowly beating with a spoon. When all has been added stir in the lemon juice.

Or heat white until stiff, adding enough sugar to spread, then add flavoring. For chocolate frosting, omit the lemon juice, and add ½ oz. of melted chocolate and ½ teaspoon vanilla or a little cinnamon.

ROYAL ICING

White of 1 egg, Juice of ½ lemon, or
2 tablespoons cold water, or Both water and juice,
1½ cups confectioner's sugar

Add water or fruit juice to unbeaten white of egg. Stir in the sugar, until thin enough to spread, more or less, as required. This makes a soft creamy icing.

BUTTER FROSTING (UNCOOKED)

No. 1

- 1 cup confectioner's sugar,
- 2 tablespoons butter,
- 1 tablespoon water, milk or cream,
- 1 tablespoon sherry, rum or brandy, or
- 1 tablespoon lemon or orange juice and a little of the grated rind, or
- 1 tablespoon strong black coffee with 1 teaspoon cocoa and ½ teaspoon vanilla, or
- 1 oz. grated chocolate melted over boiling hot water.

Cream butter and sugar well adding the liquid and flavoring in any desired proportion, until thin enough to spread.

No. 2

- 2½ cups confectioner's sugar,
- 1 cup butter,
- Yolk of 1 egg,
- Coffee extract to taste, or
- 2 (oz.) squares chocolate.

Wash butter in cold water, pat, and remove the water, then beat to a cream; add the beaten yolk and gradually the sugar and extract of coffee, or flavor with 2 oz. chocolate melted over hot water and a teaspoon vanilla.

BOILED FROSTINGS

BOILED ICING

No. 1

- 1 cup granulated sugar,
- ⅓ cup water.
- White of 1 egg.

Boil sugar gently without stirring until it threads quickly when lifted with spoon; turn slowly into the stiffly beaten white of egg; beat while turning on the hot liquid; continue to beat until stiff enough to spread; add one-fourth teaspoonful any preferred extract. If the sugar has cooked too much it will grain; then it may be made smooth by beating in a little boiling water; a teaspoonful at a time.

BOILED ICING
No. 2

1 cup sugar,
1/3 cup water,
1 teaspoon flavoring,
1 egg white (large),
1/4 teaspoon cream of tartar.

Beat white of egg until frothy, add the cream of tartar and beat until stiff and dry. Make syrup of sugar and water. When it has reached the honey stage, or drops heavily from spoon, add 5 tablespoons slowly to egg, beating in well. Then cook the remainder of the syrup until it threads and pour over the egg, beating thoroughly. Add flavoring and beat until cool enough to spread.

BOILED MAPLE SUGAR FROSTING

1/2 lb. maple sugar, or
1 cup brown sugar,
1/3 cup boiling water,
White of egg,
1/8 teaspoon cream of tartar,
1/2 teaspoon vanilla.

Prepare same as boiled frosting, recipe above.

BOILED CHOCOLATE FROSTING
No. 1

To the above Boiled Frosting No. 1, add one ounce bitter chocolate, grated, or 3 bars of Maillard's chocolate, and stir into syrup before adding the beaten white of egg.

No. 2

2 oz. chocolate,
1/2 cup cream,
2 whites of eggs,
Vanilla,
Powdered sugar.

Boil chocolate and cream and when cool add vanilla. Beat the whites to a stiff froth, add powdered sugar until stiff enough to cut. Combine the two mixtures, beat and spread.

No. 3

3/4 cup sugar,
Water to cover,
1 oz. bitter chocolate,
2 yolks.

Boil water and sugar to a thick syrup, add the grated chocolate and the beaten yolks. Thin with cream.

No. 4

1 cup sugar,
1 3/4 bars German sweet chocolate,
1/2 cup milk,
1 teaspoon butter.

Boil until a soft ball is formed when dropped in cold water. Beat until cool enough to spread.

BOILED CHOCOLATE FROSTING

No. 5

2 cups brown sugar,
⅔ cup water,
1 oz. bitter chocolate,
¾ cup butter.

Boil sugar and water until it spins a thread when dropped from a spoon. Melt chocolate with the butter, then mix it with the syrup; if it separates while stirring add a few drops of cold water.

CARAMEL FROSTING

¾ lb. maple sugar, scraped,
¾ lb. brown sugar,
Butter, size of an egg,
1½ cups cream.

Mix and boil slowly for forty minutes. Remove from stove and stir over ice until the proper consistency to spread. If too stiff, thin with cream. Dip knife in cream to spread.

MARSHMALLOW FROSTING

½ lb. marshmallows,
¼ cup milk or water,
Whites of 2 eggs,
1 teaspoon vanilla.

Break the marshmallows in pieces, add milk or water, and put in double boiler, over boiling water. Stir until melted. Take from fire and while hot, pour into the well beaten whites of eggs. Add vanilla.

NUT FROSTING

1½ cups sugar,
1 teaspoon butter,
½ cup milk,
¼ lb. chopped walnuts.

Boil the first three ingredients four minutes, beat until cool and add the chopped walnuts.

CAKE FILLINGS

NUT OR FRUIT FILLING

½ cup fruit (chopped fine),
½ cup nuts (chopped fine),
Boiled frosting.

To Boiled Icing, page 327, add one cup chopped walnuts, almonds, pecans, hickory, hazel nuts, chopped figs, dates, raisins or selected prunes, separately or in combination.

CUSTARD FILLING

No. 1

1 cup scalded milk,	1 tablespoon cornstarch,
¼ cup sugar,	2 yolks of eggs,

½ teaspoon vanilla.

Mix cornstarch and sugar, add eggs, slightly beaten and pour gradually on the hot milk. Cook in double boiler, stirring constantly until thickened. Cool and flavor with the vanilla.

No. 2

¾ cup sugar,	2 eggs,
⅓ cup flour,	2 cups milk or cream,
⅓ teaspoon salt,	1 teaspoon vanilla.

Mix dry ingredients, add eggs slightly beaten, and pour on gradually the scalded milk. Cook in double boiler. Stir constantly until thickened; cool and flavor.

Chocolate Filling same as custard filling, and add melted chocolate.

Coffee Filling same as custard filling, add one and one-half tablespoons coffee essence.

Orange, Strawberry or Lemon Filling made like custard filling, adding the desired flavoring.

Almond Custard Filling. Make like Custard Filling and when cool add 1 cup blanched, chopped almonds.

SOUR CREAM FILLING

No. 1

1 cup pecans or walnuts,	¾ cup confectioner's sugar,
1 small egg,	½ cup of sour cream,

A few drops of vanilla.

Run nut meats through meat-chopper. Beat the egg well; add the sugar and nut meats, then cream and vanilla, stirring it only enough to mix. Spread between the layers and over top of cake when cold.

No. 2

1 cup sour cream,	1 cup sugar,

¼ lb. chopped nuts.

Boil sugar and cream until quite thick, then add the chopped nuts and spread between layers of Chocolate Cake, page 346.

CARAMEL FILLING

1½ cups brown sugar,	½ cup milk,
1 teaspoon butter,	1½ teaspoon vanilla.

CAKE FROSTINGS AND FILLINGS

Put butter in sauce pan; when melted, add sugar and milk. Stir until dissolved. Heat gradually to boiling point without stirring, thirteen minutes, or until it forms a soft ball in cold water. Remove from fire, stir until it thickens to spread. Add vanilla.

CHOCOLATE FILLING

No. 1

½ cup sugar,
½ cup milk,
½ cup grated chocolate,
Yolk of 1 egg,
½ teaspoon vanilla.

Melt chocolate, add sugar and milk, and boil; when it forms a soft ball in cold water, remove from fire. Add beaten yolk and vanilla. Cool and spread between layers.

No. 2

2 whites of eggs,
¼ cup confectioner's sugar,
¼ lb. Maillard's chocolate.

Beat eggs very stiff, add sugar, and lastly the grated chocolate. Stir until smooth.

No. 3

½ cup milk,
½ cup grated chocolate,
½ cup sugar,
1 tablespoon cornstarch.

Mix dry ingredients, stir in the milk, cook until thick and when cool add vanilla to taste.

No. 4

1 cup sugar,
1 cup milk,
1 teaspoon vanilla,
3 oz. bitter chocolate.

Boil until a few drops form a soft ball in cold water. Beat until cool and spread on top or between two layers of cake.

SPONGE CAKE FILLING, Chocolate

½ lb. brown sugar,
¼ lb. grated chocolate, scant,
½ cup milk,
2 tablespoons butter,
1 teaspoon vanilla.

Mix all together and cook until thick, add vanilla when cool, and spread between 2 layers of sponge cake.

CHOCOLATE NUT FILLING

1½ cups brown sugar,
¾ cup cream,
2 oz. grated chocolate,
½ cup butter,
¾ cup chopped nut meats.

Boil sugar, cream and butter until thick; stir until cool; then add chocolate melted over hot water, and nuts, and spread between two layers of Chocolate Layer Cake, page 346.

NUT FILLING

No. 1

1 lb. grated walnuts,
¾ cup sweet milk,
½ cup granulated sugar,
2 yolks of eggs, beaten.

Mix eggs and sugar, add milk, then cook until it thickens, and then add one-half teaspoon vanilla, and the nuts and spread between layers of Walnut Torte, No. 1, page 366.

No. 2

2 yolks of eggs,
½ cup sugar,
½ cup pecan nut meats, chopped fine,
1 cup milk,
1 tablespoon cornstarch.

Wet cornstarch with a little of the milk, and place in double boiler with the rest of the milk and cook until smooth; beat yolks to a light cream with the sugar, pour hot milk gradually over, return to boiler and cook until it coats the spoon, stirring constantly; remove from fire and when cool add nut meats. Use with Lady Finger Torte, page 361.

FILLING FOR BROD TORTE

Yolks of 2 eggs,
1 cup sugar,
1 lemon, juice,
½ cup chopped walnuts,
1 white of egg, beaten stiff.

Stir yolks well with sugar, add the rest of the ingredients, the beaten whites last. Spread between layers of Brod Torte, page 355.

ORANGE FILLING

½ cup sugar,
2 tablespoons flour,
A little grated orange rind,
¼ cup orange juice,
½ teaspoon lemon juice,
1 teaspoon butter,
1 egg slightly beaten.

Mix in order given, beat up well, cook in double boiler; stir constantly until thick as thin mush; when cool it is ready for use.

ORANGE OR LEMON FILLING

2 oranges, juice and grated rind, or 1 lemon,
2 whites of eggs, beaten stiff,
1 cup powdered sugar.

To the beaten whites add the sugar gradually and then the orange or lemon rind and juice. Use between layers of Sponge or Angel Cake, pages 348 or 349.

COCOANUT LEMON FILLING

1 cup sugar,
¼ cup cornstarch,
1 cup boiling water,
Juice and rind of 1 lemon,
1 egg, beaten,
Shredded cocoanut.

Mix lemon juice and rind with sugar and the egg slightly beaten. Stir the cornstarch with a little cold water until smooth; combine the two mixtures and cook in double boiler until it coats the spoon, stirring constantly. Spread over cake, sprinkle thickly with shredded or fresh cocoanut, grated.

BANANA FILLING

1 cup banana pulp,
½ cup sugar,
Juice of ½ lemon,
1 tablespoon butter.

Cook together a cup of sifted banana pulp (peeled bananas passed through a sieve), the juice of half a lemon, or an orange, the sugar and butter; when thick and cold spread upon the cake. Or, heat the ingredients in a double boiler and then stir in an egg beaten with a tablespoonful of sugar; cook and stir until thickened, then cool. Spread on cake.

FIG FILLING

No. 1

1 lb. figs,	½ cup sugar,
1 cup boiling water,	Juice of ½ lemon.

Put figs through chopper. Mix all together and let simmer and cook slowly until it becomes a smooth paste. Let cool before using. If desired add 1 tablespoon sherry wine.

No. 2

1 lb. figs, chopped fine,	Whites of 2 eggs,
1 cup sugar,	¼ cup powdered sugar,
½ cup water,	Vanilla to taste.

Boil figs, sugar and water slowly to a smooth paste, about 15 minutes. Set aside to cool. Beat whites until stiff, add powdered sugar and flavoring, and combine the two mixtures.

MARSHMALLOW FILLING

1 lb. marshmallows,	¼ cup milk or water.
1 cup heavy cream,	

Melt the marshmallows over hot water in double boiler with the milk or water, let cool, then add the cream beaten stiff, and spread between layers of Angel Food Cake, page 349.

BUTTER FILLING (Uncooked)

1 cup unsalted butter,	1 oz. grated chocolate, melted over hot water, and
Yolk of 1 egg, beaten,	1 teaspoon vanilla, or
2½ cups powdered sugar,	Coffee extract to taste.

Wash salted butter in cold water, remove all water and then beat to a cream; add beaten yolk and gradually the sugar and melted chocolate or the extract to taste.

Use for fillings between layers of cake and for fancy pipings.

WHIPPED CREAM FILLING

¾ cup thick cream,
¼ cup powdered sugar,
White of 1 egg,
½ teaspoon vanilla.

Set medium sized bowl in pan of crushed ice to which water has been added. Place cream in bowl and beat until stiff, with wire whip or, if possible, use patent cream whipper. Whip up well that air bubbles may not be too large. Add sugar, white of egg beaten stiff, and vanilla. Keep cool.

WHIPPED CREAM FILLING WITH PINEAPPLE AND NUTS

1 yolk of egg,
2 tablespoons powdered sugar,
½ cup whipped cream,
1 cup nut kernels, or ½ cup nuts and ½ cup pineapple.

Whip cream, same as above, using one-half cupful nuts and one-half cupful pineapple, all chopped up.

CHAPTER XXXI

Cakes

GENERAL RULES

All measurements are level. For directions see page 1.
Bring all materials to the work table.
The measuring cup should hold ½ pint.
Sift flour and dip it with spoon or scoop into cup.
When measuring by the spoonful, pick up a heaping spoonful, run the back of a knife along the bowl of spoon and level off the top.
Divide level spoonful through the middle lengthwise for ½ spoonful.
Always sift baking powder with flour.
Use pastry flour and granulated sugar.
Grease pans with unsalted melted fat; then dredge with flour, invert, and shake the pan to remove superfluous flour. In filling pans have the mixture come well to the corners and sides of the pans, leaving a slight depression in the center, that cakes may bake flat. Cake pan should be filled nearly two-thirds full if the cake is expected to rise to the top of the pan.
In baking cake divide the time into quarters. 1st, The mixture should become heated and begin to rise; 2d, continue rising and begin to brown; 3d, continuing browning; 4th, finish bak-

ing and shrink from the pan. Do not move the cake in the oven while in a soft condition as that will break the air bubbles before all their cells are cooked, thereby causing the cake to fall. When done the cake will shrink from the sides of pan or will spring back quickly if pressed gently with the finger on the center of the cake.

TO TEST OVEN FOR CAKE

For Moderate Oven. A piece of soft yellow wrapping paper should burn golden grown in 5 minutes.

For Hot Oven. Paper should burn golden brown in 4 minutes.

For Slow Oven. The paper should burn golden brown in 7 minutes.

Loaf Cakes with butter (cup cakes) require moderate oven; Layer Cakes, hot oven; and Sponge Cakes, slow oven.

If cake is put in too cool an oven, it will rise too much and be of very coarse texture. If too hot, it browns and crusts over the top before it has sufficiently risen. If, after the cake is put in, it seems to bake too fast, put a brown paper loosely over the top of the pan, and do not open the oven door for 5 minutes at least; the cake should then be quickly examined and the door carefully shut, or the rush of cold air will cause it to fall. Setting a small dish of hot water in the oven will also prevent the cake from scorching.

To remove cake from pan: Loosen around the edges with a knife and rest pan on its four sides successively; then invert on wire cake cooler or on a board, covered with a piece of old linen or cheese cloth. Let the cake cool before icing it.

Cakes may be classed under two heads: Those that contain butter, Cup and Pound, and those without butter, Sponge and Torte.

CAKES WITH BUTTER

BUTTER OR CUP CAKES

In making butter cakes, creaming the butter encloses air, and makes a delicate texture. The butter should be moderately soft, but not melted in the least, or the cake will be sodden and heavy.

The oven must be ready for baking, the pans thoroughly greased with the same kind of fat used in the mixture.

Sift flour before measuring; pastry flour should be used. The flour and baking powder must be mixed and sifted several times, and if spices are used they should be sifted with the flour.

Use fine granulated sugar to make a fine texture.

Cream the butter, add the sugar gradually. The yolks and whites of the eggs should be beaten separately, and the yolks added to the butter and sugar. The bowl in which they were beaten should be rinsed with the milk. The milk and flour are added alternately, then the flavoring, and the beaten whites of the eggs. When fruit is used save a little flour to cover it and add just before the whites of the eggs.

Do not beat the mixture after adding the whites, as the mixture is so much heavier than the whites, that in the beating many of the air bubbles will be broken, the air will escape, and the cake be less light.

Bake cake from 20 to 40 minutes or until it shrinks from the sides of the pan. When taken from oven allow it to remain in the pan about 3 minutes.

Raisins quartered and seeded and sprinkled with flour may be added to the cake just before baking.

All measurements are level, see page 1.

CHEAP CUP CAKE

No. 1

2 tablespoons butter,
1 cup sugar,
1 egg,
¾ cup water,

2 cups flour,
3 teaspoons baking powder,
½ teaspoon vanilla or
Grated rind of ½ lemon.

Cream the butter, add the sugar gradually, then the egg, and beat well. Add the water and let this stand while the flour and baking powder are sifted three times. Beat all together thoroughly and bake in a moderate oven. This may be used as a loaf or as a layer cake with any preferred filling.

No. 2

2 tablespoons butter,
1 cup sugar,
2 eggs,
1 cup milk,

2½ cups flour,
3 teaspoons baking powder,
1 teaspoon vanilla, or
The grated rind of ½ lemon or orange.

Cream butter and sugar, add eggs one at a time and stir well, then add flour and baking powder mixed, alternately with the milk and vanilla. Bake in two layers in a moderate oven.

PLAIN CAKE

¼ cup butter,
1 cup sugar,
2 eggs,
1½ cups flour,
2 teaspoons baking powder,
1 teaspoon spice, or
½ teaspoon flavoring,
½ cup milk,

Mix and sift flour, baking powder and spices as directed. Cream, butter and sugar, add the beaten yolks, then the flour and milk alternately, the flavoring and beaten whites last. Beat well and bake twenty to thirty minutes. Two ounces of melted chocolate may be used, added after the yolks of eggs, or two tablespoons of cocoa mixed with the flour. Raisins quartered and seeded, and sprinkled with flour, may be added just before baking.

QUICK CAKE

⅓ cup soft butter,
1⅓ cups brown sugar,
2 eggs,
½ cup milk,
½ lb. dates, stoned and finely chopped,
1¾ cups flour,
3 teaspoons baking powder,
½ teaspoon cinnamon,
½ teaspoon grated nutmeg.

Put all ingredients in a bowl together and beat thoroughly for 3 or 4 minutes. Bake in lined loaf pan 35 to 40 minutes. Do not attempt to add the ingredients separately, if you wish a satisfactory cake. Occasionally the housekeeper has a few raisins, or nuts or figs "left over" from other preparations. These she may combine and use instead of the dates, but do not change the proportion. That should be half a pound. If figs should be used, put them through the chopper. This mixture may be baked in gem pans and served hot, as a plum or fruit pudding, with hard or other sauce, to taste.

WHITE CAKE

No. 1

¼ cup butter,
1 scant cup sugar,
½ cup milk,
Whites of 2 eggs,
1⅔ cups flour,
2 teaspoonfuls baking powder,
Flavor with orange or lemon extract or grated rind of orange or lemon.

Cream butter and sugar; sift flour and baking powder three times, add alternately with the milk a little at a time; fold in very stiffly beaten whites of eggs and ice top with Orange Icing, pages 325–326.

WHITE CAKE

No. 2

½ cup butter,
1 cup sugar,
2 cups flour,
4 teaspoons baking powder,
½ cup milk,
½ teaspoon almond flavoring
Whites of 4 eggs,

Mix and sift baking powder and flour. Cream the butter, add the sugar gradually. Add the flour and milk alternately, then the flavoring, and lastly cut in the whites of the eggs, beaten until stiff. Bake in a moderate oven.

GOLD CAKE

No. 1

⅓ cup butter,
¾ cup sugar,
1½ cups flour,
¼ teaspoon soda,
½ teaspoon cream of tartar,
⅓ cup sweet milk,
½ teaspoon vanilla,
Yolks of 4 eggs.

Mix and sift flour and soda. Cream the butter, add the sugar and beat thoroughly; beat yolk with Dover beater, when half beaten add cream of tartar and beat to a stiff froth; add this to the creamed butter and sugar and stir well. Then add milk and flour alternately and the flavoring, stir thoroughly. Place in prepared pan in a moderate oven, and bake from twenty to thirty minutes.

No. 2

1½ cups sugar,
1 cup butter,
¾ cup milk,
Yolks of 12 eggs,
Rind and juice ½ lemon,
2½ cups flour,
3 teaspoons baking powder.

Stir butter and sugar well, then add eggs, one at a time, stirring a half hour, add lemon and lastly milk and flour, alternately. Bake one hour in a moderate oven.

BLITZ KUCHEN

No. 1

1 cup butter,
1 cup sugar,
4 eggs,
2 cups flour,
½ lemon juice,
¼ lb. almonds, chopped.

Cream butter and sugar, add eggs one at a time, then add flour and lemon rind. Stir well, spread with a little unbeaten white of egg, strew with the almonds and bake in a flat tin until well done and browned.

BLITZ KUCHEN
No. 2

1 cup butter,	4 cups flour,
1½ cups sugar,	2 teaspoons baking powder,
7 eggs, beaten separately,	Grated rind of lemon.

Cream butter, add sugar and stir well; add the beaten yolks, lemon rind, flour and baking powder mixed and lastly fold in the beaten whites of eggs. Blanch and slice a few almonds and strew over the top with a sprinkling of sugar and cinnamon. Bake in a well greased spring form in a moderate oven about forty minutes.

STREUSEL FOR BLITZ KUCHENS

2 tablespoons butter,	½ cup almonds, cut fine,
¼ cup sugar,	Grated lemon rind.
¼ cup flour,	

Have butter cold and mix into crumbs, with flour and sugar, using finger tips. Sprinkle lightly over top of Blitz Kuchen Dough, No. 1, and if you wish add almonds and lemon rind. Then bake.

SAND TORTE

6 eggs,	1 cup flour,
1 cup sugar,	½ lemon (juice and rind),
1 cup fresh washed butter,	1½ tablespoon rum or
¼ lb. cornstarch,	brandy,
	2 teaspoons baking powder.

Cream butter and sugar, add beaten yolks, mix flour and cornstarch and baking powder and add to the mixture with the lemon juice and rum. Bake in a round or square loaf.

MARBLE CAKE

¾ cup butter,	4 teaspoons baking powder,
2 cups sugar,	¼ lb. chocolate, grated,
4 eggs,	1 teaspoon cinnamon,
1 cup milk,	½ teaspoon cloves,
3 cups flour,	½ teaspoon vanilla.

Cream butter, add sugar and stir well, add eggs one at a time, beating all the time, then add the flour mixed with the baking powder, and the milk alternately and stir until smooth.

Place ⅓ of the dough in another bowl, add to this the grated chocolate and the spices and flavoring; mix well.

Into a well buttered, deep cake pan, round form with tube in center, if you have one, place a layer of white dough, then a few tablespoons of the dark, then a layer of white, then dark dough and continue leaving white dough on top. Bake 45 minutes in moderate oven.

COFFEE CAKE

No. 1

2 tablespoons butter,
½ cup brown sugar,
½ cup strong coffee,
½ cup molasses,
1 egg,
1 cup seeded raisins or raisins, currants and citron, mixed,
2 teaspoons cocoa,
1 teaspoon cinnamon,
½ teaspoon cloves,
½ teaspoon nutmeg or mace,
2 cups flour,
1 teaspoon soda dissolved in 1 teaspoon warm water.

Mix the dry ingredients and sift over the prepared dried fruit. Cream the butter and the sugar, add the egg, beat well; then the molasses, coffee and dissolved soda, then combine the two mixtures and beat well together. Bake in a moderate oven in a well greased pan, dredged lightly with flour.

No. 2

1 cup butter,
2 cups sugar,
4 eggs,
2 tablespoons molasses,
1 cup cold, boiled coffee,
3¾ cups flour,
5 tablespoons baking powder,
1 teaspoon cinnamon,
½ teaspoon each cloves, mace and allspice,
¾ cup each currants and raisins, seeded and cut in pieces,
¼ cup citron, thinly sliced,
2 tablespoons brandy.

Cream butter and sugar, add eggs, one at a time; the molasses and the flour, fruit, spices and baking powder, mixed and stirred alternately into the mixture with the cold coffee, then add the brandy and bake in brick loaf pans gently, in a rather slow fire, until well baked.

COFFEE CAKE

No. 3

1 cup butter,
2 cups powdered sugar,
4 yolks of eggs,
½ cup chopped almonds,
1 cup grated chocolate,
2 cups flour,
2 teaspoons baking powder,
1 cup strong coffee,
4 whites of eggs to froth.

Cream the butter and sugar, add yolks, coffee, almonds, chocolate, flour and whites of eggs beaten to a froth. Bake in a moderate oven.

HICKORY NUT CAKE

½ cup butter,
1 cup sugar,
Whites of 3 eggs,
½ cup milk,
1½ cups flour,
¾ cup chopped hickory, walnuts or pecan meats.
1 teaspoon cream of tartar,
½ teaspoon soda dissolved in 1 teaspoon milk.

Cream the butter well with sugar, stir in the whites beaten stiff and beat until light and smooth; add milk and flour, alternately and continue stirring; add nuts, stir, then sprinkle the cream of tartar over the mixture and lastly stir in the soda dissolved in 1 teaspoon milk. Beat again and then place in well buttered and slightly floured brick loaf pan and bake in a moderate oven.

CHOCOLATE NUT CAKE

6 yolks,
1 cup sugar,
3 rolled zwieback,
1 teaspoon baking powder,
¼ lb. chocolate, grated,
¼ lb. chopped almonds,
Lemon, cloves and cinnamon,
6 whites of eggs, beaten.

Stir sugar and yolks very light and add the other ingredients, lastly whites of eggs. Can be baked in a loaf or in layers with any kind of Filling, pages 329–335.

BLACKBERRY CAKE

½ cup butter,
1 cup sugar,
4 teaspoons cold water,
1 teaspoon soda,
2 eggs,
2 cups flour,
1 cup preserved fruit, (Blackberry Jam).
1 teaspoon cinnamon,
½ teaspoon cloves,
¼ teaspoon mace.

Cream butter and sugar together until very light; add beaten yolks, water, soda, spices, preserves and flour. Stir all together, beat thoroughly, cut and fold in the beaten whites; bake in a loaf in a moderate oven about 45 minutes. When cool cover with Plain Icing, page 325.

Blackberry, Strawberry or Black Raspberry Jam may be used.

FRUIT OR WEDDING CAKE, No. 1

2 cups (1 lb.) sugar,
2 cups (1 lb.) butter,
4 cups (1 lb.) flour,
12 eggs,
1 teaspoon soda,
1 nutmeg, (grated),
½ lb. of each candied orange and lemon rind (cut fine),
½ cup black molasses,
1 tablespoon mace,
1 teaspoon ground cloves,
1 lb. almonds (blanched and chopped),
4 lbs. raisins (chopped and seeded),
4 lbs. currants (well washed and dry),
1 lb. citron (cut in long and short, thin slices).

Have fruits and nuts prepared beforehand. Line pans with three thicknesses of paper, butter the top layer.

Cream the butter, add the sugar, then the eggs, slightly beaten, and stir well. Add molasses and spices. Mix nuts and fruits thoroughly, and sprinkle half of the flour over them. Add to cake mixture, and lastly, add the soda sifted with the remaining flour.

Bake in a slow oven four hours, in deep, large pans, two-thirds full.

BAKING A FRUIT CAKE

It is often said that fruit cake cannot be baked in a gas oven. Everyone knows that is the perfect way to cook a white sponge cake, and a fruit cake cannot need more careful treatment. Still, if one has had little experience in baking, it might be safer to steam the loaves until three-fourths done and then finish in the oven, with one burner turned half on.

FRUIT CAKE, No. 2

1½ cups sugar,
1½ cups butter,
7 eggs,
3 cups flour,
½ tablespoon ground cinnamon,
½ tablespoon grated nutmeg,
¼ tablespoon ground mace,
⅓ tablespoon ground cloves
1¼ lbs. seeded raisins,
1½ lbs. seedless raisins,
¼ lb. citron,
2 tablespoons brandy,
1 tablespoon wine,
1 tablespoon rosewater.

Cut the seeded raisins in quarters; citron in fine pieces, add the seedless raisins, mix well all together, cover and mix well with the flour. Separate the eggs. Cream the butter and sugar thoroughly, add the yolks and stir well; then add the spices, wine, brandy and rosewater and lastly the beaten whites alternately with the floured fruit. Place in a large pan and bake in slow oven about 4 hours.

LAYER CAKE

½ cup butter,
1 cup sugar,
5 eggs,
1½ cups flour,
2 oz. cornstarch,
1 teaspoon vanilla,
2 teaspoons baking powder.

Cream butter and sugar, add yolks; then cornstarch, baking powder and flour, vanilla, and lastly fold in the beaten whites. Bake in two layers in a moderate oven.

MOLASSES LAYER CAKE

1 cup sugar,
2 tablespoons butter,
2 eggs,
1 teaspoon cinnamon,
1 teaspoon soda, dissolved with 1 cup sour milk,
1 cup New Orleans molasses,
2½ cups flour,
1 teaspoon cloves.

Mix the flour and spices. Cream butter and sugar, add eggs and molasses and the flour and milk alternately. Bake in a moderate oven in two layers. Frost with Boiled Icing, pages 327–328. Add one cup of chopped raisins.

DEVIL'S FOOD, No. 1

2 squares chocolate (2 oz.),
3 tablespoons water,
1¼ cups sugar,
½ cup butter, (scant),
1 cup sour or butter milk,
1 teaspoon soda,
Yolk of 1 egg.
2 scant cups flour.

Heat and melt the chocolate, water, and sugar; when dissolved, add the butter. Set aside to cool. Mix buttermilk, soda and the beaten yolk, add the melted chocolate mixture, and then the flour, and bake in two layers in a moderate oven, reserving the white of egg for the frosting.

DEVIL'S FOOD, No. 2

Part 1.

1 cup chocolate,
1 cup brown sugar,
½ cup milk.

Part 2.

½ cup butter,
1 cup sugar (brown),
3 yolks, beaten,
1½ cups sifted flour,
1 teaspoon baking soda,
½ cup sweet milk.

Melt Part 1, but do not boil. Cool it.

Mix Part 2—Cream butter and sugar, beaten yolks, then Part 1; stir well and then add milk and the flour mixed with the baking soda, and bake in layers. Chocolate Icing, page 326.

CHOCOLATE LAYER CAKE

No. 1

3 squares (3 oz.) chocolate,
3 tablespoons sugar,
1 tablespoon flour,
¼ cup water,
⅓ cup milk.

Cook all together, stirring constantly until smooth and thick, then put it away to cool; for remainder of cake as follows:

¼ cup butter,
1 cup granulated sugar,
⅔ cup milk,
2 eggs,
2 cups flour,
2 teaspoonfuls baking powder,
½ teaspoon vanilla.

Cream butter and sugar, adding a little of the milk, then the beaten yolks; remainder of the milk and flour sifted with the baking powder; then the cooked chocolate mixture, and flavoring. Lastly cut and fold in whites of the eggs which have been beaten very stiff. Bake in layers and put layers together with plain Boiled Icing, pages 327–328.

No. 2

½ cup butter,
2 cups brown sugar,
3 eggs, beaten separately,
½ cup milk,
½ cup hot water,
½ cup grated chocolate,
½ cup grated almonds,
2¼ cups flour,
1½ teaspoon baking powder.

Stir butter and sugar to a cream, add yolks, then gradually add milk, the hot water, stirred into the grated chocolate, flour and baking powder mixed and the almonds and lastly the beaten whites of the eggs.

Bake in two layers, in a moderate oven, with Chocolate Nut Filling, page 332, or Sour Cream Filling, No. 2, page 330.

CARAMEL LAYER CAKE

4 oz. butter,
1 cup sugar,
5 whites of eggs,
½ cup milk,

1¾ cups pastry flour (sift twice),
2 heaping teaspoons baking powder.

Cream the butter and add the sugar and stir well. Mix baking powder and flour and add alternately the milk and flour and lastly fold in the whites beaten very stiff. Bake in two layers in a moderate oven. Frost with Caramel Frosting, page 329.

SPONGE CAKES

CAKES WITHOUT BUTTER (SPONGE)

Sponge Cakes contain no butter and are made rich with eggs; the lightness depends upon the amount of air beaten into the eggs. In mixing sponge cakes cut and fold in the flour last, as gently as possible. If the mixture is stirred or beaten after adding the flour, many of the air bubbles will be broken and much of the enclosed air will escape.

Bake in ungreased patent pan, in a slow oven, until the cake is well risen, then increase the heat gradually until the cake is well browned over.

Press finger gently on top of cake, if it springs back and leaves no impression the cake is done. Invert the pan and let stand until cool before removing from pan.

All measurings are level, see page 1.

SPONGE CAKE (WITH WATER)

No. 1

Yolks of 2 eggs,
1 cup sugar (scant),
⅜ cup hot milk or water,
¼ teaspoon lemon juice,

Whites of 2 eggs,
1 cup flour,
1½ teaspoon baking powder,
¼ teaspoon salt.

Beat yolks until thick and lemon colored, add half the sugar gradually and beat; add milk, remaining sugar, lemon, whites of eggs beaten stiff and flour mixed sifted with baking powder and salt. Bake 35 minutes in a moderate oven.

SPONGE CAKE

No. 2

3 eggs,
1 scant cup sugar,
1 tablespoonful hot water,
2 teaspoonful vinegar,
½ teaspoonful salt,
½ teaspoonful extract of lemon,
1 cup flour,
½ teaspoonful baking powder.

Beat the yolks until thick and light; add sugar gradually and continue beating; then add water and vinegar; add the salt to the whites and beat until very stiff; sift the flour with baking powder three times; add the flavoring and fold in the flour and the beaten whites alternately as gently as possible. Bake about 30 minutes in slow oven until well risen; then increase the heat. Invert to cool, then remove from pan.

No. 3

Yolks 6 eggs,
1 cup sugar,
1 tablespoon lemon juice,
Grated rind ½ lemon,
Whites 6 eggs,
1 cup flour.

Beat yolks until thick and lemon colored, add sugar gradually, and continue beating. Add lemon juice, rind and whites of eggs beaten until stiff and dry. When whites are partially mixed with yolks, carefully cut and fold in flour, mixed and sifted with salt. Bake in an unbuttered pan, in a slow oven for 1 hour.

"BOILED" SPONGE CAKE

1 cup sugar,
½ cup water,
Yolks of 5 eggs,
Grated rind and juice of ½ lemon or orange,
1 cup flour,
Whites of 5 eggs.

Boil sugar and water until it threads when dropped from the end of a spoon, pour in a fine stream on to the yolks, beaten until thick and lemon colored; beat well, then set dish into cold water, and continue beating, until the mixture is cold, adding, while beating, the lemon or orange juice and rind. Then fold in half the whites of eggs, beaten dry, and the flour, then the rest of the egg whites. Bake in a greased patent tube pan about 50 minutes. Invert to cool, then remove from pan.

SUNSHINE CAKE

6 eggs,
A pinch of salt added to the eggs before beating,
⅓ teaspoon cream of tartar,
⅔ cup flour,
1 cup sugar,
½ lemon, or
1 teaspoon vanilla.

Sift, measure and set aside flour and sugar; then sift flour four times; separate the eggs; beat yolks to a very stiff froth; whip whites to foam, add cream of tartar, and whip until very stiff; add sugar to the yolks and beat; then add the beaten whites, gradually, and flavoring, then fold in flour lightly. Put in moderate oven at once, in ungreased pan; will bake in thirty to forty-five minutes. Invert to cool.

ANGEL FOOD

Whites of 8 or 9 eggs, or
Just 1 cup of whites,
A pinch of salt,
½ teaspoon cream of tartar,
1¼ cups sugar,
½ teaspoon vanilla, or almond extract,
1 cup pastry flour.

Sift flour once, then measure and sift three times. Add salt to the whites, beat about half, add cream of tartar, then beat whites until they will stand of their own weight; add the sugar, then flour, not by stirring but folding over and over until thoroughly mixed in; flavor. Bake in an ungreased pan, patent tube pan preferred. Place the cake in an oven that is just warm enough to know there is a fire inside; let the oven stay just warm through until the batter has raised to the top of the mould, then increase the heat gradually until the cake is well browned over; if by pressing the top of the cake with the finger it will spring back without leaving the imprint of the finger the cake is done through. Great care should be taken that the oven is not too hot to begin with as the cake will rise too fast and settle or fall in the baking. Bake 35 to 40 minutes. When done, invert the pan; when cool remove from pan.

CHOCOLATE SPONGE CAKE

Sunshine Cake Mixture,   2 tablespoons grated chocolate.

Melt the chocolate over hot water and stir in the lightly beaten yolks and sugar of Sunshine Cake Mixture, recipe above; using vanilla for flavor. Finish mixing and baking as Sunshine Cake.

DELICATE ZWIEBACK

6 yolks,	1 cup flour,
1 cup sugar,	1 teaspoon baking powder,
1 teaspoon anise seed,	6 whites of eggs.

Beat yolks until thick and lemon colored, add sugar gradually and continue beating; add flour, baking powder, anise, pounded and sifted and cut and fold in the six whites of eggs, beaten to stiff froth. Bake in flat pan, one that is high on the sides, so the cake can raise in a slow oven, about 1 hour. When baked light brown, remove from pan and keep in a dry, cool place until the next day, then slice the cake and brown or toast it on both sides. Dust with powdered sugar. This is very nice for invalids.

POTATO FLOUR CAKE

9 eggs,	1 scant cup of potato flour,
1¾ cups sugar,	½ lemon (rind and juice).

Separate the whites and yolks of eggs. Beat the whites of seven eggs very stiff. To the well beaten yolks of nine eggs and the whites of two, add the sugar and lemon juice. Beat thoroughly, add the potato flour, and beat again. Now fold in the beaten whites very carefully, and bake slowly in a moderate oven. Bake forty to fifty minutes. Nice for invalids.

MATZOS SPONGE CAKE

No. 1

6 eggs,	6 tablespoons sugar,
4 tablespoons matzos meal,	Grated rind of ½ lemon.

Separate the whites and yolks of eggs. To the well beaten yolks add the sugar, beat again, then add the lemon rind and beaten whites and lastly the matzos flour. Bake in a moderate oven in loaf or in layers.

No. 2

8 yolks of eggs,	1 cup finely sifted matzos meal,
1½ cups sugar,	8 whites, beaten stiff,
½ lemon, grated rind and juice.	

Beat yolks until light, add sugar and beat again; then add salt, the lemon, then the matzos meal and lastly fold in the beaten whites of eggs. Bake in a moderate oven in spring form or in two layers.

Nice with sweetened strawberries between the layers. Spread whipped cream, flavored and sweetened over top and sides.

MATZOS SPONGE CAKE

No. 3

12 eggs,	1 cup fine matzos flour,
2 cups granulated sugar,	1 teaspoon lemon flavor, or
1 cup potato flour,	Lemon rind.

Separate the yolks and whites of eggs. Beat yolks lightly, add the sugar, and beat well. Then add potato flour, matzos flour, lemon flavor and whites of eggs beaten thoroughly. Bake in a hot oven.

SPONGE JELLY ROLL

5 eggs,	1 cup of sugar,
The grated rind of 1 lemon,	1 cup of flour,
2 tablespoons of lemon juice,	Fruit jelly.

Beat the yolks of the eggs until very thick; add the sugar gradually, then the lemon rind and juice; fold in half the whites of the eggs beaten dry, then half the flour, the other half of the whites of the eggs and the other half of the flour. Bake in a large dripping pan about 15 minutes; turn from the pan on to a cloth, trim the edges of the cake, spread the bottom of the cake (the top as it lies on the cloth) with the jelly; then roll closely, wrap in the cloth and set aside to cool.

SOUR CREAM CAKE

1 cup sugar,	2 cups flour,
1 egg,	¾ teaspoon soda,
5 tablespoons of sour milk in cup,	¼ teaspoon salt,
Then fill cup with sour cream,	¼ teaspoon cinnamon.

Beat egg lightly, add sugar and continue beating; then add sour milk and cream. Last the mixed and sifted dry ingredients.

Bake in angel cake pan in moderate oven or in layer cake tins, and spread Sour Cream Filling, page 330, between layers.

SOUR CREAM CHOCOLATE LAYER CAKE

Yolks of 4 eggs,
Whites of 3 eggs,
1⅓ cups sugar,
1 cup thick sour cream,
1 teaspoonful soda,
A pinch of salt,
2½ cups flour,
2 squares chocolate.

Beat the yolks and the sugar until very light; melt the chocolate in part of the cream over the fire; let cool and then add it to the rest of the cream. Sift the soda into the flour and add alternately with cream to the yolks and sugar; flavor and cut and fold in the stiffly beaten whites. Bake in square, shallow pans. This will make two layers. When cool put together with Boiled Icing, page 327–328.

SPONGE LAYER CAKE

2 eggs,
⅔ cup sugar,
5 tablespoons boiling water,
1 cup flour,
2 teaspoons baking powder,
¼ teaspoon salt,
1 teaspoon vanilla, or
Grated lemon rind.

Put eggs and sugar into a mixing bowl and beat with the egg beater till very light. Add 5 tablespoons of rapidly boiling water and beat again. Mix flour with baking powder and salt. Stir this into the eggs quickly, add vanilla and when well mixed, turn at once into two well greased jelly cake pans and bake about 12 minutes in a quick oven. Reduce the heat as soon as well risen, and at the last turn out the burner, and remove the cake when firm.

CREAM FILLING

Cream Filling. Whip 1 cup of thick cream till stiff, adding powdered sugar till sweet to taste, and flavor with vanilla. Put part of it on the bottom of one cake, lay the other cake on with the top up and put the remainder of the cream on by forcing it through a pastry tube in a bag in any fanciful design.

ORANGE LAYER CAKE

5 eggs, yolks,
2 cups pulverized sugar,
Juice of 1 orange,
Grated rind of orange,
2 cups flour,
1 teaspoon baking powder,
Whites of 3 eggs,
½ cup water.

Beat yolks light, add sugar, beat again. Then add water, orange juice and part of the rind and the flour, sifted three times, and baking powder mixed. Lastly fold in the beaten whites of three eggs. Bake in layers in a moderate oven.

Icing: Whites of two eggs, beaten stiff, powdered sugar to spread and the rest of the grated rind of orange.

SEVEN LAYER CAKE

5 eggs,
¾ cup flour, sifted three times.
1 scant cup powdered sugar,

Beat yolks well with the sugar, add sifted flour and the whites beaten stiff. Spread on seven tins (one-quarter inch high), well buttered and floured. When baked, remove from tins at once.

Filling: Three eggs, 1½ cups sugar, 3 sticks Maillard's sweet chocolate, a little vanilla. Boil in double boiler, stirring constantly. When thick, set out to cool and then add one-half pound butter (scant); stir this well, spread between the layers, over top and sides. Let cool to harden.

MOCHA LAYER CAKE

6 eggs,
1 cup sugar,
1 tablespoon Crosse & Blackwell's Mocha essence.
1 cup flour,
1 teaspoon baking powder,

Beat yolks until thick and lemon colored, add sugar gradually and continue beating. Add Mocha essence and the whites beaten until stiff and dry. When the whites are partially mixed with the yolks, carefully cut and fold in flour, mixed and sifted with the baking powder. Bake in two layers in a moderate oven.

Filling No. 1: Serve with whipped cream, sweetened with powdered sugar, and three tablespoons mocha essence between layers.

Icing No. 1: Confectioners' sugar and water, stirred until smooth, and mocha essence to taste. Or,

Filling No. 2: Two cups C brown sugar. Moisten with water, boil until it strings, and add one tablespoon butter and two tablespoons cream. Boil until butter dissolves, beat until thick, and cool; then add one tablespoon essence of coffee. Spread immediately between cake.

Icing No. 2: Beat the white of an egg, one cup of confectioners' sugar, one tablespoon cold water and flavor with mocha essence.

TORTES

Tortes are cakes that contain no butter, but are made rich with nuts and light with eggs, while bread or cracker crumbs usually take the place of flour.

The nuts are chopped, rolled or ground fine, mixed with crumbs and spices. The eggs are beaten separately. Beat yolks with sugar and add nuts, crumbs and spices. Fold the whites in last. Bake slowly in moderate oven.

ALMOND TORTE

No. 1

9 eggs, separated,
½ lb. almonds, unblanched and grated,
1½ cups sugar,
1 cup flour,
1 teaspoon baking powder.

Beat yolks well with sugar and add alternately the stiffly beaten whites and grated almonds; then fold in lightly the flour mixed with the baking powder. Place in well greased spring form and bake in a moderate oven about 40 minutes.

No. 2

9 eggs,
8 tablespoons granulated sugar,
¼ lb. sweet almonds,
⅛ lb. bitter almonds,
4 stale lady fingers,
1 teaspoon baking powder,
½ teaspoon vanilla.

Beat the yolks and sugar until very light; add grated almonds, grated lady fingers, vanilla, and the baking powder, lastly the whites of the eggs, beaten to a stiff froth. Place in spring form and bake in moderate oven about forty minutes.

ALMOND TORTE WITH LADY FINGERS

10 eggs,
1½ cups (¾ lb.) sugar,
¾ lb. grated almonds, unblanched,
1 cup grated lady fingers, mixed with 1 teaspoon baking powder.

Put sugar in a bowl and beat in each egg separately, beat in all ¾ hour; then add almonds and grated lady fingers. Bake in a spring form, in a moderate oven 1¼ to 1½ hours.

Bake 3 days before using; then cut crosswise in 4 or 5 or as many layers as possible, and put the following Cream Filling between the day before using:

2 cups milk,
2 teaspoons cornstarch,
2 yolks of eggs,
A little vanilla.

Wet the cornstarch with a little of the milk, add the rest of the milk; boil; take from the stove, and pour gradually on the beaten yolks. Add vanilla to taste.

ANGEL TORTE

½ lb. powdered sugar,
½ lb. almonds,
A few bitter ones,
½ lb. dates,
5 eggs,
2 teaspoons baking powder.

Blanch almonds, chop fine or grind. Stone dates, pour boiling water over them, drain and rub to a smooth paste.

Beat the yolk of 1 egg and stir in a small portion of the date pulp and some sugar, and continue until egg, dates and sugar are all mixed. Stir well. Stir in most of the almonds and stir lightly into cake. Add beaten whites of the eggs. Bake in well greased and floured spring form in moderate oven. When cool cut in 2 layers and spread Whipped Cream, page 335, between.

BROD TORTE

5 yolks of eggs,
1 cup sugar,
1 cup almonds, blanched and grated,
1½ teaspoons baking powder,
1 cup grated bread,
2 tablespoons wine,
1 lemon, grated rind,
5 whites of eggs, beaten stiff.

Beat yolks and sugar until very light, soak the wine with the crumbs and add and mix all together, the beaten whites last. Bake in two layers, Brod Torte Filling, page 332, between.

CHEESE TORTE

No. 1

½ lb. cottage cheese (riced),
6 yolks of eggs,
5 oz. butter,
½ lb. sugar,
5 oz. almonds, blanched and grated,
Rind of a lemon,
1 teaspoon flour,
6 whites of eggs.

Cream the butter and sugar, add the beaten yolks and other ingredients, beaten whites last. Place in buttered spring form in moderate oven until well set, and when cool ice with Chocolate Frosting, page 326. If two layers are desired, double the recipe.

No. 2

1 cup sugar,
1 cup butter,
½ lb. cottage cheese (riced),
½ lb. blanched and grated almonds,
5 tablespoons grated wheat bread,
10 yolks of eggs,
10 whites of eggs,
1 lemon, juice and grated rind.

Beat sugar and butter to a cream, add yolks, put cheese through a sieve, and add that and other ingredients and mix well and bake in buttered spring form in moderate oven until well set. When cool, ice with Chocolate Frosting, page 326. May be made in two layers.

No. 3

1½ lb. cottage cheese,
1 pint cream,
1 cup milk,
1 large teaspoon cornstarch,
1 teaspoon vanilla,
5 eggs,
1½ cups sugar.

Line a spring form with Murberteig, No. 3, page 302. Put cheese through sieve. Beat yolks of eggs and sugar, add cheese, milk, cream, cornstarch, and vanilla, then the whites previously beaten to snow.

Fill in the lined spring form and bake in a moderate oven until cheese is well set and dough is well browned at the bottom.

CHESTNUT TORTE

1½ lbs. chestnuts, before shelling,
8 yolks,
8 tablespoons sugar,
8 whites,
2 oz. grated almonds,
1 teaspoon grated bread

Shell Chestnuts, page 160, then boil in a little milk until tender, and put through the ricer. Cream beaten yolks and sugar, add crumbs and nuts and lastly, the beaten whites, and add other ingredients. Bake in a spring form in a moderate oven until set.

CHOCOLATE TORTE

9 eggs (whites beaten stiff),
1 lb. powdered sugar, sifted,
1 teaspoon vanilla,
½ lb. of Maillard's grated sweet chocolate,
½ lb. grated almonds.

Beat yolks with sugar, add chocolate, almonds and vanilla, and lastly the beaten whites. Bake one hour, in spring form, moderate oven.

Icing: One-quarter pound Maillard's chocolate, one cup of sugar, one cup of milk; boil and add vanilla and yolk of one egg.

CHOCOLATE ZWIEBACK TORTE

1 cup sugar,
6 yolks,
1 cup grated chocolate,
1 cup zwieback, grated,
6 whites of eggs,
½ cup almonds, grated,
1 teaspoon cinnamon,
1 teaspoon cloves,
1 teaspoon baking powder,
½ cup almonds, grated.

Mix the zwieback and baking powder. Stir yolk and sugar very light, add other ingredients, and lastly the whites of egg, beaten very stiff. Bake in two layers, spread raspberry jelly between and Chocolate Frosting, page 326, on top.

COFFEE CREME TORTE

8 eggs, separated,
½ lb. powdered sugar,
½ lb. almonds, grated,
2 oz. coffee, pulverized,
1 teaspoon vanilla.

Beat the yolks until thick. Add the sugar; then the almonds and coffee and vanilla, and lastly fold in the well beaten whites. Bake in two layers in a moderate oven. Use the following:

Creme for Filling and Frosting:
6 oz. fresh, unsalted butter,
6 oz. powdered sugar,
4 yolks, each one added separately,
1 tablespoon coffee essence, added drop by drop.

Cream butter and eggs together, add each yolk separately, and coffee essence drop by drop. Decorate with small chocolate wafers and candied cherries. To be kept in a cold place until used in order to harden the creme. Cut with a knife dipped in hot water.

DAISY TORTE

- 10 yolks of eggs,
- 1 cup sugar,
- ¾ cup sweet chocolate,
- ¾ cup sweet almonds,
- 8 bitter almonds,
- 1 cup stale wheat bread crumbs,
- ½ teaspoon cinnamon,
- ½ teaspoon cloves,
- 1 teaspoon baking powder,
- 1 lemon, juice and rind,
- 1 teaspoon brandy,
- 10 whites of eggs, beaten.

Stir yolks and sugar together. Mix dry ingredients and add the rest, beaten whites lastly. Bake in three layers in moderate oven.

Filling: Two teaspoons of cornstarch, one cup of milk, one-fourth cup of sugar, two yolks of eggs, and flavor with vanilla. Cook all in a double boiler until thick. Cover the top layer with a Chocolate Frosting, page 326.

DATE TORTE

- 9 eggs,
- 1¾ cups sugar,
- 16 dates (sliced),
- 3 tablespoons grated chocolate,
- 1 teaspoon cinnamon,
- 1 teaspoon allspice,
- 1 heaping cup cracker crumbs,
- 2 tablespoons wine, brandy or lemon juice.

Rub the dates to a smooth paste with the wine, brandy or lemon juice. Beat two whole eggs and seven yolks, add sugar, beat again, add the dates, chocolate and spices and cracker crumbs and stir in well, and lastly fold in the beaten whites of the eggs. Bake in a good sized spring form forty minutes.

NOTE—Prunes may be used instead of dates.

DATE AND WALNUT TORTE

- 2 large eggs,
- 1 cup powdered sugar,
- 1 cup walnuts (chopped),
- 1 cup dates (cut fine),
- 2 tablespoons flour,
- 1 teaspoon baking powder.

Beat eggs very light, add sugar, nuts and dates, and lastly the flour mixed with the baking powder. Bake in a slow oven one hour. If desired for dessert, pour over a glass of wine and cover with Whipped Cream, page 335. The wine may be omitted.

FARINA TORTE

6 yolks of eggs,
1 cup of sugar,
1 cup sweet almonds (grated),
6 whites of eggs, beaten,
1 cup farina, with
1 teaspoon baking powder.

Stir sugar and beaten yolks until very light, the almonds, grated; then mix in the order given, and bake in spring form, moderate oven, forty minutes.

FILBERT TORTE

½ cup bread crumbs,
1½ cups powdered sugar,
½ cup bread crumbs,
1 lemon, grated rind,
Juice of ½ lemon,
½ lb. grated filberts or hazelnuts,
8 whites of eggs, beaten stiff.

Beat yolks and sugar until very light, add bread crumbs and the rest of the ingredients in order, the beaten whites last. Bake in a slow oven 40 to 45 minutes, in a spring form. Frost with Nut Frosting, page 329. Decorate with nuts.

Or bake in two layers, with fresh strawberries, or sweetened whipped cream, between and on top of cake.

FILLED TORTE, Cherries

½ lb. flour,
5 oz. butter,
2 oz. sugar,
1 yolk of egg,
2 teaspoons brandy.

Make a dough of above and roll out and spread in a spring form, cover with canned fruit (cherries) (not too much juice), and bake. Then cover the top with a sponge made as follows:

6 yolks,
¼ lb. sugar,
¼ lb. grated almonds,
Rind of 1 lemon,
Whites of 6 eggs, to stiff froth.

Stir yolks and sugar fifteen minutes, add almonds, lemon and whites, and bake a light brown.

FILLED TORTE, Macaroon

Murberteig,
Whites 14 eggs,
2 cups powdered sugar,
1 lb. blanched and grated almonds,
1 teaspoon vanilla.

Line sides and bottom of spring form with Murberteig, page 301. Beat whites of eggs very stiff, add sugar and beat again, until stiff and dry, add vanilla and fold in the grated almonds.

Place the nut mixture in the dough lined spring form and bake 1 hour, in slow oven, and serve with Whipped Cream, page 335.

HIMMEL TORTE

¾ lb. butter,
4 tablespoons sugar,
4 yolks of eggs,
4 cups (1 lb.) flour,
Grated rind of lemon.

Cream the butter and sugar together and add yolks of eggs, one at a time; then the flour and grated lemon rind. Bake in three layers. Spread the top of each layer with white of egg to moisten, a sprinkling of cinnamon, sugar and chopped almonds. Put raspberry jelly on top of two layers, and over all the following:

Creme: One pint thick, sour cream, vanilla, two tablespoons cornstarch and sugar mixed. Boil and lastly stir in the beaten yolks of two eggs.

KARMELITER TORTE

9 whole eggs,
2 yolks of eggs,
1½ cups sugar,
1 lb. almond, blanched and grated,
6 bitter almonds, grated,
1 lemon, grated rind,
½ teaspoon cinnamon,
½ teaspoon nutmeg,
2 cups flour.

Beat the eggs well with Dover beater, add sugar and beat again until very light, then add the other ingredients and stir well. Bake one hour in a moderate oven. Ice if desired, with Lemon Frosting, page 325.

KISS TORTE

6 whites of eggs,
2 cups granulated sugar,
1 teaspoon vanilla,
1 teaspoon vinegar.

Beat the whites of six fresh eggs to a stiff, dry froth, add the sugar a little at a time and beat, add the vanilla and vinegar.

Grease a spring form and pour in it two-thirds of the mixture. Make small kisses dropped from a teaspoon with the rest of the mixture and form in a circle on a tin, the same size and shape of the spring form. Bake forty-five to sixty minutes in slow oven. Fill with whipped cream and berries and decorate top with the circle of baked kisses. See recipe for Kisses, page 383.

LADY FINGER TORTE

6 eggs, yolks,
1½ cups granulated sugar,
9 large or
11 stale lady fingers, rolled fine,
2 tablespoons brandy,
1 cup grated almonds,
Pinch salt,
5 eggs, whites.

Beat yolks and sugar very light, until lemon colored. Add the rest of the ingredients, the beaten whites last. Bake in two layers, in slow oven, 40 minutes. Spread Nut Filling, No. 2, page 332, between layers.

LAYER TORTE

10 yolks of eggs,
1 cup of sugar,
¾ cup bitter chocolate,
¾ cup chopped almonds,
1 cup grated wheat bread,
½ teaspoon cinnamon,
½ teaspoon cloves,
1 lemon, (rind, juice of half),
A little brandy,
10 whites of eggs, to stiff froth.

To the beaten yolks add the sugar, beat well, then add the rest of the ingredients in order, and fold in the beaten whites lightly. Bake in two layers with Custard Filling, No. 1, page 330, between, and Boiled Chocolate Frosting, No. 2, page 328.

MACAROON TORTE

¾ lb. almonds,
½ lb. powdered sugar,
7 whites of eggs,
Juice and part of the grated rind of a lemon,
Murberteig, No. 1.

Steam the sugar, sifted, and whites of eggs in the double boiler for five minutes, stirring constantly. Blanch and grate the almonds, using the coarse grater; add the sugar and eggs with the lemon. Line a Torte (spring) form with the Murberteig, No. 1, page 301, spread the top of the dough with gooseberry preserves or with gooseberry or cherry conserve. Fill with the macaroon mixture. Bake about ¾ hour in a moderate oven.

MARTZEPAN TORTE

½ lb. flour,
¼ lb. butter,
2 tablespoons sugar,
2 yolks of eggs,
2 tablespoons water.

Mix flour, sugar and butter, add eggs and water, put in a cool place to harden, then roll out the dough.

Filling: One pound almonds, blanched and dried the day before, then grated. One pound powdered sugar, juice of two lemons. Place on fire until it cooks (or is very hot); then stir a short time, add the whites of eight eggs beaten stiff. Line a spring form with the dough, put in the mixture, place strips of dough over the top and bake in a very slow oven one hour. Dust with powdered sugar and candied cherries to decorate.

MATZOS TORTE

6 yolks, beaten,
1 cup sugar,
1 tablespoon wine or lemon juice,
1 cup chocolate, grated,
1 cup almonds, blanched and grated,
Grated rind of ½ lemon,
½ cup matzos meal or 1 cup cracker meal,
1 teaspoon baking powder,
6 whites of eggs, beaten stiff,
1 teaspoon each cinnamon, allspice and cloves.

To the beaten yolks add the sugar and beat well. Mix the dry ingredients; stir all together, adding beaten whites last.

Bake in spring form or in layers, with jelly between. Ice top and sides with Chocolate Frosting, page 326.

MATZOS CHOCOLATE TORTE

4 yolks, beaten,
½ cup sugar,
¼ lb. almonds, blanched,
¼ lb. sweet grated chocolate,
¼ lb. raisins,
½ cup matzo meal, sifted fine
Juice of an orange,
¼ cup wine,
4 whites, beaten stiff.

Beat sugar and eggs until very light, add almonds, grated, raisins, matzo meal, the wine and orange juice, and lastly the whites of eggs. Bake in spring form in moderate oven.

MOSS TORTE

10 yolks of eggs,
7 whites of eggs,
1 cup powdered sugar,
6 oz. almonds, grated,
A little cinnamon,
A little citron, cut fine,
Rind of 1 lemon,
Juice of ½ lemon,
1 teaspoon baking powder.

Stir yolks with sugar until light, add some of the grated almonds, lemon juice and rind; then citron, mixed with the rest of the grated almonds and lastly the beaten whites.

Bake in spring forms or in layers and put Whipped Cream, page 335, or a Custard Filling, page 330, with grated almonds between. Slow oven.

MUSHKAZUNGE

7 whites of eggs (unbeaten),
½ lb. almonds, grated and unblanched,
½ lb. granulated sugar,
½ teaspoon cinnamon,
Rind of ½ lemon.

Mix and bake 20 minutes in a long, shallow pan in a moderate oven.

ORANGE TORTE

8 eggs,
1 cup sugar,
½ lb. grated almonds,
2 tablespoons bread crumbs,
2 oranges, rind and juice.

Beat sugar with the yolks and stir until very light; add almonds, bread crumbs, juice and light grated rind of the oranges and beaten whites of eggs.

Bake in two layers, in a moderate oven ½ hour, in spring forms. When cold spread jelly between the layers and pour over the following orange icing:

½ cup sugar,
2 oranges, juice,
1 orange, sections, and candied cherries, to decorate.

Boil sugar with orange juice until it threads from end of spoon; spread over top of cake and decorate with orange sections and cherries.

Half the cake recipe may be used baked in a square shallow pan, cut into small oblongs or squares, frosted and decorated for Bunde Schuessel, page 370.

POTATO CHOCOLATE TORTE

1 cup of butter,
2 cups of sugar,
½ cup of cream,
1 cup potatoes, boiled and riced,
1 cup of almonds, grated,
1 cup of chocolate, grated,
¼ teaspoon cloves,
¼ teaspoon cinnamon,
4 yolks of eggs,
2½ cups of sifted flour,
1 teaspoon vanilla,
Rind of lemon,
2 teaspoons baking powder,
Beat 4 whites of egg.

Cream the butter and sugar together, add one yolk of egg at a time, and the rest of the above ingredients, beaten whites lastly. Bake in spring form, moderate oven, forty-five minutes. Chocolate Frosting, page 326, on top.

POPPYSEED TORTE

No. 1

1 cup poppyseed,	2 tablespoons raisins, chopped,
6 yolks,	1 tablespoon citron, cut fine,
¾ cup sugar,	1 teaspoon vanilla,
Grated rind of lemon,	6 whites,
¼ cup ground almonds, sweet and bitter mixed.	Murberteig.

Line a spring form with Murberteig, page 301, sprinkle with bread crumbs. Grind poppyseed fine in coffee mill, throw away the first bit, to lose the coffee taste. Beat the yolks with the sugar until light, add the rest of the ingredients, the stiffly beaten whites last. Fill in the form and bake in moderate oven until well set and browned at the bottom.

No. 2

8 yolks of eggs,	½ lb. ground poppyseed,
1½ cups sugar,	1 oz. citron,
¼ lb. chopped raisins,	1 lemon, juice and rind,
¼ lb. almonds, blanched and grated,	8 whites of eggs.

Beat eggs and sugar until very light, add rest of the ingredients, beaten whites last. Bake ½ hour in a moderate oven. Frost with Plain Frosting, page 325, flavored with 1 tablespoon rum.

No. 3

18 eggs,	Rind and juice of a lemon,
18 tablespoons sugar,	1½ teaspoons cinnamon,
18 tablespoons ground poppyseed,	1½ strips sweet chocolate,
¾ lb. grated almonds,	1½ teaspoons baking powder,
	1 wine glass brandy.

Mix poppyseed, almonds, cinnamon, German sweet chocolate and baking powder. Beat yolks of eggs, add sugar and stir well, then brandy, lemon and the dry ingredients, and lastly, fold in the whites beaten stiff. Bake in large greased spring form in moderate oven.

RUM TORTE

8 eggs, separated,	2 heaping tablespoons bread crumbs,
½ lb. almonds, grated,	
1 cup sugar,	2 teaspoons flour, mixed with ½ teaspoon baking powder.
Juice and rind of one lemon,	

Beat the yolks with the sugar until light. Add the almonds, bread crumbs and lemon. Then fold in lightly, the beaten whites, and the flour and baking powder mixed. Bake in a spring form for one hour in a moderate oven.

Allow the cake to cool somewhat, then cut crosswise through the center into two layers and put in a filling of 1 glass raspberry jelly and 1 cup chopped walnuts.

Frost with the following mixture:

2 cups confectioner's sugar,   2 tablespoons rum,
4 tablespoons cream.

Stirred until smooth. Spread over top and sides. (For trimming the cake use half walnuts and slices of figs.)

RYE BREAD TORTE

No. 1

½ cup butter,
1¾ cups sugar,
1¾ cups rye bread crumbs,
4 yolks, beaten,
4 whites of eggs, beaten stiff,
Whipped cream.

Cream butter and sugar, add yolks, beat well, then the grated crumbs and lastly the beaten whites. Bake in two layers in a moderate oven and when ready to serve pile Whipped Cream, page 335, between and on top.

No. 2

10 yolks of eggs,
2 cups of sugar,
1¾ cups rye bread crumbs,
1 cup grated chocolate,
½ teaspoon cinnamon,
¼ teaspoon cloves,
¼ cup chopped almonds,
A little citron, chopped,
3 tablespoons preserved or stewed fruit,
1 wineglass claret,
10 whites of egg, beaten,
2 teaspoons baking powder.

Stir the yolks of eggs and sugar until very light. Mix the dry and then add the other ingredients, beaten whites lastly. Bake in spring form, one hour, moderate oven.

No. 3

9 oz. almonds, grated and unblanched,
1 oz. bitter almonds, blanched and grated,
¾ lb. powdered sugar,
12 whole eggs, and
4 yolks of eggs,
1 lemon, rind and juice,
2½ oz. citron, chopped,
½ teaspoon cinnamon,
¼ teaspoon cloves,
⅛ teaspoon mace,
¼ lb. dry, grated and sifted rye bread,
½ cup claret.

Stir 16 yolks of eggs until thick and lemon colored, add sugar gradually and continue beating; add almonds, rind and juice of lemon. Add bread and spices and the whites of 12 eggs, beaten stiff and dry.

Bake in a moderate oven one hour or over. Remove from oven. Next day, if desired, sprinkle 2 tablespoons Tokay or Port wine over the cake and frost with Plain Frosting, page 325, flavored with Rum.

WALNUT TORTE, No. 1

1 lb. English walnuts or almonds,
1 cup sugar,
9 eggs,
¼ cup grated chocolate,
½ cup of fine cracker crumbs

Chop the nuts, reserving twenty-three halves for decorating the top. Mix the chopped nuts and chocolate. Beat yolks thoroughly with Dover beater, add sugar, and beat again. Then mix with the nuts, crumbs and chocolate, and stir well. Beat whites of eggs until stiff and add lastly, just as in sponge cake. Bake in moderate oven forty-five minutes in prepared spring form.

WALNUT TORTE, No. 2

6 eggs,
½ lb. granulated sugar,
¼ lb. grated walnuts,
6 grated lady fingers,
2 tablespoons flour,
1 teaspoon baking powder,
½ lemon juice and rind.

Beat the yolks with the sugar, add the other ingredients in given order; mixing baking powder with flour. Bake in layers in moderate oven.

Filling for Same

¾ cup milk,
1 egg yolk,
2 tablespoons sugar,
¾ lb. grated walnuts,
Vanilla or
Rum flavoring.

Beat egg and sugar and cook with milk to a custard, stirring constantly, add nuts and flavoring. Ice top to suit, or use Nut Filling, No. 1, page 332, in place of the above.

WALNUT TORTE, No. 3

8 yolks of eggs,
1 cup sugar,
½ lb. grated nut meats,
1 tablespoon grated bread crumbs,
8 grated coffee beans,
8 whites of eggs, beaten,
Vanilla flavoring to suit taste.

Beat sugar and yolks together and add the other ingredients; fold in the beaten whites last. Bake in two layers.

Filling: One cup chopped walnuts, yolks of two eggs, cooked in one cup of cream, sugar to taste, juice of a lemon. Chocolate Frosting, page 326, on top.

ZWIEBACK TORTE

¾ cup sugar,
6 yolks, beaten,
¼ lb. grated almonds,
Juice and rind of ½ lemon,
¼ lb. grated zwieback,
½ teaspoon cinnamon,
½ teaspoon cloves,
6 whites,
2 teaspoons baking powder.

Stir sugar and yolks, mix dry and add the other ingredients, beaten whites last. Bake in moderate oven, spring form, and when nearly done, put a little wine and sugar over the top.

CHAPTER XXXII

SMALL CAKES, COOKIES AND KISSES

SPONGE DROPS

3 eggs,
½ cup sugar (sifted),
½ salt spoon salt,
1 teaspoon lemon juice,
¼ teaspoon vanilla, or a grating of lemon or orange rind,
½ cup flour.

Beat the yolks until thick and creamy; add sugar and flavoring and continue beating; add salt to the whites and beat until very stiff; fold in the whites with the flour very gently; drop mixture from the tip of a spoon on ungreased tin sheet; sprinkle with pulverized sugar and bake in a cool oven about 8 minutes; put together in pairs with jelly between.

LADY FINGERS

Follow recipe for Sponge Drops, above; press the mixture through a tube on a baking sheet, covered with paper, in portions 1 inch wide by 5 inches long. Dust with powdered sugar and bake from 10 to 15 minutes, slow oven, without browning. Remove from paper, brush over the flat surface of one cake with white of egg and press the underside of a second cake upon the first.

OTHELLOS

Press Sponge Drop mixture, recipe above, through a tube on a baking sheet covered with paper, in rounds 1½ inches across. When baked spread the flat side of ½ of the cakes with jam or jelly, cover with the remaining cakes. Dip in

Chocolate Frosting, page 326, and let dry on oiled paper. Or, scrape out a small portion from the flat side of each cake, fill with Lemon or Vanilla Custard, page 330, press together in pairs and dip in the Chocolate Frosting. Let dry on oiled paper.

CREAM PUFFS OR ECLAIRS

¼ cup butter,
1½ cups flour,
¼ cup lard,
1 cup boiling water.

Put boiling water, butter and lard in a large saucepan, and when it boils turn in flour. Beat well with a vegetable masher. When perfectly smooth remove from the fire, and as soon as cold break into it 5 eggs, 1 at a time, beating hard with the hand. When the mixture is thoroughly beaten (it will take about 20 minutes), spread on buttered sheets in oblong pieces about 4 inches long and 1½ inches wide. Bake in a rather quick oven for about 25 minutes. As soon as they are done, ice with either chocolate or vanilla frosting.

Make an icing with the white of two eggs and ½ cup of powdered sugar. Flavor with 1 teaspoon vanilla extract. Frost the eclairs, and when dry, open on one side, and fill with Custard Filling, page 330. Or, they may be filled with cream, sweetened, flavored with vanilla and whipped to a stiff froth. Strawberry and raspberry preserves are sometimes used to fill eclairs.

CHOCOLATE ECLAIRS

2 squares chocolate, scraped,
5 tablespoons powdered sugar,
3 tablespoons boiling water.

Put chocolate, powdered sugar and boiling water over the fire and stir until smooth and glossy. Dip the tops of the eclairs in this as they come from the oven. When the chocolate icing is dry, cut open, and fill with the Custard Filling, page 330, or with sweetened and flavored cream whipped stiff.

BROWNIES

Bake an Angel Food or Sunshine Cake, page 349; pull the cake apart with a fork in irregular pieces about 2 inches square; take each piece on a fork and dip in hot Chocolate Icing, page 326, and let cool on a platter.

SMALL STRAWBERRY OR PINEAPPLE CREAM CAKES

Make Sponge Cake, page 347, or Cup Cake, page 337, and bake in well greased muffin tins. When cold cut off tops, scoop out soft inside. Fill with fresh strawberries, chopped or grated pineapple, or any other fresh fruit or berry. Cover with sweetened and flavored whipped cream.

CAKE BASKETS

Make Sponge, page 347, or Cup Cake, page 337, and bake in well buttered muffin tins. When cold cut off tops and carefully take out soft inside with cookie cutter and knife. Fill with ice cream or with sweetened and flavored whipped cream.

Cut rind of lemon or orange, or apple peel, in long strips ¼ inch wide. Lay a piece of either over top of filled cake, sticking ends in at sides, between filling and cake, to resemble handle of basket. Use scraps of cake for Bundte Schuessel.

BUNDTE SCHUESSEL

Sponge, or cup cake, or scraps of any stale or fresh cake,
1 tablespoon rum,
2 tablespoons corn syrup,

Chocolate, lemon, orange, vanilla and any other desired uncooked icing or Fondant,
⅛ lb. pistachio nuts,
⅛ lb. each of candied cherries, orange rind, limes and pineapple,

1 oz. each candied rose and mint leaves and violets.

By Bundte Schuessel is meant a large flat cake plate on which is arranged a variety of fancy shaped, decorated cakes. Use any desired sponge cake, cup cake or torte, that is not too delicate to handle. Bake in small fancy shaped tins or in a sheet. When baked in a sheet the cake may be cut in any square, oblong, diamond, heart or round shape with knife or cutters.

Scraps of devil's food or chocolate cake may be used by crumbling the cake and mixing it to a paste with syrup and a little rum for flavor. These are formed into small balls, rings and crescents.

Cover cakes with Fondant, pages 391–392, in a variety of colors and flavors, keeping the icing warm and creamy over hot water (in little tin cups). Slip cakes one at a time on knife into the softened icing, dip quickly, then place on oiled paper for several hours to harden. Then decorate.

Cut pistachio nuts lengthwise in slices, and green limes in small pieces, to represent leaves; cherries cut in pieces lengthwise and the violet and rose leaves, to represent flowers. Raisins may be pressed flat and cut in fanciful shapes. Dip the end of the ornaments lightly in a little warm icing to make them stick to the frosting.

When baked in a sheet, the cake may be cut in pieces, covered with white icing, and, for a musical entertainment, be decorated with chocolate icing in the form of a bar of music, pressing the chocolate through tube. Make dominoes by dipping oblong cakes, shape and size of a domino block in Chocolate Icing, page 326; when hardened decorate with dots of White Fondant or Icing (thick), page 392; pressed through a paper tube to represent the different numbers on the blocks. Small round or oval cakes are pretty decorated with almonds, blanched, sliced, and browned in the oven. The almonds may be put on to simulate a daisy.

GINGER DROPS

¼ cup butter,
¼ cup brown sugar,
1½ cup flour,
½ teaspoon cinnamon,
¼ teaspoon cloves,
Speck salt,
1 egg,
½ cup molasses,
1 teaspoon soda,
½ cup boiling water.
1 tablespoon ginger.

Cream butter and add sugar gradually, then add the egg. Mix and sift dry ingredients and add alternately with hot water and molasses. Bake in muffin pans.

CHOCOLATE DROP CAKES

2 whites of eggs,
2 oz. grated chocolate,
1 teaspoon cinnamon,
1 teaspoon vanilla,
1 cup powdered sugar,
1 cup baker's bread (crumbled).

Beat the whites to a stiff froth, add sugar gradually, and continue beating. Mix chocolate, cinnamon and bread crumbs together. Add this mixture gradually to the eggs and sugar. Add vanilla and beat well. Drop from teaspoon on buttered paper or inverted buttered tin, not near together, as they spread. Bake in moderate oven twenty minutes, first ten minutes on floor of oven and last on rack.

COCOANUT DROP COOKIES

1 lb. powdered sugar,
4 eggs,
1 tablespoon butter,
¼ lb. cocoanut,
3 teaspoons baking powder,
1½ cups flour.

Beat eggs until light, add sugar and beat again; add flour and baking powder mixed, and stir in the grated or shredded cocoanut. Drop small portions with teaspoon on well buttered pans, rather far apart, as they spread. Bake in a moderate oven from 10 to 15 minutes. Keep in covered jar.

PEANUT DROP CAKES

2 tablespoons butter,
¼ cup sugar,
1 egg,
½ cup flour,
1 teaspoon baking powder,
¼ teaspoon salt,
2 tablespoons milk,
½ cup finely chopped peanuts,
½ teaspoon lemon juice.

Cream the butter, add sugar and egg, well beaten. Sift and mix flour, salt and baking powder, and add to first mixture; then add milk, peanuts and lemon juice. Drop from a teaspoon on an unbuttered sheet one inch apart. Bake in moderate oven twelve to fifteen minutes. Makes twenty-four cookies.

COOKIES

SUGAR COOKIES

No. 1

½ cup butter,
1 cup sugar,
1 egg,
¼ cup milk,
2 teaspoons baking powder,
¼ teaspoon vanilla or any other flavor,
2 cups flour (about).

Cream the butter and sugar. Beat the eggs and add to the milk. Sift flour and mix baking powder with one cup, then add the rest of the flour, and gradually add more if needed to make a dough stiff enough to handle. Roll on a floured board one-fourth inch thick. Shape with biscuit cutter. Sprinkle with sugar, cinnamon and chopped nuts, if desired. Bake in a quick oven 8 to 10 minutes.

No. 2

½ cup butter, or
⅓ cup beef drippings,
1 cup sugar,
1 tablespoon milk or water,
2 eggs,
1 heaping teaspoon baking powder,
Flour to roll out.

Cream the shortening, add the sugar, the liquid and eggs, beaten lightly, and the baking powder, mixed with two cups of flour, then enough flour to roll out. Roll a little at a time. Sprinkle with sugar. Cut out. Bake about ten minutes.

BUTTER COOKIES (MUERBER)

No. 1

1 pound of butter,
1 cup sugar,
2 eggs,
Rind of ½ lemon,
Juice of ½ lemon, or
2 tablespoons brandy,
6 cups flour,
1 teaspoon baking powder,
1 cup almonds, chopped fine.

Cream the butter, add the sugar, then the yolks of eggs, slightly beaten; add rind of lemon, and the flour mixed with the baking powder, then the brandy or lemon juice, with only enough flour to handle. Chill dough, then roll; cut with small biscuit cutter, brush with white of egg; sprinkle a little sugar and chopped almonds on each cookie. Bake in moderate oven a delicate brown, 10 to 15 minutes. Will keep for weeks.

BUTTER COOKIES

No. 2

1 cup butter,	2 hard cooked yolks, mashed fine,
½ cup sugar,	
2 cups flour,	1 tablespoon brandy,
2 raw yolks,	½ lemon (juice).

Stir butter and sugar, then the cooked yolks, add flour and raw eggs alternately. Roll thin, cut round, square or diamond shaped, and bake in greased tins, in moderate oven 10 to 15 minutes. Chopped almonds, sugar and cinnamon on top of each cookie.

CHOCOLATE COOKIES

No. 1

½ cup butter,	2½ cups flour,
1 cup sugar,	2 teaspoons baking powder,
1 egg,	¼ cup milk,
¼ teaspoon salt.	2 squares (2 oz.) chocolate.

Cream the butter, add sugar gradually, egg well beaten, salt and chocolate (melted). Beat well and add flour, mixed and sifted with baking powder, alternately with milk. Chill, roll very thin, then shape with a small cutter, first dipped in flour, and bake in a moderate oven 10 to 15 minutes.

No. 2

1 cup butter,	¼ teaspoon nutmeg,
1 cup sugar,	¼ lb. almonds,
2 eggs,	¼ lb. sweet vanilla chocolate,
½ teaspoon cinnamon,	
¼ teaspoon cloves,	4 cups flour,
	1 teaspoon baking powder.

Grate the chocolate and almonds (unblanched). Cream butter, add sugar, eggs, one at a time and the rest of the ingredients. Mix well, roll out quite thick. Cut in rounds, place in pans; spread cakes with white of egg beaten and sugar. Bake in a moderate oven.

No. 3

4 whites of egg,	1 cup granulated sugar,
¼ lb. melted chocolate,	1½ cups flour,
	1 teaspoon vanilla.

Beat whites of egg very stiff, add chocolate, sugar, flour and vanilla, drop in buttered tins, and bake in moderate oven.

CHOCOLATE STICKS

4 eggs,
1 lb. brown sugar,
1 cup almonds,
¼ lb. German sweet chocolate,
2 oz. citron,
½ teaspoon cinnamon,
¼ teaspoon each allspice and cloves,
3 cups flour,
1 teaspoon baking powder.

Beat eggs and sugar until light, add the spices and the chocolate, grated. Blanch almonds and chop, cut citron fine; mix with the flour and baking powder and combine the two mixtures. Roll on floured board, cut into strips 3½ inches long and bake in shallow buttered pans, in a moderate oven, 10 to 15 minutes. Let cool and keep in covered jar.

CRISP COOKIES

2 tablespoons butter,
2 cups sugar,
2 eggs,
1 cup sour cream,
½ teaspoon soda,
4 cups flour.

Cream butter, add sugar, and stir, add eggs, mix well and add the rest of the ingredients, the soda, with the sour cream. Toss on floured board, roll out thin and cut into rounds.

Bake in shallow pans in a hot oven about 10 minutes.

OATMEAL COOKIES

No. 1

⅔ cup butter,
⅔ cup brown sugar,
1 egg,
1 cup rolled raw oats,
1 cup flour,
1 teaspoon baking powder.

Cream the butter, add the sugar, egg, the oats, flour and baking powder. Mix well, if too dry add a little cream. Toss on floured board, roll thin and cut into rounds. Place in buttered pans and bake 10 minutes in a hot oven.

No. 2

¾ cup butter,
1 cup sugar,
2 eggs,
2 cups flour,
1 cup oatmeal,
½ cup sweet milk,
1 teaspoon baking powder,
½ teaspoon soda,
A little salt,
1 teaspoon cinnamon,
¼ cup chopped raisins,
¼ cup chopped hickory nuts.

Cream butter and sugar, add eggs, mix the rest of the dry ingredients, sprinkle over the raisins and nuts and combine the mixtures, adding the milk. Drop on a buttered tin, a little way apart. The nuts and raisins may be omitted.

GINGER SNAPS

¼ cup butter,
¼ cup sugar,
¼ cup molasses,
1 egg,
¼ tablespoon ginger,
¼ teaspoon soda,
1½ cups flour.

Cream the butter in a warm bowl, gradually beat in the sugar and molasses, then add the ginger, soda and flour and, if needed, more flour to knead. Roll very thin on a floured board, cut with a cake cutter and bake in a quick oven.

SOFT MOLASSES COOKIES

¾ cup butter,
1 cup sugar,
1 egg,
1 cup molasses,
¾ cup hot water,
4 cups flour,
1 teaspoon cinnamon,
¼ teaspoon ginger,
1 teaspoon soda.

Cream butter, add sugar, well beaten egg, molasses and hot water, then the mixed and sifted dry ingredients. Drop from spoon in warm buttered pan; bake quickly.

SPICE COOKIES

No. 1

⅔ cup butter,
1½ cups sugar,
2 whole eggs,
1 cup seeded raisins,
2½ cups flour,
1 teaspoon cinnamon,
1 teaspoon cloves,
1 teaspoon nutmeg,
¼ teaspoon salt,
1 teaspoon soda,
3 tablespoons sour milk.

Cream the butter and sugar, add eggs, the raisins, chopped, spices, and then alternately flour, and sour milk, in which soda has been dissolved. Drop by teaspoonfuls on buttered tins and bake, in a hot oven.

No. 2

5 whole eggs,
1 lb. brown sugar,
2 teaspoons cinnamon,
1 teaspoon ground cloves,
1 teaspoon vanilla,
1 teaspoon ginger,
1 teaspoon baking soda,
3 cups flour.

Mix the above together, add enough flour to handle it, roll into small balls and bake on greased pans, in moderate oven 10 to 15 minutes.

CLOVE COOKIES

1 lb. brown sugar,	1 tablespoon chocolate,
¼ lb. butter,	2 teaspoons baking powder,
4 eggs,	4 cups flour,
½ oz. ground cloves,	1 teaspoon cinnamon.

Mix sugar and butter, add eggs, flour and the other ingredients. Roll, cut and bake fifteen minutes.

CARDAMOM COOKIES

1 cup butter,	4 cups flour,
1 cup sugar,	1 oz. cardamom seed,
2 whole eggs,	crushed,

Rind of 1 lemon.

Stir butter and sugar together, and add the other ingredients. Roll, cut and bake as other cookies.

ANISE COOKIES (Springerle)

No. 1

4 eggs,	1 tablespoon anise seed,
2 cups sugar,	3 cups flour,
1 teaspoon baking powder.	

Beat eggs very light, add sugar and beat again; add flour, baking powder and the anise seed, pounded fine. Drop by ½ teaspoonfuls in well greased pans, one inch apart. Let stand over night or about 10 hours, in a cool place to dry. Bake in a slow oven.

No. 2

4 eggs, separated,	1 teaspoon baking powder,
1 lb. powdered sugar,	¼ teaspoon salt,
Grated rind of 1 lemon,	1 tablespoon anise seed,
4 cups flour (about),	pounded fine.

Beat yolks of eggs until light and thick, whites until dry; then beat together, add lemon rind, and the sugar sifted, very gradually, beating all the time; then add flour with the baking powder anise seed and salt. Knead, cover closely and let chill 2 or 3 hours; then roll, a small piece at a time, into a sheet ⅛ inch thick; sprinkle lightly with flour, then press the wooden springerle mould down very hard upon the dough, to leave the perfect impression of the pictures on the dough. Cut out the little squares and set aside about 10 hours or over night to dry on a lightly floured board. Place on buttered tins and bake a light straw color in a slow oven.

MATZOS ANISE COOKIES

3 eggs,
1 cup sugar,
¾ cup sifted matzos meal,
1 tablespoon anise seed, pounded fine,
A little salt.

Beat eggs very light, add sugar and the anise seed pounded, then the salt and meal. Drop by ½ teaspoonfuls in greased pans. Let them stand over night, then bake in a slow oven.

PFEFFERNUESSE

2 cups sugar,
4 eggs,
6 oz. almonds,
4 oz. citron,
2 oz. orange peel,
½ teaspoon cloves,
3 teaspoons cinnamon,
4 cups flour,
1 teaspoon baking powder,
¼ cup brandy.

Beat eggs and sugar well together; blanch and grate the almonds and cut the citron and orange peel fine, or use grated rind of 1 lemon or orange. Sift dry ingredients and mix all together with the brandy. Butter hands and shape mixture into balls, size of a hickory nut; bake on buttered tins one inch apart; let stand over night. Bake in a moderate oven. Let stand two weeks before using.

FIG COOKIES

½ cup butter,
1 cup brown sugar,
2 eggs beaten,
½ teaspoon cinnamon,
2 tablespoons sour cream,
1 teaspoon soda,
1 cup chopped figs,
Flour to roll.

Cream sugar, with butter, add beaten eggs, sour cream with soda dissolved in it, cinnamon, and the chopped figs rolled in flour. Add flour to make a stiff dough; roll, cut and bake.

ORANGE COOKIES

¼ cup butter,
1 cup sugar,
2 cups flour,
Grated rind ½ orange,
4 egg yolks,
2 tablespoons orange juice,
2 teaspoons baking powder,
More flour if needed.

Cream butter, add sugar and orange rind gradually. Add egg yolks; sift flour and baking powder three times and add to egg mixture alternately with water and orange juice mixed.

Mix stiff and roll and cut. Bake 8 to 10 minutes in hot oven.

FRUIT COOKIES

No. 1

½ cup beef drippings, or
½ cup butter,
1 cup sugar,
2 eggs,
½ cup molasses,
2 cups flour (about),
2 teaspoons baking powder,
¼ teaspoon salt,
1 teaspoon cinnamon,
¼ teaspoon cloves,
1 teaspoon nutmeg,
1 cup seedless raisins,
2 tablespoons sweet milk.

Cream the shortening, add the sugar, the beaten eggs and molasses. Sift dry ingredients with one cup flour and add to above mixture; add flour and milk to roll out. Cut with cutter and bake in moderate oven. Stone raisins and chop or cut in quarters and add to mixture before rolling out.

No. 2

½ cup butter,
½ cup sugar,
1 egg,
2 teaspoons spices, mixed,
1 teaspoon baking powder,
1 cup flour,
A little salt,
⅓ cup chopped walnuts,
¼ cup each currants, citron and raisins, chopped.

Mix well, drop by teaspoon on oiled tin. Bake in quick oven.

NUT PATTIES

1 egg, beaten,
1 cup sugar,
1 cup English walnuts, finely chopped,
5 tablespoons flour.

Beat egg and sugar until very light; into this stir the nuts, then add the flour. Drop on tins with teaspoon; make the patties about the size of macaroons and bake in a medium hot oven about 10 minutes.

ROCKS

1½ cups brown sugar,
1 scant cup butter,
1 cup walnuts (chopped), or hickory nuts,
3 eggs,
1 teaspoon cinnamon,
½ teaspoon salt,
1 cup raisins (seeded and chopped),
3¼ cups flour,
1 teaspoon soda, dissolved in 1½ tablespoons hot water.

Cream the butter, add the sugar gradually, then the eggs, well beaten. Reserve part of the flour and mix with the fruit and nuts. Add the rest of the ingredients and lastly floured fruit. Drop from teaspoon on buttered tins, 1 inch apart; bake in moderate oven.

JELLY COOKIES

5½ tablespoons butter and lard,
1 cup sugar,
1 egg,
¼ cup milk,
2 teaspoons baking powder,
1 teaspoon vanilla,
½ teaspoon salt,
2 cups flour.

Cream butter, add sugar, egg well beaten, and milk. Mix and sift dry ingredients and add to the first mixture. Add vanilla. Toss on floured board. Cut out some with cookie cutter and place in the center of each cookie a teaspoon of jelly. Cut out covers with a jumble or doughnut cutter with hole in center, and place on top of cookies. Bake in a moderate oven until done.

ROLLED WAFERS

¼ cup butter,
½ cup powdered sugar,
½ teaspoon vanilla,
¼ cup milk,
⅞ cup bread flour,
Almonds, grated.

Cream the butter, add the sugar gradually, and milk drop by drop; then add flour and flavoring. Spread very thinly with a broad, long-bladed knife, on a buttered inverted dripping pan. Sprinkle with almonds. Crease in three inch squares, and bake in a slow oven until delicately browned. Place pan on back of range; cut squares apart with a sharp knife, and roll while warm, over the handle of a wooden spoon, or in cornucopia shape. May be filled with Whipped Cream, page 335, before serving.

ROLLED DATE COOKIES

½ lb. dates,
¼ lb. walnuts, chopped,
White cookie dough,
¼ cup butter, melted.

Follow recipe for Sugar Cookies, page 373. Toss dough on floured board; roll into one large thin sheet, brush plentifully with the melted butter, strew the dates, stoned and cut in small pieces, and the walnuts, all over the top; sprinkle with sugar and cinnamon. Start at one side and roll the dough over and over like a jelly roll; then cut roll into pieces 1 inch wide. Place in greased tin and bake in a quick oven.

KOUMISS BREAD

4 large eggs,
1 cup granulated sugar,
Rind of ½ lemon,
1 tablespoon lemon juice,
¼ lb. almonds, unblanched,
1½ cups flour.

Beat eggs without separating, until very, very light; add sugar, lemon juice and rind. Cut the almonds in long slices and sift the flour over them. Then, very gradually, a little at a time, stir in the egg mixture. Bake in shallow, well greased pan, in a moderate oven; cut into slices a little over an inch wide and while still warm, turn on the cut surface in pan and toast lightly on both sides.

CARD GINGERBREAD

⅓ cup butter,
1 cup sugar,
1 egg,
1⅞ cups flour,
3 teaspoons baking powder,
1 teaspoon ginger,
1½ cups milk.

Cream the butter, add sugar, then eggs, well beaten. Mix dry ingredients and combine the two mixtures with the milk. Spread out thin on buttered pan. Bake 15 minutes in moderate oven. Sprinkle with sugar and cut into squares or diamonds, before removing from pan.

HONEY CAKES

½ lb. strained honey,
½ lb. powdered sugar, sifted,
½ lb. blanched almonds, cut in half lengthwise,
2 cups flour,
1 oz. citron, cut very fine,
⅛ teaspoon grated nutmeg,
⅛ teaspoon ground cloves,
¼ cup brandy.

Boil sugar and honey, then add almonds and stir thoroughly. Add the rest of the ingredients, more flour if needed, and knead the dough well. Put away in a cool place, well covered, for a week. Roll ½ inch thick and bake in shallow greased pans, in a quick oven. When done cut into strips 1 by 2 inches long. Ice with Lemon Icing, page 325.

LEBKUCHEN

No. 1

4 whole eggs,
1 lb. light brown sugar,
2 cups flour,
1 teaspoon cinnamon,
2 oz. citron, cut fine,
¼ lb. almonds, blanched and cut fine.

Beat eggs well with Dover beater, add sugar gradually, and beat again. Mix flour and cinnamon with chopped nuts and citron, and combine the two mixtures. Bake in three flat greased pans, in hot oven. When cool, cut into regular strips one-half inch wide, five inches long. Before taking out of pans, frost with one cup confectioners' sugar, two tablespoons water and flavoring to taste.

LEBKUCHEN
No. 2

7 eggs,	¼ lb. orange peel,
1 cup brown sugar,	¼ lb. citron,
1 cup molasses,	½ lb. almonds,
1 teaspoon cinnamon,	½ lb. chocolate,
1 teaspoon salt,	2½ cups flour,
½ teaspoon allspice,	1½ teaspoons baking powder
¼ teaspoon nutmeg, grated,	2 cups powdered sugar,

A little lemon juice.

Separate the eggs, reserving the whites of 3 for the frosting.

Beat 7 yolks and 4 whites of egg very light, add the sugar and beat again; add molasses and spices, the chocolate grated, almonds blanched and grated, or ground, citron and orange peel, cut fine, and the flour and baking powder.

Spread dough 1½ inches thick in well greased, long pans, with well floured hands. Bake in a very moderate oven, and before removing from pans cut into squares and ice with Plain Frosting, page 325. Bake one week before using.

ALMOND PRETZELS

1 cup butter,	2 cups flour,
1 cup sugar,	2 yolks and
½ lb. almonds, unblanched and ground,	2 whole eggs.

Cream butter and sugar, add eggs and the rest of the ingredients. Mix and knead into one big roll. Let stand in ice chest to harden. Cut into pieces size of a walnut. Roll each piece width of your little finger and form into hearts, rings, crescents and pretzels.

KISSES

KISSES

Whites of 4 eggs, 1¼ cups powdered sugar, or 1 cup granulated sugar.

The eggs must be strictly fresh and the sugar dry. Beat the whites until stiff, and gradually add two-thirds of the sugar. Continue beating until mixture will hold its shape. Fold in the remaining sugar. Drop mixture from tip of spoon in small piles one-half inch apart, on tins. Bake a very light brown fifty minutes in slow oven with decreasing heat, or until dry. When done they leave the pan readily.

KISSES WITH WHIPPED CREAM

Prepare Kisses same as in foregoing recipe. Bake thirty minutes in slow oven. Remove soft part with spoon, and dry again in oven. When ready to serve, fill with Whipped Cream, page 335, or ice cream, putting the kisses together in pairs.

NUT AND FRUIT KISSES

To Kisses mixture, add chopped nut meats (pecans, almond, English walnut, hickorynut, shredded cocoanut), or fruit meats (chopped dates, raisins, figs or prunes), separately or in combination. Allowing 1 oz. of nuts or fruit for each white of egg ¼ cup of sugar. Bake same as Kisses above.

COCOANUT KISSES

Whites of 2 eggs, ¼ lb. shredded cocoanut.
¼ lb. powdered sugar,

Make and bake same as Kisses above, folding the shredded cocoanut in last.

HICKORYNUT KISSES

No. 1

Whites of 2 eggs, 5 oz. hickorynuts,
5 oz. sugar.

Mix and bake same as Kisses above, folding the hickorynuts in lightly at the last.

No. 2

2 yolks, 1 cup nutmeats,
1 cup sugar, 2 whites of eggs.

Stir yolks and sugar together, add nut meats and the beaten whites of eggs. Bake same as Kisses, above.

CHOCOLATE KISSES

3 whites of eggs,
½ cup sugar,
2 oz. grated chocolate,
Vanilla.

Beat whites of eggs very stiff, add sugar, chocolate and vanilla. Bake on floured tins in a slow oven about 60 minutes.

COCOA KISSES

2 whites of eggs,
1¼ cups sugar,
2 tablespoons cocoa,
¼ teaspoon cinnamon,
¼ lb. almonds, chopped and blanched.

Make and bake same as Kisses, page 383, folding in the chopped nuts last.

DATE MACAROONS

1 lb. stoned dates,
½ lb. almonds,
Whites of 4 eggs, well beaten,
1 cup granulated sugar.

Stone the dates, then weigh and chop them fine. Cut almonds lengthwise in slices, but do not blanch them. Beat the whites of 4 eggs until foamy, add the sugar, and beat until stiff; add the dates, then the almonds and mix very thoroughly. Drop mixture with teaspoon in small piles, on tins one-half inch apart. Bake 50 minutes in a very slow oven or until dry. They are done when they leave the pan readily.

Fig Macaroons. Made same as Date Macaroons using dried figs, softened by steaming, in place of the dates.

CINNAMON STARS

1 lb. grated almonds,
1 lb. powdered sugar,
6 whites of eggs,
1 lemon rind,
1 teaspoon cinnamon.

Beat whites to a very stiff froth, add sugar and lemon rind and reserve ¼ of the mixture to put on center of cookies.

To the balance, add the cinnamon and almonds, blanched and grated or ground. Roll out on board, using powdered sugar instead of flour to prevent sticking; cut into star shaped forms, place a small portion of the mixture set aside on each cookie.

Bake in a rather hot oven, with door open—in paraffined pans, or if you prefer to drop them from the spoon on buttered pans, add to the mixture the juice of the lemon and bake in a slow oven until crusty.

ALMOND COOKIES

1 lb. sweet almonds,
¼ lb. bitter almonds,
1¼ lbs. confectioners' sugar,
2 whites of eggs.

Blanch almonds and dry them over night. Then grind very fine. Sift the sugar over the almonds and mix and knead to a stiff paste with the unbeaten whites of two eggs, or more egg, if needed. Roll with hands on board, sprinkled with powdered sugar to prevent sticking. Cut into pieces size of a walnut. Roll each piece width of your little finger, form into rings, crescents, hearts, bow knots and pretzel shapes, and bake, slightly browned, in slow oven.

MARGUERITES

18 wafer crackers,
White of 1 egg,
¼ cup sugar,
2 tablespoons nutmeats.

Add the sugar to the stiffly beaten whites, and the nuts if desired. Spread on top of crackers. Place in pans in a moderate oven for a few minutes, until slightly browned.

CHAPTER XXXIII

Candies

GENERAL RULES

Syrup boiled from sugar for candies must hang from the end of a spoon to form a thick drop, and long silk-like threads hang from it, when exposed to the air. The syrup is then 238 degrees Fahrenheit, and when a drop is tried in cold water, the water will remain clear and the syrup will form a soft ball and will just keep its shape. Boil a few moments longer, and try in cold water, and if the syrup becomes brittle, and it forms a hard ball, it is at 248 degrees Fahrenheit.

When the syrup begins to discolor it is at 310 degrees, while at 350 degrees it is caramel or burned sugar. The syrup should only be stirred until the sugar is dissolved; if stirred while hot, it will grain or sugar.

SUGAR

Sugar is made for common use from sugar cane, sugar beets and maple sap. This sugar is called sucrose. Honey is the purest natural form of sugar.

CANDY

Glucose, or grape sugar, is found in honey, fresh fruits, and on the skins of dried fruits, such as raisins, dates, etc. It is also made for commercial use from the starch of corn. The sugar of milk is called lactose. Sugar made from sugar cane and sugar beets is the kind most commonly used. The products of sugar cane are molasses, brown sugar, granulated, cutloaf, powdered and confectioners' sugar. Only white sugar is made from beets. Sugar is very easily digested, as it dissolves so readily. It is a very necessary food when taken in small quantities. It produces heat and energy in the body; children, being more active than grown people, naturally crave more sweets.

EVIL EFFECTS OF TOO MUCH SUGAR

If sugar in any form is left on the teeth, it will ferment, and cause them to decay.

If too much is eaten at one time, part of it will ferment in the stomach and interfere with the digestion of other foods.

PEANUT BRITTLE

No. 1

2 cups sugar,   ½ to 1 cup shelled peanuts,
⅓ cup water.

Put sugar and water in saucepan and cook until light brown. Have peanuts sprinkled over buttered pan. Pour syrup over and when cool mark in squares.

No. 2

2 cups sugar,   ½ to 1 cup shelled peanuts.

Shell peanuts and remove the skins. Break in pieces or chop them, or take thick, unglazed brown wrapping paper, spread the peanuts over half of it, cover with the other half, and roll until well crushed with rolling pin. Line a greased pan with the peanuts. Put sugar in saucepan, and heat till it becomes a thin, light brown syrup, stirring constantly. Pour over peanuts, and mark in squares. When cool, break in pieces. Any kind of nut meats may be used.

PENOCHE

2 cups brown sugar,   2 tablespoons butter,
¾ cup milk,   1 teaspoon vanilla,
1 cup chopped nuts.

Boil sugar and milk to the soft ball stage. Remove from the fire; add butter, flavoring and nuts. Beat till creamy and thickened; pour into a greased tin, and when firm cut in squares.

FUDGES

2 cups sugar, maple, brown or white,
1 cup milk or cream,
2 tablespoons cocoa or ¾ square of chocolate.
1 tablespoon butter,
½ teaspoon vanilla, if desired

Stir the mixture all the time. Boil until soft ball in water or until you can stir it to a cream on a buttered plate. After removing from fire, cool and beat until grain changes. Put on plate and cut in squares. Put in nuts if desired. Place in buttered pan, cool and cut in squares.

Double the quantity of cocoa or chocolate if you desire.

MARSHMALLOW FUDGE

2 cups sugar,
1 cup milk or cream,
½ lb. marshmallows.
2 (oz.) squares chocolate,
1 tablespoon butter,

Heat sugar and milk, add chocolate and boil until soft ball in water. Add butter and then gradually add the marshmallows, stirring until dissolved. Cool in buttered pans, ¾ inch thick, and cut in squares.

COCOANUT CANDY

1½ cups sugar,
½ cup milk,
½ teaspoon vanilla or lemon extract.
2 teaspoons butter,
⅓ cup cocoanut,

Put butter in saucepan; when melted add sugar and milk and stir until sugar is dissolved. Boil 12 minutes, remove from fire; add cocoanut and vanilla, and heat until creamy and mixture begins to sugar slightly. Pour at once into a buttered pan and mark in squares.

SEA FOAM

2 cups sugar,
½ cup corn syrup,
½ cup water,
1 cup walnut meats,
2 egg whites,
1 teaspoon vanilla.

Boil sugar, corn syrup and water until mixture forms a soft ball when dropped into cold water. Pour slowly into beaten egg whites, beating constantly with a Dover egg beater. When it begins to stiffen, add vanilla and nuts, broken in rather large chunks, and drop by the spoonful on oiled paper.

TURKISH CANDY

Follow recipe for Sea Foam, above, and when stiff and creamy, add nuts, and place in small, deep, well buttered pan. When cold cut into slices or squares.

CHOCOLATE CARAMELS

No. 1

2 cups brown sugar,
1 cup milk,
2 (oz.) squares chocolate,
¼ cup butter.

Boil all together, stirring to prevent burning, until a drop will form a hard ball in cold water. Pour on buttered pan to cool and cut into squares with a heated chopping knife.

No. 2

½ lb. Maillard's chocolate,
½ lb. granulated sugar,
½ pint cream,
¾ cup syrup,
2 tablespoons butter.

Melt the chocolate, add sugar, cream, syrup, and when it begins to boil the butter. Stir constantly, test in cold water. This should then boil to the hard ball stage. Remove from the fire and pour on an oiled slab to the depth of ½ inch, cut in squares when cool, then wrap in paraffine paper.

OPERA CARAMEL

2 cups granulated sugar,
¾ cup milk,
Butter size of walnut,
A little vanilla.

Place the ingredients in a granite saucepan and boil; when candy forms a soft ball in cold water remove from stove and place the pan in cold water for a few minutes, then stir until creamy, pour on buttered tin and cut into squares; chopped nuts or cocoanut added while stirring makes very nice candy.

NEW ORLEANS PRALINES

1 cup brown sugar,	2 oz. butter,
½ cup New Orleans molasses,	½ teaspoon vanilla,
1 cup cream,	1 pint pecan nutmeats.

Boil the first four ingredients until when tried in cold water a soft ball is formed, stirring constantly. Pour this over the nuts and stir until it begins to sugar. Drop from tip of spoon in small piles on buttered pans.

BUTTER SCOTCH

2 cups brown sugar,   ½ cup butter,
½ cup water.

Put in saucepan over fire, boil until a drop poured in cold water forms a hard ball. Stir to prevent burning. Pour into buttered tins ¼ inch thick, and when cool mark in squares.

DAISY CREAM CANDY

3 lbs. sugar,	1 pint water,
6 oz. butter,	½ tablespoon vanilla.

Mix in sugar and water, add butter and boil without stirring until it reaches 262 degrees Fahrenheit, that is the hard ball stage, which becomes brittle. Pour quickly on ice cold buttered slab. Flavor, when slightly cooled, and pull until white, glossy and porous. Mark into squares. Will be soft and creamy next day.

Another recipe: 2 cups sugar, 2 tablespoons butter, 1½ cups vinegar. Proceed as in the above recipe. Any flavoring may be added by pouring a few drops over the mixture in the pan while cooling.

MOLASSES CANDY

No. 1

1 cup molasses (New Orleans),	1 tablespoon water,
	1 teaspoon butter,
½ cup sugar,	¼ teaspoon soda.

Melt the butter in an iron spider, add molasses, water and sugar, and stir until sugar is dissolved. Stir occasionally until nearly done, and then constantly. Boil until brittle or until it forms a hard ball in cold water. Set on back of stove, stir well, add the soda, stir thoroughly, and pour into a well greased pan. When cool enough to handle, pull until light colored and porous. Work candy with finger tips and thumbs, do not squeeze in the hands. When it begins to harden, stretch to the desired thickness, cut in small pieces with large shears, turning the candy half way round after each incision, thus alternating the direction of the cut. Cool on buttered plates.

MOLASSES CANDY

No. 2

1 cup corn syrup,
⅓ cup molasses,
⅓ cup sugar,
2 tablespoons butter,
1 tablespoon vinegar,
⅓ teaspoon soda.

Cook first five ingredients until brittle, when tried in cold water. Add soda, beat thoroughly, pour on buttered plate and when cool pull until light colored.

CINNAMON BALLS

Add ½ teaspoonful of essence of cinnamon to the molasses candy before it is pulled. Then let it cool and make into balls.

PEPPERMINT OR WINTERGREEN WAFERS

6 drops oil of peppermint or wintergreen,
1½ cups sugar,
½ cup boiling water,

Put sugar and water in granite saucepan and stir until sugar is dissolved. Boil until it threads or forms a soft ball in cold water. Remove from stove, add peppermint, beat until it thickens and looks cloudy. Drop from tip of spoon on slightly buttered paper.

Wintergreen Wafers. Add a few drops of oil of wintergreen and color with fruit red.

FONDANT, COOKED

2 cups sugar (fine granulated),
⅔ cup cold water,
⅛ teaspoon cream of tartar.

Boil all together until it makes a soft ball when tried in cold water. Turn out on a large platter, and when cool work it until creamy. Divide into portions and flavor to taste. This forms the Stock Dough, and is the foundation of many candies. Sprinkle board with confectioners' sugar, roll one-fourth inch thick, cut into squares, strips, bars, or any desired shape. It may be used with nuts, whole or chopped, dried or candied fruit; shape into chocolate creams, nut creams, cream dates and bonbons. These candies are better the day after they are made.

FONDANT, UNCOOKED

1½ lbs. confectioners' sugar,
⅕ cup pure cold water,
Vanilla to taste,
White of 1 egg.

Slip the white of a strictly fresh egg in a cup; measure the space it occupies; add the same amount of water (usually one-fifth cup), and mix thoroughly. Pour enough XXXX confectioners' sugar into the mixture to mould like dough. Flavor to taste and knead thoroughly. Use same as Cooked Fondant.

To Dip Bonbons: Put Fondant in small sauce pans or granite cups with handles, over hot water, and color and flavor as desired. In coloring, dip a small wooden skewer in coloring paste, then dip skewer in small quantity of Fondant, to get desired shade. Dip centers (nuts or candied fruits or Fondant center) on a fork in the Fondant, one at a time; stir until covered, then remove to oiled paper. Stir Fondant between dippings to prevent crust from forming. If too thick, add a few drops of water or milk; if too thin, add confectioners' sugar.

CHOCOLATE CREAM DROPS

Fondant,
4 (oz.) squares chocolate,
Cocoa butter or paraffine.

Make cone shaped forms of the Fondant, recipes above. Lay them on oiled paper to harden. Melt chocolate over boiling water, add a little cocoa butter or paraffine, take the creams, one at a time, on a fork and dip into the melted but not hot chocolate to cover all sides. Set on buttered or waxed paper to harden.

CHOCOLATE DIPPED CHERRIES

Bottle Maraschino cherries,
Fondant,
Melted chocolate,
A little cocoa butter.

Drain the cherries, but not too dry. Fill a shallow baking pan with flour or cornstarch, about 1 inch deep; press the rounded end of a stick or thimble into the flour, making as many cavities as you have cherries. Melt Fondant, page 391, over hot water and dip the cherries one at a time; drop them in the cornstarch cavities, and let stand in cool place over night to harden. Then dip as other chocolate creams in melted bitter chocolate to which a little cocoa butter or paraffine has been added. Do not have the chocolate too hot as that spoils the rich glossy look.

CHOCOLATE DIPPED GRAPES (ACORNS)

½ lb. Malaga grapes, 2 oz. bitter chocolate, scraped,
2 tablespoons granulated sugar.

Place sugar in small saucer. Wash grapes, drain dry between towels and remove stems carefully. Stir chocolate over boiling water in a small granite cup until warm and melted, but not hot. Dip stem end of grapes one at a time into the chocolate to about one-quarter the depth of the grapes, holding them by the other end with the fingers. Remove from chocolate quickly, invert to cool a moment, then roll the chocolate end in the sugar, and place chocolate side down on oiled paper to harden.

FRESH DIPPED STRAWBERRIES

1 quart fresh strawberries, 1 cup Fondant.

Select large, clean, dry berries. Dip them, one at a time, half way into Fondant (page 391, softened over hot water), holding the berry by the stem and the small adjoining leaves. Lift the berry out quickly, turning it round and round in the air a moment, tip upward, to dry; then invert berry and stand on tip on oiled paper, rearranging green leaves and stem on top. Place each berry in a little paper bonbon cup. Serve within an hour.

STUFFED DATES

With Nuts: Make a cut the entire length of dates and remove stones. Fill cavities with English walnuts, blanched almonds, pecans or with a mixture of chopped nuts, and shape in original form. Roll in granulated sugar or powdered sugar and serve on small plate or bonbon dish.

With Fondant: Fill with Fondant, page 391, or Butter Frosting, page 327, letting it project slightly, and insert in it a pecan or half a walnut. Roll in granulated sugar.

With Ginger-and-Nut: Remove the stones from choice dates, and chop together equal measures of preserved ginger and blanched nuts, chopped (hickory, pecan, or almond). Mix with Fondant or a paste of confectioners' sugar and ginger syrup. Use only enough Fondant or paste to hold the ingredients together. With this mixture fill the open space in the dates, cover securely, and roll in granulated sugar.

STUFFED FIGS

Wash figs and steam over boiling water until tender and well puffed, but not soft. Cut in halves lengthwise and fill with Fondant, page 391, or with Butter Frosting, page 327, letting it project slightly. Insert in it half a walnut or pecan. Roll in granulated sugar.

STUFFED PRUNES

Soak large, perfect prunes in cold water several hours. Steam until the skins are tender and remove stones. Fill cavity with an equal bulk of chopped figs, candied cherries and walnuts, or pecans. Roll in granulated sugar and let stand several days before serving to dry.

DATE OR FIG CHOCOLATES

Remove stone from dates or cut figs in halves lengthwise and cut off stem. Press in uniform shape and dip into melted sweet chocolate. Marshmallows may also be dipped.

DATE SAUSAGE

1 lb. dates, stoned,
½ cup walnuts,
2 oz. candied ginger.

Put dates through meat chopped and add the ginger and walnuts, coarsely cut. Knead and roll into sausage, using powdered sugar to prevent sticking. Serve cut in thin slices.

CHOCOLATE SAUSAGE

¼ lb. German sweet chocolate, grated,
¼ lb. almonds (blanched and cut into chunks),
White of ½ an egg, beaten slightly,
Sugar to roll.

Heat the mixing bowl slightly, add chocolate, almonds and the one-half of egg. Knead the mixture into a solid mass and place on board sprinkled with sugar and roll to resemble sausage. When ready to serve, cut in slices with a very thin, sharp knife.

SPANISH SWEETS

¼ lb. candied cherries,
¼ lb. raisins (seeded),
¼ lb. figs,
¼ lb. dates (stoned),
¼ lb. almonds,
½ lb. English walnut meats,
¼ lb. hickory nut or pecan meats,
Powdered sugar.

Mix all together and grind fine or chop. Sprinkle board with powdered sugar, toss on the mixture, knead well, roll like sausage or one-fourth inch thick and cut into small squares. Will keep indefinitely in a box packed in layers between paraffine papers.

ORANGE STICKS

½ cup sugar,
¼ cup hot water.
Peel of an orange,

Wipe the orange, remove the peel in quarters, and cut it in narrow strips. Place peels in sauce pan, cover with cold water, let boil up once and drain. Repeat five times, to extract the bitter taste. Heat the sugar with the hot water, and when dissolved, add the orange peel. Cook slowly until the syrup is nearly evaporated, drain and roll the strips in granulated sugar.

GLACED NUTS OR FRUITS

2 cups sugar,
1 cup boiling water,
⅛ teaspoon cream of tartar.

Put ingredients in a smooth sauce pan, stir until sugar is dissolved. Place over fire, see that the flame does not reach the sides of the pan. Heat to the boiling point, and let boil well, without stirring, until the syrup assumes a light color or just begins to discolor. Remove sauce pan from hot fire or place in large pan of cold water, to instantly stop boiling; then quickly place in pan of hot water, to keep syrup from hardening. Now quickly dip fruits and nuts, a few at a time, in the hot syrup and remove them with fork or wire spoon to oiled paper.

Glaced fruits keep but a day and should only be attempted in cold, clear weather. Oranges and tangerines are separated into sections and allowed to dry a few hours or over night before dipping. Dip fruits first and then nuts, and do them quickly.

MARRON GLACE

1 pint chestnuts,
1 lb. sugar,
¼ vanilla bean.

Shell and blanch Italian or French chestnuts (page 160), cover with fresh boiling water; boil rapidly until tender, but not soft; drain. Split good, oily vanilla bean in halves, cut it into small pieces, add seeds and all to the sugar; then add water and stir until dissolved; bring to the boiling point; let boil a minute; add the chestnuts and cook slowly without boiling, 2 hours, or until chestnuts are soft, dark and very rich. Lift each carefully with a fork, so they do not break, put them in a bottle or jar, and cover with the boiling syrup. Seal and set aside. Will keep.

GUMDROPS

Dissolve one pound of gum arabic in a pint and a half of water, strain and add one pound of white sugar. Heat till the sugar is dissolved; then flavor to taste and color all or part, as desired. When cooled to about the consistency of honey fill a shallow pan with cornstarch or flour; take rounded end of a stick or thimble and make little cavities in the starch, and pour mixture gently into starch molds till filled, when you must cut off the thick stream with a wire. Set pan in warm place for several days to harden; then dampen them a little and shape in granulated sugar.

TOASTED OR ROASTED MARSHMALLOWS

Place marshmallows on a wire broiler and toast under the gas. Turn and toast brown on both sides.

Or, build a bonfire of logs of wood and when flames have gone down, hold the marshmallow over the bright coals with a long pointed stick until browned and roasted.

POPCORN BALLS

5 qts. of popped corn,	1 cup molasses,
2 cups sugar,	2 teaspoons vinegar,
1 teaspoon butter.	

Fresh corn does not pop well. Have fire hot; have corn in popper one kernel deep, shake over fire. Do not heat corn too quick, continue shaking after it has popped to "cook" it. Put the nice, white corn in a greased pan. Boil the rest until brittle in cold water, pour over popcorn; form in balls and let cool.

SALTED ALMONDS OR PECANS

½ lb. almonds,	1 tablespoon butter,
or pecans,	Salt.

Cover one-half pound almonds with boiling water, let stand 5 minutes or until skins slip off easily. Remove the skins, place the nuts in a shallow pan in a hot oven. Let them become a delicate brown, stirring frequently so that all will brown evenly. When brown, add 1 tablespoon butter and plenty of salt, stirring the nuts thoroughly.

Salted Peanuts. Remove skins from peanuts and proceed same as for almonds.

CHAPTER XXXIV

FRESH AND STEWED FRUIT

STRAWBERRIES EN NATURAL

Pick over the berries, but do not remove stems. Place carefully in colander in a pan of cold water, so the water will cover the berries; lift colander up and down, change the water and thus wash the berries.

Place berries in small plate, on rose geranium leaves, if desired, and at the side put one leaf with a tablespoon of powdered sugar. Or omit the leaves, have small mound of powdered sugar in center of plate and surround with the berries, or stem and wash the berries, place in sauce dish and serve with sugar or with sugar and cream.

TO SERVE AN ORANGE

Cut an orange in half crosswise. Place on an attractive dish, scoop out the juice and pulp with a spoon and sweeten if necessary.

West Indian Way: Peel the oranges, taking off as much white skin as possible, then slice them off all round as you would an apple, regardless of the sections. This leaves the seed, tough, stringy central part, and most of the inner skin together, and is a much less tedious process than removing the skin by sections. Use a very sharp knife, so as to make clean cuts and not crush the fruit. Cut out each section separately, and put on a small plate in the form of a daisy. Put white sugar in center.

Oranges with Cocoanut: Pare the oranges, slice as thin as possible, place in small saucers, covering the fruit thickly with fine shredded cocoanut, then add powdered sugar, and for every six dishes of the fruit use the juice of one orange divided among them. Let stand half an hour before serving.

GRAPE FRUIT

Cut in half, with a sharp knife, remove seeds, and sprinkle with sugar, or loosen pulp, and thick, pithy white center; wipe knife after each cutting that the bitter taste may be avoided. Pour in white wine or sherry and sprinkle with powdered sugar, and let stand several hours in ice chest to ripen. Serve cold in the shell. Decorate with maraschino cherry.

FRESH PINEAPPLE

Cut pineapple in thick slices, crosswise, peel off the rind and then slice in small slices or chop, reject the hard core in the center. Place in fruit dish, sprinkle well with sugar, add the juice of a lemon and leave stand a few hours to ripen and serve cold.

MUSK MELONS

Select Rockyford melons, a very small green, firm nutmeg melon. Cut in halves, remove seeds and put where they will keep cool, tied in paper bag, in the ice chest, as the odor of the melon is quite decided and will cling to other foods.

When ready to serve, fill with crushed ice and sprinkle with powdered sugar. Serve in the beginning of a dinner, breakfast or luncheon, or fill with plain ice cream and serve as a dessert at the end of a meal.

Other melons may be served the same way, but are not so dainty.

TO SERVE WATERMELON

Cut a watermelon, chilled by standing on ice, in slices and remove the shell, or cut out the red portion with tablespoon or divide into cubes an inch square and remove seeds. If you desire, add a little wine or have ready a mixture of half a tablespoonful of ground cinnamon to half a cup of powdered sugar, and springle this over the melon; refill the melon shell. Let stand a few moments.

BAKED APPLES

Wipe and core sour apples. Place them in an earthen dish and fill the center of each apple with sugar. Measure 1 tablespoon of water for each apple and pour it around the apples. Bake in a hot oven until soft, but not until broken—20 to 30 minutes. Serve with milk or cream.

STEAMED APPLES

No. 1

Wipe, core and pare sour apples; put on a plate in a steamer and cook until the apples are tender. The juice may be strained and made into a syrup, using ¼ cup sugar to ½ cup juice; boil 5 minutes, add 1 teaspoon lemon juice and strain over the apples.

No. 2

Select 8 red apples, cook in boiling water until soft, turning often. Have water half surround apples. Remove skins carefully that the red color may remain.

To the water add 1 cup sugar, grated rind of ½ lemon, and juice of 1 orange. Simmer until reduced to 1 cup. Cool and pour over apples.

APPLE SAUCE

No. 1

10 apples,	½ cup sugar,
¾ cup water,	1 tablespoon lemon juice,

or ⅛ teaspoon nutmeg or cinnamon.

Wipe, quarter, core and pare sour apples; add the water and cook until the apples begin to grow soft, add the sugar and flavoring, and cool until the apples are thoroughly soft, press through a strainer and beat well.

No. 2

6 or 8 tart apples,	1 cup water,

1 cup sugar.

Pare, core and quarter the apples. Make a syrup of the sugar and water. When boiling, add the apples and cook a few at a time until tender, but not broken. Remove carefully. Boil down the syrup and pour over the apples.

RHUBARB SAUCE

Skin and cut stalks of rhubarb in one-half inch pieces. Scald with boiling water. Let stand ten minutes and drain. Add water to keep from burning, cook until soft, then sweeten. Flavor with the grated yellow rind of orange.

STEWED PRUNES

½ lb. prunes,	1 quart water,

¼ cup sugar.

Wash the prunes, and then soak them in cold water over night. Cook slowly in the water in which they were soaked until soft.

Add one-fourth cup sugar to every two cups of prunes and cook five minutes longer. Season with lemon juice or cinnamon if desired.

CRANBERRY SAUCE

1 qt. cranberries,
2 cups water,
2 cups sugar.

Boil water and sugar to a syrup about 10 minutes, add the cranberries, washed and picked over. Cover at first and cook until the cranberries are clear. Serve cold with meat or poultry.

CRANBERRY COMPOTE

1 qt. cranberries,
1 cup granulated sugar,
1 pt. Wiesbaden or preserved strawberries.

Enough water to well cover berries. Put cranberries and water on to boil and let them cook for about five minutes and keeping covered. Then add strawberries and sugar and cook about five minutes. Serve cold.

CRANBERRY JELLY

4 cups cranberries,
2 cups water,
2 cups sugar.

Pick over and wash the cranberries. Cook them (covered) in the water until they are soft and burst from the skins. Press through a strainer, add the sugar, and stir until the sugar is dissolved; stop stirring, and boil eight to ten minutes, or until a drop jells on a cold plate, skim. Pour it into molds or glasses which have been wet with cold water and set away to cool.

FRESH PEACH OR PEAR COMPOTE

1 dozen pears, or
2 dozen peaches,
1 cup sugar,
1 cup water,
4 small pieces stick cinnamon.

Boil sugar and water to a syrup, add the cinnamon; drop in the fruit peeled and sliced to suit, let boil slowly until tender. Serve cold with meat.

CANNED FRUIT COMPOTE

1 can strained fruit juice,
¼ cup sugar,
¼ oz. citron, cut fine,
2 dozen raisins,
1 can drained fruit.

Mix and boil first four ingredients until thick as syrup, add the drained fruit, cover for a few moments and then let boil 5 minutes more. Let cool, and serve cold with meat. Canned peach, pear, plum or pineapple may be used.

GINGERED FIGS

Wash one pound dried figs and remove stems. Add cold water to cover and juice and rind of one-half lemon, and one large piece ginger root. Stew until the figs are puffed and soft. Remove figs to dish. Measure syrup and add one-half as much sugar; simmer until thick and add one tablespoon sherry. Serve with whipped cream.

STEAMED DATES

Separate dates and wash them. Place in a colander or strainer over a sauce pan of hot water. Cover and let steam in this way for three-quarters of an hour. Cool before serving.

BAKED BANANAS

Pull down a section of the skin of each banana, loosen the pulp from the skin, remove all coarse threads that adhere to the pulp and return the pulp to the skin in its original position; lay the fruit thus prepared in an agate pan and bake in a hot oven until the skins are blackened and the pulp is softened. Remove pulp from the skin without injury to shape, bend in a half circle and dispose in a serving dish; sprinkle with powdered sugar and fine-chopped, blanched pistachio nuts and serve as a dessert dish; or pour a Currant Jelly Sauce, page 91, and serve as an entree with broiled or roasted meat.

CHAPTER XXXV

FRUIT SYRUPS, JUICES AND WINES

FRUIT SYRUPS AND JUICES

The only difference between syrups and juice is that in the syrup there must be at least half as much sugar as fruit juice.

These syrups are used for flavoring ice creams and water ices. They also make a delicious drink, when two or three spoonfuls are added to a glass of ice cold water.

Fruit juice is most desirable for drinking or for culinary purposes.

Currant juice may be sterilized and canned without sugar. This juice may be made into jelly at any season of the year.

Fruit juices that are designed for use in frozen creams and water ices should be canned with a generous amount of sugar.

For grape juice good bottles are to be preferred to fruit cans. If you can get the self-sealing bottles, the work of putting up grape juice will be light. Sterilize bottles and corks, page 423.

TO MAKE A DRIPPING BAG

Take a three cornered piece of cloth or felt, sew two sides together, and attach the third side or opening to an iron hoop. Tie stout cord to opposite sides of hoop and hang up. Place crushed fruit or juice in bag to drip.

SUGAR SYRUP

2 cups sugar, or
1 lb. brown sugar,
1 cup water (scant).

Boil till clear, do not stir after the sugar and water are mixed. Cool and serve with griddle cakes.

LEMON SYRUP

12 lemons, juice,
6 lemons, grated rind,
6 lbs. sugar,
6 qts. boiling water.

Add grated rind of lemons to juice and let stand over night. Pour water over sugar and stir until sugar is dissolved; then boil. Cool and add the strained lemon juice, squeezing as much of the oil from the grated rind as possible.

Bottle and seal. Serve diluted with an equal amount of fresh water.

ORANGE SYRUP

12 oranges, juice,
2 lemons, juice,
6 oranges, rind,
1 lemon, rind,
6 lbs. sugar,
6 qts. water.

Follow directions for making lemon syrup, in above recipe, substituting the orange juice and rind.

CHOCOLATE SYRUP

8 oz. soluble chocolate,
2½ quarts water,
8½ lbs. white sugar.

Thoroughly dissolve the chocolate in hot water, then add the sugar, and heat until the mixture boils. Strain while hot. After it has become cool, vanilla may be added.

This is a preparation for the special use of druggists and others in making hot or cold soda. It forms the basis for a delicious freshening, nourishing and strengthening drink.

UNFERMENTED GRAPE JUICE

10 lbs. Concord grapes,
2 qts. water,
2 lbs. sugar.

Pick over and wash grapes. Place in kettle, cover with the water and let boil until the seeds are free. Strain while hot through bag and squeeze thoroughly; heat to boiling point and skim. Let boil up again and skim; then add sugar, more, less or none, as preferred.

Heat to the boiling point; fill patent air tight bottles (not too full, allowing room for the corks to go down), and cork immediately. If ordinary bottles and corks are used place corks over bottles very lightly at first, immediately after filling, and, as they cool off push corks down, always a little deeper, then cover air tight with melted paraffine or sealing wax. Ordinary fruit cans may also be used, the small ones preferred.

NOTE—Grape juice is particularly good as a drink. It may be canned with or without sugar, but, except where the grapes have a large percentage of sugar, as is the case in California, some sugar should be added to the juice in canning. Almost any variety of grape may be used, and yellow, red or purple juice may be obtained, according to the color of the grape, the Muscat, Concord, Catawba, Isabella or Iowa.

Use only clean, sound, well ripened, but not over-ripe grapes.

TRANSPARENT GRAPE JUICE

If you wish a particularly clear grape juice, great care should be taken in the heating of the grapes, before pressing and in the straining or filtering. Wash the grapes and pick them from the stems. Crush the grapes well, place in a bag. Hang bag up securely and twist it, or, let two persons take hold, one at each end, and press out the juice. Place juice in a double boiler or in a large enameled pan or kettle, in a pan of hot water and heat the juice gradually until it steams; if a deeper color is desired, heat to the simmer point, do not let it boil. If you wish the juice extra clear, let it now stand 24 hours to settle. Carefully remove juice from pan, that the sediment at the bottom is not disturbed and drain through cloth or Dripping Bag, page 402.

Then pour into clean bottles, not too full, as the heat expands the juice; place the filled bottles in a steamer or a wash boiler, protected by a thin board or rack, fill boiler with cold water to within one inch of top of bottles and gradually heat until about to simmer.

Then take the bottles out and cork immediately. If ordinary corks are used place them on lightly at first and as the bottles cool off push corks down, then cover air-tight with melted paraffine or sealing wax. If corks, even of patent bottles, are forced down too quickly the bottles are apt to crack.

CURRANT AND RASPBERRY JUICE

4 qts. currants,
2 qts. red raspberries,
3 qts. water,
3 lbs. sugar.

Pick over and wash fruit. Place in preserving kettle, cover with the water and let boil until soft. Strain well through jelly bag. Measure, and to every quart of juice add 1 cup of sugar. Heat to the boiling point and immediately fill into sterilized cans to overflowing. Screw on covers of cans and when cool screw air tight. Do not fill too full if bottles with patent stoppers are used. If ordinary bottles are used, cover with cork lightly at first and as it cools off push in until air-tight and cover corks with paraffine or sealing wax, melted.

Cherry, Plum and Peach Juices—To preserve the juices of these and similar fruits, proceed as for Jelly, page 408, but adding to each quart of juice, one cup sugar. If not desired to have the juice transparent, press the pulp of the fruit to extract all the liquid.

RASPBERRY SHRUB

4 qts. raspberries,   1 qt. vinegar,   Sugar.

Take red or black raspberries, mash them and cover with the vinegar. Let stand over night or longer; strain. To each pint of juice, add 1 lb. sugar, boil 20 minutes, then put in sterilized bottles and keep in a cool, dry place. Use two tablespoons to a glass of water. Blackberries or strawberries may also be used.

BLACKBERRY CORDIAL

8 qts. blackberries, (Lawtons),
2 quarts cold water,
4 lbs. sugar,
1 tablespoon each, whole allspice, cloves, and cinnamon bark,
2 qts. whiskey or brandy.

Tie spices in a thin bag. Pick over, wash the berries. Place in preserving kettle, cover with the water, let boil thoroughly soft; then strain well. Measure and to each quart of juice add 2 cups sugar (1 lb.). Add spice bag and boil about 20 minutes or until thick. Let cool and measure again. To each quart of syrup, add 1 pint of whiskey. Bottle and cork tightly. Will keep for years, the older, the better.

CHERRY BOUNCE

1 qt. cherries,
½ lb. sugar (cut loaf),
1 pint whiskey,
1 tablespoon allspice, cinnamon and cloves (heads removed),

Wash cherries and pick off the stems. Fill a large mouthed bottle alternately with a thick layer of cherries, a layer of the loaf sugar and a few of the whole spices, continue until the bottle is almost full. Then pour in the whiskey until full. Cork and let stand in a dark closet for 2 months or more. The older it is the better.

GRAPE WINE

No. 1

Mash the grapes well and then strain and press through a cloth. Then add barely enough water to the pressed grapes to cover them. Strain the juice thus obtained into the first portion. Put three pounds of sugar to one gallon of the liquid. Let it stand in a crock or tub, covered with a cloth, from three to seven days. Skim off what rises every morning, without disturbing the contents. Put the juice in a cask, leave it open for twenty-four hours; then bung it up and put clay over the bung to keep the air out. Let young wine remain in the cask until March, when it should be drawn off and bottled. Or, if you have no cask pour wine in jugs, allowing the corks to remain very loose; when through fermenting, fill into bottles. After all signs of fermentation cease, put in the corks very tight, and tie or wire them in and seal. Keep in a cool place.

Currant, Blackberry, Elderberry or Rhubarb wines are made the same way, using less sugar for Blackberry and Elderberry wines.

No. 2

9 lbs. Concord grapes, 4¾ lbs. sugar.

Wash and pick over the grapes and place in a 2 gallon jar. Fill with cold water. Cover with cheese cloth and keep in a warm place. Stir twice a week for 6 weeks. Strain and let stand 2 weeks longer to allow wine to settle. Fill in bottles not necessarily air tight.

RAISIN WINE

2 lbs. large raisins, seeded and chopped,
1 lb. white loaf sugar,
1 lemon, cut up,
6 quarts boiling water.

Put all in a stone jar, cover and stir every day for a week. Then strain, bottle and cork. Good in 10 or 12 days.

DANDELION WINE

1 gallon dandelion flowers,
1 gallon boiling water,
3 lbs. sugar,
3 oranges, cut in small squares,
3 lemons, cut in small squares
1 oz. yeast.

Pick dandelion flowers early in the morning, taking care not to have a particle of the bitter stem attached. Pour the boiling water over the flowers and let stand three days. Strain and add the rest of the ingredients and let stand to ferment three weeks. Strain and bottle.

TARRAGON VINEGAR

3 oz. tarragon, or Estregan leaves,

1 qt. good white wine, or Cider vinegar.

Strip the leaves from the branches of the estregan or tarragon about the last of August. Put into a quart fruit can and fill with the vinegar, close and let stand 20 days, then strain. Use for salads or sharp sauces.

ROSEL, BEET VINEGAR

Place beets in a stone crock, removing greens. Cover with cold water and put in a warm place and let stand for three or four weeks or until mixture becomes sour. This is used as a vinegar during Easter or Pesach and to make beet soup, Russian style.

CHAPTER XXXVI

JELLY

GENERAL RULES FOR JELLY MAKING

Wash the fruit and remove stems and imperfections. Cut large fruit into pieces. With watery fruit, such as grapes and currants, use no water. With apples and quinces use enough water to cover them.

Cook the fruit until the juice flows, crushing it with a spoon. Remove it from the fire and strain it through a pointed bag hung from the ceiling or between two chairs. Do not squeeze the bag at first; when nearly all is strained through, the bag may be squeezed. Keep this last juice by itself; the jelly made from it will not be clear, but can be used for jelly cake, etc.

Measure the juice and put an equal quantity of sugar in the oven to heat. Boil the juice with the sugar until the jelly thickens slightly when dropped on a cold plate, or if the last drop on the spoon can be held while counting sixty. Pour into sterilized jelly glasses and set aside to harden. Then label.

Jelly must be covered to protect it from mould. Paraffine is convenient for this purpose. If fruit is fully ripe, use ¼ less sugar.

Apples, quinces, crabapples, currants and grapes make the best jellies. An acid fruit is the most suitable for jelly-making. The fruit should be fresh, just ripe, or a little under-ripe. Juicy fruits, such as currants, raspberries, etc., should not be gathered after a rain. Fruits such as strawberries, raspberries, peaches, which will not "jell" easily, make beautiful jelly, if ⅓ rhubarb or pieplant juice is used.

The jelly will be clearer and finer, if the fruit is simmered gently and not stirred during the cooking. If the syrup boils too rapidly, it will not jell.

Medium-sized granite preserving kettles are best to use in making jelly. They are lighter to handle and quickly and easily cleaned. Do not make a large quantity at a time; a quart of juice is quite enough.

FILLING AND COVERING THE GLASSES

First heat your glasses thoroughly, by standing in a pan of tepid water and allowing it to get scalding hot. Then set them on a damp cloth spread on the table or board. Pour jelly at once into these, filling almost to running over, as jelly will shrink. Let stand until cold. To prevent jelly from moulding brush the top over with brandy or alcohol. Dip a disk of thick, white paper the size of the top of the glass, in the brandy and put it on the jelly. Then pour a layer of melted paraffine over the paper. If the glasses have covers, put them on.

If paraffine is used, break it into pieces and put in a cup. Set the cup in a pan of warm water on the back of the stove. In a few moments it will be melted enough to cover the jelly. Have the coating about a fourth of an inch thick. In cooling the paraffine contracts, and if the layer is very thin it will crack and leave a portion of the jelly exposed.

CRABAPPLE JELLY

8 quarts apples,   4 quarts water,
Sugar.

Select under-ripe Siberian crabapples, a yellow pink cheeked apple. Wash, cut in halves, but do not pare or core the apples. Boil until soft. Mash and pour into jelly bag and let drip into large pitcher or jar. Do not squeeze. Take equal parts of juice and sugar. There should be about 3 quarts of juice.

Put juice on to boil, let boil 5 minutes, add the sugar, boil a few minutes longer; or until a drop jells on a cold plate.

Skim and turn into hot glasses. When cool, cover with paraffine, and keep in a cool, dry place.

Crabapple Sauce may be made by straining the drained apples, adding sugar and cinnamon or lemon juice to taste, and heating it up only long enough to dissolve the sugar.

CRABAPPLE AND PLUM JELLY

¾ peck crabapples,   ¼ peck plums.
Water to barely cover sugar,

Select under-ripe fruit. Wash and pick over, but do not pare or seed. Boil until soft. Mash and pour into jelly bag to drip. Do not squeeze. Take equal measures of sugar and juice, let juice boil 5 minutes, add sugar and boil until a drop jells on a cold plate. Skim and turn into hot glasses, cover and keep in a cool, dry place. Reserve the pulp, strain through sieve, add sugar to taste and use as sauce.

CRABAPPLE AND CRANBERRY JELLY

½ peck crabapples,   2 quarts cranberries.
Follow directions for Crabapple and Plum Jelly, recipe above.

CURRANT AND RASPBERRY JELLY

4 quarts currants,   4 pints raspberries,
Sugar.

Select the cherry currants. They should not be over-ripe nor gathered after a rain. Pick over the fruit, but do not take the stems from currants. Mash the fruit, using wooden potato masher. Cook slowly until currants are nearly white. Strain. Take equal parts of sugar and juice. Boil five minutes, add heated sugar and boil three minutes. Skim, and pour into glasses. Cover and keep cool and dry.

CURRANT JELLY WITHOUT COOKING

To make currant jelly by the cold process follow the first rule for jelly as far as dissolving the sugar in the strained juice. Fill warm, sterilized glasses with this. Place the glasses on a board and put the board by a sunny window. Cover with sheets of glass and keep by the window until the jelly is set. The jelly will be more transparent if the juice is strained through the flannel bag. Jelly made by the cold process is more delicate than that made by boiling, but it does not keep quite so well.

Or, wash and mash currants well, let stand a little while and strain. Place juice in stone jar and place in the coolest part of cellar for 24 hours. Remove scum from top, strain and to 1 pint of juice add 1 pint sugar; stir until sugar is dissolved.

Put in glasses and seal. In 24 hours you will have a perfectly transparent jelly. No heat is required.

GRAPE JELLY

An acid grape is best for this jelly. The sweet, ripe grapes contain too much sugar. Half-ripe fruit, or equal portions of nearly ripe and green grapes, will also be found satisfactory. Wild grapes make delicious jelly.

Grapes should be picked over, washed and stems removed before putting into preserving kettle. Heat to the boiling point and cook until the seeds are free, about 30 minutes. Pour into jelly bag to drip. Take equal measures of sugar and juice and boil until it jells. Skim and pour into sterilized glasses. Keep in cool, dry place.

PLUM JELLY

Use an under-ripe acid plum. Wash the fruit and remove the stems. Put into the preserving kettle with 1 quart of water for each peck of fruit. Cook gently until the plums are boiled to pieces. Strain the juice and proceed the same as for other jelly.

FILLED CURRANTS (BAR-LE-DUC)

10 cups large currants, stemmed,	10 cups sugar.

Add sugar to currants, washed and stemmed, and let cook slowly and steadily from 20 to 25 minutes. Pour in jelly glasses, cover, and keep in a dry, cool place.

CHERRIES IN CURRANT JELLY

2 qts. currant juice,
8 lbs. sugar,	2 qts. stemmed and pitted cherries.

Wash, mash and cook slowly at first as many currants, with stems, as will make 2 quarts of strained juice. Let juice come to a boil, add sugar and skim; add cherries and cook slowly and steadily from 10 to 15 minutes. Pour in jelly glasses, cover and keep in a dry, cool place.

MINT JELLY

Snow apples,	Equal weight sugar,
Fresh mint leaves.

Wipe apples, pare, remove stem and blossom ends and cut in quarters. Put in preserving kettle, add cold water to barely cover and add enough mint leaves, well washed, to give a decided mint flavor. Cover and cook slowly until apples are soft; wash, drain in jelly bag. Boil 20 minutes, add the sugar, heated; add more mint leaves, if desired, let boil 5 minutes. Skim and turn in glasses. Let stand in sunny window 24 hours. Cover and remove to dry, cool place.

CHAPTER XXXVII

PRESERVED AND PICKLED FRUIT

PRESERVES

Fruit is preserved by cooking it with from three-fourths to its whole weight in sugar.

PRESERVING SMALL FRUITS RAW

An easy and excellent method of preserving small fruits, such as currants, strawberries and raspberries, is by putting them up raw.

Look the fruit over and mash each berry carefully, or put through food grinder, then take equal parts of crushed berries and sugar and mix together. Let stand in a cool place over night to dissolve the sugar. Can the next morning in Mason jars. The success of this method depends upon mashing each berry and having the sugar thoroughly dissolved before canning.

Cherry Currants are particularly nice done up this way.

Pineapples, sliced, pared, cored, and put through the food grinder or chopped fine and allowed to stand over night in an equal amount of sugar and then packed in air tight, sterilized jars keep well and retain their natural flavor.

BAKED CRAB APPLE PRESERVES

½ peck crab apples,   a 1 gallon stone jar,
4 lbs. sugar,   1 tablespoon water.

Wash, wipe and remove the blossom ends of perfect, large red Siberian crab apples. Pour water in bottom of jar, then place in alternate layers of apples and sugar (with sugar on top). Cover with two thicknesses of Manila paper, tied down securely or with close fitting plate. Bake in a very slow oven (that would only turn the paper a light brown), 2 or 3 hours. Let stand to cool; keep in cool, dry place.

Baked Sickel Pears—May be prepared the same way. Flavor, if desired, with ginger or lemon juice.

Baked Quinces—Quinces may be wiped, cored, and quartered; sugar filled in the cavities, and baked same as crabapples, in a very slow oven 3 or more hours until clear and glassy.

BAKED CRANBERRIES OR CHERRY PRESERVES

4 quarts cranberries or sour cherries,   4 quarts sugar,
     a 1 gallon stone jar.

Pick over, wash and drain large, perfect cranberries; or stem and then stone large cherries (with new steel hairpin so they remain whole). Place a tablespoon hot water in jar, then alternately in layers cranberries or cherries and sugar (with sugar on top), cover closely. Bake in a very slow oven 2 hours. Let stand. Then keep in a cool, dry place.

Look and taste like candied cherries.

CHERRY OR RASPBERRY PRESERVES

5 lbs. cherries or raspberries,   5 lbs. sugar.

Wash berries carefully that they do not mash; or wash, pick over and stone the cherries. Place in preserving kettle, alternate layers of sugar and fruit; let stand over night. Bring slowly to the boiling point and boil slowly until thick. Put away in glasses or jars.

GOOSEBERRY PRESERVES

The berries should be picked when they begin to show signs of ripening. Stem carefully, drop them into cold water and let come to a boil. Remove from fire and pour off the water and when the berries have cooled drop them into boiling syrup (made by using just enough water to sugar to form a liquid), heating very slowly. Seal. The berries will stay quite whole and if the operation has been carefully done, will keep for years.

GRAPE MARMALADE

4 lbs. grapes,   4 lbs. sugar.

Pick over, wash, drain, and remove stem from grapes. Heat to boiling point and cook slowly until seeds are free. Rub through fine sieve. Return to kettle, and add equal measure of sugar; cook slowly thirty minutes, stirring occasionally to prevent burning. Put in jars or tumblers.

GINGER PEARS

8 lbs. pears,   ¼ lb. Canton ginger,
4 lbs. sugar,   4 lemons.

Wipe pears, quarter, core and remove the stems and cut into small slices. Add sugar, the ginger, cut fine, and the juice of the lemons. Cut the lemon rinds into long, thin strips; mix all together and let stand over night. Place in preserving kettle, on stove and let cook slowly for three hours, or until thick and clear. Put in stone jar, well covered, or in glass cans.

GINGER APPLES

1 qt. sour apples, diced,   1 lemon,
2 cups brown sugar,   2 cups water,
6 pieces ginger root.

Wipe, pare, quarter, core and cut the apples into small squares. Grate the rind of the lemon. Boil water, sugar and lemon juice 12 minutes or until clear, add the rest of the ingredients and cook slowly two or more hours until thick and brown.

Will keep for several weeks, or longer if filled while hot in airtight cans.

ORANGE MARMALADE

12 sour oranges,   ¾ lb. cut sugar,
2 lemons,   To 1 lb. fruit.

Select smooth skinned oranges. Remove peel from skin in quarters. Cut the rind of ½ of the oranges and lemons into very narrow strips, with scissors. Place shredded peel in sauce pan, cover with cold water, let boil up once, drain through colander. Repeat 4 times, to extract bitter taste of rind. Take the peeled oranges and lemons and with a sharp knife, peel as you would an apple, the thin outer skin, through to the pulp. Separate pulp from section walls, with point of knife and remove pulp, rejecting seeds, and core with tough section walls attached. Place pulp in preserving kettle; heat to boiling point, add sugar gradually and cook slowly 1 hour; add the shredded cooked rind and cook one hour longer. Fill in glasses.

QUINCE AND SWEET APPLE PRESERVES

1 peck quinces,
½ peck pears,
¼ peck sweet apples, (Tolman),
Sugar.

Wash and pick over the fruit, then peel and core. Cut the quinces and apples in rounds and the pears in quarters. Cover cores and peels with cold water, boil thoroughly and strain. For each pound of fruit allow three-fourths of a pound of sugar, add to the strained liquid and let boil until a clear syrup. Boil the rounds of quince in cold water until they can be pierced with a silver fork, remove carefully to platter and then into the boiling syrup. Add the rest of the fruit and boil slowly and steadily for three or four hours until the fruit is clear and a deep red color. Pour into crocks and cover.

RADISH OR BEET PRESERVES (Russian Style)

1 lb. beets or 1 qt. radishes,   1 qt. strained honey.

Cut radishes (black), in thin slices ¼ by 1 inch. Cook in boiling water 3 or 4 minutes. Drain and dry between towels.

If beets are used cook them and then cut same as the radishes.

To 1 cup of the vegetables take 1 cup honey and cook until the mixture is thick enough to drop heavy from the spoon. Add a little ginger to the beets.

Serve cold mixed with almonds cut in thin slices. Put away in glasses or jars.

STRAWBERRY PRESERVES

Select large, sound strawberries. Pick and wash them carefully. Place in preserving kettle alternately one quart of berries and one pound of sugar. Let stand over night. Place on stove, let cook steadily for several hours until the fruit is clear. Put in jelly glasses or jars.

SUNSHINE STRAWBERRIES

Use equal weights of sugar and strawberries. Put the strawberries in the preserving kettle in layers, sprinkling sugar over each layer. The fruit and sugar should not be more than 4 inches deep. Place the kettle on the stove and heat the fruit and sugar slowly to the boiling point. When it begins to boil, skim carefully. Boil ten minutes, counting from the time the fruit begins to bubble. Pour the cooked fruit into platters, having it about 2 or 3 inches deep. Place the platters in a sunny window, in an unused room. Cover with a piece of cheese cloth or with glass, for three or four days. In that time the fruit will grow plump and firm, and the syrup will thicken almost to a jelly. Put this preserve, cold, into jars or tumblers.

SUNSHINE CURRANTS OR CHERRIES

Select large, firm red or white fruit, remove the stems, and proceed as for strawberries. Stone the cherries before weighing.

GREEN TOMATO PRESERVES

1 quart sliced green tomatoes,
2 pints sugar,
1 lemon, sliced and seeded,
1 stick cinnamon,
or, a few cassia buds.

Place in kettle, let stand several hours to draw juice. Cook until tomatoes have a clarified appearance.

TOMATO PRESERVES

1 lb. yellow pear tomatoes, or, the red ones, slices,
1 lb. sugar,
2 oz. Canton ginger, or a few pieces of ginger root,
1 lemon.

Scald the tomatoes to peel. Cover with the sugar, and let stand over night. Pour off syrup and boil until clear and quite thick. Skim, add tomatoes, ginger and the lemon sliced and seeded. Cook until the fruit is clear. Pour into jars or crocks.

CHERRY CONSERVE

5 lbs. ripe cherries,
5 lbs. sugar,
1½ lbs. seedless raisins,
4 oranges,
2 lemons.

Wash, stem and pit the cherries. Squeeze out the juice of the oranges and lemons. Wash raisins. Mix all together and let stand over night. Then boil slowly and steadily for several hours, or, until thick and clear. Pour in cans and seal.

GOOSEBERRY CONSERVE

3 lbs. gooseberries,
3 lbs. sugar,
1 lb. seeded raisins,
3 large oranges.

Peel the oranges, grate the skin and use grated rind and juice. Mix all together and cook slowly until thick. Seal hot.

RHUBARB CONSERVE

To three lbs. of pieplant, add three lbs. of sugar and the juice of three lemons. Cook thirty minutes. Then add the grated rind of three lemons and ½ lb. of chopped almonds. Cook 30 minutes longer.

PLUM CONSERVE

No. 1

3 lbs. blue plums or prunes,
1 lb. seeded raisins,
3 oranges, cut in small pieces,
Juice of 2 lemons,
3 lbs. sugar,
1 lb. English walnuts, broken in chunks.

Wash the plums, remove the stones and cut them into small pieces. Mix. Place in preserving kettle, on stove, let come slowly to the boiling point and cook steadily until the fruit is clear and thick. Put in jelly glasses or jars.

No. 2

5 lbs. blue plums or German prunes,
1 lb. seeded raisins,
4 oranges, pared and sliced,
Rind of 2 oranges,
Sugar.

Wash the plums, cut them in halves and remove the stones. Peel the oranges, slice them fine and cut each slice in half. Cut the rind of two of the oranges into small squares. Take a measure of sugar and a measure of the mixture, place in preserving kettle on stove and let come slowly to the boiling point and cook steadily for several hours until the fruit is clear and thick.

PEAR CONSERVE

1 pk. pears,
4 lbs. sugar,
1 lb. raisins, seeded,
1½ lbs. shelled English walnuts,
3 lemons, juice,
2 oranges, juice.

Pare, core and slice the pears in large pieces, crosswise; add sugar and let stand over night. Drain off the liquid and let boil to a syrup, about 12 minutes, then add pears and the rest of the ingredients, breaking the walnuts into pieces, about the size of the raisins.

Let cook slowly until thick and clear, one hour or more. Place in jars or cans. Cover well.

PEAR AND APPLE CONSERVE

9 hard pears,
6 tart apples,
3 lemons,
⅛ lb. Canton ginger,
½ pint water,
Sugar.

Pare, quarter and core the pears. Pare apples, core and cut crosswise in ½ inch slices. Grate the rind of the lemons and add the juice to the water. Cut ginger in small pieces. For every pound of fruit allow one pound of sugar.

Boil sugar and water to a syrup, add the rest of the ingredients and boil ¾ hour or until thick and clear. Place in cans or glasses and cover well.

PEAR AND NUT PRESERVES

½ pk. Seckel pears,
½ lb. pecans,
½ lb. shelled almonds,
Sugar,
Water.

Pare, quarter and remove core of pears. For each pound of fruit allow 1 pound of sugar, 1 cup water; add water to sugar, let boil well, add the pears and boil 1 hour slowly or until clear, then add the nuts and boil 20 minutes longer. Place in jars or cans; cover well.

Hard winter pears may be used instead of the Seckel pears.

SPICED FRUIT

PICKLED APPLES

9 lbs. apples,
4 lbs. sugar,
1 pint water,
1 qt. vinegar,
¼ broken cinnamon and cloves mixed.

Select "Pound Sweets" or large Crab apples. Pare the sweet apple, leave Crabs whole, with stems.

Place fruit in crock alternately with layers of sugar and pour vinegar and sugar over and let stand over night covered. Drain and to the liquid add the spices, tied in a bag, soft heads of cloves removed. Heat slowly to the boiling point and when clear, add the apples; boil until tender but not soft. Place in heated glass cans, using perforated skimmer and cover. When apples are all cooked and in the jars let syrup boil down a little and lifting covers, pour the boiling syrup over the fruit and seal at once.

PICKLED PEARS

10 lbs. pears, peeled,
4½ lbs. sugar,
½ cup water,
1 qt. vinegar,
¼ cup broken cinnamon and cloves, mixed.

Place peeled pears, "Sickel" pears are best (leaving stems on), in a crock alternately with layers of sugar. Cover with the water and vinegar. Let stand covered over night. Drain and to the liquid add the spices tied in a bag, soft heads of cloves removed. Heat slowly to the boiling point, and when clear add the pears, boil until tender but not soft. Place in heated glass jars, using perforated skimmer and cover; when fruit is all cooked and in the can lift covers and pour the boiling syrup over the fruit and seal at once.

PICKLED PEACHES

7 lbs. peaches,
5 lbs. sugar,
1 pint cider vinegar,
2 tablespooons cloves, heads removed,
2 sticks cinnamon, broken in pieces.

Pare and weigh large clingstone peaches. Boil sugar, vinegar and spices, tied in a bag, about 12 minutes or until clear. Add peaches, only enough for one can at a time, and cook, testing with a straw, until tender but firm. Lift out of kettle with perforated skimmer, place in jars and cover to keep hot. Continue the same way until all the peaches are cooked.

Cook syrup down a little and pour hot over the peaches. Screw down covers immediately and seal air-tight.

PICKLED PLUMS

6 lbs. Damson plums,
3½ lbs. sugar,
1 pt. vinegar,
1 tablespoon cinnamon,
½ tablespoon allspice,
½ tablespoon cloves.

Remove stones from plums. Boil vinegar, sugar and spices (ground), then add plums and boil slowly 30 minutes. Place in jars and cover well.

SWEET PICKLED WATERMELON

Watermelon rind, 2 lbs.,
1 cup salt to 4 qts. water,
2 qts. vinegar,
2 cups sugar,
¼ cup mixed pickle spices.

Pare rind, remove all red meat and cut into small strips or squares. Soak in salt water over night. Next morning soak in fresh water about 2 hours, drain. Boil vinegar, sugar and spices, tied in a bag, until clear, about 12 minutes. Add the watermelon rind and boil until tender, but not soft. Test with a straw. Remove rind to jar, with perforated skimmer, boil syrup down a little and pour hot in jars over the cooked rind. Cover air-tight and keep in a cool place.

PICKLED CHERRIES

2 qts. cherries,
4 lbs. sugar,
Vinegar.

Pit the cherries and put into a large stone, cover with vinegar and leave them stand for twenty-four hours (stir it up a few times). Then drain off the vinegar. Measure the same amount of sugar as cherries, and alternate in layers, sugar on top. Stir this each day for three days, to dissolve all the sugar. Then bottle in Mason jars.

SPICED CHERRIES

6 qts. cherries, pitted,
3½ lbs. white sugar,
1 pt. cider vinegar,
1 tablespoon ground cinnamon,
½ tablespoon ground allspice,
½ tablespoon ground cloves,
½ nutmeg, grated.

Mix sugar, vinegar and spices, until dissolved and pour over the cherries. Stir well for three mornings and then can or bottle and seal.

Spiced Currants. Stem the currants and proceed same as for spiced cherries, using less spice.

SPICED GOOSEBERRIES

5 lbs. half-ripe gooseberries,
4 lbs. sugar,
1 pt. vinegar,
1 tablespoon cinnamon,
½ tablespoon allspice,
½ tablespoon cloves.

Wash and stem the fruit. Bring vinegar, sugar and the spices (ground), to a boil. Add the berries and boil slowly 20 minutes. Place in glasses and cover well.

BRANDIED CHERRIES

5 lbs. cherries,
5 cups sugar,
1 pt. brandy,
2 cups water.

Select the dark, large sweet cherries. Boil the sugar and water 12 minutes or until a clear syrup, pour over the cherries and let stand over night. Drain cherries and let syrup come slowly to the boiling point, add cherries, boil about 8 minutes. Lift out cherries with perforated skimmer and pack into hot, glass cans, then cover. Boil the syrup down 15 minutes longer, until quite thick and while boiling add the brandy. Remove from fire and pour over the cherries at once; cover and seal.

BRANDY PEACHES

No. 1

9 lbs. peaches,
9 lbs. sugar,
1 qt. water,
2 tablespoons stick cinnamon,
2 tablespoons whole cloves heads removed.
3 pints brandy.

Select large clingstone peaches. Pare and weigh fruit.

Boil sugar and water with spices tied in a bag, until clear; drop in fruit, a few at a time and let boil until tender, but not soft. They must remain whole. Place fruit on platter out to sun. Drop in the remainder of the peaches, a few at a time and place in sun.

Let syrup boil until thick, let cool, add the brandy and stir well. Put peaches in jar, cover well with the syrup. Seal and keep in a cool place.

No. 2

3 pecks choice peaches,
5 lbs. sugar,
1 qt. water,
10 lbs. sugar,
1½ qts. brandy.

Make a syrup by boiling 5 lbs. of sugar in 1 qt. of water. Peel the peaches (best Crawfords), and boil in this syrup until tender, but not soft; then put them on platters. Fill into jars and cover with a new syrup made of the 10 lbs. of sugar and the remaining water, adding the brandy, when syrup is taken from stove. Fill bottles full and seal. The thin syrup may be bottled.

Brandy Pears. Follow directions for making Brandied Peaches—only boiling the pears a little longer, as they are tougher.

CHAPTER XXXVIII

CANNING

TABLE FOR CANNING FRUIT

The sugar and water must be boiled to a syrup before adding to the fruit.

For 1 quart cans	Boil Minutes	Sugar Cups	Water Cups
Cherries slowly	5	¾	½
Raspberries slowly	6	1	½
Blackberries slowly	6	¾	½
Plums slowly	10	1	½
Strawberries slowly	8	1	½
Huckleberries slowly	5	½	½
Small sour pears, whole	30	1	2
Bartlett pears, in halves	20	1	2
Peaches, in halves	8	1	2
Pineapples, cut	15	1	1
Siberian or crab apples, whole	25	1	2
Sour apples, cut in quarters	10	¾	2
Ripe currants	6	1	½
Wild grapes	10	1	½
Tomatoes	20	0	½

GENERAL RULES

Canned fruit is preserving sterilized fruit in sterilized, airtight jars, sugar being added to give sweetness. Fruits may be canned without sugar, if perfectly sterilized, that is, freed from all germ life.

Can each kind of fruit in its season, when it is best and cheapest. Select it under-ripe rather than over-ripe. There are several methods of canning; and while the principle is the same in all methods, the conditions under which the housekeeper must

CANNING FRUITS

do her work may, in her case, make one method more convenient than another. For this reason three will be given which are considered the best and easiest. These are:

Cooking the fruit in the jars in an oven.
Cooking the fruit in the jars in boiling water.
Stewing the fruit before it is put in the jars.

When the fruit is cold wipe the jars with a wet cloth. Paste on gum labels, and put the jars on shelves in a cool, dark closet.

TO STERILIZE THE JARS

For a small family use pint jars. Buy jars with tight-fitting covers, and fit them each with new rubber rings. Old rubber becomes porous and lets in air. Fit each jar with a ring and a cover; pour water into them and invert them to see if they are air-tight. If not, do not use them. Having the jars, covers, and rings in perfect condition, the next thing is to wash and sterilize them.

Have two pans partially filled with cold water. Put some jars in one, laying them on their sides, and some covers in the other. Place the pans on the stove where the water will heat to the boiling point. The water should boil at least ten or fifteen minutes. Have on the stove a shallow milk pan in which there is about 2 inches of boiling water. Sterilize the cups, spoons, and funnel, if you use one by immersing in boiling water for a few minutes. When ready to put the prepared fruit in the jars slip a broad skimmer under a jar and lift it and drain free of water.

TO PREPARE THE SYRUP

Put the sugar and water in the saucepan and stir on the stove until all the sugar is dissolved. Heat slowly to the boiling point and boil gently without stirring for 10 minutes. Follow Table at head of Chapter, for the proportion of sugar and water used for the various fruits.

DIRECTIONS FOR PUTTING FRUIT INTO JARS

1. Take jar from boiling water and set on a wet cloth or tray.
2. Put sterilized spoon and fruit funnel in jar.
3. Pour in the boiling fruit.
4. Dip rubbers in boiling water and put them on jars quickly.
5. Fill jars to over-flowing.
6. Put on sterilized cover and screw tight.
7. Turn upside down.

CANNED FRUIT—Stewed

Boil sugar and water 10 minutes, to make a thin syrup; then cook a small quantity of the fruit at a time in the syrup; by so doing, fruit may be kept in perfect shape. It saves time to have two or more kettles of syrup on the stove, each with enough syrup for one can. Add the fruit in rotation to the boiling syrup, that one can may be taken up as soon as the last one is done. Test if soft with a wooden splinter or silver fork. Set the sterilized jar in the small pan and fill to overflowing with the boiling fruit. Slip a silver plated knife or the handle of a spoon around the inside of the jar, that the fruit and juice may be packed solidly. Wipe the rim of the jar, dip the rubber ring in boiling water and put it smoothly on the jar, then put on the cover and fasten. Place the jar on a board and out of a draft of cold air. The work of filling and sealing must be done rapidly, and the fruit must be boiling hot when it is put into the jars. If screw covers are used, it will be necessary to tighten them after the glass has cooled and contracted.

If there is not sufficient syrup, add boiling water, as jars must be filled to overflowing.

CANNED FRUIT—Baked in the Oven

In this method the work is easily and quickly done and the fruit retains its shape, color and flavor. Particularly nice for berries.

Sterilize jars and utensils. Make the syrup; prepare the fruit, the same as for cooking. Fill the hot jars with the fruit, drained, and pour in enough hot syrup to fill the jars solidly. Run the handle of a silver spoon around the inside of the jar. Place the hot jars, uncovered, and the covers, in a moderate oven.

Cover the bottom of the oven with a sheet of asbestos, the kind plumbers employ in covering pipes, or put into the oven shallow pans in which there are about two inches of boiling water. Cook berries to the boiling point or until the bubbles in the syrup just rise to the top; cook larger fruits, 8 to 10 minutes or according to the fruit. Remove from the oven, slip on rubber, first dipped in boiling water, then fill the jar with boiling syrup. Cover and seal. Place the jars on a board and out of a draft of air. If the screw covers are used tighten them after the glass has cooled.

Large fruits, such as peaches, pears, quince, crab apples, etc., will require about a pint of syrup to each quart jar of fruit. The small fruit will require a little over half a pint of syrup.

CANNED FRUIT—Steamed

Wash, wipe and pare the fruit as usual and pack it carefully into the cans. Boil sugar and water to a syrup and fill the cans solidly. Place covers loosely over cans; no rubbers. Have wooden or wire rack in bottom of wash boiler. Put in enough warm water to come to about 4 inches above the rack. Place the filled jars in the boiler, but do not let them touch one another. Pack clean white cotton rags around the jars or thin slabs of wood between, to prevent them from striking one another when the water begins to boil. Cover the boiler, place over slow fire and gradually increase the heat to the boiling point. Let berries just come to a boil, or boil slowly from 5 to 8 minutes, larger fruit from 10 to 30 minutes until sufficiently cooked. Count from the time when the surrounding water begins to boil. Draw the boiler back, lift off the cover and when the first steam passes off, take one jar at a time, add rubber, dipped in boiling water, fill up with boiling syrup and seal. Put the jars on a board and do not let cold air blow upon them. If screw covers are used tighten them when the glass has cooled and contracted.

CANNED APPLES

Make a syrup by boiling for ten minutes sugar and water in the proportion of two cups of water and one cup of sugar. Wipe, pare, quarter and core Porter apples. Add a small piece of stick cinnamon to syrup or a quince pared and cut in small pieces. Add apples and cook until just soft. Remove to jar, cover and seal.

CANNED CHERRIES

1 qt. cherries, stemmed,   ½ cup water,
¾ cup sugar,   1 qt. or 2 pt. cans, air-tight.

Select the large, dark sweet cherries; wash, stem and stone with new steel hairpin, in colander over preserving kettle to save juice. Boil sugar and water to a syrup 10 minutes, add the cherries and boil 5 minutes. Put in hot sterilized jars and seal.

CANNED PEACHES—Stewed

8 quarts of peaches,   1 quart of sugar,
3 quarts of water.

Select large early Crawford peaches (freestone).

Put the sugar and water together and stir over the fire until the sugar is dissolved. When the syrup boils skim it. Draw the kettle back where the syrup will keep hot but not boil. Pare the peaches, cut in halves, and remove the stones, unless you prefer to can the fruit whole.

Put a layer of the prepared fruit into the preserving kettle and cover with some of the hot syrup. When the fruit begins to boil, skim carefully. Boil gently for ten minutes, then put in the jars and seal. If the fruit is not ripe it may require a little longer time to cook. It should be so tender that it may be pierced easily with a silver fork. It is best to put only one layer of fruit in the preserving kettle. While this is cooking the fruit for the next batch may be pared.

CANNED PEACHES—Steamed

1 qt. peaches, halved and peeled,	2 cups water,
1 cup sugar,	1 qt. can, air-tight, or
	2 pint cans, air-tight.

Select large early Crawford peaches, a firm, yellow freestone peach with a red center.

Wipe, cut in halves, remove the stones and peel. Pack closely in clean, air-tight can or cans and add a few of the stones. Cover cans to keep peaches from discoloring.

Make a syrup by boiling the sugar with the water 10 minutes. Pour hot over the peaches, toward center of can, so as not to crack the can; place cover loosely over can.

Set the cans on a wire, to protect them from the fire, in a deep kettle with luke warm water filled to within an inch of the neck of the can. Cover the kettle or steamer closely, that no steam escapes. Let slowly come to the boiling point, increasing the heat gradually. Let boil steadily 8 minutes; lift off the cover of kettle, remove cover of cans, one at a time, slip on a new rubber, dipped in boiling water and if syrup does not fill can to overflowing, add more syrup, boiling hot, and screw down cover at once. Let cool gradually. Invert cans and when cool, screw air-tight. In steaming more fruit, separate cans, with cloth, straw or thin strips of wood.

Pears, apples and plums may be canned like peaches.

CANNED PEARS

Select Bartlett pears. Add ginger root or lemon slice to syrup if desired. If the fruit is ripe it may be treated exactly the same as peaches. If, on the other hand, it is rather hard it must be cooked until so tender that a silver fork will pierce it readily.

CANNED PINEAPPLES

1 qt. pineapple, peeled and chopped,
1 cup sugar,
1 cup water,
1 qt. or 2 qt. cans, air-tight.

Select large Florida pineapples. Cut crosswise in thick slices, and then peel and core the pineapples. Chop or slice rather fine. Mix fruit and sugar. Let stand over night. Then add the cup of water to each quart of the fruit. Pour in preserving kettle, let come slowly to the boiling point, fill the hot cans to overflowing with the boiling fruit, put on clean rubbers and covers and seal at once.

CANNED RAW RHUBARB

Cut the rhubarb when it is young and tender. Wash it thoroughly; cut into pieces 2 inches long; pull off long threads. Pack in sterilized jars. Fill the jars to overflowing with cold water and let them stand ten minutes. Drain off the water and fill again to overflowing with fresh cold water. Leave no air bubbles. Seal with sterilized rings and covers. When required for use, treat the same as fresh rhubarb.

Green Gooseberries may be canned in the same manner. Rhubarb may be cooked and canned with sugar in the same manner as gooseberries.

CANNED STRAWBERRIES OR RASPBERRIES

Place berries in colander that sets down in a deep pan full of cold water. Lift colander up and down to wash but not to crush the berries. Remove stems. Prepare the syrup. Pack the berries in the hot, sterilized jars, pour in the boiling syrup, put on covers loosely, no rubbers. Place jars on rack of boiler, with enough warm water to come to about 4 inches above the rack. Cover the boiler, place over slow fire and gradually increase the heat to the boiling point. Draw boiler back, lift off the cover and slip rubbers, first dipped in boiling water, add cover and seal, let the jars remain in the water until cooled off.

Blackberries, blueberries and cherries may be canned the same way, but baked in the oven as directed, removing cans when the bubbles just begin to rise to the top of can.

CANNING STRAWBERRIES—Without Fire

After washing and removing the hulls, fill sterilized Mason cans to the top with the berries. Then make a syrup to the preparation of two cups of water to six of sugar. Pour this over the berries slowly while boiling hot until the can is full, then close tightly, using one old rubber and one new one. Then place the cans in a kettle of boiling hot water on the table or back of the stove, cover kettle closely and let stand until the next morning, then tighten the covers once more.

Raspberries and **Blueberries** are canned the same way.

TO CAN VEGETABLES

Cook peas, string beans, beets, turnips, carrots, as for the table, in boiling water until softened so a fork can pierce them, remove from the fire, drain off the boiling water, and let cold, running water cool off and crisp the vegetables and drain again.

Pack them in hot, sterilized jars. Fill them to overflowing with water that has been boiled and cooled, add ½ teaspoon salt to each quart of water, adjust rubbers and seal, stand jars in steamer or wash boiler, the bottom of which has been protected by a rack. Surround them with cold water, cover the boiler, gradually bring to the boiling point and boil steadily from one to two hours, according to the recipes which follow. When cooked, the required time, tighten the covers and run some warm beeswax around the rubber. Set away in a cool place.

CANNING ASPARAGUS

Wash and trim the asparagus the exact length to fit the jars, Tie in bunches, tips up. Place bunches, standing tips up, in kettle of boiling water, having the water come to ½ the height of the bunches; boil 5 minutes, then add water to reach up to one inch from the tops and boil 2 minutes more, then add water to fully cover the tips and boil not more than ½ minute. Drain off the hot water and cool in running water.

Pack into jars carefully, fill with hot, salted water, adjust new rubbers to jars and seal tightly. Stand the jars in large steamer or washboiler, the bottom of which has been protected by a rack. The jars must then be entirely covered and under water, slightly warm; cover boiler, let gradually come to the boiling point. Allow quarts to boil 1 hour and 30 minutes; pints 1 hour and 15 minutes. Lift out of the water one at a time, see that covers are tight and then pour warm beeswax around rubbers.

CANNING STRING BEANS

Cut strings off carefully from sides, then cut into small pieces, crosswise or lengthwise, as preferred. Boil in salted water until tender but not soft. Cool in running water. Pack in jars, fill with salted, warm water; adjust rubbers and seal. Place jars in large boiler or steamer, protecting bottom with a rack. Cover jars entirely with warm water, then cover boiler; let boil gradually, then allow quarts to boil 1 hour and 20 minutes, pints 1 hour and 10 minutes. Lift out of boiler, tighten covers and pour warm beeswax around the rubbers.

CANNING BEETS

Select small, young, fresh beets; wash, put them into boiling water and boil carefully for 30 minutes, then remove the skins. Pack the beets into quart jars, add warm, salted water, and a little vinegar, if desired, adjust rubbers and seal. Put jars in large boiler, with rack at the bottom. Cover jars entirely with warm water and cover boiler. Let come to a boil gradually and boil for ¾ hour. Lift jars from boiler and run warm beeswax around rubbers.

Young carrots and turnips may be canned the same way.

CANNING CAULIFLOWER

Wash, trim and prepare cauliflower as for the table. Place in salted, boiling water and boil until it is tender but not soft. Cool, in running water. Pack in hot, sterilized cans, being careful not to break the flowerettes. Fill jars with salted water that has been boiled and cooled. Arrange jars in a boiler or steamer that has been protected by a rack. Place rubbers on jars, screw covers on tightly. Pour cold water in boiler to cover the jars, place cover on boiler, bring all gradually to the boiling point. Let boil 2 hours. Lift cans out one at a time, see that the covers are on tight. Pour warm beeswax over rubbers and keep in a cool place.

CANNED CORN

Select fresh, young sweet-corn, cut it down from the cobs, if you wish to retain the kernel; if you want the pulp grate it off with an ordinary grater or cut the kernel lengthwise and scrape the heart of the corn remaining on the cob.

Fill the hot, sterilized jars with corn to within ½ inch of the top, packing it solidly, add a little water and salt and sugar, if desired. Dip the rubber in boiling water and screw the covers on tightly. Place the jars in a boiler or large steamer of cold water, protected by a rack or place a layer of corn husks at the bottom of boiler, lay the sealed cans on their sides on the corn husks; if two layers are used have corn husks between the layers. The water in the boiler should completely cover the cans. Bring this to a boil gradually, and counting from the time it begins to boil, let boil 3 hours. Take it out of the water, where no draft will strike it. See that the top is screwed tight. Run some warm beeswax around the rubber. Put it away in a cool place and it will keep for years.

CANNED CORN ON COB

Cut thin cobs of fresh young sweet corn in halves, lengthwise, or cut in small pieces, crosswise. Pack them in large mouthed sterilized jars as full as you can without crushing the kernels. Cover with clear cold water. Dip rubber in boiling water, screw the covers down tightly. Place jars in steamer of cold water on a rack, or on a bed of corn husks. Lay the cans on their sides. If two layers of cans are used have corn husks between the layers. The water in the boiler should completely cover the cans. Bring gradually to the boiling point, and counting from the time it begins to boil, let boil 5 hours. Take out of water, where no draft will catch it. See that the top is screwed tight. Run warm beeswax around the rubber. Keep in a cool, dry place.

TO CAN PEAS

Boil fresh picked young peas in salt water until tender. Drain, Pack in sterilized, air-tight cans. Cover with fresh water that has been seasoned with 1 teaspoon of salt and 1 of sugar to each quart of peas. Seal air-tight. Place in steamer in a bath of cold water. Let slowly come to the boiling point and boil 35 minutes, counting from the time it begins to boil. Place out of draft to cool, pouring melted beeswax over the rubbers.

CANNED STEWED TOMATOES

Select the Acme tomato, a smooth, red, fleshy variety. Wash the tomatoes and plunge into boiling water for five minutes. Pare and slice, and then put into the preserving kettle. Heat the tomatoes slowly, stirring frequently from the bottom. Boil for thirty minutes, counting from the time the vegetable begins actually to boil. Put in sterilized jars and seal.

CANNED WHOLE TOMATOES

Select medium sized, solid tomatoes. Wash and skin them. Cut out any imperfection. Pack carefully into hot, sterilized cans. Fill the cans with water that has been boiled and cooled, or strained tomato juice, and place covers loosely on cans.

Place cans on the floor of a moderately hot oven, protected by a sheet of asbestos paper, or set in a pan of hot water. Close oven door. When bubbles form in the water in the cans and rise to the top of cans take each can separately, slip on the rubber quickly, cover tightly and place out of a draft, until cool.

CANNED TOMATO SOUP

1 pk. ripe tomatoes,
4 onions, sliced,
12 sprigs parsley,
2 bay leaves,
1 teaspooon pepper corns,
Tie spices in a bag,

1 teaspoon celery seed,
1 teaspoon cloves, heads removed.
2 tablespoons salt,
1 tablespooon sugar,
Wipe tomatoes and quarter.

Boil all together, gently at first until the juices flow, then let simmer for ½ hour. Strain, reheat, bring to the boiling point, pour into sterilized, air-tight bottles or cans to overflowing and seal at once. Use for meat, fish or vegetable gravies or for soups.

The plain strained tomatoes without the seasonings may be bottled or canned the same way if desired.

CHAPTER XXXIX

PICKLES AND CATSUPS

SWEET PICKLES

4 qts. tiny cucumbers,
1½ cups salt to 2 qts. water,
1 gallon vinegar,
2 cups brown sugar,
4 whole red peppers,
2 sticks cinnamon, broken,
2 tablespoons allspice, whole,
2 tablespoons cloves, heads removed,
2 tablespoons mustard seeds,
¼ cup horseradish root, diced.

Lay cucumbers in the salt water over night and drain. Let vinegar, peppers, sugar and whole spices come to a boil, throw in the pickles, let heat through well, over slow fire. Bottle while hot, lay pieces of the horseradish and some of the mustard seeds on top of each bottle. Cover and seal at once.

SWEET PICKLED RIPE CUCUMBER

1 doz. ripe cucumbers,
3 lbs. sugar,
1 qt. vinegar,
2 tablespoons mustard seeds,
1 tablespoon each cloves, heads removed,
Stick cinnamon.

Peel cucumbers, cut in two lengthwise, scrape out seeds with a silver spoon, salt and let stand over night. Drain and dry cucumbers. Make a syrup of the sugar and vinegar. Add the mustard seed and also the whole cinnamon and cloves tied in a bag. Boil cucumbers in this syrup only a few moments until they are glassy. They must remain crisp. Pack in jars and cover air-tight.

SLICED CUCUMBER PICKLES
(For winter use)

50 cucumbers, about 1 by 3 inches,
½ cup salt,
2 medium onions,
1 qt. vinegar,
1 cup best salad oil,
½ oz. mustard seed,
½ oz. celery seed,
2 tablespoons sugar.

Slice cucumbers, without peeling, ⅛ inch thick. Sprinkle well with the salt and let stand 3 hours, then drain. Add the rest of the ingredients, mix well and pack in jars or large mouthed bottles. Use best pickling vinegar and see that pickles are in the brine, closely covered. Will keep. Makes one gallon pickles.

MUSTARD PICKLES

Small cucumbers,
1 gal. cold white wine vinegar,
1 cup salt,
1 cup sugar,
1 cup ground mustard.

Soak in cold water to freshen cucumbers, but do not salt. Mix dry ingredients, and add vinegar gradually to dissolve mustard. Pour mixture over as many cucumbers as it will cover. Set away in crocks.

ESTREGAN PICKLES

25 pickles (large, long ones),
1 stalk dried éstregan,
1 bunch of dill (six stalks),
1 horseradish root (diced),
2 tablespoons of whole white pepper,
12 bay leaves (dried),
1 cup salt,
1 quart water,
2 quarts vinegar,
½ lb. mustard seed.

Soak pickles in cold water twelve hours, or over night. Drain and wipe. Place over each layer of pickles two or three blossom-ends of dill, three or four one-half inch pieces of estregan (stalks and leaves), a few small pieces of horseradish root, one tablespoon of whole white pepper and three or four dried laurel leaves. Make a brine of two quarts of vinegar, one quart water and one cup of salt, beat together until it foams, and pour over the pickles to cover. Cover the whole with a bag, made to fit the top of crock. Fill bag with mustard seeds, and sew up. Cover with plate and stone, and keep in a cool, dry place. Must stand five or six weeks before they are done. Keep well.

SMALL DILL PICKLES

Select pickles of from two to three inches in length and scrub well with a small brush. Pack in layers in Mason jars, a layer of pickles, a layer of dill and a few mustard seeds, placing a bay leaf and a piece of alum the size of a pea on the top of each jar.

Let one cup of vinegar, two cups of water and one tablespoon of salt come to a boil. Pour boiling hot over the pickles and seal.

WINTER DILL PICKLES

100 cucumbers, medium size,	10 qts. water,
1 small red pepper,	1 qt. vinegar,
1 big bunch of dill,	2 cups salt,
Some cherry leaves,	2 qt. Mason jars.

Lay cucumbers in salt water over night (½ cup salt to 4 qts. water). Boil water, vinegar and sugar and let cool over night. Drain cucumbers and place in cans in layers between the cherry leaves and dill. Pack cucumbers tight, add a small piece of red pepper. Cover with the brine and screw down the cover. Will keep. One cup mustard seeds and one cup horseradish root, shaved fine, may be added.

SUMMER DILL PICKLES

100 pickles,	1 cup vinegar,
5 stalks dill,	Grape leaves, or cherry,
1 oz. black peppercorns,	2 cups salt,
Bay leaves,	2 gal. water.

Soak pickles in cold water over night, or twelve hours. Drain and dry. Place in layers of two rows pickles, then three or four blossom ends of dill and a teaspoon of whole black pepper; repeat, covering top layer well with dill and adding some cherry or vine leaves. To four quarts of water, take one cup of salt. Boil, and when cool, pour over the pickles to cover. Cover with cloth. Weight well with plate, to keep under brine. Let stand in warm place to ferment for a week. One cup of vinegar may now be added. Rinse off scum that arises on cloth every day in warm weather and once or twice a week when cooler, and pickles will keep hard all winter. Keep cool, in a dry place.

DILL BEANS

1 pk. wax beans,	½ oz. black peppercorns,
4 qts. water,	6 bay leaves,
1 cup salt,	6 grape or cherry leaves,
2 large stalks dill,	fresh,
	1 cup vinegar.

Remove strings and parboil beans in boiling, salted water until tender, (1 teaspoon salt to 1 qt. boiling water). Drain and pack in layers, in a crock, add a few peppercorns, a little dill, some pieces of bay leaf; repeat, covering top layer well with dill and adding the grape or cherry leaves. Follow recipe for Summer Pickles, above.

GREEN DILL TOMATOES

Select small firm green tomatoes, follow recipe for Winter or Summer Dill Pickles, page 434, using the green tomatoes in place of the pickles.

MIXED PICKLES

2 qts. tiny cucumbers,
2 qts. large cucumbers cut in ¼ inch slices,
2 qts. small white onions,
1 qt. string beans, cut,
2 large cauliflowers, flowerettes, separate,
3 small red peppers, and
1 large green pepper sliced,
1 pt. nasturium seeds,
1 pt. radish pods,
1½ cups salt to 2 qts. water,
½ cup horseradish root, diced,
¼ lb. yellow mustard seed,
¼ lb. black mustard seed,
1½ gallons cider vinegar,
1 lb. brown sugar,
1 teaspoon red pepper, ground,
1 teaspoon black pepper, ground,
1 oz. tumeric.

Mix first 9 ingredients, pour over salt water, let stand 24 hours, drain; add next three quantities. Boil the rest and pour over pickles, let stand 2 days. Pour into jars and seal.

CHOW-CHOW

2 qts. small cucumbers,
2 qts. small white onions,
1 qt. string beans,
1 large cauliflower,
1 green pepper,
1 cup salt to 4 qts. water,
2 tablespoons tumeric,
2 tablespoons mustard,
1 cup flour,
1 cup brown sugar,
2 teaspoons celery seed,
2 qts. vinegar.

Peel onions, under cold water. String and cut the beans. Cut off leaves and stalks of cauliflower and separate flowerettes. Mix the first 5 ingredients and cover with the salt water, let stand 24 hours and then drain.

Mix tumeric with a little cold vinegar; add flour to mustard and mix to a smooth paste also with some of the vinegar. Now stir each separately into the remaining vinegar, add the sugar and celery seed and let boil thoroughly until smooth, stirring constantly. Pour over the pickles and fill in cans, closely covered. Let stand several weeks before using.

GREEN TOMATO PICKLES (DELMONICO)

No. 1

½ pk. green tomatoes, sliced,
¼ pk. skinned onions,
1 pk. salt,
3 large cucumbers, diced,
½ gallon cider vinegar,
1 oz. tumeric powder,
2 lbs. brown sugar,
¼ lb. white mustard seed,
¼ oz. celery seed,
2 tablespooons cinnamon, broken,
2 tablespoons cloves, heads removed.

Mix tomatoes and onions with the salt and sprinkle a little salt over the cucumbers. Let stand 24 hours, pour off brine, then soak 12 hours in cold water. Tie spices in a bag and place into a kettle with the vinegar and sugar, heat to the boiling point, add the pickles and let simmer slowly for 1 hour. Fill into cans and keep in a cool place.

No. 2

1 pk. green tomatoes, sliced,
6 large onions, sliced,
1 cup salt,
1 qt. vinegar with 2 qts. water,
3 qts. vinegar,
2 lbs. brown sugar,
2 teaspoons each whole allspice, stick cinnamon and cloves, heads removed,
4 tablespoons mustard seed,
6 green peppers, chopped fine.

Sprinkle the salt over tomatoes and onions separately, place in thin bags over night to drain. Boil the quart of vinegar with the water, add tomatoes, and let boil 15 minutes. Drain and throw away the liquid.

Mix with the rest of the ingredients, bring to a boil, scald thoroughly, put in jars and seal at once. Let cool gradually.

PICKLED CAULIFLOWER

4 heads cauliflower,
1 cup salt,
2 qts. vinegar,
2 cups sugar,
¼ cup mixed pickle spices.

Separate flowerettes of cauliflower, add the salt and let stand over night. Place in colander, rinse with cold water and let drain. Tie spices in thin bag and boil with vinegar and sugar, throw in the cauliflower, boil a few minutes and pour to overflowing in wide mouthed bottles or cans. Cork or cover and seal air-tight.

PICKLED BEANS

No. 1

1 pk. wax beans,	1 cup vinegar,
3 tablespoons salt,	½ cup sugar,
8 qts. boiling water,	8 pint cans.

Remove strings and cut beans into one inch pieces; wash and cook in the boiling, salted water (1 teaspoon salt to 1 quart water), until tender, but not soft. Drain beans and save the water in which they were cooked. Reserve enough of this bean liquor to fill cans, add the sugar and vinegar, let just cook up, add the drained beans, cook all together and pour boiling hot into the cans. Seal at once. Use as a salad or sweet sour vegetable.

No. 2

1 pk. of string beans cooked until tender,	1 quart water,
	1 lb. sugar,
1 quart vinegar,	1 tablespoon cloves,
1 stick cinnamon (broken).	

Wash and pick over the beans, string and cut. Boil in salt water (one teaspoon to one quart of boiling water), until tender. Drain and spread out to dry; then pack into air-tight cans. Boil until a nice syrup is obtained. Let cool, then pour in cans and seal.

PICKLED BEETS

1 qt. cold, boiled beets, sliced,	1 teaspoon brown sugar,
	1 teaspoon caraway seed,
1 teaspoon salt,	1 pint vinegar.
⅛ teaspoon pepper,	

Boil Beets, page 429, place in crock in layers, sprinkle with salt, pepper, sugar, caraway seed, if you like, and cover with vinegar.

Cold, hard cooked eggs may be placed in the vinegar, and sliced over the beets for decorations. The eggs will be red.

PICKLED CABBAGE

4 qts. thinly sliced cabbage, red or white,	¼ cup mustard seed,
	¼ cup mixed pickle spices,
4 teaspoons fine salt,	1 cup sugar,
½ teaspoon pepper,	2 qts. vinegar.

Select large, heavy cabbage, take off the outside leaves; cut in quarters and then in thin shreds, using cabbage cutter. Sprinkle the salt over cabbage, mix thoroughly, and leave stand over night. Drain slightly and add the pepper and mustard seed, mix and place in crock. Add sugar and pickle spices, tied in a bag, to the vinegar, bring to the boiling point slowly and pour boiling hot over the cabbage to cover. If after cooling the vinegar does not cover cabbage, add more hot vinegar. May be used cold or, when heated, as a vegetable, in place of sauerkraut. Will keep indefinitely.

PICKLED ONIONS

4 qts. small white onions,
1 cup salt;
2 qts. vinegar,
2 cups sugar,
¼ cup mixed pickle spices.

Peel onions under water, add salt and let stand over night. Place in colander, pour cold water over to rinse and let drain. Tie spices in thin bag. Boil with sugar and vinegar, throw in onions, let boil up and pour at once to overflowing into air-tight bottles or jars.

PICKLED PEPPERS

¼ peck green peppers,
1 large head cabbage,
1 qt. onions,
1 pt. green tomatoes or cucumbers,
1 tablespoon seeds of peppers,
½ teaspoon best salad oil,
¼ cup mustard seed,
1 tablespoon celery seed,
¼ cup grated horseradish,
1 teaspoon sugar,
12 pepper corns,
1 grated nutmeg,
½ tablespoon prepared mustard.

Select large peppers, wipe clean, cut off 1 inch from small end; remove seeds and core without breaking the peppers. Sprinkle well with salt and let stand over night. Chop cabbage, onions, tomatoes or cucumbers each separately, salt well and place in little cheese cloth bags to drain over night. Press dry and in the morning mix all ingredients in order given. Wipe peppers, fill with mixture, replace tops of peppers, tie securely with cord, pack in layers in a jar. Cover with boiling vinegar to which has been added ½ cup sugar. Cover jar closely. Ready to use in one week. Peppers may be pickled without the chopped mixture and canned as other vegetables.

MOCK OLIVES

Take plums when just beginning to ripen, but still green.
Make a brine out of sea salt or rock salt strong enough to hold up an egg. Pour the brine over the fruit, hot, cover and let stand 24 hours. Pour off and make a new brine, heat, add the fruit, heat one minute and seal in the hot brine.

SAUERKRAUT

15 heads cabbage,
2½ lbs. salt,
24 tart apples,
A wooden stamper,
A round board,
A small square of cloth,
A heavy stone,
An 8 gallon crock.

Select large, heavy cabbages, remove outer leaves, cut in halves and slice very fine on large cabbage cutter. Into a large granite pan, place 4 quarts of the shredded cabbage, sprinkle with ¼ cup of salt, mix thoroughly and then pack into the large crock; add, if desired, a cup of apples, cut fine and then pound and stamp down the cabbage with a wooden stamper, until the brine flows and covers the cabbage. Mix another 4 quarts of cabbage and ¼ cup of salt, and pack again into crock, cover with 1 cup chopped apples and pound as before until covered with brine. Continue until all cabbage is used, always pounding until covered with brine. Now cover with cabbage leaves, lay on the fitted square of cloth, then the board and stone, to help keep the contents under brine. See that the crock is large and leave enough space on top for the cabbage to swell or ferment, without overflowing.

Put in a warm place to ferment. In two weeks examine, remove the scum, if any; wash cloth, picking it up at the corners to catch all of the scum; wash board, stone and sides of crock; and return the clean cloth, board and stone over cabbage; then cover. Remove scum and wash cloth, etc., weekly.

CATSUPS AND RELISHES

TOMATO CATSUP

No. 1

½ bu. very ripe tomatoes,
2 teaspoons ground cinnamon,
⅓ teaspoon cayenne or red pepper,
2 tablespoons salt,
4 cups sugar,
¼ teaspoon ground mustard,
2 quarts vinegar.

Score the tomatoes with a knife and boil 2 hours, then strain. Add the dry ingredients and when nearly done or reduced one-half, add the vinegar. Bottle and seal.

TOMATO CATSUP

No. 2

1 peck ripe tomatoes,
½ cup sugar,
2 tablespoons salt,
2½ cups vinegar,
¼ tablespoon cayenne pepper,
¼ cup all together, of cassia buds, whole allspice and stick cinnamon.

Wash and cut up the tomatoes, add the salt and boil until soft. Strain well and let boil again slowly, 5 hours, or until very thick. Add sugar to vinegar. Tie spices in a bag and boil in the vinegar until well flavored, add to the tomato pulp and boil 15 minutes longer. Bottle while hot and seal.

No. 3

1 peck ripe tomatoes,
4 onions,
1 small section of garlic,
12 sprigs parsley,
2 bay leaves,
½ cup sugar,
2 tablespoons salt,
1 teaspoon each mace and paprika,
1 tablespoon each black peppercorn, celery seed and cloves, heads removed,
1 pint vinegar.

Boil first five ingredients until soft, strain through colander and then through sieve. Tie whole spices in bag. Add with the rest of the ingredients to strained tomatoes.

Boil slowly and steadily, several hours, until thick or reduced one-half. Remove spice bag, add 1 more cup vinegar, boil 10 minutes longer. Bottle while hot and seal.

CHILI SAUCE

50 medium ripe tomatoes,
25 medium onions,
4 red peppers, seeds removed,
1 large bunch of English celery (6 to 12 stalks),
1 qt. vinegar,
1 tablespoon whole allspice,
1 tablespoon whole cloves, heads removed,
1 tablespoon whole cinnamon,
3 cups sugar,
2 tablespoons salt,
1 nutmeg, grated.

Scald, peel and chop the tomatoes, and put in colander to drain. Chop all the vegetables. Tie the whole spices in a bag.

Mix and then boil 2½ hours; fill into bottles while hot and seal air-tight. Will make about seven quarts of sauce.

TOMATO RELISH

No. 1

1 pk. ripe tomatoes,	2 cups granulated sugar,
2 cups chopped onions,	1 cup mustard seed,
2 cups chopped celery,	½ cup salt,
2 qts. cider vinegar,	1 teaspoon black pepper,
4 red peppers, chopped fine,	1 teaspoon paprika.

Chop and peel tomatoes and put in colander to drain, add above ingredients and fill to overflowing, in Mason jars and cover tightly. Ready for use in six weeks.

No. 2

1 pk. ripe tomatoes,	¼ cup celery seed,
6 large onions,	2 qts. vinegar,
8 red or green peppers,	2 lbs. sugar,
1 bunch celery,	1 cup salt.

Put tomatoes, onions and peppers through food chopper. Place in bag over night with salt, to drain. Add celery, cut fine, and celery seed. Boil sugar and vinegar and let cool, and pour cold over mixture. Place in wide mouthed bottles and seal.

ENGLISH CHUTNEY SAUCE

1 lb. of apples, chopped,	¼ cup of mint leaves, chopped,
¾ lb. of raisins, chopped,	1 oz. of white mustard seed,
1 dozen ripe tomatoes, chopped,	¼ cup salt,
2 red peppers, chopped,	2 cups granulated sugar,
6 small onions, chopped,	1½ qts. vinegar, boiled and cooled.

Salt the chopped tomatoes and let drain in a bag over night. The rest of the ingredients may be put through the meat chopper. This sauce requires no cooking, but should be kept in a crock for ten days, in a convenient place, that it may be stirred every day. Place in wide mouthed bottles, cork and seal.

GREEN TOMATO RELISH

2 qts. green tomatoes,	2 tablespoons salt,
4 qts. chopped cabbage,	1 lb. sugar,
½ dozen medium onions,	3 pints vinegar,
2 small red peppers,	½ oz. tumeric,
½ oz. celery seed,	½ oz. white mustard seed,
1 bunch table celery,	½ oz. whole allspice.

Chop the first 5 ingredients fine. Mix with the rest and boil 20 minutes. Fill in cans and seal.

CUCUMBER RELISH

No. 1

2 cucumbers,
Salt,
1 cup vinegar,
¼ cup sugar,
½ cup celery, cut fine,
1/16 teaspoon cayenne pepper,
6 tablespoons horseradish,
2 tablespoons onions, chopped,
1 tablespoon mixed spices,

Peel and chop 2 large, thin cucumbers, sprinkle with salt and let stand 2 hours in thin bag. Let drain. Add chopped onion and celery. Place in a small jar or wide mouthed bottle. Heat the rest of the ingredients with the vinegar, and spices in a bag, bring to the boiling point, let cool, and pour over the chopped vegetables. Seal.

No. 2

6 ripe cucumbers, peeled,
6 large green tomatoes,
6 large onions,
3 green peppers, seeded,
3 red peppers, seeded,
½ cup salt,
½ cup sugar,
½ cup white mustard seed,
1 tablespoon celery seed,
Cold vinegar to cover.

Press the first five ingredients through the food grinder or chop them fine. Drain in colander. Place in large pan, add salt, sugar, mustard and celery seed; mix thoroughly, cover well with cold vinegar and pack in pint cans, air tight.

CORN RELISH

20 ears corn,
1 medium head cabbage,
4 green peppers,
6 red peppers,
4 onions, chopped,
1 teaspoon celery seed,
½ cup salt,
2 cups sugar,
½ cup flour,
½ teaspoon tumeric,
¼ lb. Coleman's mustard,
1 qt. white vinegar.

Cut corn from cob; cabbage, onion and pepper through food grinder. Mix flour, tumeric and mustard. Stir in the vinegar gradually at first, then let come to a boil. Add the rest of the ingredients and boil ½ hour. Bottle, add more vinegar if necessary. Seal.

GREEN PEPPER RELISH

6 green peppers, cut fine,
3 small onions, cut fine,
2 tablespoons sugar,
1 tablespoon salt.

Cover with cold vinegar. Bottle and seal.

BEET AND HORSERADISH RELISH

No. 1

2 qts. boiled beets, chopped,
2 qts. cabbage, chopped,
1 cup horseradish, grated,
2 cups sugar,
2 teaspoons salt,
Pepper to taste.

Boil Beets, page 429, mix ingredients, add cold vinegar to cover, and place in gallon jar. Will keep.

No. 2

3 cups cold, boiled beets,
½ cup horseradish root,
¼ teaspoon pepper,
1 teaspoon salt,
¾ cup vinegar,
2 tablespoons sugar.

Boil, peel and grate beets, page 429, and horseradish; season with salt, pepper and sugar. Add all the vinegar, the horseradish and beets will absorb, and place in covered jar or glass and it is ready for use. Will keep a long time.

MUSTARD FOR THE TABLE

1 teaspoon sugar,
⅛ teaspoon salt,
1 tablespoon salad oil,
2 tablespoons ground mustard,
2 tablespoons vinegar.

Mix salt and sugar and stir in the oil thoroughly. Add the vinegar to the mustard and combine the mixtures. If too thick add a little boiling water.

Or, take the dry, ground mustard and add to it gradually cold water or vinegar to make a smooth paste.

HORSERADISH FOR THE TABLE

1 lb. horseradish root,
2 tablespoons sugar,
White wine vinegar.

Scrub the horseradish root, pare and grate over hot stove, or out of doors. Mix and add all the vinegar that the horseradish will absorb. Bottle in air-tight cans and take out only enough at a time for immediate use.

CHAPTER XL

INVALID COOKERY

In preparing food for an invalid the following points should be kept in mind:

The food should be served in the most pleasing manner possible. It should be served in small quantities, suit the digestive powers of the patient, and satisfy hunger or furnish needed strength.

In a severe illness the doctor prescribes the kind and amount of food to be given. In long and protracted illness it is necessary to take nourishing food in small quantities at frequent intervals. In short spells of illness it is sometimes best to go without food for a day or more, so as to give the system complete rest.

The following foods are easily digested and are given to invalids: Milk, eggs (raw or slightly cooked), beef tea, gelatinous jellies, gruels, well-cooked cereals, raw oysters, juice of oranges, grapes or other fruit.

SERVING FOOD

Use the daintiest dishes in the house. Place a clean napkin on the tray, and, if possible, a fresh flower.

Small quantities are more tempting to a delicate appetite.

Try to surprise the patients by some unexpected food and in this way induce them to take nourishment.

Serve hot food hot, and cold food cold.

Remove the tray as soon as the food is eaten, as food should never be allowed to stand in a sick room.

MILK

Milk is the natural food of the young. Its value in the dietary of adults is often overestimated. Solid food is essential. One obtains the greatest benefit from milk when taken alone at regular intervals between meals, or before retiring, and sipped rather than drunk. Hot milk is often given to produce sleep.

In feeding infants with milk, avoid all danger of infectious germs by Sterilization, page 20, or Pasteurization, page 20.

To prevent acidity of the stomach, add from one to two teaspoonfuls of lime water, to each half pint of milk.

Vessels used for milk must be thoroughly cleansed; tins should be rinsed in luke-warm water and washed thoroughly with hot water, then rinsed in boiling water. Cover milk with muslin and keep in a cool place.

Modified milk is put up by physicians' prescriptions; the milk is separated into its parts, and re-combined in different proportions to suit the needs of individual cases.

Certified milk is fresh, clean milk put in the most sanitary manner in bottles.

LIME WATER

Pour 2 quarts boiling water over an inch cube unslacked lime; stir thoroughly and let stand over night; in the morning pour off the liquid that is clear and bottle for use. Keep in a cool place.

MILK FOR THE SICK

Where milk cannot be taken alone, add soda, seltzer, apollinaris, or Vichy water; give in small quantities, at frequent, regular intervals.

ALBUMENIZED MILK

½ cup milk,
White of 1 egg.

Put white of egg in a tumbler, add milk, cover tightly, and shake thoroughly until well mixed.

KOUMISS

1 qt. milk,
1½ tablespoon sugar,
⅓ yeast cake,
1 tablespoon lukewarm water.

Dissolve the yeast in the lukewarm water. Heat the milk until lukewarm; add the sugar and dissolve yeast cake. Fill airtight bottles, (patent tops), to within one and one-half inches of top; cork and invert. Let stand for 6 hours at a temperature of 80° F. Chill and serve the following day. If ordinary bottles are used, tie the corks down firmly with strong twine. Use for fevers and gastric troubles.

EGG NOG

Beat the yolk of one egg, add one tablespoon sugar, and beat until light. Add ½ cup milk. Beat the white of the egg well and fold it in lightly. Add ½ teaspoon vanilla, a little grated nutmeg or 1½ tablespoons lemon juice.

MILK PUNCH

No. 1

½ cup milk,
Sugar,
A few gratings nutmeg,
1 tablespoon whisky, rum or brandy.

Mix ingredients, cover and shake well.

No. 2

1 egg,
1 teaspoon sugar,
1 tablespoon Sherry wine or brandy,

Or, ½ tablespoon Sherry and 1 tablespoon rum,
A nutmeg, grating,
Hot milk.

Separate egg. Beat yolk until very light with sugar, add white, beaten stiff, then the liquor. Fill up the glass with the hot milk. Grate the nutmeg on top. Serve hot for colds.

ICE CREAM FOR ONE

½ cup cream,
4 teaspoons sugar,
¼ teaspoon vanilla,

Use a toy freezer, or make a freezer of a one-half pound baking powder tin, a thick 8-inch bowl, or a small wooden pail, to form the outside of the freeze. Chop the ice fine. For each layer use one-third cup rock salt and one cup of ice. The can must be water-tight.

Stir the ingredients until sugar is dissolved, and pack in can. Beat, and as it freezes, scrape from the sides of can with wooden spoon. Beat the mixture again, cover, turn the can back and forth until more of the cream is frozen. When frozen throughout, drain off water, beat the cream again, pack evenly, and put on cover. Repack in ice and salt to cover can, and let stand in fireless cooker, if you have one. Drain off water as it melts.

JUNKET CUSTARD

1 cup milk,	¼ junket tablet,
2 tablespoons sugar,	1 teaspoon cold water,

1 teaspoon brandy.

Heat milk until lukewarm, add sugar and brandy, when sugar is dissolved, add tablet dissolved in cold water. Turn into small moulds and let stand in a cool place until firm.

LEMONADE OR ORANGEADE

2 tablespoons sugar,   1 cup water,
Juice ½ lemon or orange.

Extract the juice of ½ lemon or orange. Add sugar and water and stir until dissolved. Or the sugar and water may be boiled to a syrup, allowed to cool and then added to the juice. Serve hot or cold.

APPLE WATER

1 large sour apple,	2 teaspoons sugar,
1 cup boiling water,	1 teaspoon lemon juice.

Wipe, core and pare apple. Put sugar in cavity and bake until tender; mash, pour over water, let stand ½ hour and strain, add lemon juice if desired. Or, slice the raw apple and boil in the water and strain without squeezing.

GRAPE OR CURRANT JUICE

No. 1

2 tablespoons grape or currant juice,	Or 2 teaspoons grape or currant jelly,
Sugar to taste,	1 cup hot water.

Mix fruit juice with cold water and sweeten to taste or dissolve jelly in hot water and sweeten to taste. Beat jelly with fork, then measure.

No. 2

2 tablespoons grape juice,   1 white of egg.

Place juice in wine glass, add egg beaten stiff and a little chopped ice. If the grape juice is not sweet, sprinkle sugar over top.

RHUBARB WATER

3 stalks rhubarb, ½ cup sugar,
2 cups water.

Wash the rhubarb, without peeling, cut in one-half inch lengths. Into a bowl, add sugar and boiling water. Cover and set away to cool. Strain and serve cold. Pink stalks will give the water a pretty color.

TOAST WATER

Equal measures of stale bread toasted and boiling water, salt. Cut bread in ¼ inch slices, put in pan and dry thoroughly in a slow oven until crisp and brown. Break in pieces; let stand 1 hour, strain through cheese cloth and season. Serve hot or cold.

LEMON WHEY

1 cup hot milk, 2 teaspoons sugar,
1 small lemon.

Heat the milk in a double boiler, add the juice of the lemon. Cook until the curd separates, then strain through a cheese cloth. Add the sugar. Serve hot or cold.

WINE WHEY

½ cup milk, ½ cup Sherry or Port wine.

Scald milk, add wine, let stand five minutes, or until the curd forms. Strain and serve, or heat before serving. Sweeten to taste.

BARLEY WATER

3 tablespoons barley, Salt,
4 cups cold water, Lemon juice,
Sugar.

Pick over barley and soak in water over night or for several forms. Strain and serve, or heat before serving. Sweeten to taste and serve.

RICE WATER

2 tablespoons rice, Milk or cream,
2 cups cold water, Salt.

Pick over rice, add to water and boil until rice is tender; strain and add to rice water, milk or cream, as desired. Season with salt and reheat. A half inch piece of stick cinnamon may be cooked with rice and will assist in reducing a laxative condition.

IRISH MOSS LEMONADE

¼ cup Irish moss,   Juice 1 lemon,
2 cups boiling water,   ⅓ cup sugar.

Wash, pick over and soak until soft, Irish moss in cold water to cover. Pick over and wash again, add the 2 cups boiling water and cook 20 minutes, until dissolved, in double boiler, then strain; add lemon juice and sugar to sweeten.

FLAXSEED TEA

1 tablespoon flaxseed,   Juice of 1 lemon,
1 tablespoon sugar,   1 cup cold water.

Wash the flaxseed thoroughly, put it with the cold water into a sauce pan. Let it simmer one or two hours. Add lemon juice and sugar to taste. Serve hot.

BEEF TEA

No. 1

½ lb. round steak of beef,   Salt to taste.

Select a piece of steak from the rump or upper part of round. Broil or warm slightly one or two minutes to set free the juices, then squeeze out the juice by means of a press or lemon squeezer, into a slightly warmed cup. Salt, if necessary, and serve at once. Prepare only enough to serve, as it does not keep well.

No. 2

½ lb. round steak, scraped,   Salt to taste.

Scrape one-half pound lean, juicy beef to a fine pulp. Put it into a double boiler, with cold water in the lower part, heat gradually, and keep it simmering 1 hour, or until the meat is white. Strain and press out the juice, season with salt to taste, and serve hot.

No. 3

½ lb. round steak, shredded,   1 cup cold water,
½ teaspoon salt.

Shred one-half pound lean, juicy beef, and place it in a double boiler, with one cup of cold water and one-half teaspoon salt. Let it stand one hour. Then put boiling water in the lower part of boiler and cook five or ten minutes, until the juice is brown. Strain and press the meat to obtain all the juice. Serve hot, salt to taste.

MUTTON BROTH

1 lb. lean mutton, chopped very fine,
1 pt. water, cold.

To make this quickly for a sick person, pour the cold water over the mutton, let stand until the water is very red, then heat it slowly and let it simmer 10 minutes; strain, season with salt and serve hot.

BROWN FLOUR SOUP

1 tablespoon butter,
1 tablespoon flour,
1 cup boiling water,
½ teaspoon salt,
⅛ teaspoon nutmeg, grated,
1 teaspoon caraway seed.

Brown the butter in a spider, add the flour, let cook, but not burn, until well browned, then add seasoning, and gradually the boiling water. Cook a few moments longer and serve hot. Good to reduce a laxative condition.

WINE SOUP

1 pint white wine,
2 tablespoons sugar,
2 yolks of eggs,
Croutons.

Boil wine and pour very gradually over yolks, beaten very light. Add Croutons, page 81, and serve at once.

RED WINE SOUP

1 cup red wine,
½ cup water,
2 tablespoons sugar,
3 whole cloves,
3 small sticks cinnamon,
1 yolk of egg.

Boil wine, water and spices 10 minutes and pour boiling hot, gradually, over the well beaten yolk of egg. Serve hot or cold.

CREAM WINE SOUP

1 cup white wine,
½ cup cold water,
7 lumps loaf sugar,
3 whole cloves,
3 small sticks cinnamon,
1 cup sweet cream,
2 yolks eggs.

Boil water, wine, sugar and spices 10 minutes. Heat the cream, pour it gradually hot over the well beaten yolk and then pour in the boiling wine, stirring constantly, to prevent curdling. Serve hot or cold.

SCRAPED BEEF

Cut a piece of tender steak one-half inch thick. Lay it on a meat board and with a sharp knife scrape off the soft part until there is nothing left but the tough, stringy fibres. Season the pulp with salt and pepper, make into little flat, round cakes one-half inch thick, and broil them two minutes. Serve on rounds of toast. This is a safe and dainty way to prepare steak for one who is just beginning to eat meat. When it is not convenient to have glowing coals, these meat cakes may be broiled in a very hot frying pan, or in the broiling oven of a gas stove.

PREPARED FLOUR BALL

2 cups wheat flour,
Boiling water,
2 tablespoons powdered flour,
2 tablespoons cold milk or water,
1 cup boiling milk,
A little salt.

Tie 2 cups flour in a stout cloth, put into boiling water and let boil 5 hours. Turn out the flourball, scrape off the doughy part. The inside is hard and dry and will grate to powder.

Grate a tablespoonful from the ball when wanted. Wet it with 1 tablespoon milk or water. Stir, add another tablespoonful and rub to a smooth paste, add it to the boiling milk, boil 5 minutes. Add a little salt. For infants, very astringent.

OATMEAL GRUEL

½ cup coarse oatmeal,
1 teaspoon salt,
3 cups boiling water,
Milk.

Add the oatmeal and salt to the boiling water, and cook 3 hours in a double boiler. Strain and dilute with milk or cream. If rolled oats is used, cook 1 hour.

FARINA GRUEL

3 tablespoons farina,
1 teaspoon salt,
1 cup boiling water,
1 cup milk.

Place upper boiler directly over the fire until the water boils. Add farina slowly. Boil up once, then place over boiling water 15 minutes. Add milk, cook 15 minutes longer. Sweeten if desired.

CRACKER GRUEL

4 tablespoons powdered cracker crumbs,
½ teaspoon salt,
1 cup boiling water,
1 cup milk.
Boil up once and serve.

Gruels:—Any cold mush that is thinned with cream, milk or water and served very hot, is a gruel.

Gruels must be thoroughly cooked, strained, seasoned and served very hot.

They are flavored with sugar, stick cinnamon, whole cloves, meat extracts and stimulants.

SACCHARIN SOLUTION

½ teaspoon saccharin,
¼ teaspoon baking soda,
1 pint distilled water or water boiled to precipitate lime.
Heat to the boiling point and bottle.

One teaspoon is equal to 1 teaspoon of granulated sugar. Use exactly as sugar, but in cooking custards and the like add when taken from the fire. Do not let it come in contact with tin or iron—use enamel, glass, china or silver ware and utensils, as iron and tin affect the flavor. For Uric Acid Patients.

SENNA PRUNES

24 prunes,
1 pint boiling water,
2 tablespoons senna leaves.

Steep senna in the water, where it will keep hot for 2 hours; strain, wash stew pan, add senna water and prunes. Cover and simmer until prunes have absorbed the water. Put in jar, use as required. Will keep. To produce a laxative condition.

FRUIT TABLETS

2 oz. raisins,
2 oz. figs,
2 oz. dates,
2 oz. prunes,
1 oz. senna leaves.

Wash fruit, remove all seeds and hard portions; chop fine or grind. Spread thin, cut in squares, wrap each in wax paper and put in a glass or tin can. Will keep. To produce a laxative condition.

A QUICK MUSTARD PLASTER

Trim the crust from a thin slice of light bread, then sprinkle it thickly with ground mustard. Spread a very thin cloth over the mustard, and dampen with vinegar or water.

RECIPES

RECIPES

RECIPES

RECIPES

www.ingramcontent.com/pod-product-compliance
Lightning Source LLC
Chambersburg PA
CBHW080538230426
43663CB00015B/2634